MW00667249

illustrated dictionary of POTTERY FORM

illustrated dictionary of

POTTERY FORM

ROBERT FOURNIER
drawings by sheila fournier

VNR VAN NOSTRAND REINHOLD COMPANY
new york cincinnati toronto london melbourne

Copyright © 1981 by Litton Educational Publishing, Inc.

Library of Congress Catalog Card Number 80-36664
ISBN 0-442-26112-8

All rights reserved. No part of this work covered by the copyright hereon may be reproduced or used in any form or by any means—graphic, electronic, or mechanical, including photocopying, recording, taping, or information storage and retrieval systems—without written permission of the publisher.

Printed in United States of America
Designed by Dana Kasarsky Design

Published by Van Nostrand Reinhold Company
A division of Litton Educational Publishing, Inc.
135 West 50th Street, New York, NY 10020

Van Nostrand Reinhold Limited
1410 Birchmount Road
Scarborough, Ontario M1P 2E7, Canada

Van Nostrand Reinhold Australia Pty. Ltd.
17 Queen Street
Mitcham, Victoria 3132, Australia

Van Nostrand Reinhold Company Limited
Molly Millars Lane
Wokingham, Berkshire, England

16 15 14 13 12 11 10 9 8 7 6 5 4 3 2 1

Library of Congress Cataloging in Publication Data
Fournier, Robert 1915-
Illustrated dictionary of pottery form.
Bibliography: p.
1. Pottery craft—Dictionaries. I. Title.
TT919.5.F67 666'.3'321 80-36664
ISBN 0-442-26112-8 AACR1

This book is dedicated to all the fine museums and publications that have made it possible.

ACKNOWLEDGMENTS

I wish to express my appreciation and thanks to the following: the staffs of many museums and particularly to Cleo Witt of Bristol Museum, Tiffany Hunt of Salisbury Museum, and Mr. Ken Annable of Devizes Museum for allowing me to disrupt their displays in order to photograph exhibits; Mike Seaborne for his splendid photographic processing work and John Anderson for the use of some of his pictures; Jon and Kate Catleugh, Pam Margerison, Molly Watkins, Sybil Houldsworth, and May and Leslie Savage; the staff of the Craftsmen Potters Shop; the Sloane family with their fine collection of antiquities; Barley Roscoe of the Crafts Study Centre at Bath; Murray Fieldhouse; Pan Henry of the Casson Gallery, London; Eileen Lewenstein and Emmanuel Cooper, editors of *Ceramic Review*; Angela Cook for her advice on modern Greek pottery; and all who have helped me amass the daunting number of illustrations that were necessary; nor would the book have been possible without my wife's research and her clear, charming drawings and silhouettes. Recent photographs from public and easily accessible collections have been credited with the illustrations. In addition many of the drawings have been based on pieces in the British Museum, London; the Lewes Museum, Sussex; the Horniman Museum and the Museum of London; the York County Museum, York; the Victoria and Albert Museum, London; and the Abbey Museum, Leeds. The Barlow Collection is now at the University of Sussex, Brighton.

INTRODUCTION

The prime objective of this book is to be a source of ideas, inspiration, and interest to the craftsman. In the making of it, however, in the fascination of discovering ever-widening applications of the invention and genius of the potter, the scope has widened and has resulted, I hope, in a dictionary that will be of use to a larger public, to museums and collectors, and to those to whom a pot is an object of contemplation and enjoyment, regardless of its time or place of origin.

Shape is basic to pottery. Other factors such as glaze and decoration are the clothes, important to a pot's character and interest, but unable to exist separately. It would have been possible, therefore, to limit illustrations to silhouette and line, but this omits the vital element of volume. Also, the subtleties of profile and detail in such a plastic art often defy the scissors or pencil. A measure of photography was, therefore, considered essential, but the choice has still been made in the primary interests of form. To quote from two great potters, Bernard Leach and Michael Cardew: "The form of a pot is of first importance" (Leach), and "There is a mysterious thing about shape . . . to know what it means" (Cardew).

Certain preferences on the part of the author are inevitable. The most lively and exciting work comes straight from the hands; examples from the industrial world of molds and mechanization are thus in short measure. For the same reason, pottery without glaze, sometimes even without decoration, such as the work of early civilizations and the later peasant or folk earthenware, which had to rely on form alone to give pleasure, is well represented. "For all those cultures that used no glaze, it is obvious that the pots had to stand . . . by the clearness and excellence of their shape," says Margaret Wildenhain. Useful pots also far outnumber the purely decorative or sculptural work, although both these qualities may be present in a useful pot, and invention and fantasy abound.

There has always been an instinctive and, more recently, an intellectual agreement on the close relationship between function and form in ceramics, and the modern desire for self-expression is not excluded from this unity. Michael Casson, for instance, has said, "I believe that being a potter making useful pots gives you a chance to use every facet of yourself." In addition there must be that spark without which a pot will not, as Harold Guilland puts it, "transcend the common." A similar thought has been well expressed by Margaret Wildenhain: "Just as with some faces, some pots have a clearer, more characteristic and distinct expression because something in the relationship of form elements and their proportions is exceptional and more personally expressive."

The dictionary style has been adopted partly because it is otherwise difficult to track down a particular shape or vessel (the indices of books are notoriously poor on references to form), but it was also done for another important reason. To give an object a name is one way of enabling the mind to isolate and consider it separately from the multitude. The importance of "naming" is central to the human consciousness; it was Adam's first task. As befits a dictionary, I have tried to trace the origins of the terms in an attempt to define them, but have also taken common usage into account. The references and illustrations of examples cannot, of course, be exhaustive and are intended to direct the reader's attention to a far wider range in books and museums. References from one heading to another are printed in **bold letters.** In many cases the referred-to heading may be illustrated, but it was felt that cross-references of all pictures would be too cumbersome to be useful. Also, rather than filling the dictionary with the many titles of books from which information has been gathered, a code for each source follows the text. The Booklist at the beginning of the book gives the code, title, and publisher of each source.

Finally, may I say along with Mao, "Let the past serve the present," and hope that potters working today, at any level, may find new directions or a fresh view of their current work from the many fine pots shown in this book, not in order to produce a pastiche, but to try to understand the practical and aesthetic principles, to widen horizons, and to give a glimpse of the infinite application and variety of pottery shapes.

BOOKLIST

In order to save space in the body of the dictionary the books have been coded with the initial of the author's surname and initial letters from the title. Some of the books referred to are not easily available, but have been included for the sake of completeness. The list could be many times as long, but these are the ones I have found useful in the compilation of this book.

A.FAR Allinne, M. *Faiences Anciennes.* Rouen: Lestringant, 1928.

B.AC Brown, A. C. *Ancient Cyprus.* Oxford, U.K.: Ashmolean Museum, 1975.
A very reasonably priced paperback with excellent and inspirational photographs of Cypriot pots.

B.AMP Birks, Tony. *The Art of the Modern Potter.* New York: Van Nostrand Reinhold Co., 1976.
Recently reissued. An examination in depth of nine famous potters of the 1960s.

B.APP Bushnell and Digby. *Ancient American Pottery.* London: Faber & Faber Ltd., 1955.
Authoritative and very well illustrated.

B.CECP Brears, Peter. *Collector's Book of English Pottery.* Devon, U.K.: David & Charles Ltd. 1974.
One of the best books on English country pottery and the nearest equivalent in England to Guilland (G. EAFP). I am deeply indebted to Peter Brears for much information and entertainment.

B.DA Boger, Louise A. and H. Batterson. *Dictionary of Antiques and the Decorative Arts.* New York: Charles Scribner's Sons, 1979.
Some references useful, but largely industrial pottery.

B.GAH Burton, Elizabeth. *Georgians at Home.* London: Arrow Books Ltd., 1967.
Some of the background to the design and use of household articles in Georgian England.

B.GEC British Museum. *Introductory Guide to the Egyptian Collection.* London: British Museum Publications, 1930.

B.GRPL Bailey, Donald. *Greek and Roman Pottery Lamps.* London: British Museum Publications, 1972.

B.MPS Barker, P. A. *Medieval Pottery in Shropshire 1066–1400.* Shropshire Archeological Society, 1970.

B.PDA Bray, W. and Trump, D. *Penguin Dictionary of Archeology.* Middlesex, U. K.: Penguin Publishing Co., Ltd., 1970.
A valuable reference book, but only occasional line drawings.

B.PiE Barton, K. J. *Pottery in England 3500 B.C.–1730 A.D.* New York: A. S. Barnes, 1975. Devon, U. K.: David & Charles Ltd., 1975.
A useful history with sectional drawings and some photographs.

B.TP Billington, Dora. *Technique of Pottery.* London: B. T. Batsford Ltd., 1962.
Includes wise words on pottery form.

C *Crafts.* London: The Crafts Council, from March, 1973, on.
The glossy British bi-monthly crafts magazine. Sometimes rather way-out, but providing a picture of contemporary work.

C.APP Cushion, John P. *Animals in Pottery and Porcelain.* London: Studio Vista, 1974.
Some very attractive illustrations from a wide field.

C.B Cole, B. *Boxes: Collecting for Tomorrow* series. London: Pitman Publishing, Ltd., 1976.
A few pottery boxes.

C.CC Mrs. A. Clark Collection. Sotheby Catalogue.

C.DPMP Celoria, Francis. *Dated Post-Medieval Pottery.*

London: H.M.S.O., 1966.

C.ESD Cooper, Ronald G. *English Slipware Dishes, 1650–1850.* Levittown, N.Y.: Transatlantic Arts, 1972. London: Alec Tiranti, Ltd. 1968.
The best book on the subject. More decoration than form, of course.

C.HP Cooper, Emmanuel. *History of Pottery.* Essex, U. K.: Longmans Group, Ltd., 1973.
History for potters, concise and well illustrated.

C.HRNC Chinese government. *Historical Relics Unearthed in New China.* 1972.
Some fine specimens.

CM *Ceramics Monthly.* Columbus, Ohio: Professional Publications.
An excellent on-going review of pottery in the United States and elsewhere. Later issues have good color plates.

COQ *Craftsmen of Quality.* London: The Crafts Council of Great Britain.
An occasional publication illustrated with examples from each craftsman member.

C.PBT Casson, Michael. *Pottery in Britain Today.* London: Alec Tiranti, Ltd., 1967.
Pottery in Britain yesterday, but still useful as a picture of British work.

C.PP Cardew, Michael. *Pioneer Pottery.* New York: St. Martin's Press, Inc., 1976. London: Longmans, Green & Co., Ltd., 1969.
Sound (and entertaining) advice on many aspects of pottery form.

C.PPC Clark, Kenneth. *Practical Pottery and Ceramics.* London: Penguin Books, 1972.
Some advice and diagrams on shape.

C.PPGT Charles, Bernard H. *Pottery and Porcelain, a Glossary of Terms.* Devon, U. K.: David & Charles Ltd., 1974.

CR *Ceramic Review.* London: Craftsman Potters Association of Great Britain, from February, 1970, on.
A bi-monthly magazine. A very wide-ranging review of contemporary pottery with excellent illustrations.

CTCD *Chambers Twentieth Century Dictionary.* Edinburgh, U. K., W & R Chambers, Ltd.

C.WC Charleston, Robert J. (Ed.) *World Ceramics.* Middlesex, U. K.: The Hamlyn Publishing Group, 1968.
A treasure house of pots, fairly conservative in choice, but none the worse for that.

D.AJ Drew, R. *Apothecary Jars.* London: Faber & Faber Ltd., 1978.

D.EBYC David, Elizabeth. *English Bread and Yeast Cookery.* New York: The Viking Press, 1980. London: Allen Lane.
Her descriptions and preferences with respect to cooking vessels make entertaining reading.

D.HBM Davey, Norman. *A History of Building Materials.* Canaan, N. H.: Phoenix Publishing, 1961.
A splendidly illustrated survey, touching on ceramics quite frequently.

D.PA *Discovering Art.* Milan: Fratelli Fabri Editoria. Bristol, U. K.: Purnell & Sons, 1961.
A part-work, issued in monthly parts.

E.ACJ Elisseeff, V. *Ancient Civilisation of Japan.* London: Barrie & Jenkins, 1974.
Some stunning pots of great imaginative power.

EB *Encyclopaedia Britannica.* Chicago and London: Encyclopaedia Britannica Ltd., 1951 edition.

E.ED Early, A. K. *English Dolls.* London: B. T. Batsford, 1955.
A few references to ceramic dolls.

F.CBW Frank, Ann. *Chinese Blue and White.* London: Studio Vista, 1969.

F.DL Fournier, Robert. *David Leach: A Potter's Life.* Wiltshire, U. K.: Fournier Pottery, 1979.
A dozen or so examples of this gifted potter's work.

F.DPP Fournier, Robert. *Illustrated Dictionary of Practical Pottery.* New York: Van Nostrand Reinhold Co., 1977. (paperback) 1980.
A number of good pots illustrated incidental to technique.

F.EC Fisher, Stanley. *English Ceramics.* London: Ward Lock, 1966.

F.PA Forman, W. and B. *Prehistoric Art.* Middlesex, U. K.: Spring Books.
Very dramatic photographs of some excellent pots.

F.PAA Fagg, William. *The Potter's Art in Africa.* London: British Museum Publications, 1978.
Lively and varied pots.

F.SB Foster, Kate. *Scent Bottles.* London: The Connoisseur Studio and Michael Joseph, 1966.
The early chapters especially show some interesting pottery bottles.

F.SOC Fujioka, Ryoichi. *Shino and Oribe Ceramics.* Tokyo: Japan Art Library, Kodansha International Ltd., 1977.
A revelation in variety, invention, and treatment.

G.CRNE Gilliam, J. P. *Types of Roman Coarse Pottery Vessels in Northern England.* Northumberland,

U. K.: Oriel Press, 1957.

G.CW Gompertz, G. St.G.M. *Celadon Wares.* London: Faber & Faber Ltd., 1968.
Also by this author are books on the great Yi period of Korean ceramics and on Koryo. All are in the Faber Monograph series.

G.EAFP Guilland, Harold F. *Early American Folk Pottery.* New York: Chilton Book Company, 1971.
A "must" for any study of household pottery. Slightly flat photographs, but many show the influences on folk culture in Colonial America, and there are many fine down-to-earth pots. Any potter will want to return to the book again and again.

GOC *Genius of China Exhibition Catalogue.* London: Royal Academy, Times Newspapers, 1974.
Small pictures, but strong on the early wares up to Han.

GOE *Gold of Eldorado Exhibition Catalogue.* London: The Royal Academy, Times Newspapers, 1966.

H.CAC Honey, William B. *Ceramic Art of China.* London: Faber & Faber Ltd., 1945.
A conservative collection of fine pots, the earliest periods rather neglected.

H.CECP Haggar, R. G. *Concise Encyclopedia of Continental Pottery and Porcelain.* London: Andre Deutsch, 1960.
Mainly factory ware, but some nice pictures.

H.EPP Honey, W. B. *English Pottery and Porcelain.* London: Adam & Charles Black, 1952.

H.FYP Holland, Fishley W. "Fifty Years a Potter." Tring, U. K.: Pottery Quarterly, 1958.
Some splendid first-hand glimpses into the life of a potter during the early years of this century.

H.GIP Robson, R. L. *Guide to Islamic Pottery in the British Museum.* London: British Museum Publications, 1932.

H.LCB Hedges, A. A. C. *Let's Collect Bottles.* London: Jarrold and Sons Ltd.
A few everyday pottery bottles.

H.MC Hettes, Karel. *Modern Ceramics.* London: Spring Books, 1965.
Obviously now rather out-of-date, but a worldwide survey.

H.MMA Higgins, Reynold. *Minoan and Mycenean Art.* Oxford: Oxford University Press, 1967.
Some of the best pots of the period are illustrated.

H.PBC Hughes, G. B. *Pocket Book of China.* Country Life, 1965.
Masses of tiny drawings, giving ideas, but a lot of industrial ware.

H.PPFE Hobson, R. L. *Handbook of the Pottery and Porcelain of the Far East* (in the British Museum). London: British Museum Publications, 1948.

J.ASP Johns, Catherine. *Arretine and Samian Pottery.* London: British Museum Publications, 1971.

J.LCP Jenyns, Soame. *Later Chinese Porcelain.* Bridgeport, Connecticut: Merrimack Book Service, 1971. London: Faber & Faber Ltd., 1971.

LG *Larousse Gastronomique.* Middlesex, U. K.: Hamlyn Publishing Group Ltd., 1977 (translation)

L.GP Lane, Arthur. *Greek Pottery.* Bridgeport, Connecticut: Merrimack Book Service, 1971. London: Faber & Faber Ltd., 1971.
A well-illustrated history, though it is difficult to find one's way about it. Text often stimulating.

L.GPBA Lacey, A. D. *Greek Pottery in the Bronze Age.* Methuen, 1967.

L.HP Leach, Bernard. *Hamada, Potter.* |Tokyo:| Kodansha International Ltd., 1975.
The definitive work on Hamada with many color illustrations.

L.LIP Lane, Arthur. *Later Islamic Pottery.* Bridgeport, Connecticut: Merrimack Book Service, 1971. London: Faber & Faber Ltd, 1971.

L.PB Leach, Bernard. *A Potter's Book.* London: Faber & Faber Ltd., 1940.
The wisdom and experience in this book needs no gloss from me.

L.PCA Lothrop, S. *Pre-Columbian Art.* Oxford, U. K.: Phaidon Press, Ltd., 1957.

L.PW Leach, Bernard. *A Potter's Work.* Tokyo and San Francisco: Kodansha International Ltd., 1967. London: Adams and Dart, 1967.
Leach's drawings of pots are more revealing than many photographs.

L.SiP Lane, Arthur. *Style in Pottery.* London: Faber & Faber Ltd., 1948.
Both text and pictures still provoke discussion.

M.CAP Mitsuoka, Tandanari. *Ceramic Art of Japan.* Tokyo: Japanese Travel Bureau.
Small photographs, but a number of interesting ones.

M.CEEP Mankowitz and Haggar. *Concise Encyclopedia of English Pottery and Porcelain.* London: Andre Deutsch, 1957.

M.CP Medley, Margaret. *Chinese Pottery.* Oxford, U. K.: Phaidon Press, Ltd., 1976.
A brave attempt to show the history of Chinese pottery from a practical point of view.

M.HCA Medley, Margaret. *Handbook of Chinese Art.* New York: Harper & Row Publishers, Inc., 1974.
Line drawings only, but useful for reference.

M.K Marshall, Jo. *Kitchenware.* London: Pitman Publishing Ltd., 1976.
A few pottery utensils.

N.GERP Nicholson, Felicity. *Greek, Etruscan, and Roman Pottery.* London: Cory Adams & Mackay, Ltd., 1965.
A small book, but with some nice illustrations.

OBPP *Observer's Book of Pottery and Porcelain.* London: Frederick Warne, Ltd., 1973.

P *Potters.* London: Craftsman Potters Association of Great Britain.
An occasional publication. Illustrations of work of most members.

P.ATP Prodan, Mavis. *Art of the T'ang Potter.* London: Thames and Hudson, 1960.

P.BP Poor, Henry Varnum. *A Book of Pottery.* London: Pitman Publishing, Ltd., 1958.

P.OBP Poulteney. W. J. *Old Bristol Potteries.* Wakefield, U. K.: EP Publications, 1920.

P.PA Piccolpasso, Cavaliere Cipriano. *The Three Books of the Potters Art.* Circa 1551 Victoria and Albert Museum, facsimile edition and translation from Italian, 1934.

PQ *Pottery Quarterly.* Edited and produced by Murray Fieldhouse, Tring, Herts, England.
One of the pioneer pottery magazines, first published 1954. A fund of valuable, professional information.

R.ANME Du Ry, Carel J. *Art of the Ancient and Middle East.* New York: Harry N. Abrams, Inc., 1969.
A general history with some exciting ceramics.

R.APE Rose, Muriel. *Artist Potters in England.* London: Faber & Faber, Ltd., 1955/1970.
The more traditional pottery well covered.

R.C Rawson, Philip. *Ceramics.* Appreciation of Art 6. Oxford, U. K.: Oxford University Press, 1971.
A wide and stimulating analysis of ceramics, carefully if intellectually considered. A number of drawings and photos.

R.EDP Ray, Anthony. *English Delftware Pottery.* Bridgeport, Connecticut: Merrimack Book Service, 1968. London: Faber & Faber Ltd., 1968.

R.MEP Rackham, Bernard. *Medieval English Pottery.* Bridgeport, Connecticut: Merrimack Book Service, 1948. London: Faber & Faber Ltd. Revised edition, 1972.
Still the best survey of this great flowering of the potter's art in England.

R.NP Ross, Sylvia Leith. *Nigerian Pottery.* Lagos, Nigeria: Ibadan University Press, 1970.
Many unusual and fine pots.

R.PF Rhodes, Daniel. *Pottery Form.* New York: Chilton Book Company, 1976.
The only deeply considered book purely on the practical aspects of pottery form. All illustrations are of Rhodes's work in progress.

S.AC Spiteris, T. *Art of Cyprus.* New York: Reynal & Co., 1970.
One of the great fountainheads of pottery form and decoration, Cyprus is here shown in all its glory.

S.C Stratton, Deborah. *Candlesticks.* London: Pitman Publishing Ltd., 1976.
Only occasional ceramic examples.

S.DA Savage, George. *Dictionary of Antiques.* New York: Mayflower Books, 1978.

S.IM Scott-Taggart, John. *Italian Majolica.* Levittown: N.Y.: Transatlantic Arts Inc., 1972.

S.M&C Stratton, D. *Mugs and Tankards.* New York: Charles Scribner's Sons, 1977.

S.PP Schofield, J. F. *Primitive Pottery.* Cape Town, S. Africa: South African Archeological Society, 1948.

S.WJC Sanders, H. H., *The World of Japanese Ceramics.* Tokyo: Kodansha International, Ltd., 1968.

TIA *The Incomparable Art.* Manchester, U. K.: City of Manchester Art Gallery, 1969.
A nicely selected catalog of the Gregg Collection, strong on 17th/18th centuries.

V.IP *Guide to Islamic Pottery.* London: Victoria and Albert Museum, 1969.

W.DSAE Whitehead, J. and C. *Designs of Sundry Articles of Earthenware.* Hanley, Stoke-on-Trent, U. K.
Historically interesting, but rather naively and badly drawn.

W.ENEP Watkins, Lura W. *Early New England Potters and Their Wares.* Hamden, Connecticut: Shoe String, 1966.
A booklet which covers some of the ground more widely surveyed in G.EAFP.

W.PFE Wildenhain, Margaret. *Pottery Form and Expression.* New York: Van Nostrand Reinhold Co., 1962.
A practical craftswoman's inquiry into the aims and motivation of the potter and aspects of pottery form.

W.SYPP Wyke-Joyce, Max. *7000 Years of Pottery and Porcelain.* London: Peter Owen Ltd., 1958.

A NOTE ABOUT FILMS

Appreciation of the development of pottery form can be greatly assisted by watching films that deal with the various processes. A splendid reference book of United States titles and sources has been published by Neal-Schuman Publishers, Inc. (New York). It is titled *Craft Films: An Index of International Films on Crafts,* compiled by Kay Salz for the New York State Craftsmen Inc., and it should be in every library. A smaller booklet on British sources of international titles was compiled by the author for the Craftsman Potters Association of Great Britain and is called *Films on Craft Ceramics.* It is available at 75p (2 dollars) plus postage from The Tanyard, Lacock, Wilts, SN15 2LB, England.

A few of the titles published in these volumes are mentioned in the text. They are:

Isaac Button, Country Potter and *Raku English Style*
Both were made by John Anderson and Robert Fournier. Write to: 12, Chase Hill, Enfield, Middlesex, England.

Big Ware
This film deals with another old Yorkshire potter at work. For more details write to: The Crafts Council of Great Britain or the American Federation of Arts.

Women of Aibon and *Legend in Clay*
These films deal with the potters of New Guinea and are issued in Great Britain by The Scottish Central Film Library, 16, Woodside Terrace, Charing X, Glasgow, Scotland.

illustrated dictionary of POTTERY FORM

A

ALABASTRON, Alabastros, Alabastos

An oil or scent bottle from Corinthian and classical Greece, produced in great numbers, especially during the 7th to the 3rd centuries B.C. It was similar to an **aryballos,** but usually taller, with a handle springing from a flat rim to the shoulder. It often has a rounded base.

This is the typical alabastron silhouette. The "tear drop" shape has a parallel in one of its uses (see **tear jar***). The average height is only about 3 inches/75mm.*

Lane's book on *Greek Pottery* contains examples with straighter sides and sloping rims, in addition to modelled ones; e.g., in the form of a boy. In his book *World Ceramics,* Charleston describes the shape as "elongated" with two **lug handles,** but the more typical form has only one handle. L.GPBA (see Booklist) has an illustration of a very squat late-Minoan alabastron, while a small, round bottle with a straight neck in "glazed fritt" from 10th century B.C. Egypt is also called an "alabastron" in the Fitzwilliam Museum. Here the name is obviously given by virtue of its use, rather than by its form. The strong, flat rim is a feature which could well be adapted by modern potters. See illustration D under **aryballos.**

ALBARELLO

The term is possibly a corruption of *el barani,* which is Arabic for "a drug pot," but it may also be from *al barello,* "a little tree," after the **bamboo** containers in which drugs were imported from the Orient.

A B C D

A. The rounded Turkish albarello silhouette.
B. A typically tall and elegant Spanish version of the shape. From Manises, about 12 inches/300mm high.

E

F

C. A two-handed Italian albarello from Faenza, circa 1475.
D. Common Italian proportions.
E. Italian, Deruta, 1507. The decoration shows a deep **mortar** *being used for grinding medicines. (Victoria and Albert Museum.)*
F. A jar by John Reeve in the basic albarello shape.

The form originated in the Near East and was introduced into Spain by the Moors. It became very common in Italy and throughout the Mediterranean in Medieval times. It has, typically, a vertical concave wall and a fairly wide mouth and foot; it is, in fact, a **jar.** It is rarely lidded; the short neck and pronounced flaring rim allowed a covering of parchment to be secured with string. There is great variety in proportion among albarelli, the tall 17th century examples from Talavera are especially handsome. Normally, the albarello has no handle (though a few have two opposed handles—see illustration C), the shape itself being easy to grip and allowing room for the fingers to slide between adjacent pots on a shelf.

Often made in elaborate "sets," rows of gaily painted albarelli formed a very decorative background in the old pharmacies, which were favorite meeting places. At a later date, similar pots were used for spices in grocers' shops. There are variations—some taper towards the base; a Swiss form has a flaring foot; etc.—and the basic shape occurs in some modern pottery jars. It is related to the **diabolo.**

ALCARRAZA

This porous, unglazed **bottle** or **jug** with a long

A. A landscape *alcarraza from 10th century Columbia.*
B. A modern type from Spain.

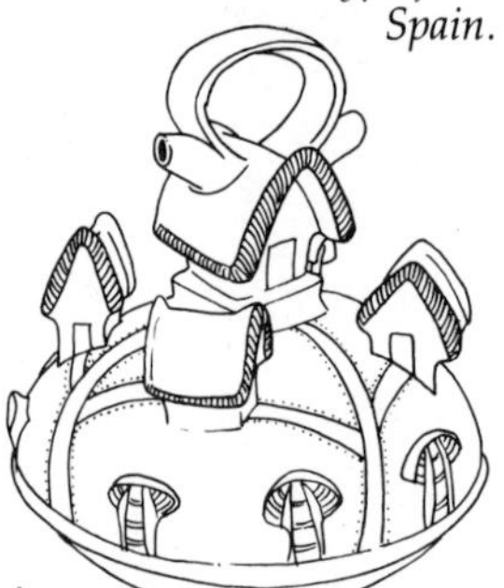
A

B

neck came to Europe via Spain. The name comes from the Arabic *al kourraz,* which means "a pitcher." In the "Gold of El Dorado" Exhibition (Royal Academy, London, 1979), an ornate pot with two spouts (illustration A), made by the Colima tribe, was called an "alcarraza." Simple single-spouted variations are still made on the Iberian Peninsula. To drink from an alcarraza, liquid is directed into the mouth with the lips not touching the spout. Some English **harvest jugs** were used in a similar manner.

ALEMBIC

A primitive still used for distilling spirit from wine. Like so many terms in pottery, the word derives from the Middle English *biker,* meaning a **beaker.**

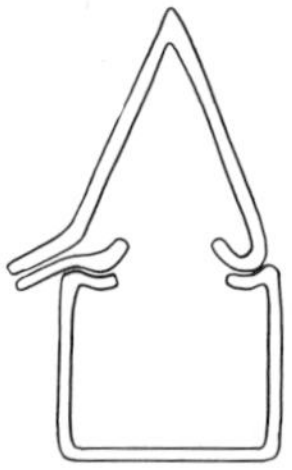

The diagram shows the principle of the alembic and not any particular model. The evaporated spirit condenses inside the lid and exits through the spout from the internal gully. There were other designs with domed tops, etc., all of which are designed to give the maximum cooling area.

More exactly, "alembic" refers to the cap, or operative top section, of the still. The lower half would contain the wine, the cap being a tall cone with an internal gully. The warmed wine was condensed to spirit in the lid, then ran into the gully and out of the spout, which pierced the cap. A crude spirit called "burned wine" or "brandy wine" was made in this way in the 17th century (and probably has been since!). There is evidence of the distilling of medicines and perfumes, and even of crude oil, as early as the 17th century.

ALI BABA

An English nickname for a large stoneware jar for acids, which can contain over 9000 gallons. These noble pots remind one of the grain jars of ancient Crete. See **storage jar.**

An ali baba, about 5 feet 9 inches/1.75m high, which sits outside the Bradford Industrial Museum. (Photograph: John Anderson.)

ALMS DISH

Many small bowls have been used for begging. A very explicit example on display at the Sheffield City Museum (England) has the single word "Money" trailed across it "possibly for use in a church." See also **offering dish.**

ALTAR VASE

Two-handled pots were made specifically for this purpose in the Netherlands in the late 15th century.

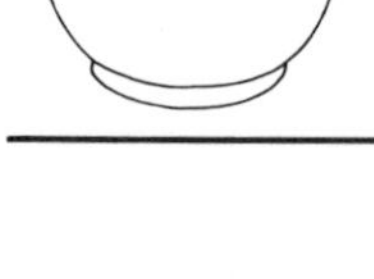

A Dutch thickly tin-glazed altar vase.

AMPHORA

From the Greek *amphi,* meaning "both sides" (in this case referring to the fact that it is two-handled) plus *phoreus,* "a bearer."

This is a form that was very common in the Mediterranean area throughout ancient times. It displays a wide variety of proportion and outline. Normally used for transport and, therefore, fairly large, the typical amphora has two handles set high on the shoulder, the form tapering to a narrow base. One explanation of the narrow base is that it helped to concentrate wine dregs. Sometimes the base was actually pointed and was housed in holes cut through a stand in the hold of a ship. Later,

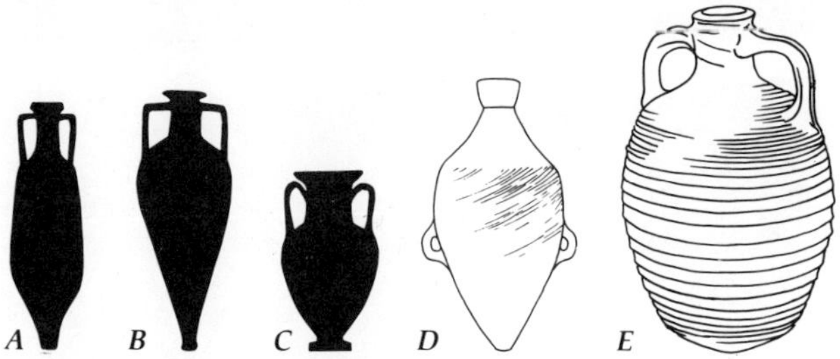

A. A Roman type of amphora, unusual in that its widest section is near the base.
B. The high-shouldered amphora, common throughout antiquity and shown in F.DPP (see Booklist), still made in Cyprus as late as 1970. Note the button base.
C. The more "classic" type of amphora, as given to the contestants at the Panthenaic games.
D. A splendid, strong form from 4500 B.C. China.
E. Another powerful version from 5th century A.D. Nubia.

the more decorative Greek amphoras were frequently filled with oil and given as a prize at the Panthenaic Festivals. These had a spreading foot on which to stand more firmly.

The standard Attic amphora held nearly 9 gallons; the Roman, also known as a "cadus," nearly 7 gallons. That they were also used for solid materials is proven by the remains of almonds found in the ancient Greek ship recovered off Kyrenia in Northern Cyprus. There is mention of fish pickle sauce being carried in amphoras. Each Aegean island and port had its typical amphora variation and a ship's journey can be traced using the amphoras as evidence.

Although most amphoras are shown lidless today, LG (see Booklist) mentions amphoras "surmounted by a lid in the same material, ending in a point." Similar forms are found as far apart in place and time as Shang-Yao China from 5000 to 4000 B.C. and the Rhineland from 800 to 1200 A.D., where it was used for Rhenish wine exports. In Minoan pottery the shape resembles a modern **cider jar.**

In Cyprus the amphora is thrown in two parts, the top half first. This is later reversed onto the wheelhead (complete with handles); a pointed base is thrown onto it with extra clay in the form of a cylinder, this being tapered and closed over. (See F.DPP in Booklist for working illustrations.)

The illustrations given here show something of the great variety of the amphora form.

AMPULLA

A diminutive of **amphora.** It is an earthenware flask with a globular body and two handles, used in ancient Rome for perfume, oil, or wine. Later, the word was used to describe a vessel for holding consecrated oil, etc.

ANALYSIS OF FORM

The classic analysis of pottery form, as exemplified in two Chinese pots, is to be found in Leach's *A Potter's Portfolio* and is reproduced elsewhere.

In relation to more humble pots, in his excellent book *Early American Folk Pottery,* Guilland quotes the principles of proportion, balance, unity, and harmony. He states that balance may be established by symmetry or by "asymmetry, which is the placement of unequal elements at different distances from the central axis," and also deals very cogently with the elements of line and space in the appreciation and analysis of pottery. "Line, as used in defining pottery, refers first to the contour line which forms the boundaries of the shape . . . [although] . . . it is impossible to separate line and shape. Line encloses shape, which is the two-dimensional aspect of the pot and defines its height and width; . . . space, when not limited to shape alone, is three-dimensional and refers to the defined area within the object as opposed to the limitless space around it. Both the positive space (the object) and the negative space (the area around the object) provide contrasting shapes for the viewer to enjoy."

The word "line," used by some theorists to indicate pure profile, is used by others, such as Leach in his famous *Potter's Book,* to suggest more than two dimensions: "The ends of lines are important . . . lines are forces . . . vertical lines are of growth, horizontal lines are of rest, diagonal lines are of change . . . curves for beauty, angles for strength . . . enduring forms are full of quiet assurance."

Arthur Lane in his stimulating and controversial *Style in Pottery* tends to view pots as eye-level outlines. The potter "usually expresses his sense of form through the vertical curves, angles and straight lines of the vessel seen in profile." In fact, a thrower normally works above a pot and can rarely see it in strict profile. He is, anyhow, concerned more with volume than with outline. In an attempt to bring the infinite subtleties of pots into some intellectual order, Lane repeats what has often been stated elsewhere that "all . . . [thrown shapes] . . . are based on the sphere, the ovoid, and the cylinder." While it may be useful to think in these terms, these are essentially mathematical concepts, and a pot can only suggest or approximate them. Rawson, in *Ceramics,* takes a different view, warning against geometric curves in the profile of a pot. He maintains that, since the plan of a thrown vessel is normally circular, any repetition of this geometry in the vertical plane leads to dullness and a lack of vitality. "The great danger to all potters in articulating their forms, the indecisive, evenly undulating contour whose curves are virtually arcs, is a trap particularly alluring to those Europeans who are under a strong impression from the Far East."

Rawson also gives a morphological analysis of form deriving from a rounded pot, a cylinder, and a flat dish, and discusses "body images," tracing a "female element in the somatic reference of pots," emphasizing, like Leach, the anthropomorphic names for the elements of pots—the neck, the belly, the foot, etc. Perhaps most importantly, he analyzes three approaches to form—the juxtaposition of units as in Greek pottery, smooth continuity as in Chinese stoneware and porcelain, and thirdly "overlap and elision . . . by far the subtlest . . . in that quite large stretches of the surface may belong ambiguously to two [formal] units at once."

There is also the question of emphasis and accent. A pot may appear unsatisfactory to the eye because it consists of too many equally important sections, in which case the potter has failed to decide where the main accent should lie. In a pitcher, for instance, the curve of the shoulder often comprises the dominant feature, but, if the neck and lip are pronounced, the curve may take second place. Guilland presents the same idea in reverse terms: "The principle of subordination means that the character of the work is set by a single element around which the lesser parts are organized." In W.PFE (see Booklist) Margaret Wildenhain stresses the more personal involvement in form. "When work and life have a really deep relation . . . when the spiritual content transcends the material knowledge, real form will then grow silently as the natural result of a man struggling with his materials, his techniques, his emotions, his ideas, and his knowledge. Those forms will have something of the growing qualities of forms of nature."

ANIMAL FORM

A

A. The aquamanile type of vessel has been modelled in animal form from very early times. This bull from 1000 B.C. Iran has an open spout for a head.
B. A pot from ancient Ecuador barely altered to suggest a bear lying on its back. (The University Museum of Archeology and Anthropology, Cambridge.)

B

Pots have been made throughout history in the shapes of birds and animals. The range is too wide to be adequately illustrated here, though many other examples will be found throughout this book. Many share an essential simplification and styli-

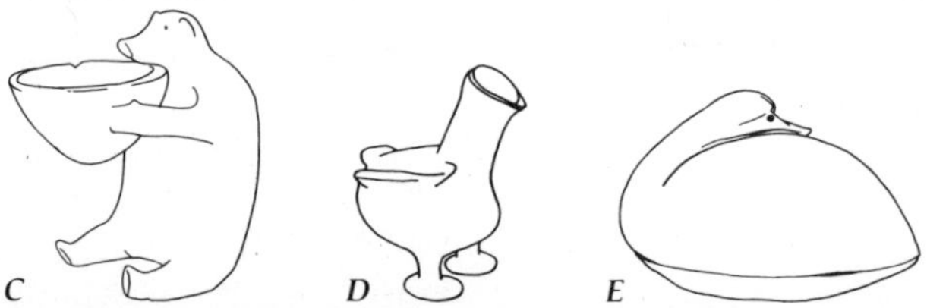

C D E

C. Here this Bronze-Age Aegean creature is holding a bowl, rather than forming a pot in itself.
D. Mainly by its stance, this pot from Lesotho suggests a chicken.
E. A splendid Japanese incense box *in the form of a swan, which manages to imply the weight of the bird, as well as its grace.*

zation combined with an insight into the characteristics of the creature portrayed. Apart from models of the animals themselves—hippos, locusts, porcupines from Egypt, for instance—and the truly ceramic coiled creatures of Rosemary Wren in our own times, they have been used formally to decorate countless pots; e.g., the dragons found on the necks of Sung porcelains, or the pretty swan incense boxes from Japan. (See illustration under **bath rasp** for a very powerful crocodile model.)

F

F. This creature is by no means a pot, but is conceived and executed in a purely ceramic way. By Denise Wren, circa 1959.

Perhaps the most effective animal forms are those in which the merest allusion to the stance, shape, or character of the animal is incorporated with a typical pot shape. There are many fine examples shown in C.APP (see Booklist).

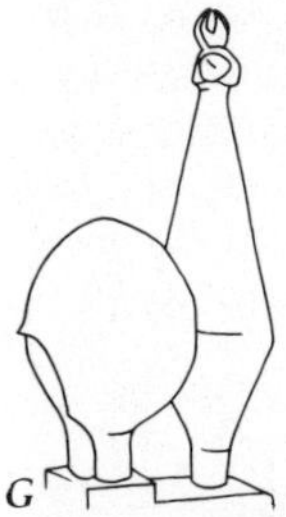

G

G. Constructed from thrown pieces by Julie Horova, Czechoslovakia.

Examples of animal spouts, handles, lugs, or other details will be found under the appropriate headings. See also **bear jug, bird tureen, cow creamer, fish form, frog mug, hound-handled pitcher, money box, owl jug/pot, pig, rhyton, snuff box.**

ANTHROPOMORPHIC POTS

See **human form.**

APALA

"A sort of pie dish with cavities of various sizes hollowed out in it for cooking eggs, which seems to prove that the Romans knew all about poaching eggs." (See LG in Booklist.)

APPLE BUTTER POT

A 19th century American container in red earthenware for a sauce of apples stewed in cider. It has a wide mouth and a slightly narrower base. Those intended for storage of the sauce had no handle. See G.EAFP (Booklist) for illustrations.

AQUAMANILE, Aquamanale

The word is derived from the Latin which literally translates as "water for the hands." The form, often

This stocky creature is a fairly typical Medieval aquamanile. The drawing is a reconstruction from the broken example in the Scarborough (Yorks) Museum. It is from the 13th/14th centuries and is 14½ inches/370mm long.

very intricately modelled, was probably borrowed from silver work. Before the days when forks became common, it was a semihorizontal jug/pitcher used for the washing of fingers at mealtimes. It has a long history from early Mesopotamia through Persia to Medieval Europe and was often modelled in the form of a lion, ram, stag, or mounted knight. It is very decorative.

See **animal form,** and also similar vessels under **askos, cadogan teapot, ewer.**

ARBOR GROUP

The form consists of simple modelled figures set in a niche or leafy rococo arbor with a seat, the main form often being made from a domed pot cut through vertically. They were made at Frankenthal and other potteries in Europe, and were allied to English **pew groups** of the mid-19th century, although some Dutch variations were considerably more bucolic. A very pretty group of lovers under an arching tree in white salt-glaze can be seen in the Brighton Museum (England). A number of modern potters have produced similar groups.

ARTISTS' IMPRESSIONS OF POTTERY

It seems that graphic artists often find difficulty in actually seeing the ceramic forms of their own times and painting what they see. In Charleston's fine book, *World Ceramics,* he shows a Medieval painting of peasants bringing water from a well by means of jug/pitchers which resemble no contemporary form, being shaped like tall urns with a little flaring foot, probably metal shapes. Breugel is much more accurate, although his flaring pitcher feet appear to have knobs on them, instead of being depressed by the thumb which was the usual case in many Medieval pieces. Today many artists are still in the classic revival as far as pot representations go; the **amphora** is still the favorite shape. There are honorable exceptions, of course, such as the fine pots painted by Velasquez.

ART NOUVEAU

A movement in force at the beginning of the 20th century, which combined a feeling for "natural" flowing forms with rococo and Gothic overtones. It was often asymmetric in feeling, although this was more often the effect of the decoration, and was typically sinuous or flamelike, the elements of

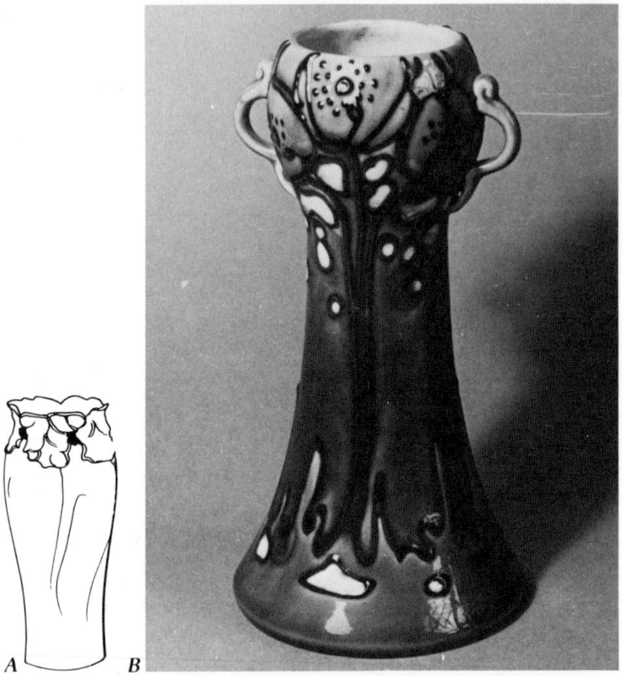

A. An Art Nouveau vase from Rorstand in which the floral decoration of pansies is modelled into the rim, circa 1900. B. A Minton vase designed by Wadsworth and Solon 1900–14. Although there appears to be an imbalance between the parts, they add up to a distinctive style.

form losing separate definition and flowing one into another. It was rich in linear rhythm, but also liable to exaggertion and excess. A number of pots, mostly semi-industrial, were designed in the Art Nouveau style, which has recently enjoyed something of a revival.

ARYBALLOS, Aryballus

An attractive small Greek pot common in the Corinthian "orientalizing" period of 800 to 600 B.C. typically with a rounded body and a bold, wide, flat rim. Described (I think unfairly) as a "globular and baggy bottle" in EB (see Booklist), it was used by athletes for holding oil, which was applied at the bath for cleaning the skin, or for holding perfume. It even had a purpose at funerals (see **tear jar**). It was often suspended by a cord from the wrist. A rather taller form is also found, and an Egyptian variant in the shape of a hedgehog is shown in C.APP (see Booklist), but most examples are squat with a short handle from the wide rim to the shoulder. The rounded body and wide rim

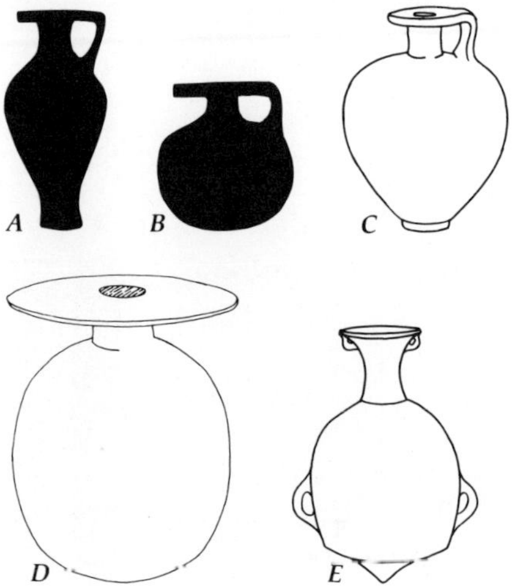

A/B. Typical silhouettes of Greek Corinthian aryballoi. These are 2½ inches high.
C. A Greek style with a less pronounced rim—a handsome little pot.
D. While not suggesting direct influence, this pot by Hans Coper shows a possible modern adaptation of the form. It is also quite small, approximately 4½ inches/115mm high.
E. The ancient American Inca form called an aryballus *by archaeologists. Circa 1500.*

is reflected in some of Hans Coper's pots. It is a strong and uncompromising shape.

A different shape, with two low handles and a pointed base from the Inca period of Peru is known as an **aryballus.**

ASHTRAY

Almost any small, shallow dish can be used for smokers' debris, although the typical ashtray will have indentations in the rim in which to rest cigarettes. This is difficult to design in an aesthetically satisfactory way. Some, more considerate smokers, use an ash and stub **box,** which lessens contamination.

ASKOS

Originally, this was the skin of a small animal made into a bottle, a type of container still used in the 20th century for carrying *moustos,* "grape juice," on pack horses. The pottery askos was an asymmetric vessel from early Helladic and later Greek times, usually with a handle and often bird- or even boat-shaped. A similar form from prehistoric 6th century

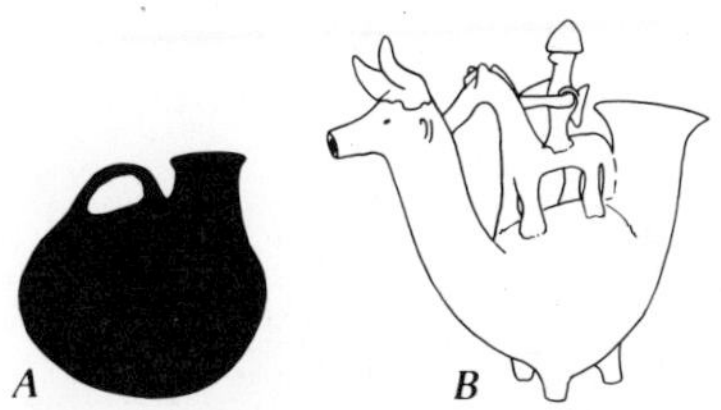

A. A typical askos form. This one is from Aulia, which was colonized by the Greeks, circa 700 B.C.
B. A 6th century B.C. *askos from Bologna as mentioned in the text.*

B.C. Italy is in the form of a man on a horse on a bull—an odd combination of Mediterranean and Hallstatt cultures.

ASPARAGUS DISH/TRAY

A simple two-sided tray for serving this delectable and expensive vegetable. It has been made mainly in the 19th and 20th centuries.

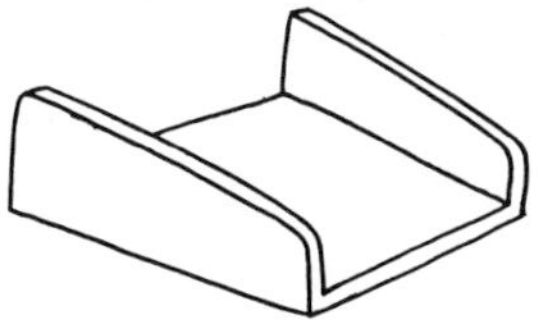

Surely one of the simplest forms in all ceramics!

ASYMMETRY and IRREGULARITY

"Living as we do in an environment of predominant symmetry of form and pattern it is difficult for us Westerners to appreciate the subtle asymmetry of these teabowls. Yet this very quality is one of the most valuable and characteristic in Japanese art." Since Leach wrote this in *A Potter's Book* in the 1940s we have become more accustomed to the pleasures of asymmetry, although it still occupies only a minor place in the generality of Western ceramics.

Although the *Shorter Oxford English Dictionary* gives the definition as "want of symmetry or *pro-*

A. A typical Japanese asymmetric or irregular pot is this water jar from Oribe. The character of many Japanese pots is partly determined by the use of stick-operated low-mass wheels.

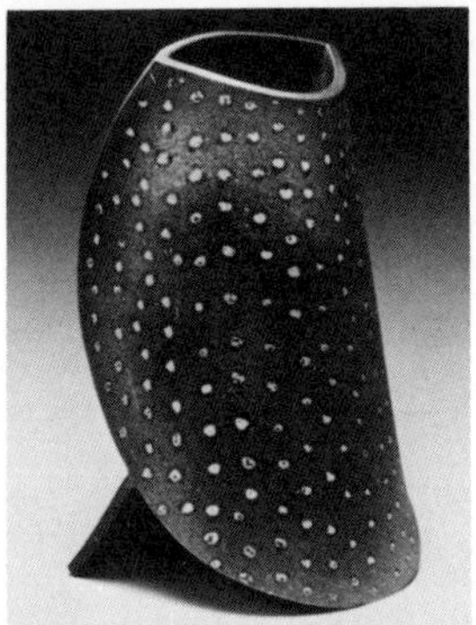

B

B. A cast form by Jaqueline Poncelet, which needs a rather unclaylike foot to make it stand.

C

C. Hand-built bottle by the author, with a subtle asymmetry of the body profile and neck.

portion" asymmetry, in a more positive sense, is a less obvious balance than that of equal weights around a central axis, which is symmetry, but a balance all the same. It is based on the physical fact that a small weight at a distance from a fulcrum will balance a greater weight nearer to the axis or point of balance. In practice, asymmetry is more involved and intuitive than this simple precept, but the final proof is still a physical one—whether the pot will stand steadily on its own base. In *Pottery Form* Rhodes suggests that "crookedness and waywardness [in throwing] tend to be abberations . . . a departure from symmetry which is different from the growth of form in an object which is essentially asymmetrical." Asymmetric pottery forms, therefore, tend to be coiled or modelled. Although thrown forms can be altered when half dry, the result is rarely fully satisfactory. Overt asymmetry is seen in a number of modern pots, such as the Poncelet "container" or the author's bottle, as illustrated. A rather stronger term is required to describe the attacked and "destroyed" shapes which some extreme potters practice. See illustrations for **split and slashed forms, beaten shape, distorted form.**

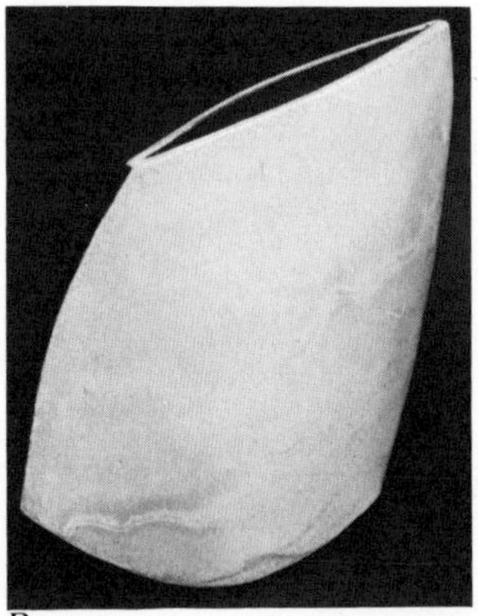

D

D. Asymmetry is the raison d'être of this envelope *pot by Val Barry.*

Irregularity is a rather different quality, being inherent in the nature of craft ceramics. To quote a review in PQ40 (see Booklist): "The subject of irregularity cannot be aired too often as far as the potter is concerned. Yanagi distinguishes between irregularity and deformation in art, the latter craze he does not see as a path towards true beauty."

AVOCADO DISH

An ovoid dish on a firm foot, the better to control this delectable fruit while it is being scooped out. The avocado should fit snugly, but, in England at any rate, the dishes are often too large (or the avocados too small!) so their usefulness is minimized.

An English industrial avocado dish with a lobed *rim.*

B

BACINI

The word literally means "basins," specifically, Italian painted earthenware plaques set into the walls of churches. They are found not only in Italy (Ravello, Rome, etc.), but also in the Near East and in Spain. They represent an aspect of the cooperation between potter and architect, once so fruitful, which has been largely lost, and which could be revived to the benefit of both professions.

BAIL

An arched handle, from Middle English *baile,* "to

bend." Pottery bail handles have been used on various types of pots, such as the **currant washer,** or on **basket** forms, but are most commonly found on **teapots.** Pottery bail handles give a firmer grip than **cane** ones, but are more vulnerable.

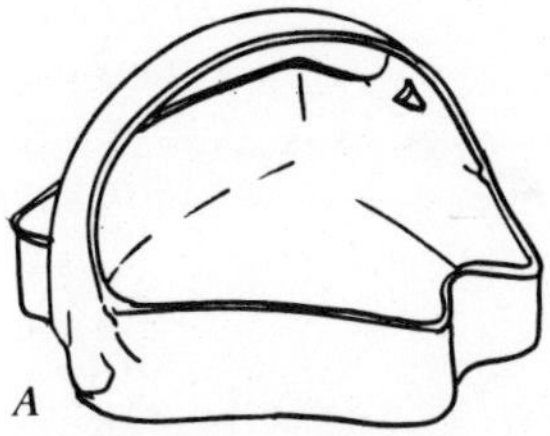

A

A. An Oribe bail-handled mukozuke *dish.*

B

B. A spirited teapot handle by Bill Brown, with an unusual handle stop *on the top.*

BAKER

A shallow dish or cover used upside down over food to be baked on a preheated flat stone, in its turn to be covered with hot embers and turf. In use until the end of the 19th century in Cornwall, it could be developed and used as a "safari" item today. See also **oven, egg baker.**

BAKING DISH

A/B. Two modern baking dishes, both thrown, the first beaten into a rectangle, the second made into an oval by the "cut center" method. Made by the author and Ray Finch.

A

B

This covers a wide field, but, specifically, the term indicates a more or less straight sided, flat-bottomed dish for top-crust pies and such. It would not have a lid. It has been an essential utensil in the kitchen since ovens came into general use. Watkins in W.ENEP (see Booklist) says of 18th century America: "Baking dishes were turned out in almost as many depths and widths as they are today" from small dishes "for muffins and custards to receptacles for large puddings." They are not infrequently oval or rectangular in shape, the former often an altered thrown dish, the latter press-molded. There is a fine example in the Guildhall at Lavenham (England) with two lug handles and standing on four feet, but these additions are unusual. See also **divided dish, fish dish,** etc.

BALSAMARIA

A collective Italian term for the perfume or balsam unguent bottles of antiquity, such as the **alabastron** and **aryballos.** See also **scent bottle.**

BALUSTER FORM

The word comes from the Italian *balustra,* meaning "the blossom of wild pomegranate"; hence also balustrade, which has a similar form.

A

A. A 13th century English baluster jug, about 16 inches/ 400mm high. (Victoria and Albert Museum.)

Both Medieval European and Chinese cultures produced this triple-curved form described in the *Concise Oxford English Dictionary* as "slender above, pear-shaped below." The upper part usually has a slight swell, but one which is less pronounced than that of the lower belly. The shape terminates in a flaring foot. It is typified by English 14th and 15th century jug/pitchers. A related form, but one less subtle and satisfying, is known as the **double gourd.**

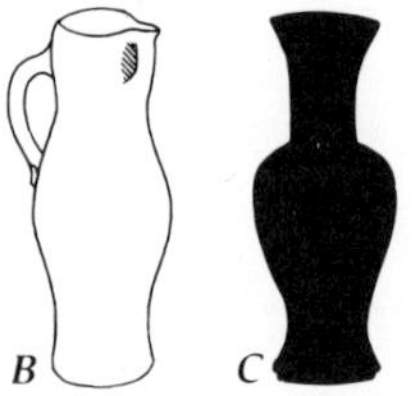

B. This form (similar to A) by Sam Haile (1947, 13 inches/325mm) is in no sense a slavish copy, but a fresh look at an old form.
C. The Chinese baluster form, more angular and defined.

Medley in M.HCA (see Booklist) gives a slightly different shape for a Chinese "baluster." She describes it as a high-shouldered, slightly flaring-footed body, with a long, wide neck spreading at the top. It is, again, basically treble-curved, but with a sharper juncture between shoulder and neck, and thus it resembles the "balustra" less closely than do the Medieval pots.

BAMBOO FORM

Based on the jointed construction of the bamboo, this form was adapted to ceramics in the Far East and was especially popular in Japan. Drugs were exported from the Orient actually packed in bamboo sections, and this may have been the origin of the **albarello.** Industrial potters in Europe enthu-

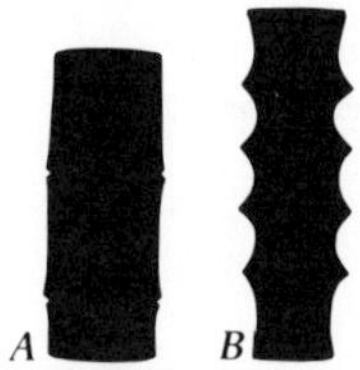

A. Very subtle use of the bamboo form in a Japanese Hirasa pot.
B. A more explicit and exaggerated version by Dan Arbeid, circa 1966.

siastically took over the style, which came to a climax during the "Japanese period" of the later 19th century. Wedgwood's "cane ware," while possibly referring to the buff color, was also often made in the form of cane or bamboo, sometimes forming the wall of a pot side by side like a fence, or grouped to make candlesticks, etc. Thrown pots, luted together, can give a similar effect, and some modern potters, Dan Arbeid for instance, have used the shape effectively.

BARBECUE

From the Spanish *barbarcon,* which was a framework set on posts over a fire, on which meat was dried, smoked, or cooked, the beast often being roasted whole. Now, especially in the United States, the term indicates an open-air feast with the cooking of food over a grill on a simple, usually charcoal-burning stove, although the meat, alas, has for the most part diminished from large hogs to small

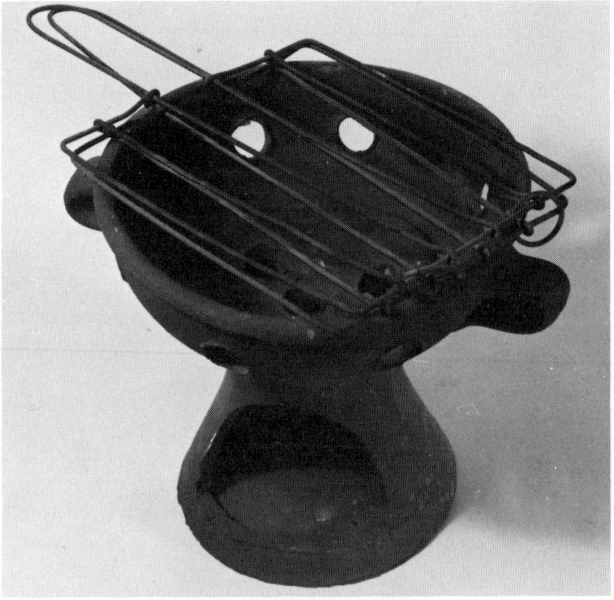

A simple pottery grill or barbecue from Portugal.

frankfurters! Very simple variations, some in pottery, are found all over Europe.

The construction of a barbecue stove is a challenge to the potter's invention. A body with some thermal shock resistance (unglazed, low-fired earthenware often fulfills this requirement), together with a design which allows for adequate ventilation, are essential.

BARBER'S BASIN

Once an essential piece of equipment for the barber-cum-surgeon, this was a wide-rimmed plate or basin, sometimes oval in plan, and with a semicircle cut from the rim so that it would fit against a customer's neck for shaving, or his arm for bleeding. It is found all over Europe and in early United States pottery, often decorated in tin-glaze. The

Late 18th century Bristol tin-glaze barber's basin, 10 inches/250mm in diameter. (Victoria and Albert Museum.)

idea of a curve or curves cut from the side of a bowl or dish could be adapted by the modern potter. See also **monteith** and illustration F under **rim.**

BARM JAR

At the beginning of the 20th century, Fishley Holland (see H.FYP in Booklist) tells us, "women did their own baking using barm, obtained from the local pub, for leavening. This meant keeping a barm jar which had a bung at the top." With the resurgence of home bread-making, perhaps a modern barm (yeast) jar would again be a welcome kitchen container. In Bedfordshire, England, it was tall and cylindrical and was known as a "dicky pot."

BARREL SHAPE

The Sussex "harvest barrel" in the 19th century was about 11 inches/275mm high with double bungholes and a thin, flat handle. Miniature barrel shapes were made in Bristol tin-glaze, 4 to 6 inches /150mm long, with a stopper in the side. Barrellike containers, much larger, often oval in plan, and used for wine and spirits especially, were widely made industrially and can be very handsome. The **costrel** was sometimes barrel shaped, the Roman type very much so. See also **flask.**

A

A. A charming 18th century Bristol barrel form reputedly used for spirits, although it is difficult to see just how it was used in practice. (Bristol Museum.)

B

B. A magnificent 17th century salt-glazed ale barrel. A small tap would have been inserted in the spout.

BARTMANN JUG

A Rhenish salt-glazed bottle/jug with a bearded mask, in common production since the 15th century. See its better-known later title of **bellarmine.**

BASE

The base of a pot will control its overall character; a wider base can give stability and dignity; a narrower one, elegance and "spring." Too wide a base in relation to the curve of the wall can render a pot earthbound or can even give the impression that it is sitting in a hole rather than on the surface. This is a common fault in students' early pots. A slight emphasis at the base of a pot, either inwards or outwards, or a curve or bevel, can alter the whole impression.

When turned over, the base of a pot should present as acceptable a form and surface as the more visible parts. See Leach on this subject under **foot.** A tap on the base at the leather-hard stage, giving it a slight concavity, will greatly assist stability and will impart some form to it.

BASIN

The word is originally from the Latin *bacchinon* and the Old French *bacin.* There is some overlapping in the meanings of basin and **bowl.** The *Concise Oxford English Dictionary,* in fact, gives bowl as a "more poetic alternative to basin." A basin, however, may be more or less hemispherical in profile, or may have a flat area, as in a pudding basin, or

The typical 19th/20th century pudding basin form.

may even be platelike, as is the **barber's basin.** A basin is used for the mixing of foods and liquids (although "mixing bowl" is a common term); for waste materials (e.g., slop basin); or for washing water (Shakespeare mentions "basons and ewers to lave her dainty hands"). Almost any large, open vessel which is shallower (or less elegant) than a bowl, but deeper than a plate, is liable to be called a "basin" in books on the history of ceramics. In the 18th century the practice of drinking tea from teabowls and later from deep saucers led to the expression "to take a basin of tea."

BASKET

It is often asserted that the earliest pots were formed inside coarse wicker or rush vessels, although the impressions found on some early shards could well have been **skeuomorphic.** The term is applied to some early pots with handles over them; e.g., the late Mycenean "basket vase" referred to in L.GPBA (see Booklist).

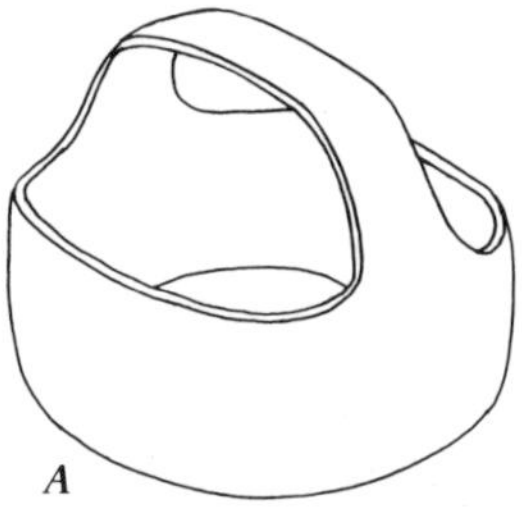

A

A. Simple and attractive, this pottery basket form was by Kenzan; 18th century Kyoto.

B

B. A basket or pail *form by Colin Kellam.*

Baskets, often with fruit or flowers, were made starting in 16th century in Italy and elsewhere. Industrial pottery abounds in realistic impressions of baskets, often with open wickerwork, which are ceramic tours de force (though not always aesthetic ones). A slipware imitation of a rustic log basket, which has a certain innocent attraction, is shown in the York County Museum (England) and was made at the curiously named Saladine Nook Pottery near Huddersfield, circa 1870. The example could be multiplied many times. A more restrained and subtle Japanese interpretation of the form is illustrated. See also under **well** for a similar form, and under **bail.**

BATH

Some Chinese vessels, often up to 4 feet/1.25m wide, are called "baths," although they are more likely to have been fish bowls. Minoan remains abound in bath-shaped terra-cotta vessels which are almost large enough to be used as tubs. They are

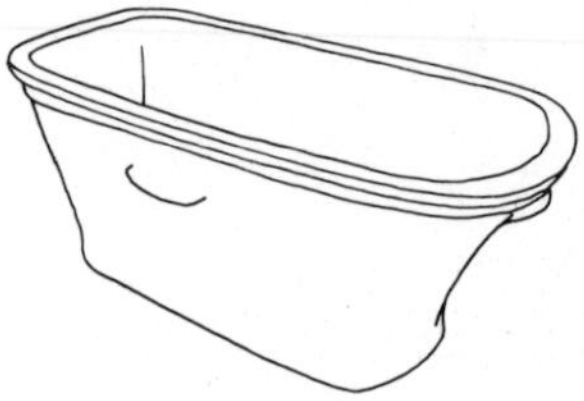

From 1400 B.C. this Minoan pottery bath or larnax stands about 18 inches/450mm high and is very reminiscent of the modern shape.

decorated with fish, etc., which suggests an association with water, although similar shapes known as **larnax** were made for the burial of the dead. Today we accept full-size ceramic baths as commonplace, but in earlier times legends sprang up in China regarding the making and firing of these relatively smaller efforts.

BATH RASP

Pottery in the form of sitting birds, ladies' slippers, crocodiles, etc., with one flat side roughened for scrubbing the body and feet, was made in Egypt and other countries in the Near East at least as far back as the 16th century. The crocodile illustrated, in very severe modelling, is from 19th century Egypt, made in a red, burnished earthenware.

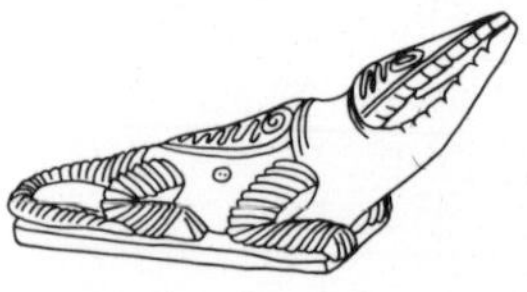

The crocodile is from 19th century Egypt. The rasp would be underneath the base, the head acting as a handle. This is a remarkably powerful piece of modelling.

BATTER BOWL

In this unusual vessel, from 19th century America, which appears to have been constructed from half a thrown cylinder, batter was mixed and poured onto a griddle via the spout in the end.

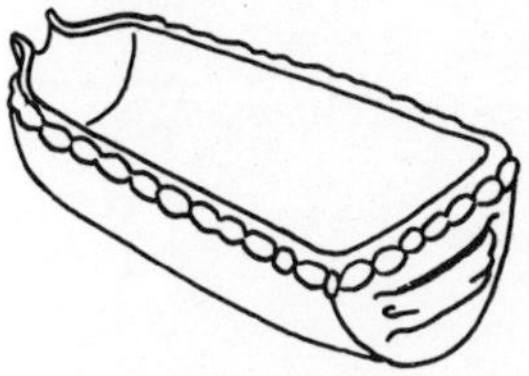

Batter bowl made in the United States, 19th century.

BATTER JUG

Another American vessel, illustrated by Guilland in G.EAFP (see Booklist) in the form of a spouted pot some 10 inches/250mm high, not unlike a teapot, but with a wire handle and a metal drop-over lid. It was probably used for the temporary storage of mixed batter, and was made in Pennsylvania in the mid-19th century.

BEAD

The word "bead," as in "rosary" or "prayer beads," comes from the Saxon *biddan*, meaning "to pray."

A row of ancient Minoan beads in the form of tiny pots, probably originally covered with gold foil, is illustrated in H.MMA (see Booklist). Glazed steatite beads were made in Mesopotamia, and Egyptian paste (confusingly called "faience") beads in blue-greens and browns were very common, the latter having been used on mummy wrappings, as well as for adornment. This type continued into the Roman period. One in the form of a melon is shown

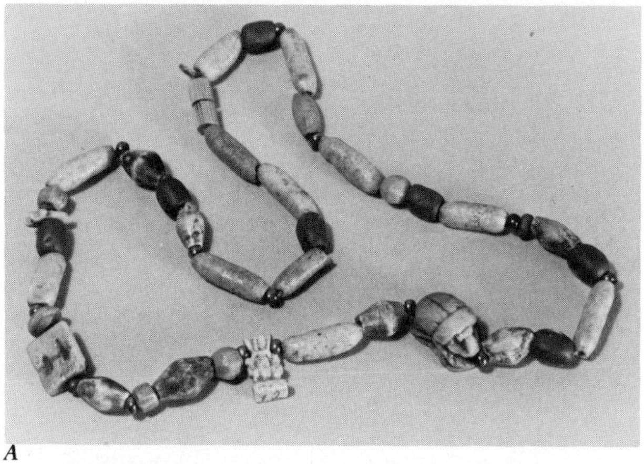

A

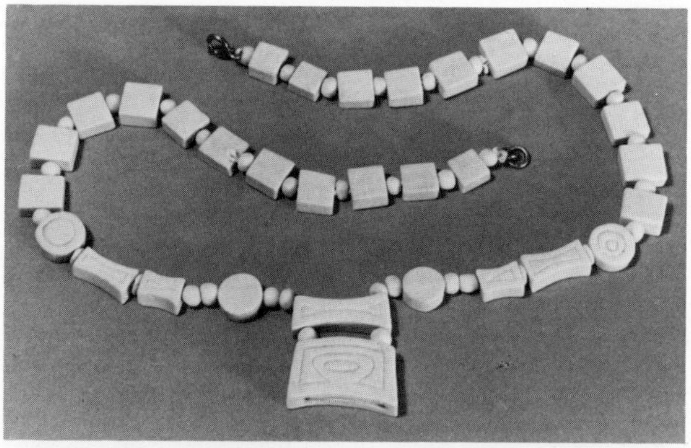

B

C

D

A. Beads from New Kingdom Egypt, circa 1200 B.C., which include the Eye symbol, a small figure of a god, and a scarab, with various mummy beads and others
B. A necklace of unglazed porcelain by Sheila Fournier. The beads have the crisp angles and outline suitable to the material.
C/D. In contrast, these earthenware beads, fired on wire, depend mainly on their decoration or glaze finish. Made by Sheila Fournier and Ruth Davies.

in EB (see Booklist), and they have even been found in English Wiltshire burial barrows.

There is little record of other pottery beads until comparatively modern times, but considerable numbers have been made by craftsman potters;

e.g., the unglazed porcelain necklaces of Sheila Fournier and the many glazed earthenware beads fired on wires.

BEAD RIM

An archaeologists' term for a rounded-section **rim.**

A well-defined bead rim on a late Iron Age British jar. (Devizes Museum.)

BEAKER

The word is derived from a variety of similar words—the Middle English *biker,* the Medieval Latin *bicarius,* etc. *Webster's New Collegiate Dictionary* defines it as a "drinking cup with a wide mouth and sometimes supported on a standard," which sounds

A

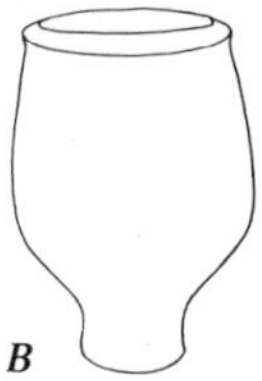

B

C

D

E

F

G

H

I

J

more like a **goblet.** A very old dictionary associates it with "beak," hence, the wide mouth, but this may have been inspired guesswork. Most authorities stipulate "large," and the *Encyclopaedia Britannica* refers to "a flaring foot," though the latter is by no means a common feature in pottery beakers.

In historical and archaeological books on pottery a great variety of tallish, wide-mouthed vessels are labelled "beakers." In general usage the term refers to drinking vessels, often without a handle, larger and taller than a **cup,** but smaller than a **tankard.** It is almost synonymous with **mug,** although the latter is usually thicker walled and rather less sophisticated. In narrower scientific usage, a beaker is of glass or porcelain and has a lip for pouring.

Excellent early forms are those of the so-called Beaker Folk of the 2nd millenium B.C., a culture found throughout Europe and England. These beakers vary from 5 inches/130mm to a massive 10 inches/250mm high. The Near East, from Sumerian times onward, has produced very elegant and interesting beaker shapes. Roman types were more squat, but were still very lively (especially those with a narrow foot as illustrated) and included the Romano-British **folded form,** which is unique.

Most tableware potters today make beakers, many with a handle, which renders them more useful for hot drinks; and the range of forms is very wide. A slightly concave or waisted profile, with a flare at the lip, is common to many. The squat barrel is probably the least satisfactory. As mentioned above, a certain slenderness and even elegance separates the beaker from the mug.

A. Strongly shaped and well designed, this beaker was made perhaps 4000 years ago by the Beaker Folk. The handle is nicely accommodated in the slightly concave section of the profile.
B. Full-formed and yet with some elegance, this type of small beaker was made in Roman Britain around 200 A.D.
C. A curious tyglike late Medieval form of beaker.
D. A simple but well-proportioned flaring form from 12th century Persia, called a "beaker" by historians. (Ashmolean Museum.)
E/F. Two modern variations on the beaker silhouette. Example E is nearer to a cup or mug.
G. The charming cup/beaker typical of many made in 17th century England.
H. A sturdy and practical handleless beaker by one of the earliest pioneers of the modern craft movement, Denise Wren. The form has some affinity in its stem base with illustration B, but, in character, they are worlds apart.
I. A modern, more rounded version of illustration G, by Danny Killick.
J. A very fine beaker by Ray Finch in which carinations in the silhouette provide junction points for the handle.

BEAN POT

This may be exclusively an early U.S. vessel, used for the baking of beans on hot coals. This was often done by potters for the surrounding villages during

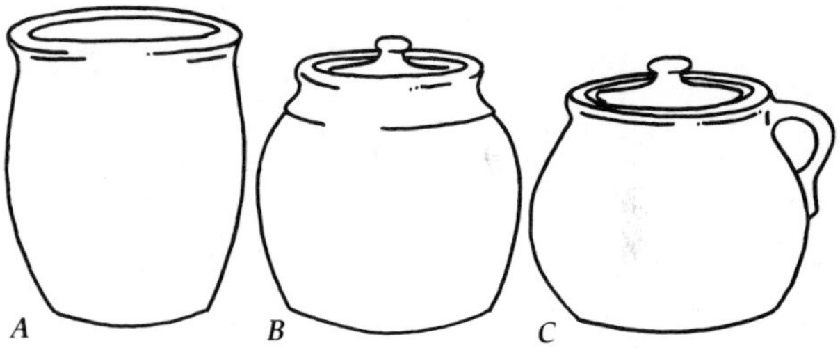

A/B/C. Illustration A shows the earliest open jar type of bean pot; B is a later form with the addition of a lid to retain moisture during cooking; and, finally, C is a more squat shape with a handle to facilitate moving the pot on a hot stove.

a firing. G.EAFP (see Booklist) gives this quote, "Baking done as usual and the smallest favours gratefully acknowledged," from an advertisement by a Connecticut potter in 1788. From Guilland's excellent book, *Early American Folk Pottery,* we cull the above "evolution of the bean pot."

BEAR JUG

In the 18th century **jug/pitchers** modelled as bears, each with a removable head to form a cup, were

A

B

A/B. This amusing figure from the Bristol Museum is typical of those made in salt-glaze and other finishes in mid-18th century England, although in this case the bear is not maltreating a dog. Illustration B shows the head used as a cup. Both pieces are designed to stand upright with the openings uppermost.

fairly common. The creature was often hugging (fatally, not lovingly) a dog; bear-baiting was a favorite sport. There are well-known English bear jugs in white salt-glaze, also in brown, and with varying degrees of efficiency in the modelling. One from Staffordshire has a spigot in the belly.

BEATEN SHAPE

In B.AMP (see Booklist) Bryan Newman more breezily calls these "bashed pots." A pot, whether

A

thrown or built, can be given an altogether new character by beating with a bat or paddle. It is difficult to say how much the technique was used in earlier times, although we do find harvest flasks in the 18th century, for instance, that were obviously beaten into a rectangular shape, and there are beaten bottles from the Japanese Yedo period; but the technique is certainly well favored by modern potters the world over. Hamada and Leach use

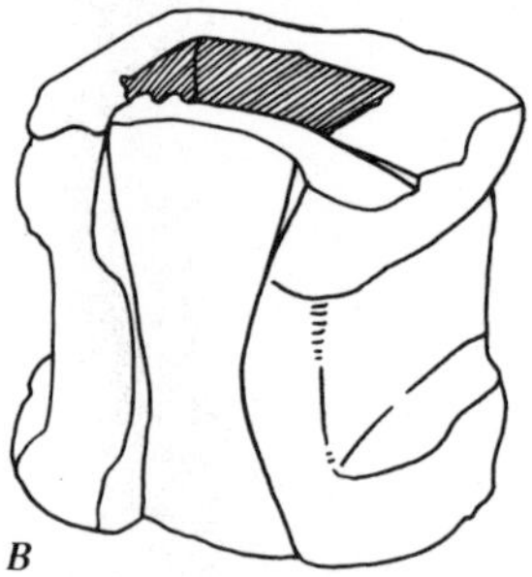

B

C

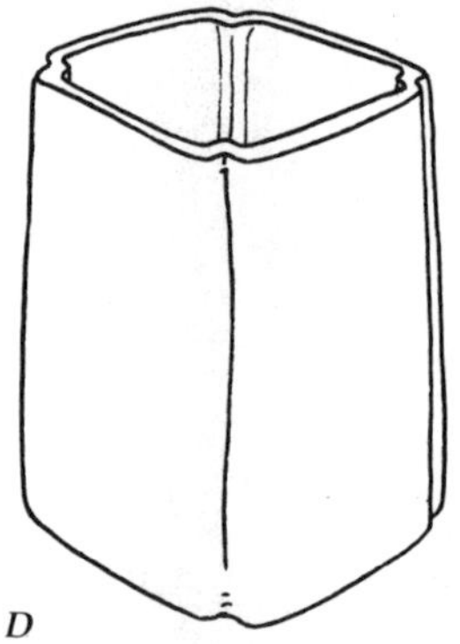

D

E

A. The flattened area on this bottle by Hamada forms the base for the decoration. Made in 1963.
B. A cleverly "bashed" plunge pot by Brian Newman; the indentations are at right angles to one another.
C. A beaten and scored pot by Janet Leach. Made at Tamba.
D. A squared thrown Shino (17th century Japan) vessel with the corners sharply beaten inwards.
E. Bernard Leach's hexagonal stoneware vase, probably beaten, but with a more regular angular form than is common with the technique. The flat surfaces may have been subsequently planed. The vase stands 8 inches/200mm high. (Crafts Study Centre, Bath.)

it extensively, usually to form slightly flattened facets on thrown pots, while the more recent trend is to attack the clay in a more violent fashion, distorting almost to the point of destruction in some cases. See also **compressed form** and **distorted form.**

BEEHIVE

Circular slabs of clay, about 10 inches/250mm across, with a 1-inch hole set near the perimeter, served as beehive covers. Mostly 19th century from Iran and the Near East, their main attraction lies in their decoration.

This English preRoman full-formed pot with holes in the lower belly is said to have been used as a beehive. (Devizes Museum.)

A "bee super" is a Cornish bottomless closed-in bottle shape, with a knob on the top and a small door in the lower wall. It was placed over a straw skep in which bees would store honey. For a beehive proper, however, we can go back 2000 years to preRoman England to find the well-shaped pot illustrated.

BEER BOTTLE

Usually of salt-glazed ware, the humble beer bottle took on a variety of shapes; it was, however, always fairly tall, with a well-defined rim that enabled the cork to be securely tied down. It usually had straight sides with a sharp angle at the shoulder, but could also resemble the modern milk bottle, with long sloping shoulders and sometimes curved sides. See also illustration A under **ginger beer bottle.**

BELL, Bird Bell

Pottery bells, whether of well-fired earthenware, stoneware, or porcelain, can give an excellent ring. Celadon-glazed bells were made at least as early as 1550 in China. Salt-glazed bell-ladies were made in England in the 1740s, and table bells were used to summon servants for a fresh course. The strikers can be of pottery, although Jonas Hanway in 1753, speaking of the little Meissen bells on clocks, insisted that "hammers must be made of wood."

A. A mid-18th century salt-glazed figure with a bell-like skirt. This type of model is a favorite exercise with student beginners.
B. A section through a thrown bird-feeder bell.

The bell should be surmounted by a knob or handle, often a modelled figure, so that the hand does not damp the vibrations. It is difficult to achieve a particular pitch without extensive trials. Tubular "bells" struck from the outside are easier to tune. See also **musical instruments.** A common teaching project is to construct a figure from thumbpots, the wide skirt of which acts as a bell.

A bird bell is a **bird feeder,** so-called because of its bell-like shape. It is filled with fat and scraps, so that it can be hung mouth down for birds to feed from. It requires a fairly full form, with a rim slightly wider than the pot wall to help the small claws to grip.

BELLARMINE

The name given to a splendid line of salt-glazed wine or spirit bottles bearing a bearded mask on the neck. They were made in all sizes, from a few inches high to 18 inches/450mm and more, and were used for the carriage and export of liquor, etc. The smaller ones have also been known to contain mercury and other liquids.

Known earlier as "Bartmannkruger" ("Barbman" in France, "D'Alva Bottle" in the 17th century), the term "bellarmine," an English nickname according to Haggar (see H.CECP in Booklist), is supposedly derived from the mask representing an unpopular Cardinal of the late 16th century. But Leach suggests that the mask may have stemmed from Bacchus, a much more appropriate subject. In fact, a bellarmine-type bottle in the Welsh Folk Museum has a pair of Bacchic figures in place of the usual mask. They were also known as "Greybeards," under which title, according to Hughes (see H.PBC in Booklist), they were made in London in the late 16th century for use in the Royal Household. The earliest known bellarmine with both a date and a mask is marked "1550," the latest "1699." The form was copied by Dwight of Fulham, London, after 1671 and later by Hubert Schiffer of Raeran, Ger-

A. A large 16th century German bellarmine. The necks of these fine bottles are often awry as in this case; 20 inches/500mm tall.

A

B. In the smaller masked bottles the proportions vary; the neck is often longer and the body rounder than in the larger specimens.

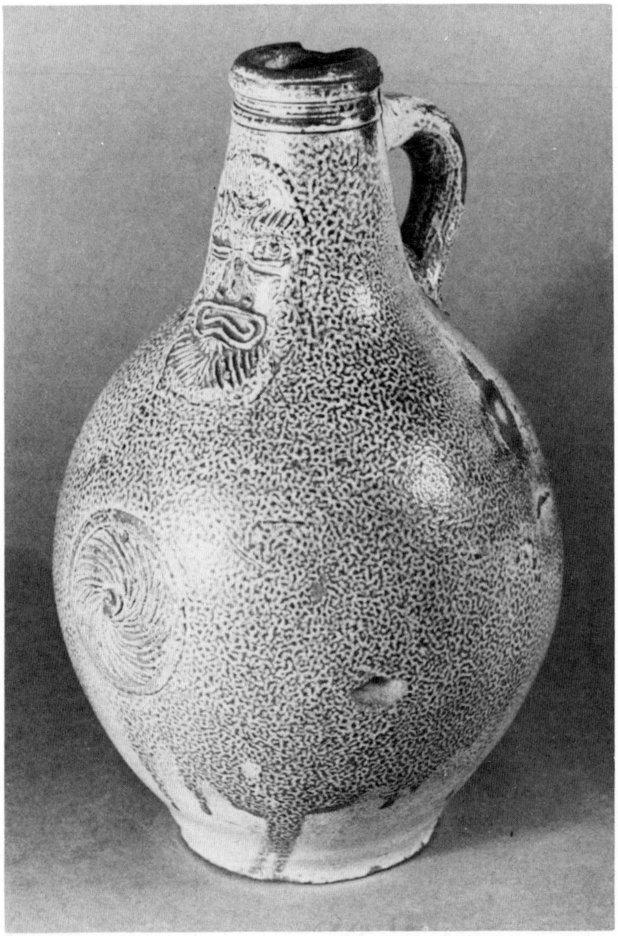

B

many. The latter copies can be recognized by their molded handles. The original centers of manufacture were Aachen and Westerwald.

There are associations between witchcraft and bellarmines and examples are occasionally found full of nails and with "positive urine tests," according to the Ipswich Museum. See also under **wine bottle.**

While the glazes on these pots are very attractive, the forms are even more so, typifying a power and directness of throwing rarely equalled before or since.

BELL BEAKER

The most commonly found Beaker Folk form. The vessels were buried with the dead (for a drink on the last journey?) and many have survived whole. See also under **beaker.**

The bell beaker varied in size and form, but this outline is typical. England, late Neolithic.

BELL RINGERS' JUG

As one who suffers from the tireless energies of campanologists in my local church, I have wondered how they keep it up. The jug illustrated, some 18 inches/500mm tall, helps to explain the enthusiasm.

This large, generous jug/pitcher for thirsty bellringers is inscribed with these words: "If you can fill me well, 'twill help to ring the bell." The double handle is unusual. (Salisbury Museum.)

BELLY

The widest section of a pot, which has a fairly low main curve; the area of greatest curvature. Applied only to the central or lower part of a pot. If the widest part is high, it is known as the **shoulder.**

BEUTELFLASCHE

A rather squat and lumpy German **flask** with a wide neck.

BIBERON

An Italian drinking vessel with a bulbous body and one or more drinking spouts. (See C.PPGT in Booklist.)

BIDET

This aid to female hygiene was invented in the 17th century and "became and object of ceremony, ladies apparently holding court and receiving guests while enjoying its comforts." (See H.CECP in Booklist.) They were sometimes wittily inscribed and were also called "biddies."

BIRD BELL

See **bell.**

BIRD CAGE

Nothing it seems is beyond the skill and fancy of the potter, and we find elaborate bird cages complete with towers and castellations, some 17 inches/425mm high, being made at Delft in the 18th century. There is a remarkable example in the Fitzwilliam Museum, England.

BIRD FEEDER

A

A. Naive and simple, this bird feeder was made in 18th century Bristol. (Bristol Museum.)

In earlier times various simple "sparrow pots" and other types, with a twig set in the rim, were made not so much for conservation, but for trapping nestlings and adult birds for eating! The little Bristol pot illustrated may have had a kindlier function.

B. An ingenious modern bird feeder by Karen Karnes.

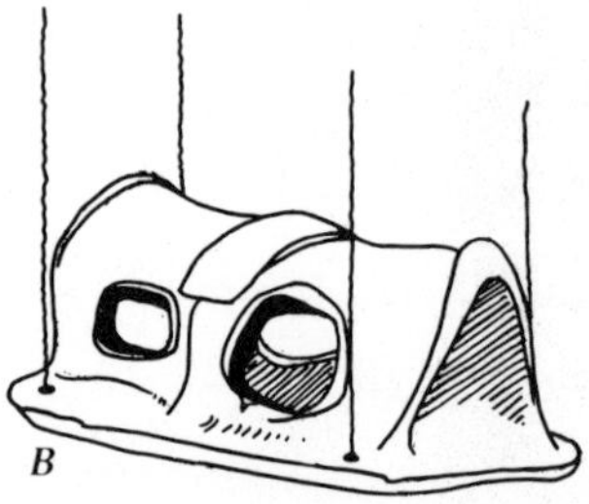

The modern bird-feeding table is very adaptable to play of the imagination, and pottery feeders make a change from the ubiquitous wooden tray with its little hut. Karen Karnes shows two ingenious and attractively designed feeders in CR50 (see Booklist). See also **bell.**

BIRD FORM

See **animal form.**

BIRD TUREEN/CASSEROLE

Tureens in the shape of birds—duck, goose, etc. (to hold the appropriate fowl?)—were commonly made in the 18/19th centuries. In recent times, Rosemary Wren and others have made hand-built **casseroles** in similar forms, while a charming variation is seen in the work of Barbara Colls.

A

B

A. More compact than many 18th/19th century examples is this French turkey tureen.
B. More like a bird on a nest than the usual bird tureen is this small bird dish or casserole by Barbara Colls.

BISHOP BOWL

A miter-shaped bowl, the rim rising to two arching points, for **punch.** Known in Scandinavia as a "Bishop." (See C.PPGT in Booklist.)

BLEEDING BOWL

A dish or bowl, often with a flat horizontal handle, used to receive blood drawn in primitive surgery. Bleeding bowls are found all over the Western world, with especially attractive forms from Spain, decorated with luster. They were in use as early as the 16th century in England. The later **barber's basin** was also used for this purpose. Although blood is now taken in a more sophisticated fashion, these bowls are strong and decorative and repay study by the potters of today. See the illustration under **escudelles ab orelles.**

BLOCK HANDLE

A **handle** so designed that a solid vertical strip of clay is available for fixing it to the vessel, instead of merely top and bottom joints. It is generally molded and used on industrial cups or mugs for extra strength.

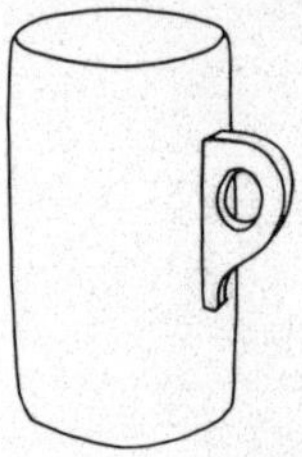

The illustration shows the general type, though many are more rounded, sometimes with a built-in handle stop.

BLUE DASH CHARGER

By reference to the decoration on their rims, this name has been given to a series of largish plates of sturdy form made at Lambeth and other centers in the 17/18th centuries. See also **charger.**

BOAT

In the Ipswich Museum there is a splendid, though crudely made, Neolithic Egyptian boat (marked circa 8000 B.C., apparently by the donor) with animal heads at each end and an elephant with a raised trunk across the middle. Another attractive and more flowing shape, dated more realistically at circa 3500 B.C. (Naguada period), is in the Ash-

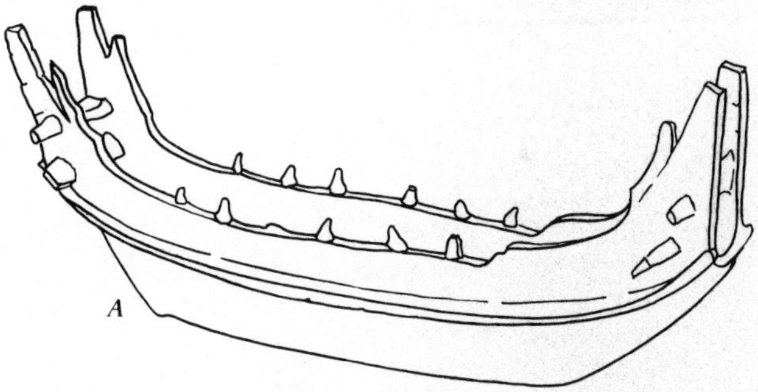

A

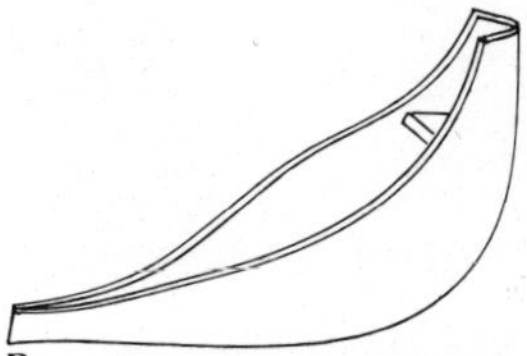

B

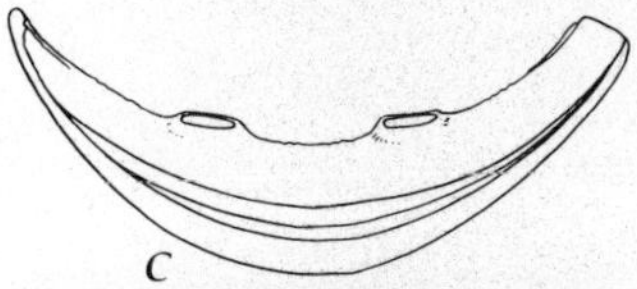

C

D

E

A. A 4th century Iron Age pottery boat almost 3 feet long from Japan. Realistic and detailed.
B. In contrast a more stylized form, made in preDynastic Egypt.
C. A boatlike modern Japanese pot with 2 apertures.
D/E. Two modern ship models: the first (left), a box by Peter Philips, in full sail and with unlikely fungilike additions; the second (above), by Ian Gregory, is totally fantastic, with house, boat, and town all in one, which is perhaps an elaborate pun on the word "houseboat"?

molean. The early Greek **askos** was sometimes boat shaped. Boatlike water pots for the mixing of ink were made in Sung China. Tomb sculpture from 500 A.D. Japan also includes boats in clay, some 3 feet/1m long.

In such highly maritime cultures as ancient Crete and modern England, however, clay boats or ship-inspired pots are quite rare. A nicely made realistic "coble"-type of fishing boat in earthenware is shown at the York County Museum, made at Stockton. The traditional tureen is vaguely boat shaped, but probably not deliberately so. Today Bryan Newman is especially known for his stylized boat forms, often as well loaded as the Egyptian cargo mentioned above, with houses and other unlikely objects. See also **Noah's ark.**

BOGGLE

From the Scottish *bogle,* meaning "a phantom" or "goblin." It is a Scottish jug or pitcher in human form.

BONE EDGE

A Staffordshire term for a nicely rounded rim. See illustration A under **bead rim.**

BONSAI BOWL

The term probably derived from the Japanese *pun-sai,* which means "planted in a tray." Rhodes also mentions the original Chinese *p'en ching,* translatable as "pot-scape" and similar to *sakei,* "living landscape" in miniature.

A

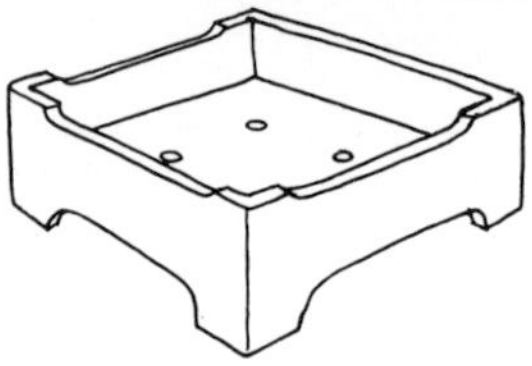

B

A. A planted bonsai bowl by the Yates' Peter and Dorothy of Yardley-Hastings. (Photograph: Yates.)

B. A typical slab-built bonsai bowl.

The bowls or trays are shallow containers of almost any decorative plan, with drainage holes, for growing miniature or dwarfed trees and plants. The holes are also used for anchoring the plants with wire during training. The formal possibilities are wide and some modern potters make a speciality of these containers; the Yates of Yardley-Hastings, for instance.

BOOTS, SHOES, and FEET

Pots in the form of feet or footware have been made throughout the history of pottery. Examples are known from Neolithic Moravia, for instance, or from the Hittite potters, right through to the more sentimental adaptations from Delft and Bristol.

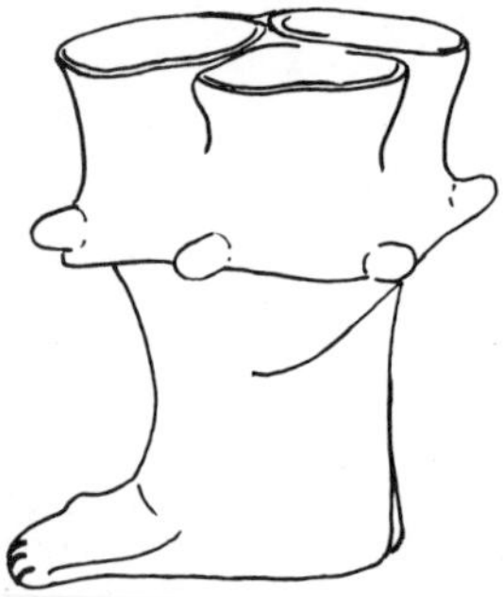

A

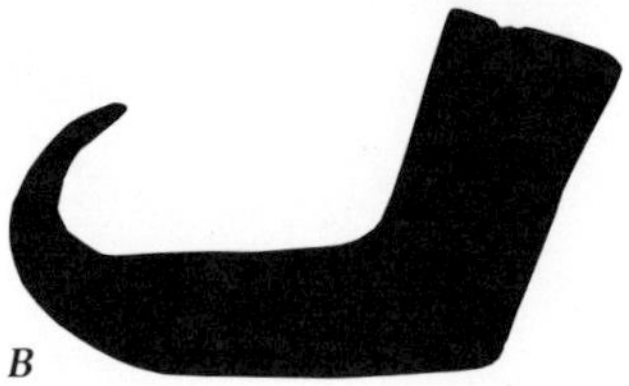

B

C

A. An astonishing construction from Neolithic Moravia, about 13 inches/330mm high.
B. An Anatolian drinking rhyton, *like a jester's shoe from 1900* B.C.
C. Many decorative boots and shoes were made in the 18/19th centuries. These were from Lambeth, circa 1690.

Attenuated foot forms from the 19th century were used as **hot-water bottle** boot warmers, one of the rare practical applications. Today boots appear as "ceramic sculptures," not even open at the top, made by art school students and others. See also **scent bottle, eggcup.**

BOSS, Embossed

A more or less circular, protuberant ornament, usually decorative, but often influencing the form.

A

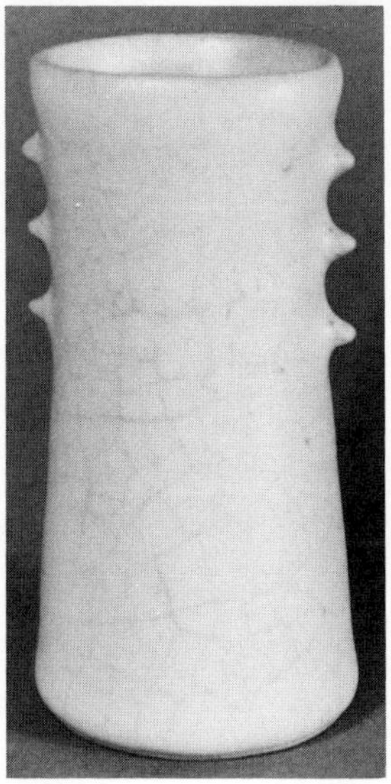

B

A. Decorative bosses on a so-called bulb bowl from Sung China. (Barlow Collection.)

B. Small bosses which break and sharpen the silhouette of this flattened porcelain pot. By the author.

A

A. A fine Chinese Sung bottle in black Honan stoneware. Note the firm, slightly rolled *base. (Barlow Collection.)*

Bosses are found on ceramics as far apart in space and time as a Sung Chun bowl, the Saxon **buckelurnen,** and a 19th century Zulu spherical pot. A Bronze Age pot from eastern Germany is strikingly embossed with large, conical forms (see C.WC in Booklist). Embossing is not widely practiced today, although Dan Arbeid and Gordon Baldwin have used the form in their individual ways.

BOTTLE

See **jug.** The term is derived from *buticular,* a diminutive of *butis,* "a butt." It is, therefore, intimately connected with spiritous liquors, the containing of them, rather than the drinking of them, although the latter use was made of small bottles such as **costrels, flasks,** etc.

The bottle usually has a narrow neck to take a cork or stopper. In the West the **bellarmine** typifies the bottle. Sometimes the word **jar** is used, as in wine jar, but a true jar normally has a wider neck. In the United States the word "jug" is applied not to a wide-mouthed pouring vessel, as it is in England, but to typical bottle shapes—even those without a pouring lip. It is impossible to reconcile these terms. Therefore, where a form is mentioned which would be called a "bottle" in England, but a "jug" in the United States, it is then described as a "bottle/jug."

Referring to the bottle/jug shape, Rhodes in *Pot-*

B. A contrasting bottle from late Roman Britain. The low belly contracts naturally to a long neck, as in the Chinese bottle vase. *(Devizes Museum.)*

C. Two large pinched bowls were used to construct this bottle, the neck being coiled on. It was fired in sawdust. By Sheila Fournier.

B

tery Form states: "The elements of form which make up a bottle, a voluminous body surmounted by a small neck . . . create a dynamism or tension more pronounced than the more relaxed proportions of the jar or vase." There are, however, many variations on, and departures from, the full symmetrical shape that Rhodes was considering—the low-bellied bottle, such as the **aryballus,** etc.; straight-sided **beer** and **ink** bottles; flat-faced **flasks;** asymmetric forms, such as those derived from skin or leather bottles (the Greek **askos** or stoneware from T'ang China, for instance); bottles in which the main form is horizontal, such as those from Archaic Corinth or the modern **hot-water bottle;** and many more.

Fine bottle/jugs came from Europe and from the early settler days of the eastern United States. Today Cardew, Finch, and others exploit this generous form, strongly based, but springing up and

C

over to a satisfying shoulder and a firm rim. With other potters the shape can be much more delicate, the neck perhaps longer and assuming greater importance. Many have lost their function as stoppered containers and are purely decorative. See under **asymmetry.** More distantly related forms are sometimes called "bottles," where no other description is available and where the neck is narrower than the body; e.g., Joanna Constantinidis's snaking thrown and altered shapes. See also **bottle vase, bridge handle, cruet, saki bottle,** etc.

BOTTLE VASE

A name given by Margaret Medley (see M.HCA in Booklist) to a low-bellied, "pear-shaped" long-necked bottle on a foot. This appeared in late T'ang times and is called *" 'Yu-hu-ch'un p'ing' "* in Chinese. The shape has been used by a number of modern potters, including Bernard Leach.

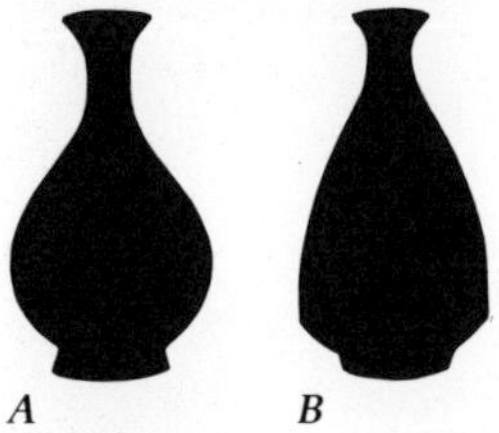

A/B. The typical Chinese bottle vase silhouette compared with a variation by Bernard Leach.

BOTTOM

Is the bottom of a bowl or pot subtly different from the **base?** Certainly the word can refer to the inside or outside of the base, such as the decoration in the bottom of a bowl, and it is also used to denote the underneath of round-based pots, which strictly have no "base." Perhaps bottoms are always rounded!

BOWL

The etymology is suggestive of the form, its origins probably in *bul,* meaning "to swell," or *bol,* "a round object." The *Concise Oxford English Dictionary,* gives bowl as a more poetic word for **basin,** although, in general usage the latter has taken on a more restricted meaning. From R.PF (see Booklist) we learn (certainly more poetically) that the first bowl was, according to Greek legend, shaped over the breast of Aphrodite.

Normally a full, open form, proportionally wider than it is high, its practical uses through the ages have been many—for eating and drinking from; for the temporary storage of foods, generally liquids; for scooping; for serving food; etc. It is also obvious from the wide variety of forms that the bowl has been an article of visual pleasure, as well as usefulness, and history (and many modern potters; see illustration H) often refutes Rhodes' statement that "the form of the bowl offers relatively little scope for sculptural complexity." China had terms for distinct types of bowls—*kung wan,* a rice bowl; *t'ang wan,* a shallower soup bowl; *ch'a wan,* a covered **teabowl;** etc. See also **bubble cup.**

It is at once the simplest and most subtle of pottery shapes. It is difficult to analyze the difference, for instance, between a Sung bowl and a Ch'ing imitation of it, although the difference is quickly appreciated. Utility bowl forms are to some degree controlled by their use: open and strong-rimmed for mixing food in; taller and more enclosed for soups, cereals, etc.; wider and flatter for fruit bowls; in-turned for bulbs; and so on. The range is immense, from a large generosity of curve to sharp angularities of outline.

The inside of a thrown bowl is normally clean and definitive; the most common fault is a sag just where the wall should start to rise. The whole fabric should be of a reasonably even thickness. It is impossible to discuss bowl forms in isolation from the **foot** or **foot ring,** which can impart to similar curves of the body heaviness or elegance, liveliness or dignity, according to width, shape, height, and slope. Great care must be taken with the *rim,* which should not only represent a definite termination of the curve of the wall, but must also be in harmony with the general style and purpose. The rims of Sung bowls are splendid object lessons.

Hand-built bowls are comparatively rare, al-

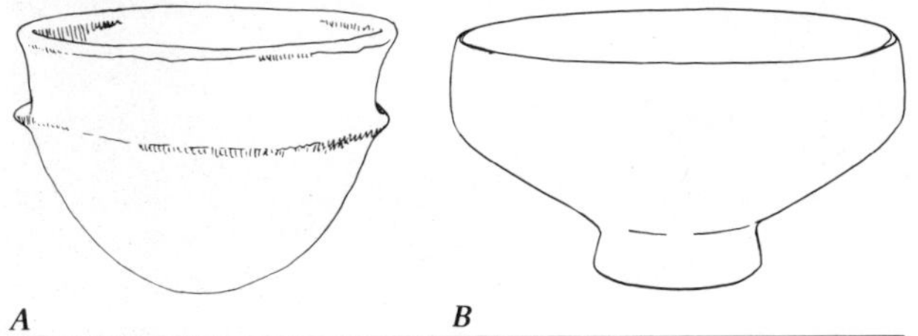

A. A very subtly carinated hand-built bowl from Neolithic Sussex.
B. The sturdy lines and beautifully proportioned foot of a 12th century Persian bowl.

C

C/D/E. Three Sung Chinese bowls which, although different in character, all share an outward flare of the rim: well defined in D, very gentle in C and E. (Barlow Collection.)

D

E

F

though in modern times Ruth Duckworth and others have produced original and powerful forms. In pinched bowls, whether of porcelain or other materials, the rim is often of great importance to the form. The main problem with pinched bowls is the

F. Generous and beautifully finished, this rounded form by Katherine Pleydell-Bouverie reminds one of a ripe seed pod. (Crafts Study Centre, Bath.)

G

provision of a foot, which often looks merely applied and not integrated with the general form.

See also illustrations under **cylinder, split form, punch bowl, folded form, ladle, spouted bowl, bulb bowl, boss, bubble cup, flange, crucible, cut-sided bowls, milk ladle, pancheon, pinched pot form, plant form, scoop, square-mouthed bowls, stacking pots,** etc.

G. A practical, but typically well defined and proportioned 12th century Romano-British basinlike bowl or pie dish. (Devizes Museum.)
H. Much more brutal, but equally indicative of the ideas and character of the potter, is this bowl in lead-glazed earthenware by Peter Smith.
I. A hand-built layered form by Sheila Fournier. Here the bowl is a purely sculptural object.

H

I

BOWL SANCTUARY

Bowls, sometimes as large as 15 inches/375mm across and crowded with models of stylized people, animals, and other objects are found in early cultures, notably in 3rd/2nd millennium B.C. Cyprus. They have inspired modern potters to create their own small worlds within the confines of bowls and other open forms. Ian Godfrey's work was seminal in this field. See also **landscape.**

A. A typically crowded ceremony, modelled in a hand-built bowl from 3rd millenium B.C. Cyprus. One figure (without an admission ticket?) is peering over the wall.
B. A very decorative lobed bowl with a sanctuary *by Ian Godfrey.*

A

B

BOWL STAND

These often very decorative Chinese and Korean stands are complete pieces in themselves, although they were originally used as a sort of saucer for bowls; or they may have been decorative or ceremonial stands for fine ceramics. See also under **cup stand.**

A

A. In celadon porcelain this Korean Koryu bowl stand is obviously inspired by the water lily, though highly stylized and ceramic in conception.
B. A much simpler, more saucerlike stand from Sung China. (Barlow Collection.)

B

BOX

A container, usually for solids, the lid of which is often as wide and sometimes as high as the containing section. Pottery boxes are usually fairly small and, because of the difficulty in obtaining a snug fit between base and lid, often circular. They do not occur widely in very early pottery. Charming examples are found in T'ang and Sung Chinese and Korean stonewares and porcelains. Some of the **hill jars** and **incense burners** could be included as boxes. Squared forms are found, but more commonly among later Japanese wares. The width of the lid combined with the fact that pottery boxes are not often in everyday use has led to extensive modelling, especially of the **knob.** Boxes are also hand-built, most commonly with slabs. See also illustrations under **buildings, plant form, pyxis, lid seating.**

A

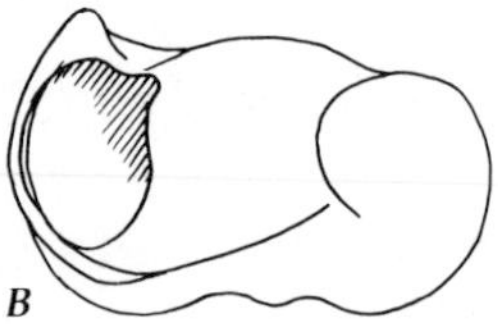

B

C

D

A. A curious little Japanese 18th century incense box.
B. Not immediately resembling a box, this strange form (its convolutions only suggested in line), is, surprisingly, from ancient Greece. It is 6 inches/150mm long and in the shape of a knuckle; possibly it was a container for the pieces for the game of "knuckle bones."
C. A charming thrown incense box by Hamada, its wide stumpy knob very much in character with the main form.
D. In the depressed form *much favored by the Koreans, this elegant box by David Leach is, nevertheless, essentially modern in detail and finish.*

E

F

E. Sharply modelled and basically simple in form, this box in Parian ware (1924) is based on the Queen's dolls' house.
F. Like the ancient box shown in illustration A under lid, *small lugs are used here with string to complement the shallow seating and to form a hinge. By John Maltby.*

G

G. Double boxes are rare. This pretty pair of birds come from Sung China.

BRAZIER

In the *Shorter Oxford Dictionary* the origin of the word is given as the French *braise,* "hot coals," indicating a flat pan for holding burning charcoal. *Webster's* varies this with "a utensil in which food

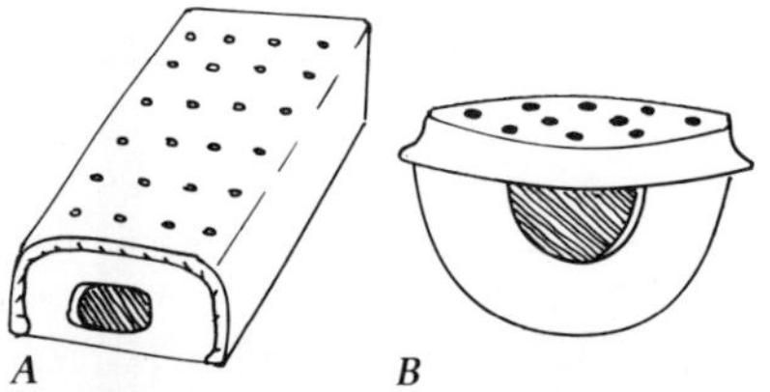

A B

A/B. Two contrasting earthenware braziers, the first from ancient Pompeii, the second from modern Africa.

is exposed to heat through a wire grill." Neither of these definitions includes the once well-known roadman's pierced dustbin!

The **barbecue** is a form of brazier. See also **oven, stove.** R.NP (see Booklist) refers to simple pot braziers of Nigeria as illustrated here. Portable pottery braziers are known from very early Neolithic China and from Mycenae and Pompeii. Hand and foot warmers of various types have been made throughout Europe since Medieval times. See **chad pot, fire pot.**

BREAD CROCK, Bread pan, Bread bin

This is usually a fairly large, deep, wide-mouthed pot with a lid. It is traditionally of earthenware, glazed inside and over the rim. The lid is often pierced with a central hole or with more than one hole equally spaced. Different parts of England had their distinctive bread crocks. In the Northwest there were vertical, cylindrical pots 18 to 24 inches/450 to 600mm high by 12 to 15 inches/300 to 375mm wide; in the North and Midlands there were fuller shapes and a lid pierced with three holes; the South, tended to broader and lower forms and a raised lid with conical sides, a flat top, and a **strap handle.** (See B.CECP in Booklist.) The high mortality rate among bread crock lids suggests the substitution of a turned wooden one. This would be quieter in use and would give craftsmen a chance to cooperate. See illustration C.

In D.EBYC (see Booklist) the author recommends earthenware for bread bins, unglazed outside (as she does for most of her cooking vessels), but these are now rarely made by studio potters. A few potters in Stoke-on-Trent, of all places, are trying to fill this gap. A large kiln is required to make these pots a commercial success. Brannam's of Devon also still supplies them in England. Elizabeth David also suggests a triangular wooden base upon which to stand the crock to keep it sweet and dry.

A

B

C

A/B. The Yorkshire potter Isaac Button's bread bins drying in his workshop. Note the absolute regularity of height and form achieved in about 4 minutes of throwing time. Illustration B shows a completed glazed bin, circa 1960. C. Made in 1979, but thrown and finished in the traditional manner, this simple, but satisfactory, Stoke bread pot is fitted with a wooden lid, as suggested in the text.

D

D. The knob and lid are more emphatic on this well-rounded crock by David Lloyd Jones.

There is obviously great scope for formal and decorative variations by the modern potter. David Lloyd Jones and Mick Casson among others make bold stoneware bread bins. A quizzical comment by Bernard Leach on one of Mick's more ornate bins was, "Not bread, Mick—cake!"

BREAD OVEN

See **oven.**

BREWING VAT

These great containers were the largest wares made by the English "coarseware" country potters. They were made in rounded and straight-sided styles, held about 70 gallons, had a wide mouth, a spigot near the base, and two, four, or six horizontal handles. Their manufacture ceased at the end of the 19th century.

BRICK

The building brick need not concern us here, although Cardew suggests that a clamp of 25,000 bricks is "about right" as a start for a workshop and kiln, and this is the way he had to begin in Africa. Decorative cut and modelled brickwork has, however, been a feature of many cultures. The most famous early use of brick relief, where each brick carries a small section of the design, is at the Ashtar Gate at Babylon, which was built by the Assyrians. There are also superb examples of Han Chinese brick or pottery slabs—friezes of very active figures harvesting, salt-making, etc., and of high-relief buildings. Byzantine and Medieval buildings are rich in three-dimensional decoration. Brick relief work is, of course, a heavy-weight and extensive operation, but not beyond the scope of a large pottery studio working with an architect.

Slightly tapering, closed-in pots called "bottle bricks" were used in the construction of domed roofs at Dover House, Whitehall, and by John Sloane at the Bank of England. The pots are about 7 inches/175mm long. Hollow pottery tubes and cones were also used for similar purposes in various parts of Europe and the Near East.

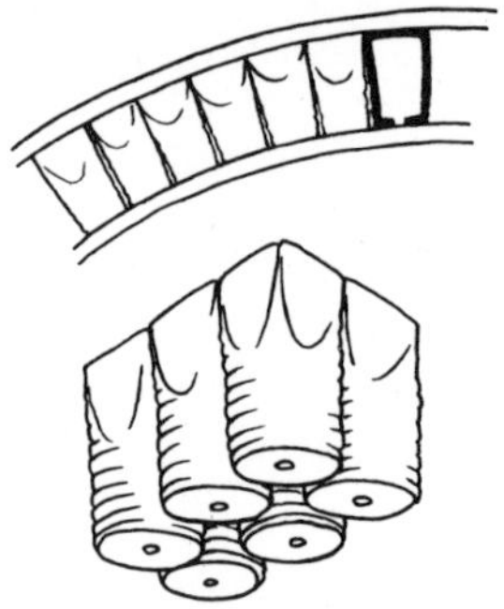

A strange use of pots to form rib supports to a dome or curved ceiling; see text. (From drawing by Norman Davey; see D.HBM in Booklist.)

The term "brick" is also used in other ways in pottery—to describe brick-shaped pots for flowers (see **flower brick** illustrations A and B) and for specialized cooking vessels. See **fish brick, chicken brick.**

BRIDGE HANDLE

A strap handle spanning two spouts on a closed-in pot. A form fairly common in preColumbian American pottery and also occurring in Etruscan wares.

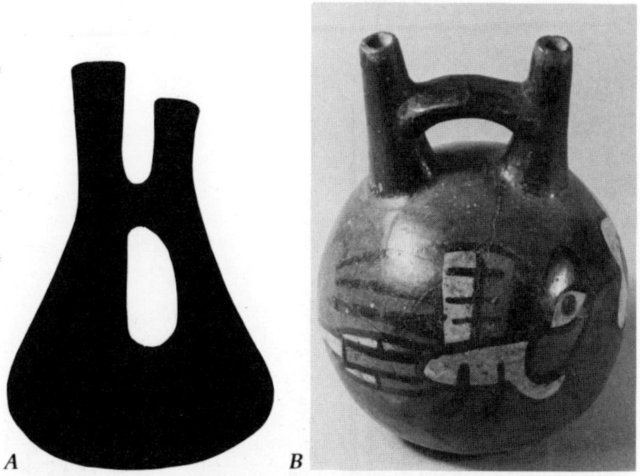

A. A modern student's coiled pot, using the same idea as illustrated in B, but in a very different way, and for appearance rather than for convenience of carrying.
B. A small Nasca pot with a handle connecting the 2 spouts.

BRINE PAN

A large, open bowl or tub used in the salting and preserving of meat and other foods. They were often the largest articles made by the country potter and represent a tremendous feat of throwing. Some were constructed on a beaten-out base. See also **salter.**

This 19th century Welsh brine pan is 20 inches/500mm across. It is roughly but sturdily constructed.

BRONZE FORM

A number of early pots are reputed to have derived from bronze precursors. Some Han Chinese shapes and details, especially **lugs,** and some tripod pots show such origins. See **hu, tou.**

Metal shapes are naturally angular and rather severe, but the potter quickly adapted them to forms more natural to clay. It may be thought, from their rigid outlines, that Greek pots were modelled on metal shapes, but Arthur Lane (see L.GP in

This powerful Han Chinese pot is the ceramic equivalent of the bronze hu, a wine vessel. The handle ring, free and of practical use in the original, is built into the pottery form and is now purely decorative—a skeuomorph. *The pot is about 16 inches/400mm high.*

Booklist) vehemently denies this. See at-length discussion under **metal form.**

BRUSH JAR/REST

The jar is a deep cylindrical porcelain vessel for holding writing brushes, known as a *Pi-t'ung.* It must have been in general use among scholars and artists of the Far East but is rarely mentioned in history books. Brush rests, usually in the form of

The basic outline of the very decorative "Five Mountains" brush rest.

"five mountains," the highest mountain in the center, are very decorative and are more often mentioned and illustrated.

BUBBLE CUP

A term given by historians to a type of small full-formed, slightly inturned Chinese Sung and later-period bowl, also sometimes known as "palace bowl."

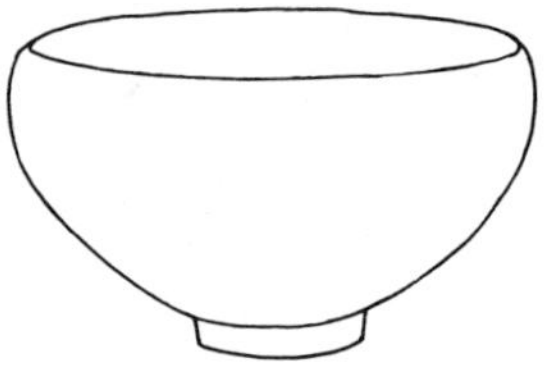

The typical outline of the bubble cup or bowl.

BUCCARO/BOCCARO WARE

This is not strictly a form, but is applied to a type of polished unglazed pottery imported from China. The teapot shape, however, is unique and worth a mention here. For the curious scented boccaro see **scent bottle.**

The unique outline of the small, polished Chinese teapot imported into the West with early tea consignments. It has a lot of lively movement.

BUCKET

See **situla, pail.**

BUCKELURNEN

A name given by archaeologists to a handsome, heavily embossed pagan Saxon funerary vessel from the 8th to 10th centuries. Wavy loops and **bosses** were pressed out from the inside. See under **cinerary urn** for illustration.

BUD VASE

In the United States, the term refers to a tall, slender pot for the display of a single flower. English equivalents are not so succinct—perhaps "single rose vase" would be the appropriate term.

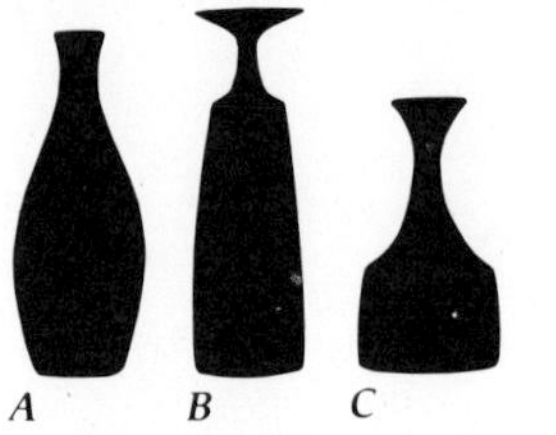

A/B/C. Three possible silhouettes incorporating the narrow neck of a bud vase. The third shape is based on a small vase by Rosemary Wren.

BUILDINGS

Pots and containers in the form of stylized houses and other buildings date back more than 5000 years. In Palestine, 3500 B.C., we find house-shaped burial urns. Other types of dwellings from all over the world include many from Han tombs—five-storied houses. of great magnificence; and smaller, very detailed models with doors, roof finials, windows, and shutters, etc.; a house on legs from 3rd to 6th century Japan has a pot neck incorporated in the roof. There are "hut urns," models of simple houses with thatched roofs from Iron Age Europe, reed and mud houses from preDynastic Egypt (which indicate an oblong dwelling with a door and two windows), a Mexican house with a very handsome

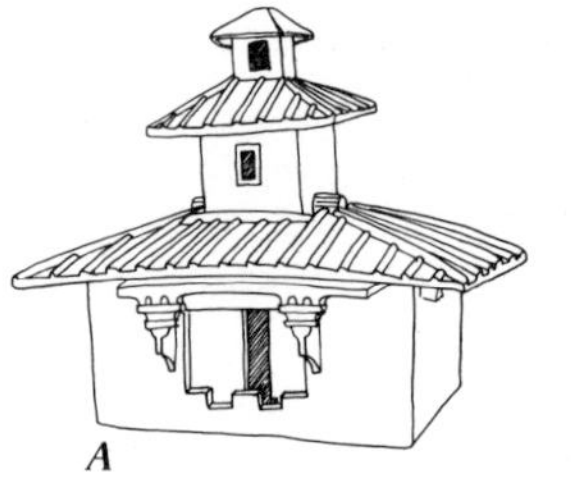

A. An elaborate Han Chinese pottery model, accurately observed.
B. The ancient Egyptians provided their dead with a "soul house" complete with furnishings and utensils. This one probably was that of a small landowner. Note that even the water spout was included.

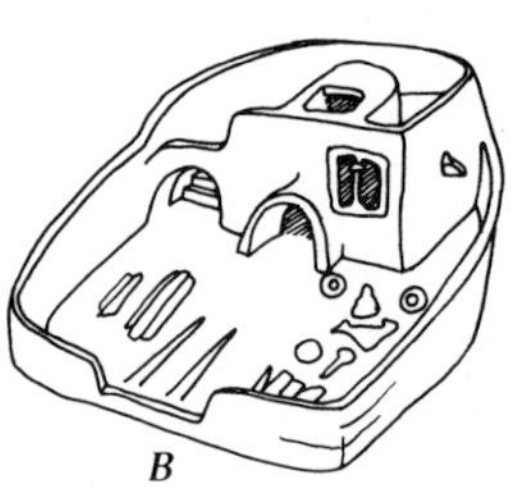

C. A strange, primitive little dwelling, mostly roof, from an ancient Colombian site.

thatched roof and outside staircases crowded with inhabitants at every point, rather Eastern-looking structures from ancient America, and so on. Nearer our own times (19th century) the English cottage was sentimentalized, but there were also a great variety of other buildings, including elaborate dovecotes (see also **furniture**), which some of Ian Godfrey's pieces recall; a fairgound menagerie tent illustrated in F.EC (see Booklist); a house with doors

D

D. "Castle with outside well" is the title of this slab-built and crisply modelled box by Paul Huber.

E

and windows of many shapes, including pointed ovals with the point downwards (!) from the Pill Pottery, Bristol; and, among the more macabre curiosities, the 19th century **murderers' houses.** B.CECP (see Booklist) illustrates a squat Nelson's Column on a dish base filled with fruit, a dog, hens, etc. (which one is unlikely to find in this vicinity today) and he comments: "As an architectural model the column fails miserably, but what it lacks in classic beauty it makes up in sheer exhuberance."

Today a number of potters work in this field. Pamela Nash's "house" with naked female figures scrambling up walls and into windows containing men, makes the opposite comment to the usual one (see COQ1978 in Booklist). Bob Rogers carves whole cities on his rocky bases. Terraces of houses by Ian Beamish compete with those of Tessa Fuchs and others, while Jane Birchenough's "castles" are a cross between buildings and fungi. These are only a few of the many potters in the United States, as well as in England, who use buildings to express their sometimes amusing, sometimes surrealistic, sometimes realistic or nostalgic, view of life. See also **box, town, kiln, watch pocket.**

E. Possibly the most extravagant invitation to a sale, this model by Ian Godfrey (1978) of the Martin Brothers workshop, with smoking kilns in the background, was sent to each of 100 collectors. Each one was slightly different.

F/G. Two modern versions of the cottage or small building: the first by Jane Holmes is a fairly straightforward, nicely potted box (compare to illustration E under box*), the second (possibly a little chapel?) in 2 sections to reveal the interior, by Liz Raeburn.*

F

G

BULB BOWL

The only formal aspect which differentiates a typical bulb bowl from other bowls is the slightly inturned rim, which helps to prevent the growing bulbs from lifting themselves out of the soil. For the same reason the bowl should be fairly deep. It needs to be firmly based. In the 19th century a perforated cover was used.

So-called Chinese bulb bowls have a distinctive form, often with bosses round the wall, and are shallow and set up on three or four decorated feet. See illustration A under **boss.** These may have been stands for flowerpots. In the 19th century Wedgwood made porcupine models with holes in the back in which to plant bulbs, and this idea has continued in various forms until the present day.

BUNGHOLE, Spigot block

A thrown or coiled ring is often attached to the rim of the hole in a cider bottle or similar vessel in order to strenghten it to take a tap or spigot which needs to be driven in. This can be a formally decorative addition, often tooled or thumbed round. In several U.S. bottle/jugs of the last century the block is square, which sets off the central circular hole.

BURIAL URN

See **cinerary urn, casket, buckelurnen.**

BUSSA

A deep and rounded pan for pickling pilchards in Devon and Cornwall. (See B.CECP in Booklist.) See also **salter.** The bussa may also be oval in plan.

BUTTER CROCK/POT

Guilland in *Early American Folk Pottery* illustrates a straight-sided jar of almost square elevation with **lug handles** and a sunken lid, glazed inside. Brears (see B.CECP in Booklist) quotes an Act of English Parliament whereby Burslem butter pots were to hold at least 14 pounds, while the pot was to weigh not more than 6 pounds. The pots were used for packing butter with salt between layers. They tapered slightly towards the base, had two lug handles, and a firm rolled rim. The early butter pots were reputed to have been made of a coarse gray body, which was impervious to water even when unglazed.

BUTTER DISH

This may be a fairly deep dish, often thrown and then beaten into an oblong plan, with upright or slightly sloping sides, or a flatter dish or plate with a cover. An 18th century salt-glazed example has an imitation wickerwork cover with a tiny cow lying on top, the cover being perforated. French butter dishes were made so that the butter could be kept under salt water, (see illustrations B and C), or the dish had a porous cover which could be soaked in water to keep it cool. Similar evaporation **coolers** were made until recently and would still make a good compromise between the oil that butter becomes in the summer and the rock that comes from a refrigerator. See also **cheese dish.**

A/B. A rather involved type of dish by Michael Cardew designed to keep butter cool and based on a French model. The butter is kept in the funnel in the lid, which is inverted into iced water in the body of the pot. (Crafts Study Centre, Bath.)

A

C. A true butter dish *(the original inscribed in large black letters "PURE BUTTER"), 19th/20th century, probably for use in shops in the making up of butter blocks and pats (see also* butter stamp*). The top is recessed to a depth of about ¾ inches/ 14mm and it is 12 to 14 inches/320mm across.*

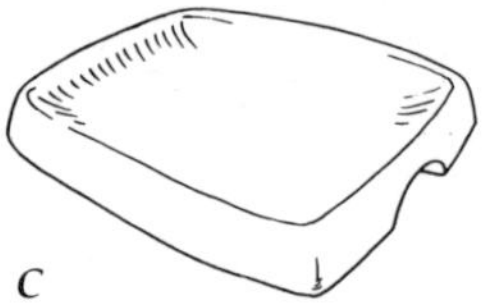

C

B

BUTTER STAMP/PRINT

Butter pats and blocks decorated with intaglio patterns have a long history, going back at least as far as 1616. They were an attractive feature of grocers' shops until well into the 20th century. The stamps, in fact, were identification marks or trademarks of a particular dairyman. The stamps with which the designs were made were often of wood, but also sometimes of earthenware, and such pottery stamps were made in Pennsylvania and New England in the 19th century.

A

A/B The type of butter stamp in use in the 19th century. The face would have been cut in a similar way to the wooden stamp shown.

B

With the spread of "personalized" goods, similar stamps could today become fashionable again. The design is, of course, cut intaglio into the face of the stamp.

BUTTON

Buttons were made in the 19th century from tough

Hard earthenware buttons made by Sheila Fournier, engraved through tin-glaze to a black body.

"ironstone" china and also in bone china. They are reputed to have been fired in ten minutes. Art Nouveau and Art Deco designs were made. They are not widely made by craft potters, although there should be a wide field open for them.

BUTTON BASE

A slight emphasis at the bottom of a pointed-based pot, like a small button on the end. Found on some **amphoras** (see illustration B) and **flasks.**

C

CADDY

From the Malayan *kati,* meaning "the weight of a small packet of tea." The caddy originated in the East and was a feature of the Japanese Tea Ceremony, in which it is called a "chaire" or "chaki." It often has a double lid and a small opening in order to prevent the escape of tea fragrance. Delft and stoneware caddies from the 18th and 19th centuries are found in the West, often made in sets to hold different teas, and with the addition of a sugar bowl.

Although tea is the favorite beverage, pottery tea caddies are comparatively rare in England. The most common form is a straight-sided container

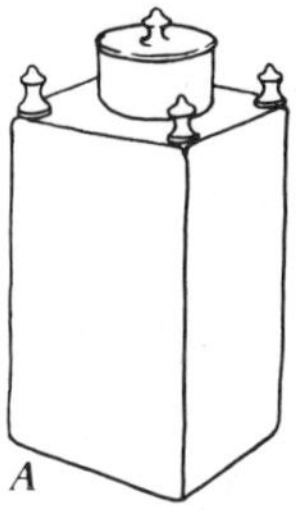
A

B

C

A. A Staffordshire caddy in salt-glaze, 1759. On a simple rectangular body the knob is repeated ornamentally at each corner.
B. The caddy is part of the Japanese Tea Ceremony equipment, and this example, well designed both for holding tea and for gripping with the fingers, is from the Oribe kilns.
C. The little octagonal Bristol tin-glaze caddy shows the typically small neck, but is without its covering lid. (Bristol Museum.)

with a lid, which may be equipped with a cork collar to keep it airtight. In the United States the word "caddy" has been used since the 1880s for a metal can with a lid.

CADOGAN TEAPOT

The industrial (Swinton) teapot, or hot-water pot, in pear-shaped form and which could be filled only

A

through a hole in the base, was by no means the first of its kind. It was, in fact, named after a lady who brought a similar type of pot to England from the Far East at the end of the 18th century. Some Sung Chinese **ewers** were filled from the base, as

B

A. A base-filled pot with an animal-head spout with 2 holes, from 16th century Persia. It is 6 inches/155mm high. These are sometimes called **aquamaniles.**
B. From Piccolpassa (see P.PA in Booklist), the little diagram of his "vaso," showing the conical stem set into a rounded pot and forming the spreading base.

were Islamic pots, and Piccolpasso (see P.PA in Booklist) describes in detail the making of a "vaso" that can be filled through the base. A hollow stem from the base hole, extended almost to the top of the pot, prevented the liquid from escaping when the vessel was returned right way up after filling.

CADUS

A Roman **amphora.**

CAKE MOLD

This circular dish with a hollow spout rising from its center was preferred to a metal tin in 19th century America. The spout allowed hot air to circulate, cooking the center of the cake, which must have looked like a large ring doughnut when turned out. Like many half-forgotten pottery utensils, though still commonly made in metal, this could become quite popular again and would be an amusing piece for the modern potter to make. The molds varied from 6 to 12 inches/150 to 300mm across and 2 to 4 inches/50 to 100 mm high. They are also known as a **ring mold** or **Kugelhopf.** Guilland also illustrates a combination mixing bowl and inverted funnel, each of which could be used separately or together, to form a cake mold. Modern metal types are more rounded and are called "Savarin" dishes.

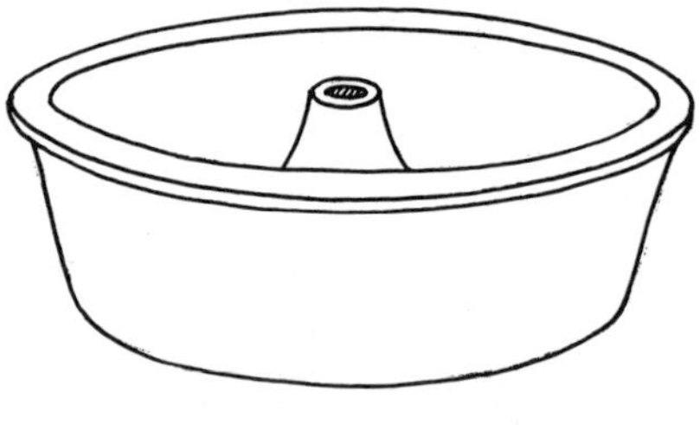

A typical pottery cake ring mold.

CALABASH FORM

A number of African tribes and others have made pots in imitation of the calabash, even including, as surface decoration, a representation of the strapping or harness by which the original vessel was carried. A vivid example of a **skeuomorph.** See also **plant, gourd.**

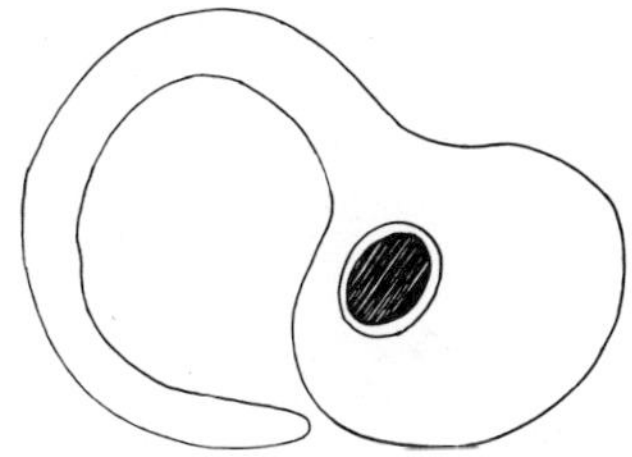

An African clay pot of almost sculptural quality based on a calabash ladle, probably Ugandan in origin. Its height is 8½ inches/215mm.

CALIX

A Roman drinking **cup.**

CAN, Coffee can

Certain squat **mug** shapes with straight vertical sides were called coffee cans in the late 17th and early 18th centuries.

CANDLESTICK, Candleholder, Candelabrum

In ancient times the oil **lamp** was more common than the candleholder. However, there are attractive "pricket" candlesticks (with a point in the center on which to impale the candle) from late Minoan times, and several types from China, including lion, bear, and elephant models, with holders on their backs, as well as gobletlike forms with wide rims. A pleasant stemmed candlestick, with a tray to catch drips of wax, from 17th century England, is

A

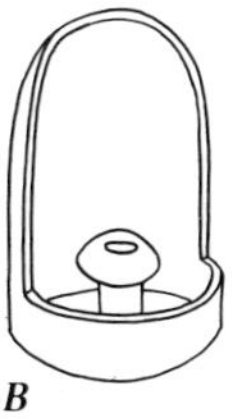

B

C

D

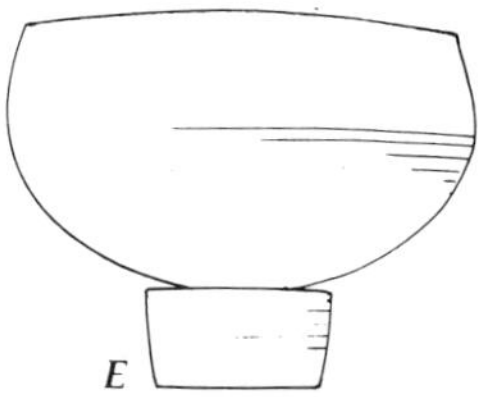

E

F

A. The "Chamber Stick" of the 19th century: a holder set in a straight-sided cup, circa 1830, from Staffordshire, 5½ inches/140mm in diameter.

B. A simple 19th century holder with a reflector, in tin-glaze blue and white from Glamorgan, Wales.

C. The typically elaborate and convoluted style of Art Deco, from the Poole Pottery, 1925.

D. A modern approach: a tree and landscape *holder by Jill Main.*

E. One of the splendidly architectural candlesticks by Hans Coper for the new Coventry Cathedral.

F. A massive free-standing candelabrum by Ruth Duckworth. It is 24 inches/600mm wide.

exhibited in Colchester Museum, and there is one in York of a century later that has two trays on the stem, the lower tray being wider than the upper one. Candleholders in slipware, often elaborately decorated with strips and coils of clay, were made at Wrotham and Lambeth. An 1830 example is set in a straight-sided cup (illustration A) with a handle. Wedgwood made a model dolphin with the candle set on its tail. Some Art Deco candlesticks in the "Bizarre" range (Newport Pottery) by Clarice Cliff are strange, but interesting.

The most impressive modern examples are the massive candleholders made by Hans Coper for Coventry Cathedral, England. A variety of candleholders were shown at the C.P.A. London shop in 1978, including (to quote Ismay's review) "Tall, stark shapes clothed in dry ash glazes from Eileen Lewenstein . . . a water-filled majolica bowl with a central candle and floating night-lights from Aldermaston, and candle bottles by Mary White." (See CR33 in Booklist.) Sheila Fournier's **night-light holders** are designed to throw circles of light.

Candelabra are less common in pottery. There is a T'ang multicandle stand set on a lotus base, and several modern potters have attempted the form. Wall sconces for several candles were made at Sevres and elsewhere.

The following illustrations here indicate something of the limitless scope open to potters who take on the simple, functional problem of keeping a candle upright.

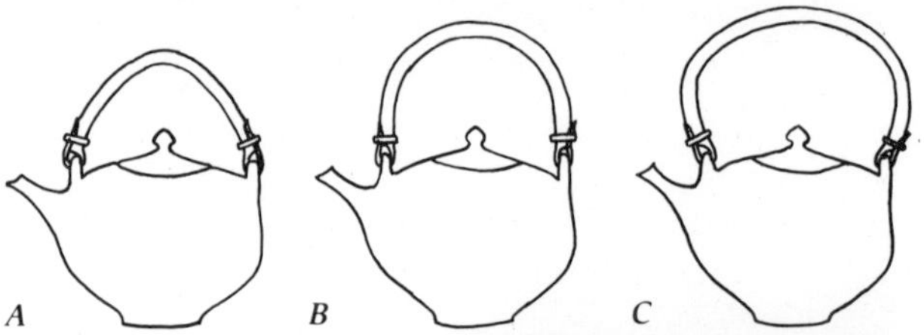

A *B* *C*

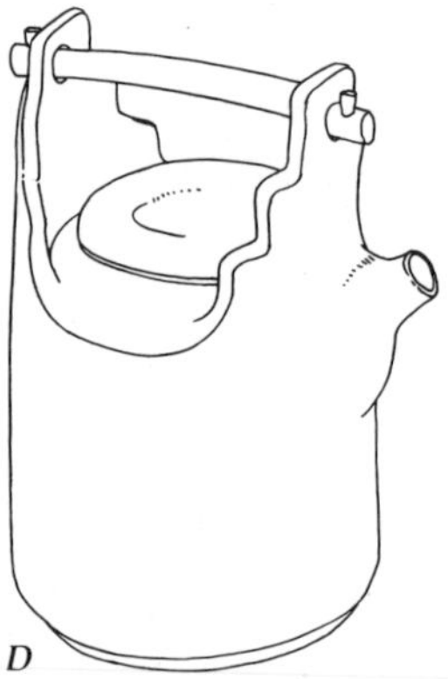

D

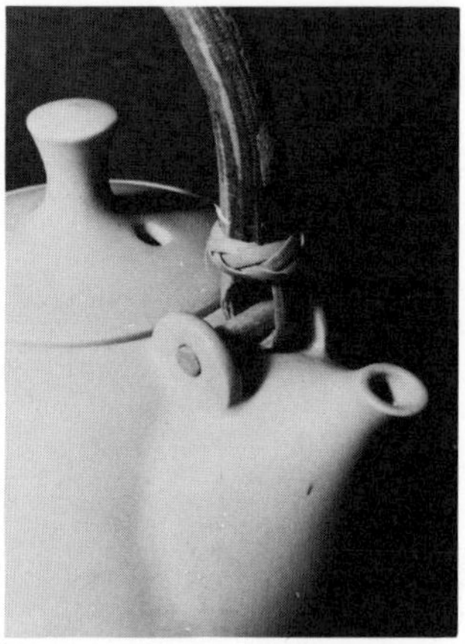

E

A/B/C. At first glance these may look like three different teapots, but the bodies are identical; only the curve of the cane handle varies, altering the character of the whole.
D. A very simple use of cane which does not necessitate steaming and bending. Teapot by Trish Phillips.
E. Another ingenious lug for a cane handle, by Roger Perkins.

CANDY MOLD

See **confectionary mold.**

CANE AND SWORD HANDLES

Both were made in porcelain in the 18th century at Vincennes-Sevres.

CANE HANDLE

These are not, of course, pottery forms (except for some imitations of cane and bamboo on Chinese and 18/19th century English pottery), but are so commonly used on modern stoneware and porcelain as to warrant an entry here. The precise size and curve of a cane handle will fundamentally affect the overall impression of a teapot or jar and should be carefully considered in relation to the pot silhouette. See also under **teapot, basket.**

CANISTER

From the Latin *canna,* meaning "a reed." A box or case, originally made in cane or wicker, but later in other materials for tea, coffee, etc. Pots used for storing and preserving meats, etc. were known as "canisters" in Sussex. (See B.CECP in Booklist.) In Jo Marshall's *Kitchenware,* preserve jars, raisin jars, etc., all lidded and sometimes with a wire handle attached to lugs, are called "canisters."

CANOPIC JAR

See **funerary urn.**

CANTAROS

Although the word is very similar to the ancient **kantharos,** this is, apparently, not a cup, but a drinking bottle similar to a **goglet.** In Spanish South

America the root *cantar* is used with various suffixes to describe a much wider range of shapes. Thus a cantaro can be a great storage jar, 5 feet high, or a pitcher. A smaller vessel is a *cantarito*, and there is also a narrow-necked *cantillo*. Many are illustrated in the excellent book by Gertrude Litto *South American Folk Pottery*, published by Watson-Guptill.

CAPUCHINE

A tall cup with a slightly flaring rim, illustrated in a 1700 Nottingham stoneware potter's catalog, is called a capuchine. The shape is probably derived from the inverted form of a hood.

CARAFE

From the Arabic *gharrafah*, meaning "a big-bellied flask." *Webster's New Collegiate Dictionary* describes it as "a bottle with a flaring lip." The carafe is usually of glass, but the term is also applied to pots made for serving wine, water, etc. It is also known as a "decanter."

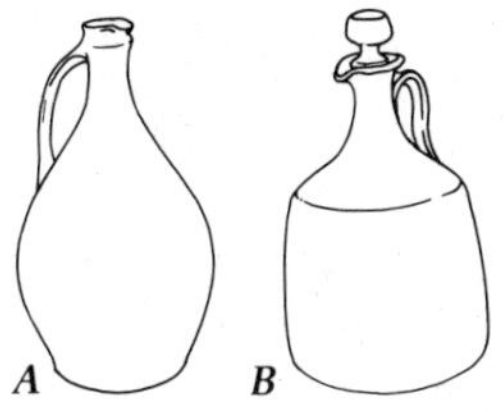

A/B. Two types of a modern carafe: the first based on a form by Bernard Leach, the second by the author.

CARINATION

From the Latin *carina*, "a keel or keel-shaped ridge"; hence, a ridge-shaped structure. This is a word beloved by archaeologists to describe a sharp alteration in the curve or direction of a profile, so that a ridge or sharp angle is formed. A Neolithic

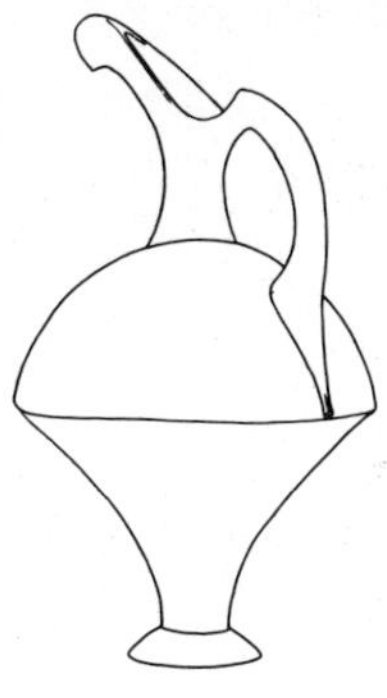

A quite violently carinated form from the 18th century B.C. Hittite culture, uncompromisingly severe.

cup from China is carinated to such an extent that it resembles a concertina. There are also common Roman and African examples among many others.

Some modern potters who produce carinated forms include Robin Welch, Derek Davies, Dan Arbeid, and others. See also **bamboo form.**

CARPET BOWLS

Called *taws* in Scotland, where many of them were made, these are earthenware or stoneware balls of apparently solid clay, about 4 inches/100mm in diameter, that were used in the game of "bowls" played in a carpeted corridor. One plain ball and six with colored rings made up a set. They were

A Portobello "taws" ball with painted rings.

made from the early 19th century at Sunderland, Portabello (Scotland), etc. Some modern potters have made sets in variegated clays and other finishes. See also **sphere.** See illustrations in CR9 and CR50 (see Booklist) for bowls 2 to 5 inches/50 to 130mm in diameter by John Walker and Michael Bayley.

CARVED FORM

See **cut-sided bowls.**

CASK

The derivations are not very satisfactory: Middle French *casque*, "a helmet"; Spanish *casco*, "a potsherd"; etc. In general usage it is normally a small **barrel,** and as such, has been imitated in pottery. There are larger stoneware examples, about 18 inches/450mm high, with a hole in the top for a cork and a spigot hole in the lower part of the curve. **Flasks** are sometimes made as tiny cask shapes. With the popularity of home wine- and cider-making there should be opportunities for the stoneware potter to replace the dismal plastic objects currently in use.

CASKET

A little cask or case. It is often used in connection with funerary ash boxes or containers (*Webster's* gives "a fancy coffin" as the definition), but it is also used for jewelry boxes, etc. See also **cinerary urn, box, chest.**

CASSEROLE

Although etymologically a diminutive of Middle French *casse* or *cassa* meaning "a ladle" or "pan," the term is now used to describe a fairly large, covered dish for cooking food in the oven. The food is usually meat and vegetables and is often served at the table in the same dish.

A late Minoan covered dish with handles on lid and base closely resembles its modern counterpart, and shapes very similar are found in 6th century B.C. Greece, with horizontal handles like large lugs set high on the bowl. The modern form may have developed from the early 19th century **piecrust ware** or "crock pies"; thus, the fairly deep lid on many casseroles. The word is also used to describe a deep porcelain dish with a handle that is used in laboratory work.

The need to endure repeated heating and cooling suggests a well-rounded form in which the tensions can be more readily relieved. The early potters knew this instinctively when they made round-bottomed **cooking pots.** Glazes are more slippery when hot

A

A. Obviously influenced by his years in Africa, this powerful casserole is by Michael Cardew. The deeply inset neck and vertical handles are unusual.
B. A forthright, firmly designed casserole by Colin Pearson.
C. The body form can be such that lug handles are not strictly necessary. This well-undercut shape by the author can safely be gripped with a cloth or gloves when hot.
D. This slip-cast shape *shows a completely different approach, with depressions in the wall for gripping. Designed by Philip Bedington.*
E. Hand-built casseroles are not common, but this example by a part-time student, is simple and successful.

B

C

D

E

and a full form is thus an advantage when handling the casserole from the oven. The opening is usually wide and the container may, therefore, be described as a deep bowl. Care should be taken in designing the lid and the knob so that they are suitable for use in the average oven. Rhodes (see R.PF in Booklist) advises that the casserole be not too shallow or the food will dry out, but stresses that the emphasis of the form is, nevertheless, horizontal. The inside should be smooth; the area under the flange especially should be without a sharp angle. For easy cleaning, in fact, the **flange** could be put on the lid. See also **chicken/fish brick, food warmer, bird tureen, stew pot, fish form.**

CASSOLETTE

A vase with a pierced cover for use with "pastils," which were small rolls of aromatic paste popular as far back as the 17th century, especially in France. The perfume was sometimes evaporated by gentle heat from a spirit or oil lamp. Charcoal impregnated with perfumed substances was also used. The purpose was similar to that of a **potpourri.** Many box and pot shapes have been and still could be adapted to this attractive use.

Larousse Gastronomique, however, gives a very different use for the word "cassolette"; i.e., "little dishes of fireproof porcelain" used for hors d'oeuvres, etc. The word also indicates the actual food, sweet or savory, which was served in the dishes.

CASTER, Castor, Dredger

Usually a small container with a perforated top, it was originally used in the 17th century for sifting pepper, but later was used also for sugar, spice, salt, etc. Larger dredgers are made for flour. The 18th century pepper caster had a domed top and a spreading foot. See also **cruet, shaker.**

Castor can also refer to a trolley wheel, and these have also been made in porcelain.

CASTLE

See **building.**

CAUDLE CUP

From Middle English *caudel* or *caut*, meaning "warm." These are two-handled vessels usually with covers and saucers, and, in the 17th and early 18th centuries, narrow, curved spouts, as well. Caudle is a hot drink of some antiquity, comprising thin gruel with wine or ale, sweetened and spiced. It was given to sick people and to their visitors. Caudle cups were often given as birthday gifts.

An enormous straight-sided open "caudle cup" (approximately 10 inches/255mm wide), with a lip and a small handle, is shown in the Brighton Museum; but Cleo Witt, of the Bristol Museum, is of the opinion that a true caudle cup is small with two handles. See also **posset pot.** Charles (see C.PPGT in Booklist) mentions **sallibube cup, wassell cup,** and **skinker** as similar forms. It is possible that the larger vessels were for communal use and the smaller ones for individual helpings. The connection between form and use is not always tidy.

CHAD POT, Fire pot

This was a pot with perforated walls, filled with hot ashes, and used to keep seated women warm under their skirts—central heating indeed, but hardly in keeping with modern regulations on safety at work. See also **fire pot.**

CHAFING DISH

From *chafen,* Middle English for "to warm." This is a utensil for keeping food warm, especially at the table. The Tudor pottery chafing dish took the form of a bowl set on a hollow base, which had a large opening. The bowl also had either holes or bosses around the body and points or knobs on stems around the rim. In all, it was a very curious form.

The natural assumption, from the evidence of the hollow base, is that it held some form of heater, but Brears (see B.CECP in Booklist) states that charcoal was burned in the dish itself, while another vessel containing the food was set on the points or knobs around the rim—somewhat precariously so, one would have thought. Designs were copied by the English from the French in the 15/16th centuries.

Probably from York Place, Westminster, circa 1530. This dish is in 2 sections; the top ring lifts out. The supports are sturdier than on many others and look more capable of supporting a large dish of food.

Of several Tudor specimens I have seen, all are elaborate, some hideously so. Some are more attractive to our present-day tastes, but all are of interest. Modern **food warmers** have been developed on similar lines, but without knobs.

CHALICE

A bowl on a stem. The term now generally applies to the Eucharist wine cup, but it is also used to describe a general form which has persisted in great variety of proportion and shape for several thousand years. Early Minoan **stem cups** are described

An "integral base" chalice by Luke Harris, a strong, broadly based shape.

as chalices by Lacey (see L.GPBA in Booklist), some with handles or trefoil bowls; a tall, handsome 13th century B.C. Egyptian **goblet** shape is called a "chalice" in the Fitzwilliam Museum; a much wider and squatter form is known as the "Etruscan bucchero chalice." The form is akin to the Greek **kylix,** or kalyx, from which its name probably derives. In CR52 (see Booklist) there is an article by Fr. Luke Harris describing the throwing of an "integral based chalice" in one piece. Certain modern goblet/beakers are also thrown in a similar way.

CHAMBER POT

A bedroom vessel once common to households the world over. The essential characteristics are a wide mouth, adequate depth, and a comfortable rounded rim! "Coach pots" were made in oval and square designs. A 16th century example has a flange around the rim, which suggests that it may originally have been equipped with a lid. The chamber pot has been featured in all potters' catalogs since that time and until very recently. In the Brighton Museum there is a very large "chamber-pot-type vessel" with a modelled bust of Napoleon and the word "Pereat" inside (Staffordshire, circa 1795).

CHAR DISH

A flat-bottomed dish, with slightly in-sloping sides decorated with fishes in tin-glazed earthenware (18th century), used for potted "char" or small trout. It is simple and charming.

CHARGER

From Middle English *chargen,* meaning "to charge"; i.e., to put a load on. This archaic, but splendid, name is for a large dish or "a flat platter." *Webster's New Collegiate Dictionary:* "capable of holding a large joint," (see CTCD in Booklist), "often oval in plan." The term "Blue Dash Charger" was applied by Father Domonican, an avid collector of the 17th century Lambeth ware, to a type of circular plate with broad, blue brush strokes around the rim.

Large **joint dishes** with gravy runnels, shown in Leach's *Potter's Book,* could well be called chargers. See also **trencher.**

CHECKERS, Draughts

Known as "checkers" in the United States and "draughts" in England, this game is known to have been played in some form since the times of the early Pharaohs of Egypt. There are now twenty-four circular pieces, half light- and half dark-colored, and sixty-four squares on the board. The pieces can be thrown or pressed into a single-piece mold. Formal variety is limited as the top surfaces must remain level for "queening." Checkers is also an old name for **chess.**

CHEESE DISH/COVER

The traditional form is a cover, triangular in elevation, set on a shallow square or oblong dish. Tall,

A

B

C

A. A simple type of plate and cover which serves equally well for cheese or butter. (Fournier Pottery.)
B. The traditional wedge-shaped cheese-dish cover. A cheese board in pottery, turned up at each end to provide a grip for lifting, is a possibility, as suggested in the drawing.
C. An ornately molded 19th century cover and plate for a whole cheese.

circular covers for whole Stilton cheeses were also made.

Modern potters have varied the form: by using the triangle as plan instead of section; by modelling the cover (a mouse is the most obvious); by using a deep-thrown cover on a wooden base; etc. A shallow dish with a central handle makes an effective server.

CHEESE PRESS, Strainer, Wringer

Guilland (see G.EAFP in Booklist) mentions a black-glazed earthenware cheese strainer from 19th century Pennsylvania. He describes it as a straight-

A

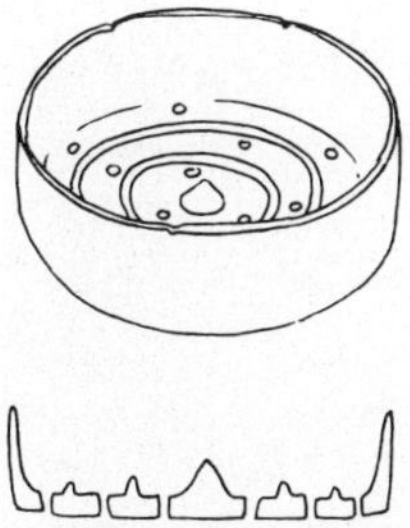

B

A. This quite elaborate early English cheese press was found in the bed of a stream in London. It is approximately 5 inches/125mm wide.
B. A small cheese strainer made in 1979.

sided pot with numerous small holes in the walls, set up on three feet, and with a strong rim and a side handle. The pot would have been lined with cheesecloth, filled with curds, and a round wooden board placed on top under a heavy weight. A cheese might be allowed to "cure" for two weeks in this fashion. A deep dish with slightly in-sloping sides and a vertical projection in the center, the outer walls and base pierced with small holes, has been described as a "cheese wringer." At Halifax there is a small "cheese press" about 9 inches/230mm high by 7 inches/180mm wide, again with small holes and set on three feet. With the return to "self-sufficiency" small versions are again on sale and ingenious variations could be devised.

CHESS

Many potters have made chessmen. Wedgwood's consisted of Shakespearean characters, and there is a set known to have been made by the Martin Brothers. The formal possibilities are almost limitless. Thrown chessmen offer a challenge to the imagination, but in whatever way the pieces are formed, the design should stand up to fairly rough handling—great passions are sometimes engendered. There are 32 pieces: 16 black or dark-colored, 16 red or lighter-colored. Of these, eight on each side are pawns, with two each of knights, castles (or "rooks"), and bishops, plus a king and a queen. There are traditional turned forms, but the pieces can be modelled using any distinctive attribute of

A

the piece. See the shield for the pawn and miter for the bishop in illustration B.

CHEST

From the Old English *cest*. It is usually a box with a lid, fairly deep and typically oblong. Minoan and Mycenean peoples buried their dead in terra-cotta chests known as **larnax.** Today John Maltby, for instance, specifically calls his oblong boxes on short legs "chests," while "chests of drawers" and other models of **furniture** are widely made.

A. A porcellaneous stoneware chess set by Bernard Leach, 1939. (Collection of Mr. Thayer Lee-Elliot. Photograph: Victoria and Albert Museum.)
B. Rather fragile, but well delineated, earthenware chessmen by Sheila Fournier.

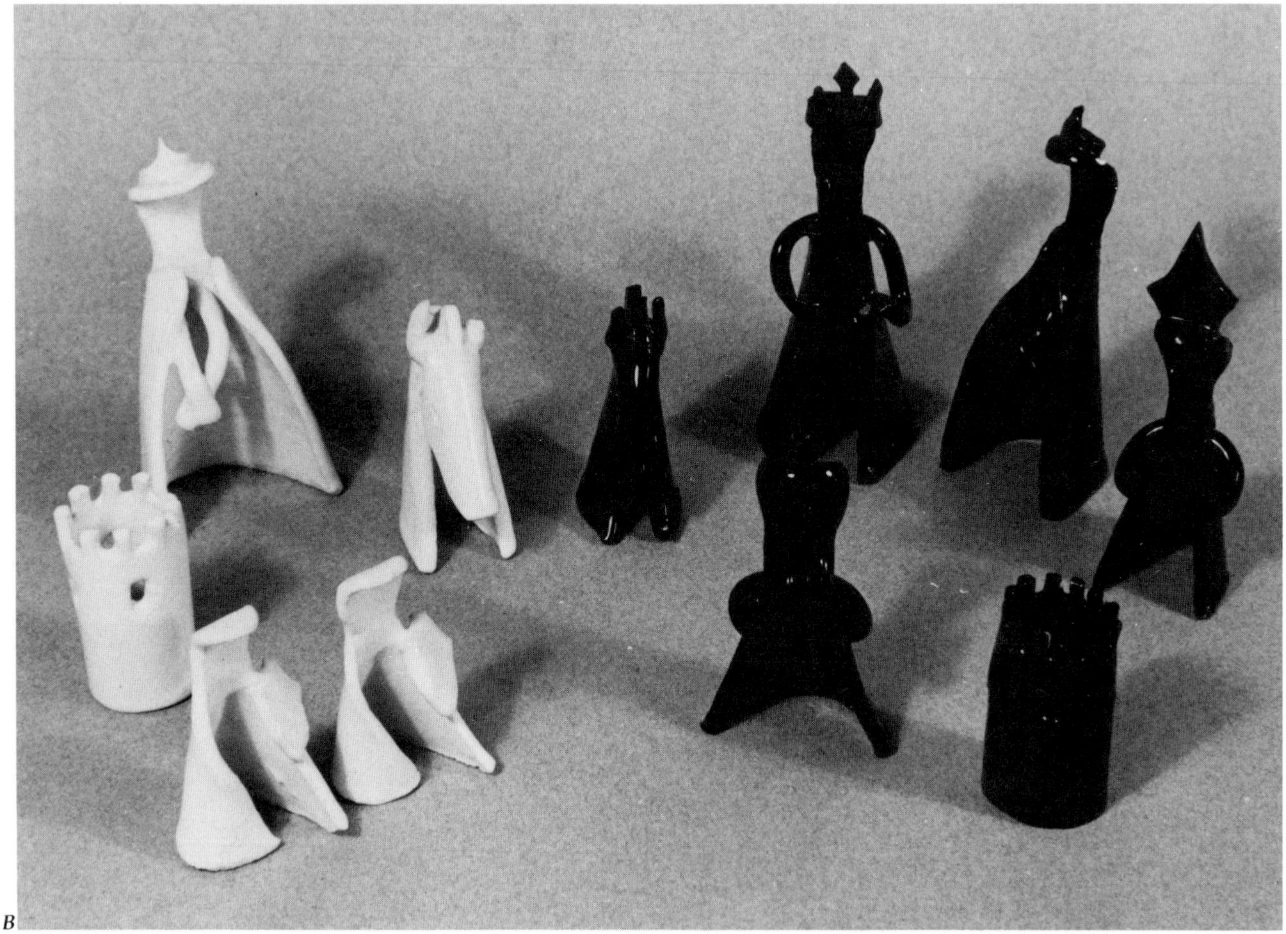
B

A

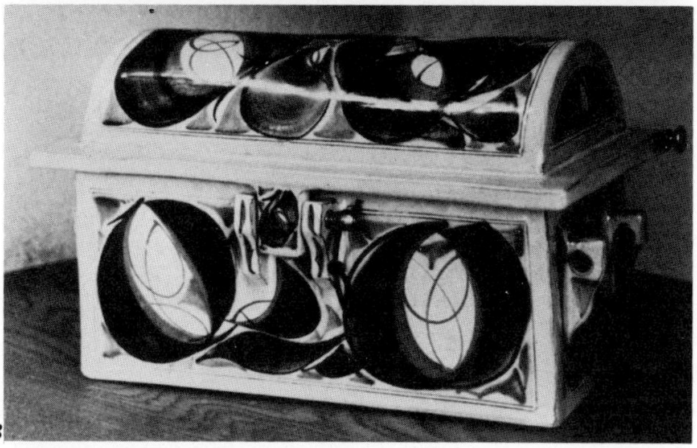

B

A/B. Two pottery chests, similar in form, but far apart in conception and finish. The first, in stoneware, is by John Maltby, the second, by Alan Caiger Smith, is in tin-glazed earthenware.

CHESTNUT ROASTER, Basket

A squat, wide-bottle shape, roughly pierced with holes, from Pereruela in Spain, is shown in an article by Shan Bristow in CR41 (see Booklist) and is called a "chestnut roaster."

Much more sophisticated containers resembling **casseroles** with high-domed lids, each perforated in elaborate patterns in both lid and base, were made in Creamware in the late 18th century. These were called "chestnut baskets," but were unlikely to have been used for roasting.

CHEVRETTE

A French chemist's jar in faience. It is oblong in shape, with a wide mouth and a projecting spout and handle. At one time only apothecaries were allowed to display these jars. (See LG in Booklist.)

CHICKEN BRICK

A simple **casserole** form in unglazed earthenware, usually thrown upright, but used on its side, the pot cut through to form a lid (see illustration). It must be large enough and of a suitable shape to hold a whole chicken. It is cleaned after use with salt. Still quite widely sold and used in England and popular in Scandinavia, chicken bricks have been made by John Leach among modern craftsmen potters. See also **fish brick.**

A modern chicken brick by C & M. Hemstock of Stoke-on-Trent. The neck is not open, but simply serves as a handle.

CHICKEN FEEDER, Waterer

One type was so designed as to form a reservoir which kept a small projecting cup at the base filled as the water or corn was consumed by the chickens. A simpler, though less hygienic type, used a flat thrown dish with a number of concentric ridges.

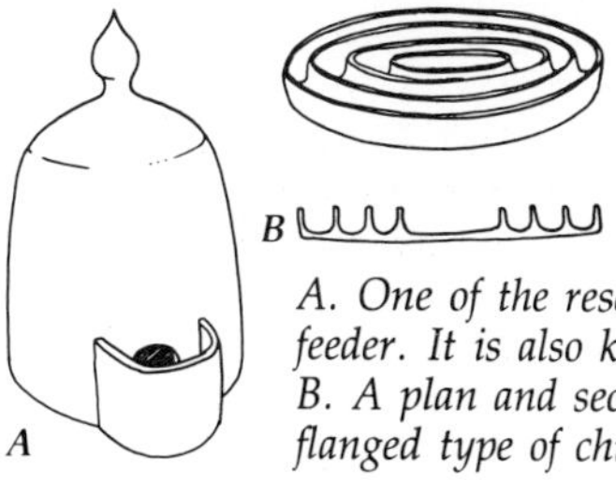

A. One of the reservoir types of chicken feeder. It is also known as a "hopper." B. A plan and section of the thrown, flanged type of chicken feeder.

CHILLS

A Cornish type of lamp in use up to the end of the 19th century.

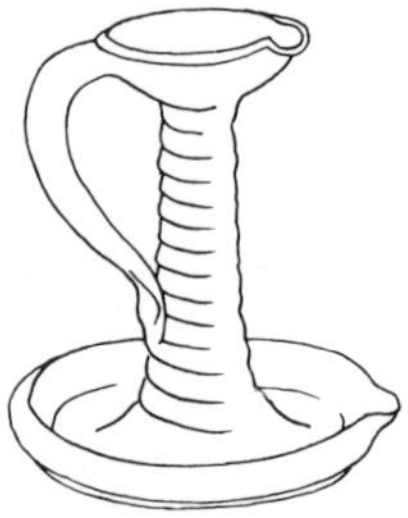

The Cornish "chills" from the 19th century. The wick would be set in the lip. (From a drawing in B.CECP—see Booklist.)

CHIMNEY POT

There is an infinite variety of chimney pot shapes and designs. Some are simple and some are elaborately modelled and have ingenious arrangements for increasing the draft. This in itself offers many an idea and inspiration to the potter. The Mediterranean countries are especially rich in strange forms, but in any land, one can find imaginative shapes and proportions. There is a 13th century English chimney in the form of a king, the top of the pot shaped as his crown. He is resplendent in rolled curls, but, surprisingly, is clean shaven.

In CR20 (see Booklist) an article on northern English chimneys shows magnificent pots, some press-molded, others thrown, with such evocative names as Long Knight, Tall Boy, Hooded Halifax, and Leeds Bishop.

A. A literal chimney "pot" from the 13th/14th centuries. One cannot believe it would have been very efficient.
B/C. Two splendidly ornate chimney pots from the North of England; on the left, a Long Knight, on the right, the Champion.

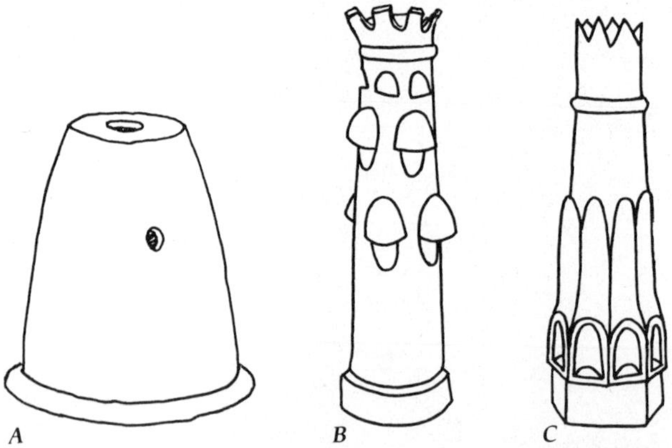

A B C

D

D. A 19th century chimney from the London South Bank, put to a new use as a plant pot.

CHOCOLATE SET

These sets were popular in the 18th century when chocolate was drunk at breakfast and in coffee houses. We can see them in a number of paintings of the period. The pieces were, on the whole, smaller than those in coffee services, but the cups were tall in comparison to their width, often had two handles, and were occasionally very elaborate in design. The pot usually had a projecting handle at right angles to the spout and had a hole in the center of the lid to accommodate a whisk. A very elegant lidded cup and stand by Wedgwood, the cup having two handles, is illustrated in L.SiP (see Booklist).

CHUEH

Originally a tripod bronze vessel of the Shang period in China, it developed, in ceramics, into a type of jug/pitcher, sometimes on feet or legs, and with the handle and lip set at right angles to one another.

An early Chinese jug form derived from the bronze chueh.

CHURN

Once common to every country household, this was a large (up to 7 or 8 gallons), firmly based, wide-mouthed pot for making butter. In G.EAFP (see Booklist) fine shapes are shown, some rather "slack"

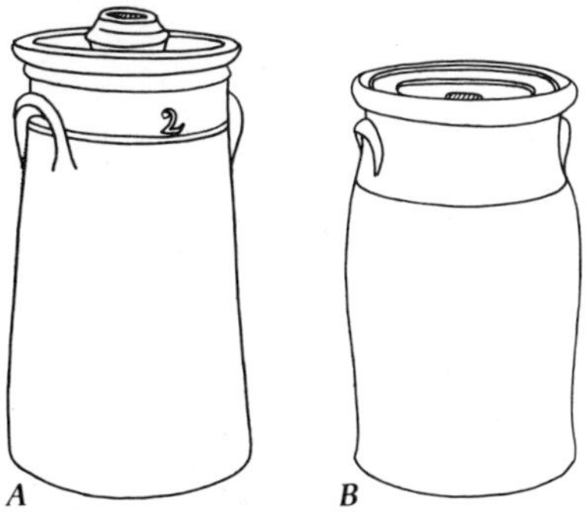

A *B*

A/B. Two American 19th century churns, both good, strong forms. The first holds 4 gallons, the ridging indicating capacity; circa 1870, 16 inches/405mm tall. The second is from New York State and is slightly smaller.

and wavy in profile, others straight-sided and more rigid in feeling. There is an inset lid with a central hole to take the churning stick. A saying is quoted by Guilland: "Butter commends the housewife, good cheese, the cow." Salt-glazed churns were also made in Great Britain in the 19th century and good specimens can be seen at St. Fagan's Welsh Folk Museum.

CHYTRA

"Among the principal kitchen utensils used by the Greeks was the chytra, a sort of earthenware **marmite** used for cooking meats and stews. It was apparently in these utensils that the famous Spartan broths were prepared." (See LG in Booklist.)

CIDER JAR/JUG, Bottle

As mentioned under **jug/pitcher,** there is some confusion between the U.S. and the U.K. terms for those typical full-bodied, narrow-necked vessels, with a spigot or tap-hole, used for storing relatively small quantities of liquor in the home or behind the bar of an inn. The term "cider-jar," though often used, is something of a misnomer in this respect, since **jar** usually denotes a wide-mouthed

This springing shape by Ray Finch sums up the typical features of a cider bottle—a firm base, generosity, and vigor.

vessel. The handle of a cider bottle is normally short, spanning the neck and upper shoulder, although an American example of 1860 shows two more out-standing handles on a 3-gallon pot. The general form is similar to that of the **bellarmine.**

All the old country potters made these fine bottles. Isaac Button's throwing time, using 28 pounds/12 kilos of clay, was about 3 minutes (see the film *Isaac Button, Country Potter*). There are many types in both earthenware and stoneware, and it is a favorite form among many modern tableware potters, notably Michael Cardew and Ray Finch.

CINERARY URN

Pots of many shapes and sizes were used to contain the ashes, sometimes the barely burned bones, of the dead. They were common objects in early and primitive cultures, and a good deal of effort was often lavished upon them. Some of the finest pots, which manage to be at once monumental and (to us at least) amusing, come from ancient Colombia (see illustration A).

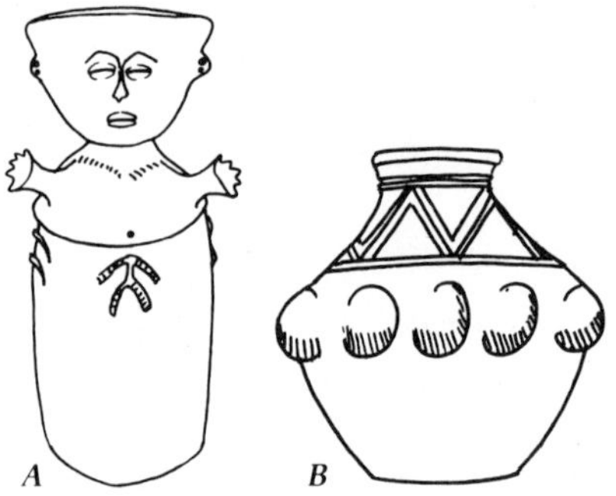

A. Pre-Columbian Tamalameque burial urns are large, up to 4 feet/1.2m high and feature rather surprised-looking anthropomorphic lids.
B. The Saxon buckelurnen *is always full-formed and is distinguished by the large* bosses *and other protuberances, which are pushed out from the inside.*

Many potters have at some time been asked to make such a vessel, though often called a different name and not surprisingly, since cremation has become so widespread in the West. The "urn" is now usually in the form of a box and is called a "casket." A simple restrained design seems called for. There is no reason why the potter today should not compete with the mass-produced article, so making our "gardens of rest" as interesting as our older cemeteries often are.

CISTERN

An artificial reservoir for storing liquid, especially water (see *Webster's New Collegiate Dictionary*). Rackham (see R.MEP in Booklist) mentions "cistern" to describe two very different forms, both having a similar function—the water storage trough of rectangular shape familiar to most households as a metal receptacle, and, also, a large, squat **jug/pitcher** with a bunghole either in the lower front area or near the handle base. Both are for storing and dispensing water. In silverware we find a "wine cistern" and there is an 1815 reference to a pottery "cistern of punch." Enormous pots that were made in the 12/13th centuries, each with a wide mouth and two bungholes, one above the other, have forms reminiscent of Saxon pottery in sturdy weightiness. They were made up to 24 inches/600mm high and, surprisingly, have slightly convex bases.

CLIBANUS

"Used by the Romans . . . an earthenware utensil, with holes pierced in it, which was used for cooking various dishes, mainly pastry, in the hot ashes." (See LG in Booklist.)

CLOCK, Clock face

Clock cases and faces have been made in earthenware and porcelain since the 18th century, especially in Europe. They are often too modelled and ornate for modern tastes, though some of the less sophisticated folk pottery wares are attractive. A

A. A small clock case from 18th century Holland, quite elaborate in detail, but fundamentally an open box. (Bristol Museum.)

A

few modern potters make clock cases, but the clock is more often treated in a "philosophical" fashion in formal comments on time itself.

B

B. A typically surrealistic modern approach to the clock, by Oldrich Asenbryl. (Photograph: Eileen Lewenstein, Emmanuel Cooper.)
C. An Adam and Eve clock face in relief modelling by Chris Hall.

C

CLOUT

A Derbyshire (England) name for a **jug/pitcher.**

CLUSTER VASE

See **kernos, composite pot.**

COCKROACH TRAP

This strange object looked like a truncated beehive, with horizontally ribbed walls. The insects could easily climb up the sloping walls, but the concave top area was glazed so that they slid down through a hole in the middle. The trap was baited with molasses and water. A 19th century U.S. roach trap is illustrated in G.EAFP (see Booklist).

COCOTTE

A French name for round or oval dishes of various sizes, with or without a straight handle. Food is cooked in the dish as in oven-to-table ware, and it is then known as "en cocotte." See also **egg baker/ poacher, soufflé dish, skillet.**

COFFEE CUP

Like the **coffeepot,** the traditional shape of a coffee cup is taller than it is wide and often straight-sided, but this form is now often varied. After-dinner cups for black coffee are smaller.

A

B

C

A/B/C. The traditional 19th century coffee cup is shown in A. B and C are modern variations. B is by Marianne de Trey, C (in porcelain) is by the author. All are designed to minimize the escape of heat.

C. A jug-type coffeepot by Danny Killick. It has a strainer behind the spout.

C

COFFEEPOT

The simplest coffeepot, favored by many craft potters today, is a lidded **jug/pitcher.** The traditional form, however, has a long low-set spout, though why this should be so is not clear, since coffee grinds sink to the bottom, and the pots do not normally have a grid at the base of the spout as do teapots. Perhaps early coarse-ground coffee tended to float?

The pots are often straight-sided (or nearly so), tall, relatively slender, and they contract a bit towards the top. A 1705 Lambeth pot illustrated in R.EDP (see Booklist) has a pleasant forthright shape, a traditional spout (but not as long and swanlike as most), with a handle at right angles to it, similar to those on **chocolate sets.** See the illustration under **handle.**

A

B

A. A rather elaborate French filter coffepot with a teapotlike base.
B. The traditional silhouettes

COFFEE SET

See **tea and coffee set.**

COFFIN

See **larnax.**

COILED POTTERY

This is, of course, a technique, rather than a form, but one which often influences the type of shape produced.

Coiled pots, when well and honestly made, tend to have a more monumental character than do the more rapidly formed and tauter thrown shapes. The very structure of the clay material is different. In unskilled hands, however, coiling can degenerate into heavy shapelessness. In his book *Pottery Form*, Rhodes remarks that "the tendency is for an overall bumpiness to develop and a lopsidedness in the form, whether it is intended to be sym-

A

A. Made by the traditional method of coiling, beating, and smoothing, these lovely pots show no signs of Rhodes' "overall bumpiness." Made by the Kwali tribe of Nigeria. (Photograph: Shan Bristow.)

B. Done by Ewen Henderson, one of the most individual and uncompromising of modern hand-builders, this coiled pot is timeless.

metrical or not . . . the inherent freedom of the method is seldom realized in practice . . . it can have a sense of becoming rather than that of finality." This is not true of the great coiling cultures of Africa and elsewhere, nor of the precise results achieved by several modern potters (see illustration C).

Coiling is often combined with beating, stroking, or throwing, and is normally reserved for large or very large pots, as in the well-known Cretan, Cypriot, Korean, and African examples. Several modern

B

C

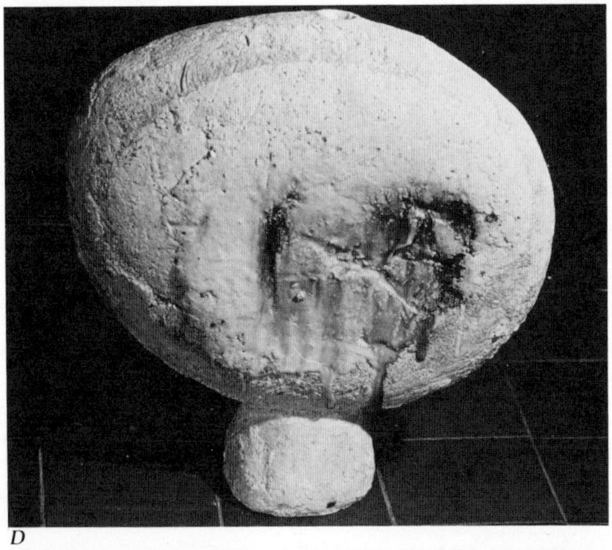

D

C. The usual weightiness and comparatively thick walls common to many coiled pots are nowhere evident in these 2 stylish flattened bowls by Dave McCall.
D. At the other extreme is this large 18-inch/450mm wide coiled form by Ruth Duckworth.

potters use coiling to develop distinctive styles—earthy and irregular as in the work of Ewen Henderson, smooth and precise as in the earlier animal modelling by Rosemary Wren, or solid, but sophisticated, as in the work of Elizabeth Fritsch.

To give a last quote from Rhodes which sums up the reasons for the continuing popularity of coiling, "Slowness is really the virtue of coiling . . . it is a more meditative, a more attentive way of handling clay."

COLANDER, Sieve

From the Latin *colare,* meaning "to strain." The colander is a perforated vessel, usually a deepish bowl, sometimes with a foot or feet, used as a strainer in cooking, wine making, etc. Examples of this fundamental item of culinary equipment are found throughout history in the ancient world, in the Roman Empire, in Saxon England, and on to today.

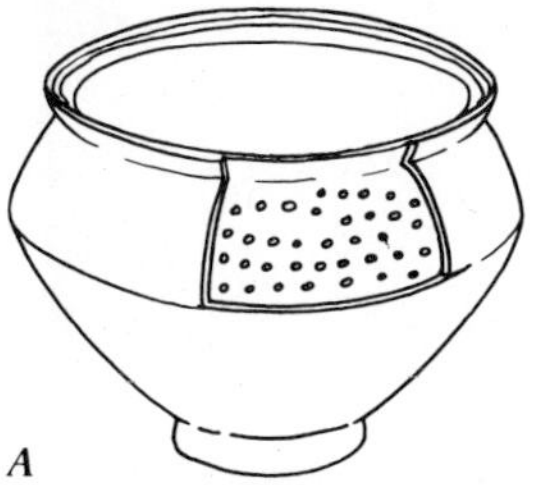

A

A. A colander or strainer built into the upper wall of a British copy of a Romano-Gallic type, 1st century A.D. *It is an ingenious arrangement which could well be adapted today. The wall is cut back to half thickness over the area of the holes.*

B. The Bristol colander-bowl form mentioned in the text. (Bristol Museum.)

C. A well-designed salt-glazed colander on a cut foot. The holes are decorative in themselves and the whole shape sturdy and practical. By Andrew and Johanna Young.

C

B

Two of many variations on the basic shape are shown in the illustrations of the Roman colander or strainer built into the side of a bowl, and in an 18th century deep bowl covered over by a concave, pierced top, which acted as the strainer, while an opening near the rim allowed the liquid to be poured off. The latter was used for fruit and spices in making punch (see **punch bowl**). Among the country potters, Fishley Holland, working in the early 20th century, tells us that "our colanders are in great demand." (See H.FYP in Booklist.) They were decorated with slip-trailing. Strangely the article is not mentioned by Guilland as being used in 19th century America.

Many attractive modern colanders are made today.

COLLARED URN

A term given by archaeologists to an open, fairly large pot, with a turned-back rim, from late Bronze Age and Saxon times in England.

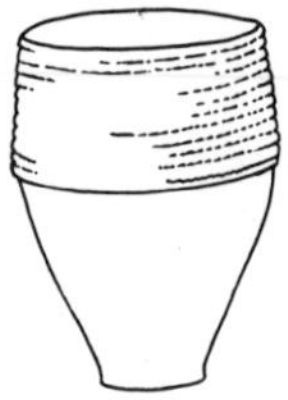

A coil-built Middle Bronze Age collared urn from Saxon England.

COMPORT, Compote, Compotier

A high, pedestaled fruit or dessert dish, originally for serving "compote," or whole fruits cooked in syrup. See also **p'an, fruit dish/stand.**

COMPOSITE POT

A pot is normally a single, continuous whole; but, apparently many potters from the earliest times have felt this to be a constriction of invention and have constructed more involved forms from several separate shapes, or have cut parts of shapes, joining them together into more sculptural and composite forms. In some cases the pots retain much of their original form as in the **kernos** or "cluster vase," which is said to have had religious significance although a very similar assemblage set on a pierced cup is shown in F.EC (see Booklist) and called a **puzzle jug.** These are more accurately referred to as **multiple pots.** Medley (see M.CP in

A

A. A nicely balanced combination of bowls and jugs into a sculptural whole, from Bronze Age Cyprus.

B. An interesting composition of 2 thumb pots connected by wings, or flanges, *which give a double or false outline to form. By Alex Watson, circa 1950.*
C. Remarkably, this "bottle" by Johanna Constantinidis is built up from thrown sections, not hand-built in the usual sense.

B

C

Booklist) mentions "a number of massive vases constructed from 4 or more thrown parts" in 6th century China. Joined and constructed pots were common in preColumbian America, and there are remarkable and technically brilliant examples from Africa.

The simplest composite pots are those built from two or more pinch-pots. Press-molded pots may be given additions of thrown necks and feet. Strictly speaking, a teapot is a composite, but the word generally indicates a construction which is more decorative and "abstract" (in the sense of "useless"!). Among modern potters, Hans Coper cuts and joins thrown shapes into fresh and exciting forms; the famous Picasso **water pot** in the form of a horseman is built of thrown shapes and strap handles; and there are countless others.

COMPRESSED FORM

A system of beating and then hollowing out clay shapes described by Rhodes in *Pottery Form*. Similar to **plunge pots.**

CONFECTIONARY MOLD, Candy mold

Roughly made little molds for making sweets in a great variety of shapes were produced in Italy in the 19th century, finished in various colored glazes. They are very attractive little vessels in themselves.

Three of the many shapes of sweet (candy) molds in bright colored glazes from Italy. They average 2 to 3 inches/50 to 75/mm long. (Victoria and Albert Museum.)

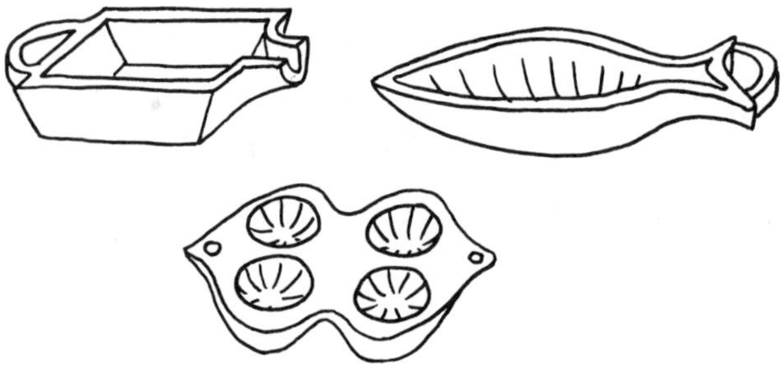

CONFINEMENT SET

In Italian majolica, around the 16th century, this would have consisted of a bowl with a plate/cover given as a gift to pregnant women or new mothers.

COOKING POT

The term could be applied to many forms, but specifically is applied to a wide-mouthed, generally round-based and full-formed, almost spherical, often hand-built vessel used in preparing food over an open fire. Splendid examples are found in most early cultures—in Africa, in early Britain and Europe, and in the Far East. It is the archetypal pot.

A

A. Splendidly rotund, and with the 3 legs frequently found on these pots, is this 14th century cooking pot. This one is glazed inside, which is unusual.
B. A mid-1st century Romano-British cooking pot influenced by the preRoman "butt beaker" shape—an interesting variation. (Devizes Museum.)

B

The early Medieval cooking pots were less rotund, but retained a slightly convex base. See also **casserole, stew pot, chicken brick, fish brick, kebab pot.**

Mollie Poupeney in CMdec78 (see Booklist) gives advice on adapting the older-style stove-top cooking pot to modern use by tempering, low firing, and soaking in water prior to use.

COOLER

Most early unglazed water pots were porous, and so, due to evaporation were also coolers. Their lugs indicate that they were hung, probably in the doorway of a dwelling, to increase the effect. The Grecian double-walled wine cooler was known as a **psykter.** Before the coming of the refrigerator, milk, butter, etc. were kept cool by means of earthenware covers which had been soaked in water. These would be an acceptable short-period compromise between the oil that butter becomes in a hot kitchen and the rock it freezes to in the refrigerator. See also **butter dish.**

A

A/B. Two varieties of milk cooler, common in the early 20th century. The cooler in A is still available in England in 1979, and this type must be soaked in water before placing it over a milk bottle. The cooler in B has its own reservoir, which can be topped up with water, the resulting form is quite attractive.

B

CORN DISH

An oval dish specifically designed for serving corn on the cob. A U.S. term.

CORN MEASURE

See **measure.**

CORNUCOPIA

See **wall vase.**

COSMETIC POT/BOWL

These have always been essential items for the wealthier woman (and often for men). In ancient Egypt cosmetic vessels were modelled as animals, etc. or were small containers in "Egyptian paste."

A

B

C

A. A set of Chinese Han period cosmetic bowls. The flanged boat-shaped bowls are each 4¼ inches/100mm long. (Barlow Collection.)
B. For rouge, this 18th century tin-glazed earthenware bowl, 2 inches/50mm wide, is attractively shaped and sturdily made.
C. A kohl (the equivalent of today's mascara) tube from 1800 B.C. Middle Kingdom Egypt.

From China we find green-glazed oval dishes with a widening of the rim to form handles. These would probably have been set in groups of four or so on lacquer trays. Straight-sided or flaring majolica jars for ointment, rouge, etc. were common in Europe from the 15th to 18th centuries, and many industrial designs, often porcellaneous, have been developed since. See also **scent bottle, aryballus, plant form.**

Today glass and plastic have taken over, but there is still a wide field for the potter. The attraction of the container psychologically affects the effectiveness of the contents.

COSTREL

Originally from the Middle French *costier,* "at the side," (in this case, worn at the waist), and Old French *costerel,* meaning a **flagon.** We find it in Chaucer: "And here withall a costrel taketh he / and said 'Here of a draught, or two, or three.' " It was, therefore, a **pilgrim bottle** for water, or something stronger, with suspension loops to enable it to be worn from the waist when travelling.

It had several forms, the most common being a fairly deep, flattened pear shape. One side was often quite flat, the other **mammiform** or convex. Early barrel shapes, with lugs on each side of a short neck set in the center of the curved wall, were common in Roman times and either persisted or returned barely altered in Medieval England and

A

B

A. A very roughly thrown and finished 17th century English costrel, the flanges not even pierced for thongs as they are normally. (Salisbury Museum.)
B. An upright, bottle-type of costrel with thick lugs.

Italy. The strap loops on some costrels were modelled as lions' heads, etc. Dismissed by Honey in *English Pottery and Porcelain* as "artistically of slight importance" it is, nevertheless, a varied and interesting vessel. See also **flask.**

COTTAGE

See **building.**

COUP

Rhodes in R.PF (see Booklist) uses this term to describe the inside curve of a plate—a "high coup" for a deep plate, a "low coup" for a shallow one, the former curving from the center, the latter having a wider and flatter central area. The *Shorter Oxford English Dictionary* gives a suggestion of "tilting," but not in this sense. Charles (see C.PPGT in Booklist) gives coup as a Chinese ink pot, but see **coupe.**

COUPE

An 18th century name given to a Chinese beehive or dome-shaped pot with a small, flaring mouth, used for cleaning brushes. Charles (see C.PPGT in Booklist) reverses "coup" and "coupe" (see above) and gives the latter as a shallow dish or plate without a rim. Neither meaning is supported by the *Shorter Oxford English Dictionary* or *Webster's New Collegiate Dictionary*.

A typical Chinese brush-washing jar, or "coupe."

COW CREAMER

An 18th century **jug/pitcher** in the form of a cow. The tail provided a handle and the liquid was poured from the mouth, the back lifting off as a lid in some cases. (So much for anatomy!) Similar forms have persisted until today. See also **aquamanile.**

This unusual 18th century Straffordshire creamer, complete with milkmaid, is in the Higgins Art Gallery, Bedford, England. The tail has not been formed into a handle, as is usual on these pieces.

CRABSTOCK HANDLE

A handle, often used on teapots, in the form of a gnarled branch or twig, as a crabtree growth. It is reputed to have been taken up by the Chinese from the early 18th century and re-exported at a later date. See illustration G under **handle.**

CRADLE

From the 17th century on, miniature pottery imitations of wicker and wooden cradles were given as christening presents, perhaps filled with candies, etc. They were made in slip-decorated and tin-glazed earthenware and in salt-glaze and other stonewares. Later they appeared in creamware. In a Newcastle (England, 1800) example we find a child modelled in the cradle, but this is rare. Some were fitted out as pincushions. This is a pleasant little custom which could well be revived. See also **furniture.**

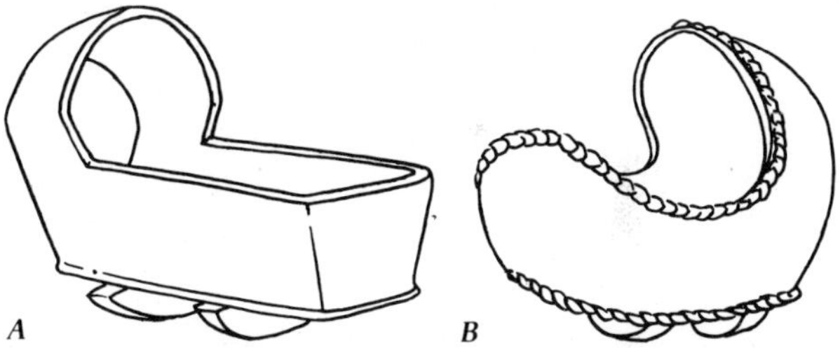

A/B. Two cradle types from the 18th/19th centuries: a squared, slab-pot-like form, which is also often decorated with little knobs at the corners and other additions; and the more rounded, perhaps originally thrown, shape, in this case with an edging of twisted clay rope. Both cradles have rockers underneath.

CREAMER

The *Concise Oxford English Dictionary* gives creamer as "a flat dish for skimming cream from milk," although this might be better described as a **cream pan.** *Webster's* gives "a small vessel for serving cream" as the definition and this agrees with U.S. usage as a small pitcher; in England it is called a "cream jug." (Photo: page 64). See **cow creamer.**

Everything a creamer should be—lively, practical, and balanced by John Lomas. (See page 63.)

A

A. Cardew calls this large and noble lidded pot, made in 1929, a "crock." It is earthenware, galena glaze, 19 inches/480mm tall. (Crafts Study Centre, Bath.)

CREAM PAN/POT

The pan is fairly large, usually straight-sided, with the walls sloping outwards, like a wide-bottomed, shallow **pancheon.** It is used for skimming cream from milk or for making clotted cream. Cardew (see C.PP in Booklist) mentions the form in connection with "a lip which pours well and does not distort the circle of the rim." See also **milk skimmer, milk pan.**

The cream pot, according to Brears (see B.CECP in Booklist) was lidded, short with convex sides, and varied from 9 inches to 2 feet (225 to 600mm) in height. Two horizontal handles and a generous lip allowed it to be lifted and the cream poured into a **churn.** It held 3 to 4 gallons.

CRESSET

A Medieval **lamp** in the form of a shallow bowl with a little foot or a central spike. The cresset (more usually in metal) was often mounted on a pole.

CROCK

From the Old English *crog,* the Icelandic *krukka,* etc., all indicating "an earthenware pot." Many books lump together all wide-mouthed vessels, usually, but not exclusively, of earthenware, as "crocks," and, indeed, it was a very general term in the 18th and 19th centuries—hence **crockery.**

The sides may be straight up and down, or curved, usually with a high shoulder and a slightly turned-out base. The crock can have a lid, or, if without, provided with a grooved or turned-out **(everted)** rim to give the necessary grip for string when tying on a cover. See also **bread crock.** It is usually fitted with two opposed **lug handles** set fairly high. Normally, it is a largish vessel 7 to 15 inches/175 to 360mm high. **Butter crocks** were common in the 19th century and in U.S. folk pottery.

B

B. Another impressive crock with a wider mouth, by Richard Batterham.

CROCKERY

A collective noun derived from *crock*. The definition given by *Webster's New Collegiate Dictionary* is simply "earthenware," but the *The Shorter Oxford English Dictionary* is a little more forthcoming: from "crocker," hence "crocks collectively, especially earthenware vessels." CTCD (see Booklist) goes further with "vessels of baked clay [synonymous with] pottery." In general usage, crockery indicates particularly tableware—cups, saucers, plates, etc.

CROCK PIE

Another name for **piecrust ware.**

CRUCIBLE

A melting pot, in profile, often a flattened hemisphere. Chemists' crucibles are of porcelain with a heat-resistant body and, like many practical lab-

These attractive, probably pinched-out crucibles are from a Norman English site near Salisbury, circa 12th century. The larger has a small hole in the side. (Salisbury Museum.)

oratory vessels, are attractive in the simplicity and severity of their forms. Crucibles may also be made of coarse saggar clay for the melting of frit, etc. In the Colchester Museum there is a set piece illustrating bronze casting in early Britain, which includes a simple, roughly made cylinder with a lip for pouring the molten metal. It would have been picked up with tongs. Crucibles with blow spouts for running gold and gold alloys were used in ancient America.

CRUET

A diminutive of the Old French *cruie,* meaning "a pot." In a strict sense it means a small bottle with a stopper, for vinegar or oil used at the table, or for water or wine in celebration of the Eucharist. A cruet stand was used in the 18th century to hold not only the bottles, but also **casters (shakers)** for condiments, and, in time, the whole group became known in England as a cruet set or simply as a cruet. By extension, a salt and pepper set, perhaps also with a **mustard pot,** but without a stand or the original oil and vinegar bottles, has also become known as a cruet or cruet set.

The term is not often used in the United States where "shaker" is preferred for salt and pepper pots. *Webster's New Collegiate Dictionary* and, therefore, presumably, American usage, returns cruet to its original meaning as a bottle for oil or vinegar. The bottles have often been linked into a single, interlocking form in such a way that either can be poured separately. This design appears in the ear-

A

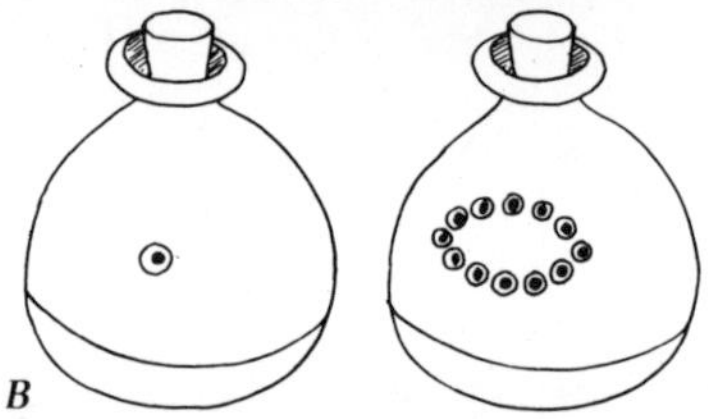

B

C

D

A/B. Similar in form, but used for different purposes are these cruets: illustration A shows oil and vinegar bottles—a cruet in the older sense of the word—from Coxwold Pottery; B shows salt and pepper shakers. It is unusual to fill shakers from the top.
C/D. Two approaches to the base-filled cruet set: simple, well-designed cylinders by West Marshall, and slab-built pieces by Sheila Fournier, with a mustard pot and spoon also included.

liest European attempts at producing porcelain in the 17th century.

The shaker/cruet demands careful design and finish; the provision of the cork is always something of a problem. Salt is liable to lift the glaze from crazed earthenware. Craft potters have, however, made ingenious and effective sets in a great variety of forms.

CRUSE

A small earthenware jar or pot for holding liquids. In Old English, *cruse* was "a pitcher."

CUP

A distant derivation through Old English *cuppe* of the Latin *cupa*, meaning "a tub" or "vat." *Webster's New Collegiate Dictionary* calls it "an open bowl-shaped drinking vessel." The precise distinction between cup and bowl, or between beaker, mug, and cup, is sometimes ambiguous. A cup is normally smaller, wider, rounder, and more finely potted and designed, but there are exceptions.

The Greek "cup" equivalents are the **kylix, kantharos,** and the **kyathos;** in Roman times, the **calix.** These were often raised on a high foot and had two handles; they were more like shallow **goblets.** The Corinthian cups, except for the two horizontal handles, are nearer to modern forms. Small drinking vessels are, of course, found earlier than this: a double-handled cup from Neolithic China is shown in C.HRNC (see Booklist) and dates back to before 4000 B.C.; a late Minoan cup is in a familiar form and has a squared, single handle. T'ang China produced some severe angular cups and also sets of eight bowl-shaped cups on a tray, grouped round a larger central bowl. Elaborately **lobed** "cups" with a more familiar side handle were made in Medieval times, but are fairly rare. During the 16th century, wooden cups, which had prevailed for some centuries, went out of fashion. Potters began making cups in green-glazed earthenware to take their place

A

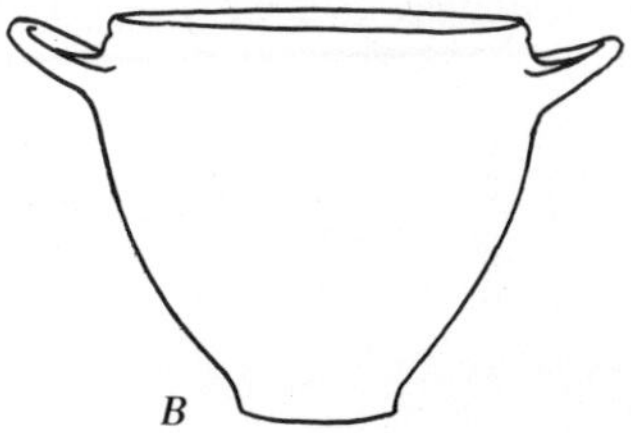

B

C

D

E

A. A rigid and uncompromising form from the Czechoslovakian Bronze Age.
B. An Etruscan or Greek import, this cup of circa 660 B.C., *with the opposed handles, is typical of the whole classical Greek period.*
C. With its elaborately capped handle and lobed form, this Ming Chinese cup looks more decorative than useful.
D. In contrast a much more straightforward tin-glazed cup from Lambeth (circa 1700), possibly used for chocolate, which was then a favorite breakfast drink.
E. Full-formed and simply conceived, this very satisfactory "open bowl-shaped drinking vessel" (Webster's New Collegiate Dictionary) *was made at Bristol in the 18th century. (Bristol Museum.)*

and, in so doing, earned the name of "cuppers." In 1533 an edict was passed forbidding cuppers to take clay from closer than 8 feet from a roadway. They had been in the habit of despoiling the road

F

F. The Staffordshire "thistle" shape in slipware, with a charming low-set handle.

surface by taking clay, which had been well-trodden and churned up by the traffic!

In 17th and early 18th centuries in Europe, tea was drunk from **tea bowls** from the Far East, rather taller than the average bowl, and, of course, without handles. Later cups were larger, and the tea was drunk hotter, so that handles became necessary, but there are few examples before 1775. Despite the Classical Revival, the single-handled cup became standard, the handle usually fairly slim and finely potted and subject to a good deal of fanciful design. The charming 17/18th century Staffordshire cup/beakers, with a slight waist and a midway handle, repay study. C.PPGT and LG (see Booklist) specify a coffee cup as "small—4 ounces," a teacup as "medium—7 ounces," and a breakfast cup as "large—9 ounces."

Rhodes is rather dismissive about the cup: "Such a simple form . . . just a small cylinder or bowl-like vessel. Its functional aspects are few." Any potter who has attempted them, however, knows that there is more to a fine cup than appears from this assessment. The balance, the placing of the handle, the width and height of the foot, the comfort of the rim to the lips, are all problems with many answers. I agree with his further remark that "a cup works best if height and width are about the same," and that the rim may slope a little outwards, but may never turn in. Discussing the recent history of the cup in America (not so true for England), he says that as a craft pottery shape it suffered serious eclipse until the mid-1960s when Ron Nagel "almost rediscovered it: in his hands the cup regained its status as a ceremonial form."

The inimitable George Curtis champions "the earthenware" for cups in the film *Big Ware.* "You see now, you try stoneware and you'll find that you can't tell whether you are drinking tea, coffee, or cocoa out of it, in my opinion . . . I've tried it and I can't say I like it at all. We've stuck to earthenware right the way through." It is certainly true that materials and forms affect one's enjoyment of beverages. See also **cup and saucer, coffee cup, punch bowl, tea and coffee set.**

CUP AND SAUCER

The earliest quoted cup and **saucer** in England was an import from Canton, about 1728. From then on, they came more and more to be considered as a single unit, although, in the mid-18th century, it was the saucer one drank from, not the cup.

There has long been a difference of opinion as to whether the saucer should have a central well to hold the cup in place. Most are designed with a well, but some potteries make a flat-bottomed saucer, which can then double as a small plate. They have even been made with a raised circle over which the cup fitted, this arrangement having the advantage of draining tea spillings away from the cup foot, but it is rather awkward in use. If a well is provided, it should fit the cup foot fairly snugly or it will serve no purpose. Between cup handle and saucer there should be sufficient room for the fingers to lift the cup without tipping it, and there should also be room to accommodate a spoon. A successful cup and saucer represents a good deal of thought and care. See also **tea and coffee set, cup.**

A

B

C

A. This elegantly balanced porcelain cup and saucer is by Harry and May Davis and has many of the essential qualities: room for the fingers under the handle, a snug fit in the wall, a smooth and slightly everted *rim, etc.*
B. A flatter, more attractive design by Sheila Fournier.
C. An interesting and well thought out cup and saucer by Sally Dawson.

CUP STAND, Cup plate

Quite elaborate forms, some based on the lotus or water lily were made during the Sung period in China and Korea, and are known as **cup** or **bowl stands** (under which term two are illustrated). They are, in effect, an early type of saucer, but not a very convenient one.

In the mid-18th century, in the West, it was customary to drink tea from a deep saucer, and small, flat plates, 3 to 4 inches/75 to 100mm across, were sometimes provided to place the cup on.

CURFEW

An order was made in the early Medieval period that fires must be extinguished at the ringing of a bell at nightfall. The curfew was thus, literally, "cover-fire," a large earthenware cover used to quench a hearth fire at night, while just allowing

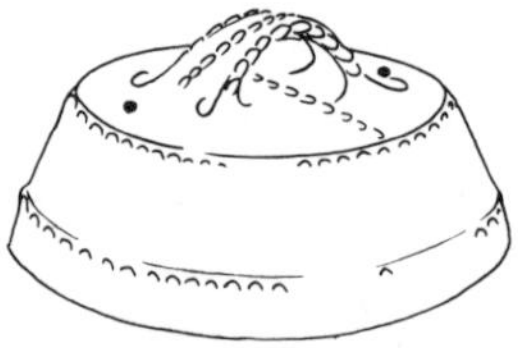

A fine 18 inches/450mm wide curfew, decorated with thumbed-down strips of clay, from a 13th century kiln site at Laverstock (Wiltshire, England).

enough air to flow through small holes to keep it smoldering. Curfews are rare: a fine example can be seen in the Museum at Salisbury (England).

CURRANT WASHER

In form, a cross between a **colander** and a **cheese press,** this paillike vessel with perforated walls, displayed in the St. Fagans Folk Museum, Wales, was reputedly designed for the washing of currants.

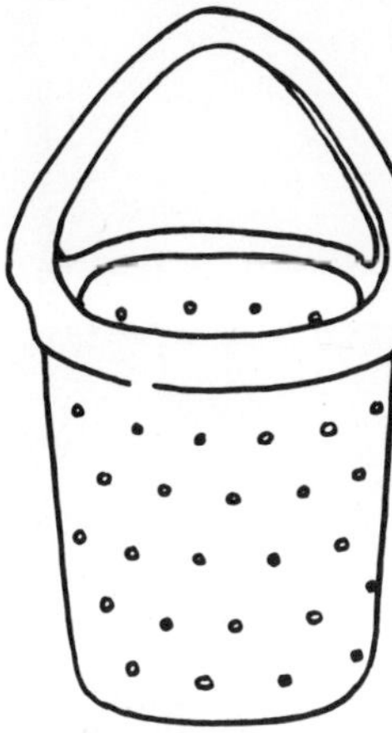

A Welsh currant washer.

CUSPIDOR

See **spittoon.**

CUSTARD CUP

In the Brighton Museum a Chelsea-Derby two-handled cup is so titled. In the Victoria and Albert Museum, however, a 19th century covered pot, as illustrated, is called a "custard cup." Custard, after all, is quite an obliging fluid.

CUTLERY HANDLE/BOX

Knife and fork handles, chiefly of porcelain, were quite widely made in the 18th and 19th centuries.

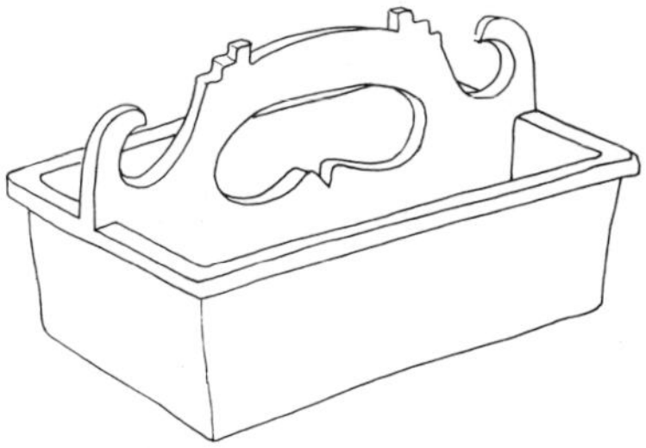

An English mid-19th century cutlery box with a center handle, made in glazed earthenware.

A potter would need to work with a silversmith or cutlery firm. The range of formal options is subtle, rather than wide.

Pottery cutlery boxes were not uncommon among the folk potters of 18th and 19th century America and England. They were generally slab built with two sections and a handle in the middle, or with a high back and a sloping lid.

CUT RIM

Carved and cut rims appear throughout history, but earlier examples are almost always regular and evenly spaced in their design, such as the Chinese **sunflower bowl.** See also **lobe, chimney pot, monteith.** Rims are also cut to form high and often

A

A. A wide-rimmed hexagonally cut dish from Bristol, 18th century. The slight lift of the rim gives the appearance of curved edges. (Bristol Museum.)

B. The form of a pot altered by cutting and overlapping in an uncompromising fashion, by Peter Smith. *B*

C

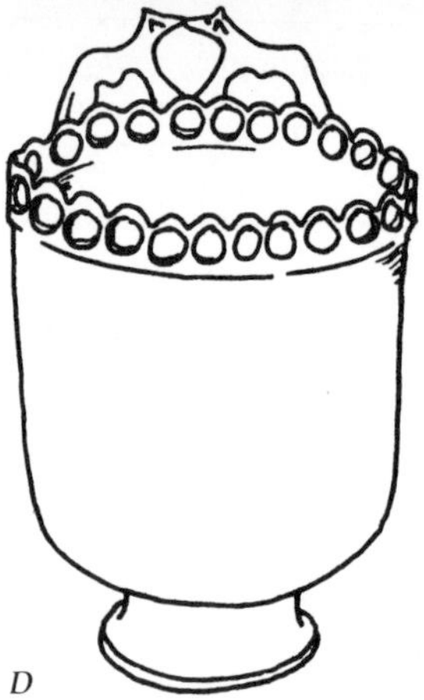

D

C. A porcelain dish rim cut into a cloudscape, by Peter Lane.
D. A decorative "jar" (Victoria and Albert Museum) with an intricately cut rim, 7 inches/180mm tall, from 12th/13th century Rayy (Persia).

exaggerated, spoutlike **lips** (see illus. at **carination**).

The technique is still practiced by modern potters but often in an asymmetric fashion and for decorative purposes. See also **split and slashed form, fish dish, coiled pottery, rim.**

CUT-SIDED BOWLS/POTS

Thrown shapes can be cut or sliced to produce flat panels. Often the wall is slightly beaten before cutting; otherwise, if the panels are to be more than a couple of inches wide, it will need to be very thick to avoid cutting right through. The character of the result depends on the tool used (wire, knife, plane, etc.) and the speed and directness of the cut.

The technique seems to have been little used in China (a rare Han example is illustrated in H.CAC—see Booklist) but there are some splendid Swankhalok pots, irregularly and beautifully cut, and also Korean and later Japanese cut wares. Hamada, Tomimoto, and others have used the method to great effect. Many modern potters produce cut wares today. Richard Batterham has used the method extensively. (Photographs: facing page.)

A

A. A thrown pot with very directly cut facets by Hamada, 1963.

B. Cut faces, which more subtly influence the form, by Denis Moore, 1958.

B

C

C. Here the cutting has been smoothed or glazed over until it resembles beating or even cast ware. Chinese, Sung. Barlow Collection.)

D. A bold and effective cut cylinder by John Reeves. Note the effect on the rim, which greatly adds to the interest of the shape.

E. The next page shows three boldly cut or carved pots by Col Levy of N.S.W. Australia. Here the potter has gone further than mere facets and has produced a sculptural form. (Photograph: David Moore.)

D

E

CYLINDER

A figure with a circular plan and, normally, vertical parallel sides. It is a basic pottery form which relies largely on proportion for its interest. A thrown shape is rarely perfectly cylindrical and the slight variations can give life and vitality to apparently cylindrical shapes. To quote Rhodes (see R.PF in Booklist) "The potter soon learns that clay . . . resists the straight line or flat plane. . . . As this variation from the exact geometric occurs . . . the cylinder moves into another realm . . . the shaped form with movement and rhythm."

A

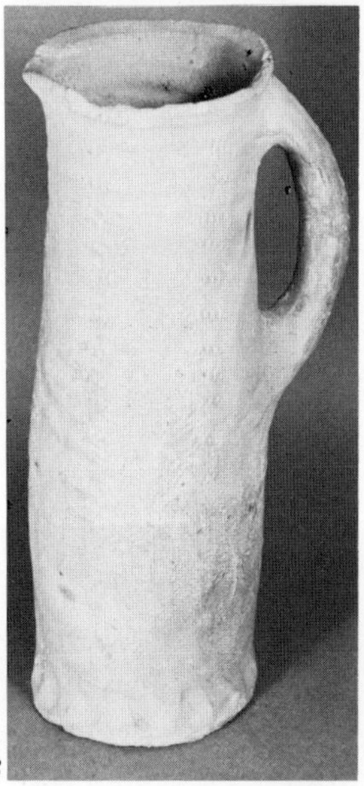

B

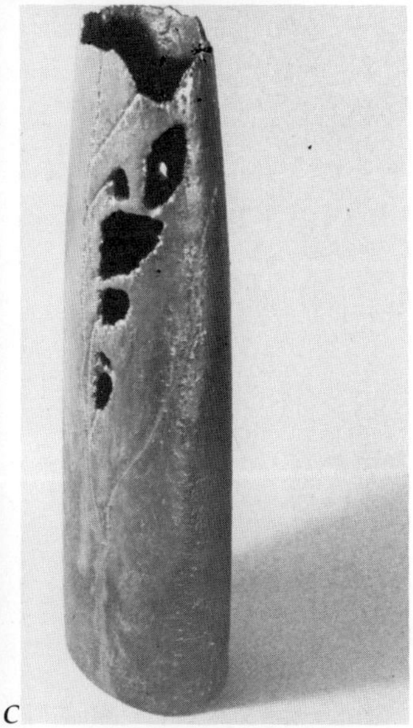

C

A. Two bowls, by Mick Casson, which show how strong the cylinder form can be, even when applied to shallow vessels. Note the sturdy rims in keeping with the shape. (Photograph: Eileen Lewenstein.)

B. In the greatest contrast to the Casson bowls is this unusual English Medieval jug/pitcher, direct and lively. (Salisbury Museum.)

C. Formed as a slab cylinder, but subsequently beaten, cut, and planed into an oval, slightly tapering form, which gives it life and interest. By Sheila Fournier, 1979.

Robin Welch's cylinders, however, eschew evidence of the hand at work and rely on the proportions of their parts, a largely intellectual effect. Casson's cylindrical bowls, while almost as "pure" in form, manage to retain more humanity. The cylinder is not common in historical pottery, although the Medieval **jug** illustrated comes very close.

Many theoreticians, writing on ceramic form, "read" cylinders into pot shapes. While this may be useful for analysis, it is essentially a geometric and finally a nonvalid approach. See also **slab plate/dish.**

D

DAFFER

A folk name for **crockery** in Cornwall (England).

D'ALVA BOTTLE

A 17th century name for a **bellarmine.**

DAVAS

A flat-bottomed oven dish from modern Greece, with an upright wall and a rounded rim.

DEFINITION AND FORM

If there is one characteristic that is shared by all good pots and, I hope, evident in the multifarious approaches to form illustrated in this book, it is the quality of definition, the feeling that the potter has made his idea truly explicit. This does not imply any aggressiveness or rigidity, but a feeling of wholeness, finality, and intention. It is most easily recognized in a handle or a crisply cut foot, but the simple curve of a bowl can also exhibit the quality or lack it.

It is often the most obvious difference between the work of the struggling beginner and the experienced professional, although it arises as much from character and sensitivity as from practical skill. I feel sure that the ideal of a well-defined form was uppermost in the mind of Leach when he discussed line and suggested his **laws of pottery form,** and it is implicit in the **analysis of form** by Honey and others.

Definition alone, of course, is not sufficient, but

the most imaginative and creative work may fail without it. As well as the more obvious application to rim, foot, lid, knob, etc., it is equally essential, and more difficult to realize, in the curves of a wall of a pot and in the relationship of one area to another. While some shapes and inventions may be controversial, they can all share the self-confidence that comes from the firm realization in space of the potter's creative idea.

DEMITASSE

Literally a half-cup; a small cup for black coffee, usually cylindrical.

DEPRESSED FORM

A term sometimes used by historians to describe very flattened-down shapes, such as some Korean **boxes.** A Roman oil flask in the Ipswich Museum would qualify for this description, as would the squared I'Hsing teapot illustrated in CMoct78 (see Booklist). Thrown boxes made today, particularly those made in porcelain, are sometimes too shallow to have much practical use, and are valued for their tactile and decorative pleasures.

A fine Sung pot, which might be described by some writers as "depressed." An attractive piece, which would sit beautifully in cupped hands.

DESSERT SERVICE

Traditionally, this consists of a large bowl, six or twelve smaller bowls, a fruit dish, a cream jug, a sugar bowl, and a sauceboat.

DIABOLO

A shape with in-curving walls; the name is derived from the toy known as "the devil on two sticks." Strictly speaking, a diabolo reduces in width to a sharply defined central waist, but the term is useful to describe many concave-walled forms.

It is rarely seen in prehistoric and early pottery, where containment was the prime aim, and the pots, therefore, tended to assume a fuller shape. See illustration A under **cup,** however, for a squat, but definitely diabolo, shape from the early Bronze Age. There are also Aztec examples and some early European pitcher shapes approximate it. In Eastern pots it appears in imitation of the Bronze **ku,** and later in Japan as a shape for holding flowers. There is an attractive mid-18th century celadon example illustrated in C.WC (see Booklist).

A number of modern potters have used the shape, generally, for decorative pots, although the author based all his tableware range on a modified diabolo for several years, and beakers especially are often designed in this form. A low-set handle can look very satisfactory. Hans Coper and Lucie Rie use variations on the shape in some of their pots, and Janet Leach uses it in various proportions to set off her freely poured glazes. See also **drum.**

A. Three free variations on the diabolo by Janet Leach. (Photograph: Leach Pottery.)

A

B. The form adapted to a box. By Sally Somerville.
C. This is nearer the true diabolo form, emphasized by the decoration. By Waistel Cooper.

B

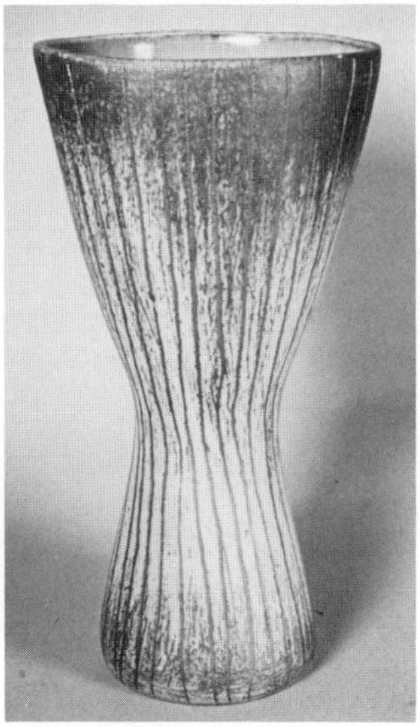

C

DINNER SERVICE

According to OBPP (see Booklist) this consists of soup bowls, salad bowls, jugs/pitchers, small hors d'oeuvres dishes, and a cruet set. *Webster's New Collegiate Dictionary* defines dinnerware as "tableware other than flatware," but flatware has a wider meaning in the United States than it has in Great Britain (see **flatware**). To the average potter in either country a dinner service would most probably include two or three sizes of plates, vegetable dishes, and a meat dish. There might also be a casserole.

DISH

A shallow, normally flat-based vessel, most commonly used for holding food at meals. It is often oblong or oval, although a thrown vessel may be called a "dish" if it is too shallow to be a **bowl** and too deep to be a **plate.** Etymologically, it should be round, since it is derived from the word "disc," but general usage has decreed that it is often applied to an irregular plan, triangular, etc. in addition to those mentioned above, possibly to differentiate it from "plate." See **baking dish, pie plate, pressed dish/bowl, fish dish,** etc. Certain other uses of the term are ambiguous, such as *cheese dish,*

A. A powerfully designed dish from Sung China made with total assurance. (Barlow Collection.)

A

B

B. Equally assured, but in direct contrast, an asymmetrical form by Ruth Duckworth, which could be called a "dish."

which is more often a plate with a cover. A "dished" surface is one with a slight hollow in it.

Few pottery dishes survive from Medieval or earlier cultures (they were mostly of wood or metal), although they were fairly common in Roman times. Flat dishes, oval in plan, with vertical edges, have been found in Roman Britain, and there are early dishes with subtle, almost Chinese Sunglike, rims, subtly everted and **beaded.** In the Ipswich Museum there is an interesting dish from the 13/14th centuries. It is very elongated, almost pointed at both ends, about 10 inches/250mm long. From the evidence of its rim, it appears to have been thrown and then reshaped, perhaps using the cut-center technique, although there is no direct evidence of this. There is also a very large English dish—some 22 inches/550mm wide by 6 inches/150mm high—from the same period. In Far Eastern history, dishes of a rather sophisticated type are common, and there must have been many in everyday use among the poorer people, but these do not find their way into glossy histories of the times. In 18th century Europe the term "dish" replaced **cup** (or **saucer**) for a time as in "a dish of tea."

Dishes formed by means of hump or hollow molds are a staple part of the output of amateur and evening class potters. Some professionals use the method, too, although baking dishes and such are more often thrown and then beaten or cut to form noncircular shapes. These are always livelier than the results of press-molding, although Siddig El'Nigoumi has specialized in delightfully decorated and very satisfying pressed dishes and plates.

DISTORTED FORM

Some early pots are uneven or lopsided, but it is unlikely that this was due to any deliberate act, except in very rare cases and then for a specific practical purpose (see **scoop**). The techniques of beating and **folding** alter the form, but this is something different from distortion. The Chinese saw little virtue in carelessly warped or damaged pots and these would probably have been weeded out and broken. The later Japanese veneration for the irregular or even for the flawed pot arose from the sophisticated man's yearning for the "natural" life, but, even here, deliberate, acute distortion for its own sake was rarely practiced (see **asymmetry**). It is the modern potter who bashes and tears at pots in an attempt to express himself and society.

Violent distortion is more often practiced in America than it is in England, and Rhodes, in *Pottery Form,* deals with it in some length. He says:

A

A. This Oribe tea bowl probably came from the wheel fairly lopsided, but has been further distorted to what is called "shoe-shaped" in F.SOC (see Booklist).

B. A pot by Jaques Laroussinie (described as a teapot!), bashed and cut almost to destruction.

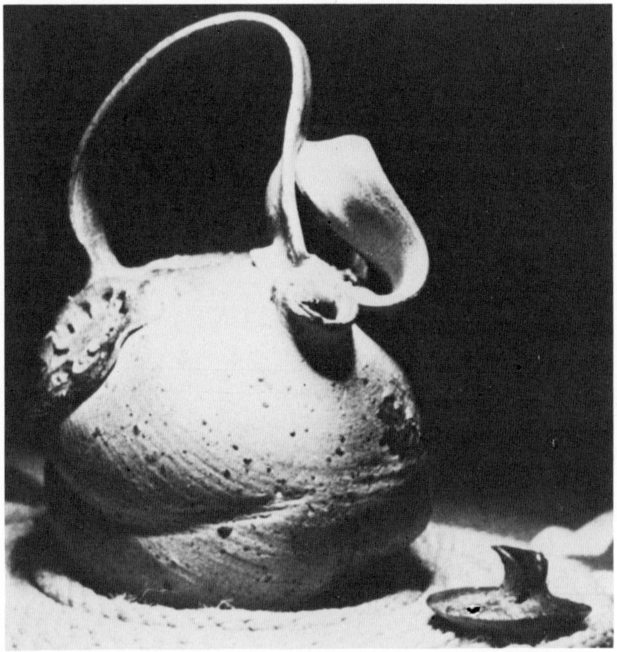

B

C

C. A large bowl, by Lucie Rie, apparently distorted from a thrown shape at the soft clay stage.

"Distorting the freshly made soft pot gives a quality of form quite different from changes . . . after the clay has stiffened. Soft flowing transitions are possible as well as folds, wrinkles, creases, tears, ripples, and pleats," but he warns that "altering can easily be overdone. . . . Total freedom of the restraints of formal relationships may lead merely to chaos." According to Rhodes, one of the extreme potters in this field is Voulkos whose "destructive impulses [make the pots] look like survivors of a war . . . gaping holes . . . rims of plates ripped and torn." See also **split and slashed form.**

DIVIDED DISH

The most common divided dish, historically speaking, is the two-section oblong pie dish, usually slip-trailed, which was made in quantity by country and

A

A. A well-proportioned slipware divided dish, probably early 19th century English.

B

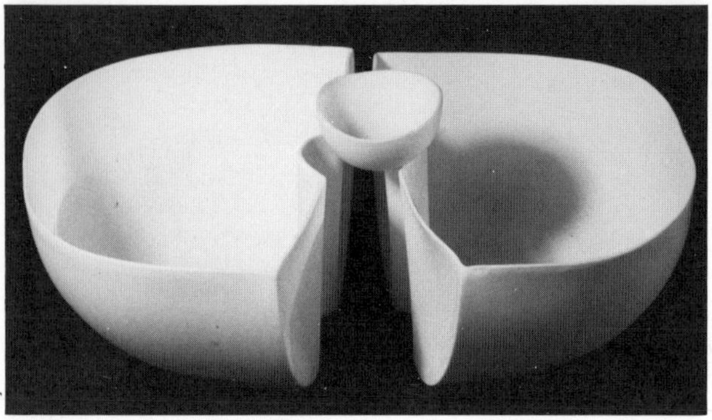

C

B. Less common, this fine, large, circular divided dish is shown in the Salisbury Museum.
C. A truly "divided" slipcast container in porcelain by Jaqueline Poncelet.

folk potters through the last three centuries and more. Circular Roman dishes were made with a central section and four radiating dividing walls; these also have a flange on the rim, which may indicate a lid. C.ESD (see Booklist) discusses the mathematics of the divided oblong dish in a way which I am sure would have surprised the old potters. Very attractive elliptical divided dishes were made in 19th century Stoke and elsewhere.

The divided dish is still a popular form, especially among amateur potters, although it has its shrinkage problems.

DOD HANDLE

A handle made by extruding clay through a die from a dod box or pugmill, which would then be the same width from top to bottom.

DOLL

The derivation of the word "doll" is apparently unknown. The word "idol" springs to mind, but no dictionary mentions it. Most suggest only a pet name for Dorothy. Its earliest recorded use was in 1560. Early doll-like figures usually have a religious connotation, although jointed dolls, apparently intended for children's play, are known from Greek and Roman antiquity. **Bell** dolls from Boeotia were hung at religious festivals. A fairly sophisticated "doll" from Pompeii is illustrated in CMdec78 (see Booklist).

Early dolls may have been entrusted to children, but as sacred objects, rather than playthings. Little figures are found in children's graves from all periods. Christian dolls were made for Nativity scenes and the like. There is an illustration in E.ED (see Booklist) of potters making clay dolls for St. Bartholomew's Fair, circa 1490. These were later known as "Bartholomew Babies," although by then they had assumed the shape of adult females! Doll fig-

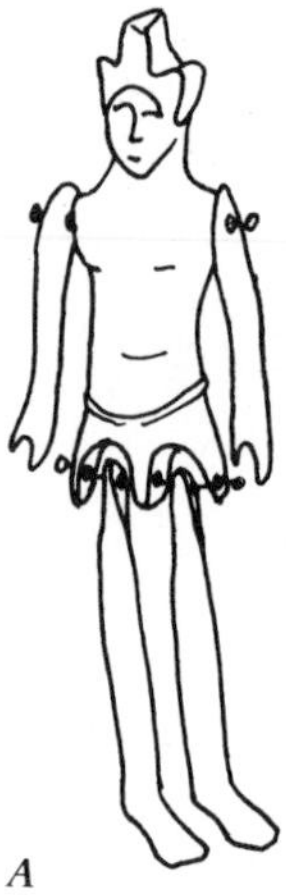

A

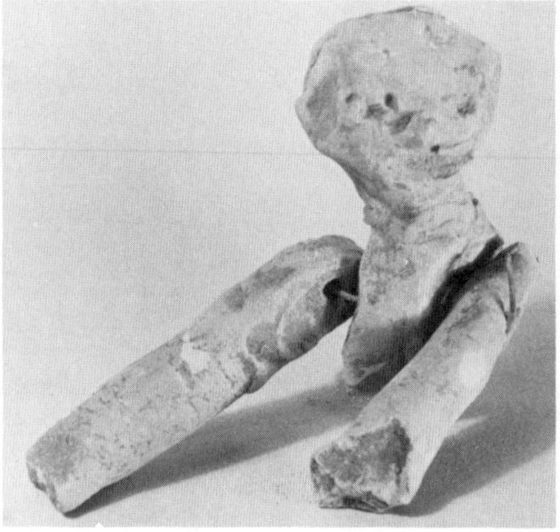

B

C

A. A clay dancing doll from 5th century B.C. *Corinth. The headdress is described as a helmet, but the effect is very much that of a jester.*
B. This fragment of a crudely made, articulated doll was surely created either by a child or by a potter to quiet an infant. It was found behind an ancient building in Lacock, Wiltshire, England.
C. Ceramic head and limbs in the 19th century style by Karen Gregory, 1979.

D

ures were also made in Nuremberg and other places as early as the 14th century. Few examples have been found at folk pottery sites, but potters certainly must have made crude figures for their children and one such figure was dug up in the author's neighbor's garden.

In the 18th century frankly secular play-dolls were made, with porcelain heads and busts; all through the 19th century, play-dolls in Parian body and in more or less flesh-colored biscuit were made. All-china dolls, some with articulated limbs, were made at Stoke-on-Trent in the late 19th century and early 20th. A modern terra-cotta doll with movable arms and legs by John Nowers was illustrated in CR14 (see Booklist), but they are not widely made today. See also **toy, Noah's ark.**

D. A white earthenware doll, 1976, by Fiona Heaney. It is hand-built and decorated with enamels on glaze. The hair is applied wool.

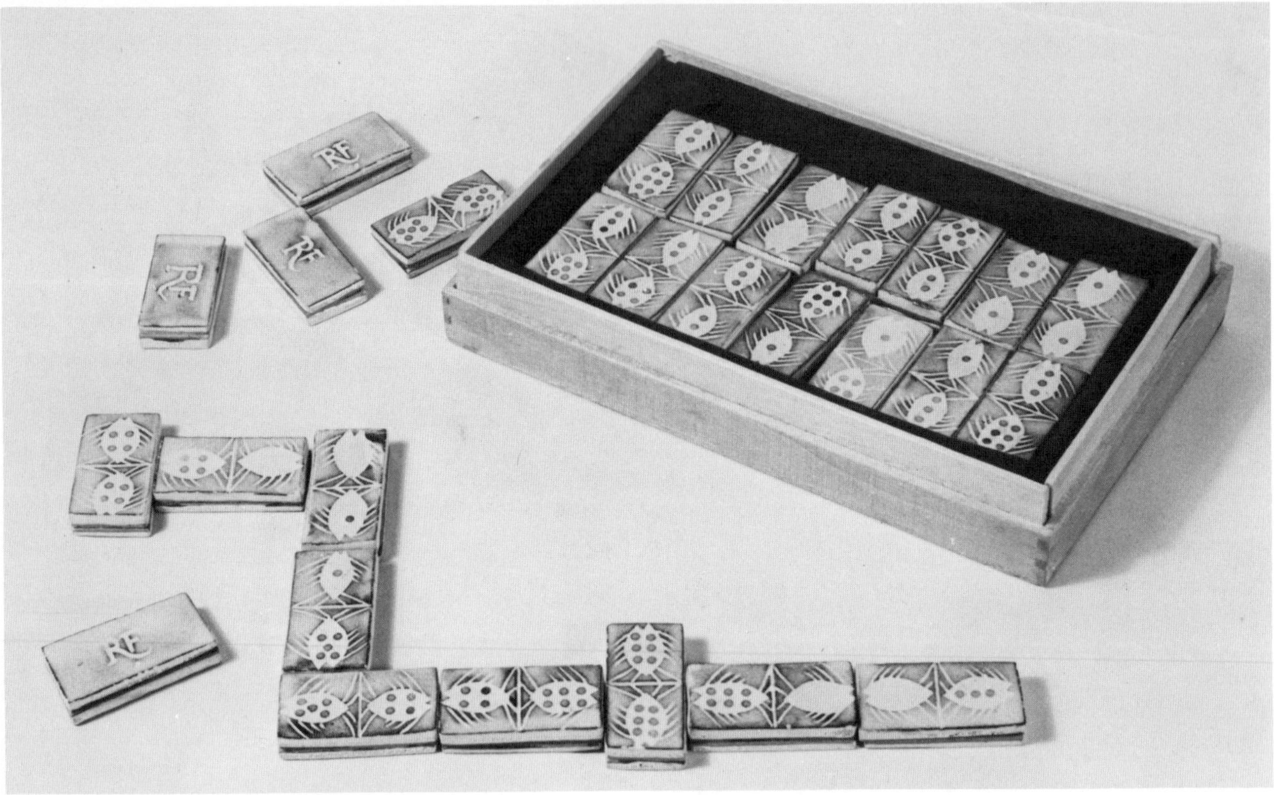

A very pretty domino set made for the author by Mary Ball. The dots are set in fish shapes, and on the reverse of the pieces are the initials R F. The set is tin-glazed earthenware.

DOMINOS

Most board games can be made in pottery. Domino sets, which consist of twenty-eight brick-shaped pieces, each about 2 by 1 by ⅜ inches/50 by 25 by 10mm, can be cut from slabs or pressed into a simple mold. Ceramic dominos, even in earthenware, make a very satisfying clacking noise in use. The twenty-eight pieces are marked in dots with all the possible variations of the numbers 1 through 6 on the two halves of each piece; e.g., 1 and 0, 1 and 1, 1 and 2, all the way up to 1 and 6; then 2 and 0, 2 and 2, etc.

DOOR KNOB/HANDLE/PLATE

Handles and knobs for doors and drawers were made in porcelain in the 18th century and were almost standard equipment until recently. They were sometimes fitted with a metal center to take the strain of turning a latch shaft, but satisfactory handles have been made in stoneware alone by modern potters. The range of forms, plain or modelled, is wide and largely unexplored.

There is little formal value in a door plate, although its outline can be varied. Its attraction lies in the decoration it provides. A relief pattern is possible and would help grip, but the nature of its use dictates that it be fundamentally flat.

DOUBLE-GOURD VASE

This form has been used by potters of several cultures in both the East and the West. It is perhaps natural to experiment by luting one pot on top of another, but the result is seldom completely integrated. It was used by the Chinese as early as the 3rd millenium B.C., in T'zu Chou ware, and during Ming and later periods, and by the Japanese Ninsei potters and others. A milk vessel from Botswana

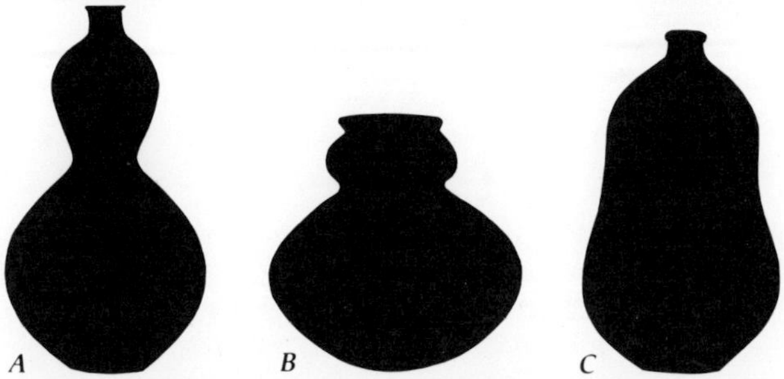

A/B. This example of a double gourd from 19th century Japan (Satsuma ware) is more integrated than many Chinese and European versions. It is not unlike an excessively curved baluster. On the other hand, the African shape is frankly 2 pots, one upon the other.
C. A very restrained use of the double curve from 17th century Japan.

illustrated in P.PA (see Booklist) is a squatter version of the shape. It does not occur so frequently in Europe. The **baluster** is an associated but more flowing and satisfactory variant on the double-bulge form.

DOUBLE-NECKED POT

There are two main types—those with two necks almost joined together and those with separated necks. Those of the first type are frequently found in Cypriot and Anatolian pottery of the 1st millennium B.C., with two adjacent spouts and necks joined to the body by a single handle. Similar pots of greater antiquity from Lapithos (Cyprus) are shown in the Fitzwilliam Museum (England).

Those of the second type demonstrate a more obvious logic: the air can enter at one spout while liquid is poured from the second. The most common of these are found in great numbers from

B

B. A lenticular *hand-built pot with 2 necks, by the author.*

preColumbian American cultures, sometimes with two simple, tapering spouts, but more often with one spout highly decorated with figures of animals, other creatures, and frequently human forms. The spouts are usually bridged by a strap handle. See **bridge handle.**

A

A. Two necks flowing into a single handle give a proud and distinguished form to this Bronze Age Cypriot pot.

DRAINER

See also **colander.** In a specific sense, this is a useful piece of kitchen equipment, consisting of a small dish or similar form, pierced with holes, and used inverted in a vegetable dish to keep the food from contact with the liquid draining from it.

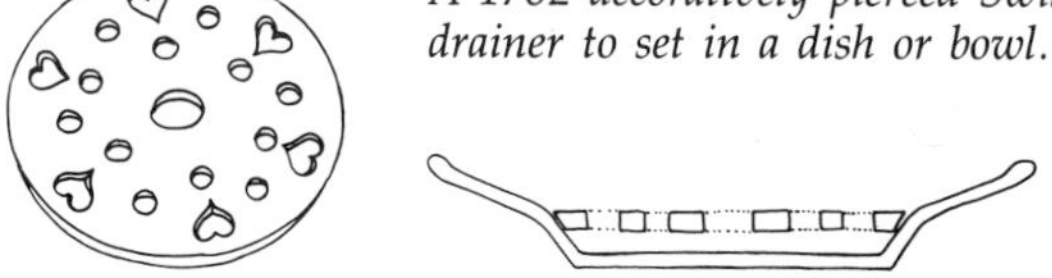

A 1782 decoratively pierced Swiss drainer to set in a dish or bowl.

DRAIN PIPE

This type of large industrial ceramic is outside the potter's field, but there have been, especially in the distant past, a number of interesting forms used for this plebeian function. Often the pipe consisted of a number of bottomless pots, placed base into mouth, building up into a silhouette which could give inspiration to modern potters. Norman Davey's beautifully illustrated *A History of Building Materials* shows some of these.

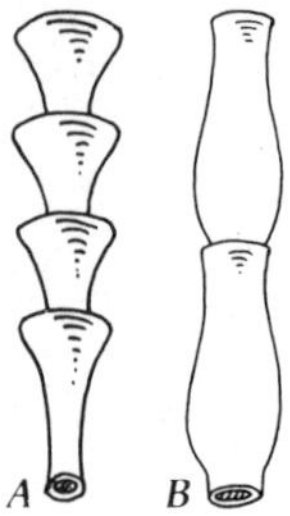

A/B. A stylish series of connected flaring forms make up this drain pipe from Ur, while the Greek pipes from Olympia make a more curvaceous silhouette. (See D.HBM in Booklist.)

C. Though designed for a purely mundane and practical purpose, this sewer pipe junction seating provides a very vigorous form.

DRAPED FORM

This is a type of molding in which a slab of clay is wrapped over any suitable object. This may be natural, such as a stone or a piece of wood, or more consciously shaped, such as a core of paper, foam rubber, cut, modelled, or built clay, and the like. The result is a softened, more hazy, image of the original, with the possible addition of pleats and folds. Shrinkage and other strains on the clay limit the technique. Rhodes recommends fiberglass filaments in the clay, such as the English commercial Newclay. See R.PF (in Booklist) for further discussion.

DRAUGHTS

See **checkers.**

DRINKING JUG/PITCHER

Some Medieval lipless pitchers were probably used for drinking, as were Tudor green-glazed examples. A strange German **baluster** shape with several handles, like a monstrous **tyg,** is illustrated in C.WC (see Booklist) and was used as a drinking jug.

DRINKING WATER POT

In the days of well and spring water supplies for drinking would have been stored in a large open **crock,** similar to a **bread crock.** An example in the Lavenham Guildhall (Sussex, England) is labelled "used in every household before piped water." Presumably, it was covered with muslin or something similar, as there is no lid. Water would have been scooped from this type of pot, but larger **cisterns** were also used with a tap. See also **water fountain.**

DRUG POT/JAR

Apart from the ubiquitous **albarello,** there have been several distinctive vessels made for the storage of drugs and ointments. Broad, little **ointment jars** were common in the 17th century and later, as were **pill slabs.** Pear-shaped drug jars, deriving from Delft, were made at Lambeth. Those for oils and syrups had a spout and handles. They were also made in baluster form and as slender-necked bottles. Many of the shapes can be traced back through Spain and Italy to the Islamic world. Tiny cylindrical

An elegant 18th century Bristol tin-glazed jar for liquid medicines.

pots for the rarer drugs are also common. English pots filled with arsenic were found at Newarke House. See also **bellarmine, mercury pot.**

DRUM

Pottery drums, often finely shaped, are found in Africa and Asia. A certain fullness of form seems

A

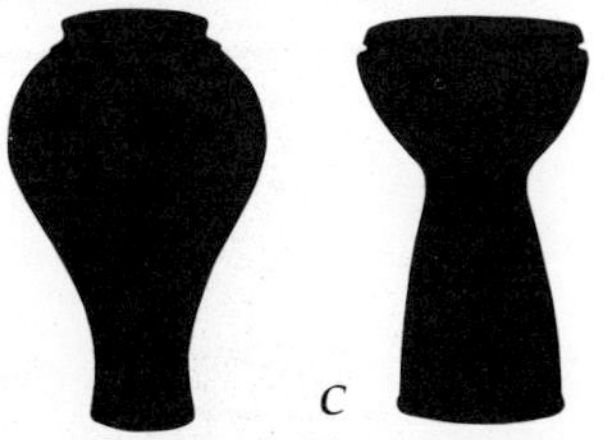

B C

A. A subtly proportioned 8th century Shosoin Japanese drum.
B/C. Two of the very fine forms of what are known as "goblet drums." (British Museum.) The first is from Tunis. The skin is stretched over the wide mouth, a groove or everted rim making this possible.

desirable, but there are many variations and possibilities for variety and invention. The **diabolo**-shaped hand drum from Japan is an unusual example. There are fine Ebo drums in the Downing College Museum at Cambridge, England. Friction drums vibrated by the fingers or by a friction cord or stick were made in Europe.

DUTCH OVEN

See **roaster.**

E

ECUELLE

A deep dish for serving vegetables. In the Bristol Museum the term is also applied to a two-handled covered dish.

EFFIGY POT

See **human form, face pot.**

EGG

Pottery eggs were made as early as 3500 B.C. in Egypt. Pottery and porcelain egg-shaped boxes, usually in celebration of Easter, were made in Russia and Germany in the 19th century.

A

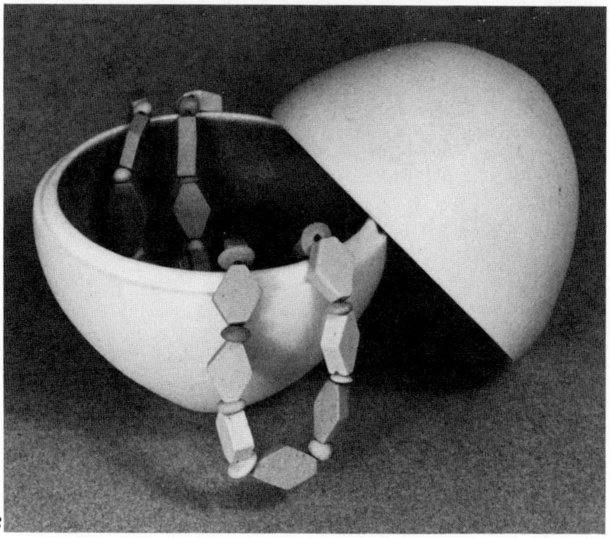

B

A. A stoneware egg in interlocking halves containing an embryonic figure, by Eileen Lewenstein. Strong in overtones of fertility.
B. A porcelain Easter Egg gift box for a porcelain necklace, by Sheila Fournier, circa 1968.

The form is occasionally used by modern potters. An "egg form" by Val Barry is illustrated in CR42 (see Booklist); Sheila Fournier's "Easter Eggs" in porcelain each contain a porcelain necklace (see **bead**).

EGG BAKER/POACHER

Usually a small, shallow stoneware bowl, with a straight, out-standing handle. It was commonly

An attractive, womanlike egg poacher by the Leach Pottery. One of their long-running designs.

made by studio potters and was a regular item in the St. Ives Pottery catalog from its early days. In LG (see Booklist), little, slightly flaring dishes for cooking eggs in water in the oven are called **cocottes.** These are also used for meat. See also **apala.**

EGGCUP

The traditional British shape resembles a small **goblet** on a splayed foot. Although *Webster's New Collegiate Dictionary* agrees with the definition that an eggcup is "for holding eggs to be eaten from the shell," the form more generally current in the United States is a larger, more genuinely cuplike

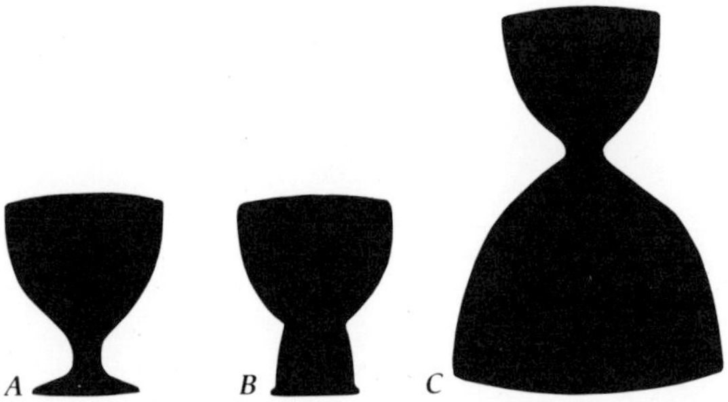

A/B/C. Three types of eggcups in general use: the first, the traditional English silhouette; the second, a similar type, but with different proportions of cup and stem; and the third, the reversing type, one end for an egg in its shell, the reverse for mashing the egg.

D

D. Original and simple slab-built eggcups by Sheila Fournier. These are fine for kitchens with limited space.

E

E. A "fun" egg-cup by Ruth Franklin.

container, used to mash the shelled egg in. Also common is a double cup (illustration C), the small end for serving the egg. In 19th century New England a large cup on a stem was made. The U.K. type of egg holder is capable of many variations, such as the flat, square example shown. In the Brighton Museum there is a dish containing ten covered eggcups shaped as partridges, each with a salt container, made at Longport in about 1800.

EGG STAND/SERVER

The simplest form is an inverted thrown or slab-built tray or dish with more or less vertical sides,

A

B

C

A. A straightforward slab-built egg stand by Sheila Fournier. The arches in the sides enable it to be easily lifted.
B. A more decorative egg server with a bail handle *by Andrew Young.*
C. A 4-egg server with a central handle. (Fournier Pottery.)

the flat top being pierced with holes about an inch/25mm wide. An early Staffordshire example is circular, the base being cut into a series of wide legs. The holes, however, seem made for super-eggs—perhaps goose eggs. LG (see Booklist) illustrates a shallow dish set on a pedestal, with a ring handle in the middle. Holes are cut around the dish for the eggs to sit in, and it is used for serving boiled eggs at the table.

ELBOW DISH

Made with an ancient Japanese technique, this was a small shallow dish formed over the crooked elbow of the potter. Elbow dishes were frequently used as oil lamps before the family shrine. Larger dishes were made over the knee. The Mashiko potter Totaro Sakuma said, "A potter's work must receive affection from his hands. All forms come from the human body." There is a series of photographs in S.WJP (see Booklist), showing the making of elbow dishes today.

EMBOSSING

Ornamentation with **bosses** in relief; also loosely used to indicate other patterns in heavy relief. Although a decorative technique, large bosses will obviously alter and influence a form. The Saxon **buckelurnen** (see illustration B under **cinerary urn**) and early English **grape cups** are cases in point.

ENVELOPE FORM

Usually slab-built, but sometimes thrown and altered, this form consists of two shallowly curved walls coming together at an acute angle or to a very sharp curve at each end; an excessively **flattened form.** It is essentially a modern development and is popular among craft potters, notably Val Barry, Gillian Lowndes, and Hans Coper, among many others. See also **asymmetry.**

A. Two delicate "landscape" envelope pots in porcelain, by Val Barry. The gently cut-away rim adds interest to the shape.

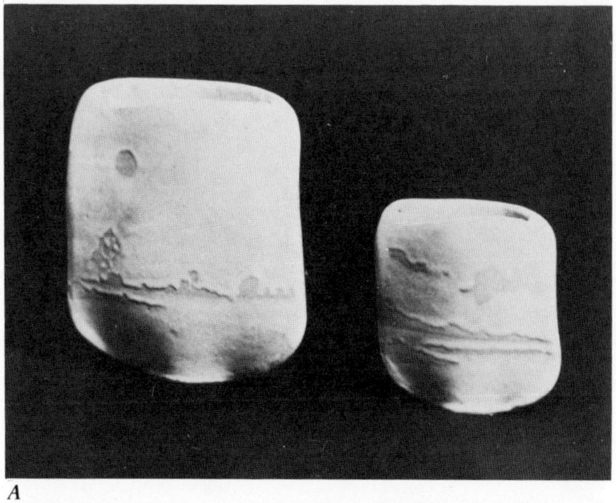

A

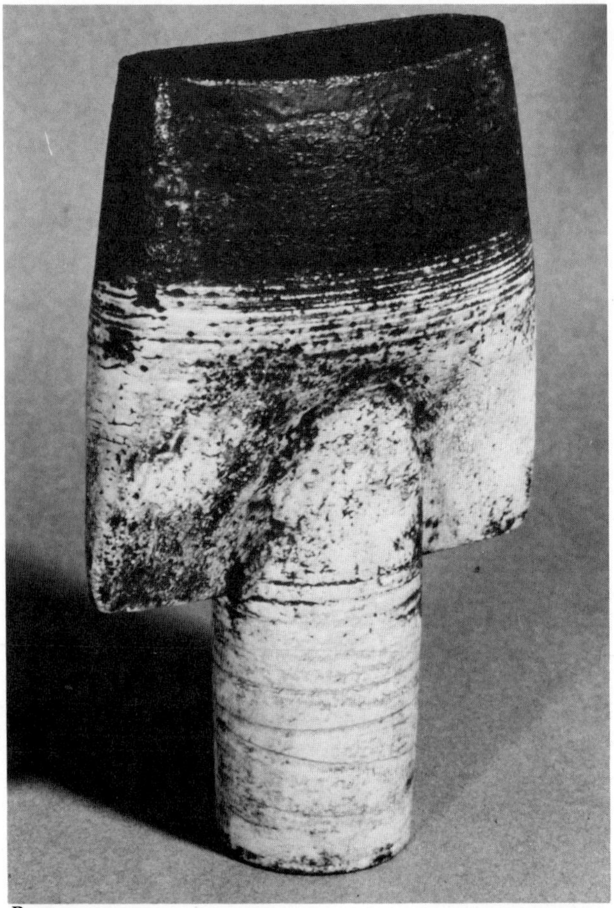

B

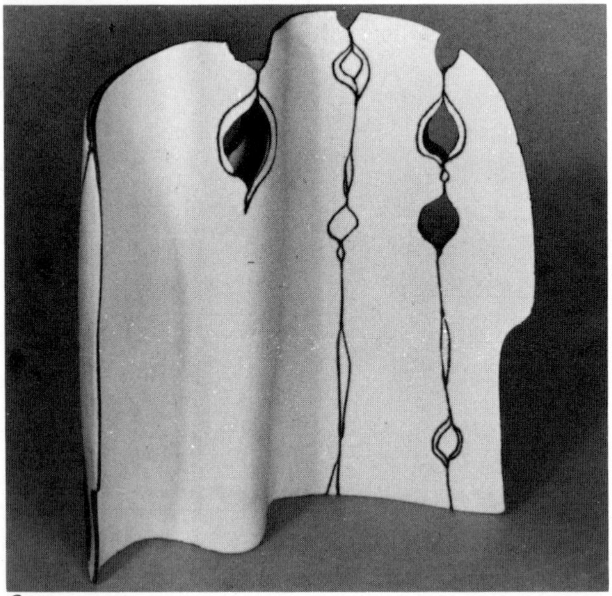

C

B. A construction of 2 thrown pots, the top flattened and altered and set on a cylinder. A scultural form by Hans Coper.
C. A quite different approach by Sheila Fournier, slab-built in porcelain.

EPERGNE

Though more often made in silver, these centerpieces for the dinner table were also made in pottery from the 18th century. They were sometimes designed as a branching form, each arm supporting a small dish or flower vase. "Grand Epergnes filled with fine pickles" (1761). They may also have been used as candelabra. In the late 19th century the catalog of Harris of Farnham, Surrey, country potters, advertised "Rustic epergnes . . . 9/— [45p or roughly one U.S. dollar] a dozen." (See B.CECP in Booklist.) These would have been rather less elaborate!

ESCUDELLES AB ORELLES

The term literally means "dishes with ears," and is applied to a very attractive 15/16th century Spanish luster bowl with ear-shaped horizontal lug handles.

This strongly formed escudelle may have been a bleeding bowl. (Victoria and Albert Museum.)

EVERTED

The term means "turned outwards, or inside out." and is used to describe rims, etc. that turn over to show the inside.

A

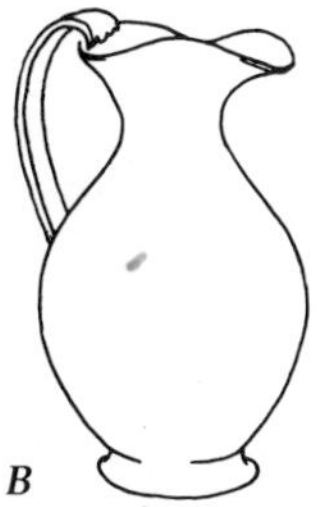

B

C

A. An elegant T'ang ewer with a chicken spout. (Barlow Collection.)
B. By the 19th century the ewer came to resemble a large pitcher with a high handle and an exaggerated lip, and it was used mainly for washing water.
C. Horse models similar to the example shown are found all over Europe and the Near East. Sometimes they were made into whistles, *but this example is described as a Turkish ewer.*

EWER

Probably from *aqua,* "water," and the French *eau;* hence, *eaurer,* or ewer. It is now a little-used term for water vessel. The ewer had two main forms—one with a wide mouth and often a lid and a spout, and one similar to a bottle/jug, but with a pronounced pouring lip which was sometimes added as a separate form or cut away from the neck. The latter is described in *Webster's New Collegiate Dictionary* as a "vase-shaped pitcher or jug." There are, however, many variations, the term referring to a use rather than a form.

Delicate, long-spouted, **coffeepot**-type vessels from the Far East are called "ewers." At the other extreme, pots in the form of animals (see **aquamanile,** with its closely related use), common in Europe and the Near East, are often referred to as "ewers." Ewers were common in T'ang China, especially in the southern region, and in 13th century Persia and later in Turkey. Numbers of very much earlier vessels with pronounced lips or spouts are described as ewers. In England a ewerer was one who carried water for washing hands at meals, and there was even a ewer's room—the ewery. The ewer was small in the 18th century, but later developed into a large pot paired with a basin for washing-water in the bedroom.

EXTRUDED FORM

Many industrial ceramics are shaped by forcing clay through a pierced die, and the technique is occasionally practiced by the craft potter, using a pug mill. Forms are limited; the walls of hollow ware extruded, as a continuous hollow tube must necessarily be parallel. Cylinders, and oval, square, and oblong shapes are possible. It is a mechanical and rather savage way of handling clay, and the resultant pots are unlikely to be very lively. There are technical problems with some clays. Extruded shapes need not, of course, be hollow, and other forms have been used in constructed and modelled pottery and on three-dimensional tile work.

FACE POT

F

The oldest ceramic pieces known are rough effigies of the human figure, and so it is not surprising that vessels incorporating the human face should appear early in pottery history. There is a famous pot with a beard and handlelike ears from Jericho dated around 1700 B.C., and a four-legged pot with a human face is known from preDynastic Egypt. **Cinerary urns** from ancient Colombia are built with human head lids, and realistic and strongly modelled ones are common throughout early America, especially among the last great tribes of the Incas and the Aztecs. A head from Chancay, Peru, has a clown-type hat with a creature squatting on the side, probably an elaborate piece of symbolism. The true face pot, however, occurs most commonly in Roman times throughout the Empire, and with a multitude of fine examples from Roman-Britain. They are often found in cemeteries and so may have had religious significance. On the other hand, these may have been the only places where they stayed whole. Fairly primitive, but very lively, faces are found on many Medieval pitchers from England and elsewhere, sometimes effectively modelled onto the top terminal of the handle. Among the best known of the 15/16th century face pots are the **bellarmines,** although here the face is applied as a sprig and is not integral with the form of the pot. Face beakers were made in Oxford, England, in the 15th century and as rum **measures** in the 19th century. Face pots are not common in the Far East, although there are vigorous examples from the early Jomon period of Japan.

A few more recent potters have adapted the style. The Martin brothers continued the realistic tradition of the **Toby jug** with grotesque, leering masks. Margaret Wildenhain has transformed a bottle into the swathed face of a woman (see CMmar77 in Booklist), although she has not been entirely successful in integrating the neck of the vessel into the modelling. Face pots are not widely found in craft ceramics.

B

C

A. A simplified and integrated face on a 2nd century Romano-British pot, rough slashes indicating the hair and ears.
B. Medieval pitchers were often decorated with faces, on the front or side, or several small heads around the rim.
C. A very different approach to the face pot. A cylindrical slab pot with one edge of the wrapping cut as a bearded face and the eye pierced right through, by Sheila Fournier. (Photograph: John Anderson.)

A

FACETED FORM

See **cut-sided bowls/pots, beaten shape, flattened form.**

FEEDING CUP/Feeder

There is some argument as to whether the small vessels with a short spout or nozzle found in earlier cultures are baby feeders or oil droppers. It is probable that, up to the 18th century, there was little or no artificial feeding of infants. A large, double-curve Roman pot with a **mammiform** boss and teat is illustrated in J.ASP (see Booklist). **Posset pots, caudle cups,** and a number of other interesting and sometimes very handsome forms were developed from the 17th century and used in the feeding of children and invalids.

FILTER

Tall, pointed-based Minoan and Greek pots with a small hole in the bottom were once thought to have been used as **sprinklers,** but are now considered to have been used for filtering wine, the lower part being filled with charcoal. Somewhat similar pots, also known as "Valentine's Flasks," are sometimes called "filters" in books on Medieval pottery. The typical 19th century water filter is a tall, cylindrical, salt-glazed jar with a lid, a tap set low in the wall, and two lug handles about one-third down. With their good proportions and simplicity of form they have a sturdy attractiveness. Doulton has made many with such names as "The Doulton PURO Water Filter."

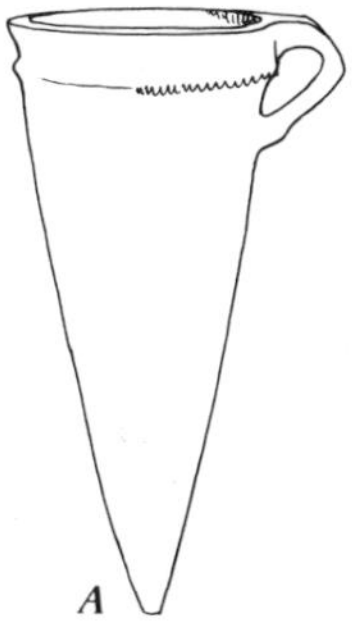

A

A. Inverted cone-shaped pots such as this were common in the 2nd and 1st millennia B.C. *in the Mediterranean countries, and are thought to be wine filters. They are satisfying and elegant shapes for such a mundane operation.*
B. Fulfilling a similar function, but usually for purifying water, great numbers of these attractive and decorative filters were produced in the 19th century. This is a particularly well-proportioned example.

FINGER BOWL

Originally a large bowl, later a small individual bowl for rinsing the fingers at table.

B

FINGER VASE

A vase with five flower holders arranged like the fingers and thumb of a hand. They were made at Delft, in European faience, and in England. The Leeds type was advertised as a "Quintal Flower-horn"! (Photograph: page 90.)

FINIAL

See **roof tile.**

A typical finger vase (see page 89) in Pearl ware, circa 1810. (Bristol Museum, England.)

FIRE POT/BOWL, Chad pot

From B.CECP (see Booklist) we learn that a fire pot (or **chad pot**) was "shaped rather like a chamber pot with small holes pierced through its walls near the rim." It was filled with hot ashes and placed beneath the skirts of lacemakers and others to give them "central heating"!

Another type of fire pot, or bowl, is found in some primitive societies where the preliminary igniting of a fire was difficult. Deep bowls containing burning embers were taken on journeys, even by boat, as can be seen in the films *Women of Aibon* and *Legend in Clay* concerning the peoples of Borneo.

FIRING AND FORM

Wildenhain in W.PFE (see Booklist) says: "That firing techniques have to be taken into account as an essential part of the form-idea is self-evident. The transformation of the material itself, its shrinkage to a smaller size, the change . . . of the whole character of the clay is so important that it cannot be stressed enough." Stoneware firing certainly does, in some degree, squeeze the richness from a shape; curves are less sensuous, proportions less striking than they appeared to be in the wet-clay state. On the other hand, certain beguiling surface qualities induced by firing, especially a rich salt-glaze, can temporarily mask an indifferent form, although this weakness will eventually make itself felt.

FISHBOWL

There are very large bowl or tub forms from 17th century China that are described as **baths** or fishbowls. They are sometimes 4 feet or more in width and there are miraculous stories concerning their making and firing. Many shapes are possible for fishbowls, and imagination can come into play so long as one provides for the creatures a comparatively dark place to hide. See also **water garden.**

FISH BRICK

Like the **chicken brick,** these are unglazed earthenware lidded dishes, or **casseroles,** made by throwing an upright closed-in form with a knob at the top, then laying the pot on its side, flattening the wall to a new base, and cutting horizontally about two-thirds of the way up to form a lid onto which two lug handles are fixed for lifting. The fish is cooked in the closed "brick." It is difficult to clean these vessels, as only salt can be used, but they are still quite widely available in England today.

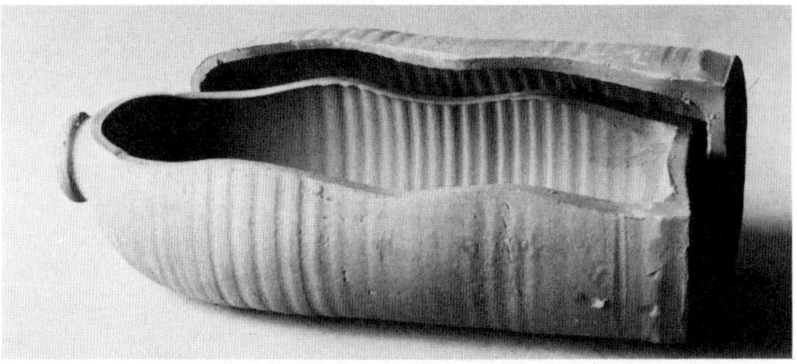

A modern fish brick, simple and directly formed from a closed-in pot. The direction of cut helps the lid to stay in place. It would be bound with string in use.

FISH DISH

Rather handsome 16th century English fish dishes, generally with two flat handles, as shown in the illustration, and lips at each end, feature in a number of museums. A somewhat similar leaf-shaped dish with two lips and a handle, 15 inches/375mm long, is mentioned in B.CECP (see Booklist). They were made from the 17th to the 19th century.

Apart from **fish bricks,** few utensils seem to have been made specifically for fish, although the piscine form lends itself readily to ceramic adaptation. A Roman dish for fish was called a **patella.** Very realistic, often covered dishes in fish and crustaceous forms were made in soft paste in Chelsea and elsewhere. In ancient America we find crayfish modelled vessels of great power.

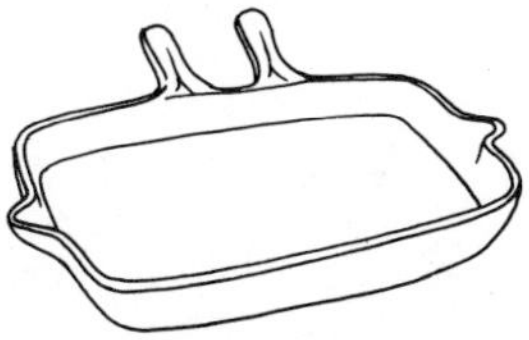
A

A. A large, handsome, two-handled 17th century fish dish, which might have been designed at any period, including our own.
B. Here the fish shape is used in a decorative way to give interest to the rim of a thrown dish. By the author.

B

FISH FORM

In spite of its somewhat potlike form, the fish has not been very extensively used as a basis for pottery form, not even for knobs or spouts for which they might be appropriate. A few small bottles are known from ancient Egypt; there are some slightly tortuous fish vases from the later Chinese dynasties

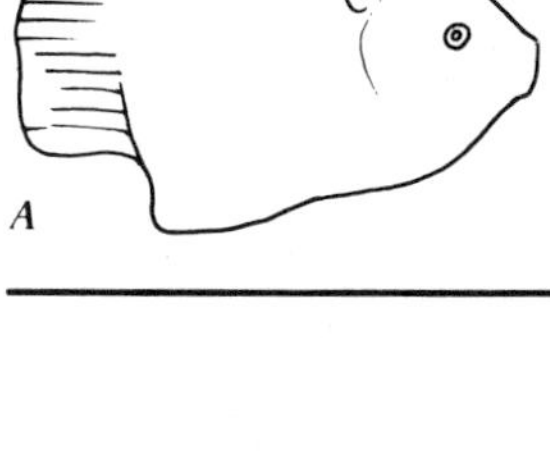
A

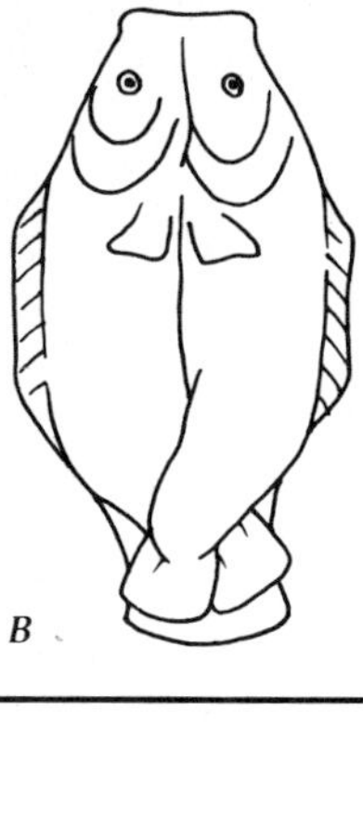
B

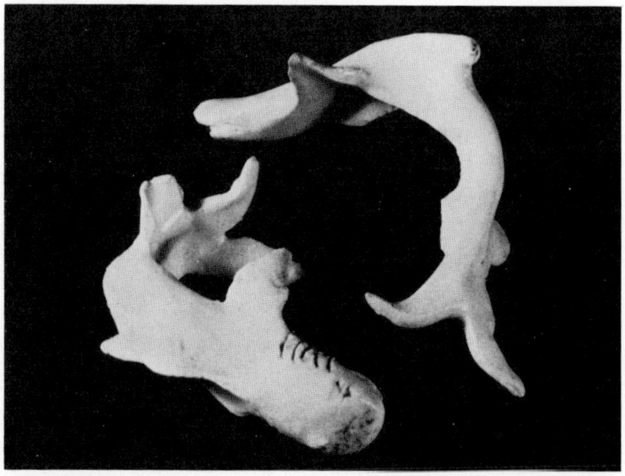
C

D

A. A nicely modelled bottle probably for unguent or ointment from New Kingdom Egypt. Turquoise "paste."
B. A double-fish vase, denoting happiness, from Kuang-tung, 18th century China.
C. Two tiny porcelain sharks to be used as earrings, by Molly Watkins.
D. Fish whistles were fairly common in Europe. This a roughly modelled, but quite effective, peasant potter production.
E. An amusing hand-built fish casserole by Rosemary Wren. (Photograph: Pottery Quarterly.*)*

E

A

and from Europe, but there is no parallel to the wide use of birds and animals that has continued from the earliest times.

FLAGON

From Late Latin *flascon*, "a bottle," and similar words in several languages, from which **flask** is also derived. It is normally a large, handled, sometimes spouted and lidded pot for serving liquors at the table. Many have long necks and a handle straight down from rim to body; others are nearer to jug/pitcher or bottle/jug forms. The flagon has been partly replaced today by the **carafe** or decanter. The name is also applied to a flattened globular shape with a shorter neck—nearer the original "flask," in fact. *Webster's New Collegiate Dictionary* calls it a "bulging, short-necked bottle."

A/B/C. Three varied shapes of Romano-British flagons, distinguished by their generous, yet crisp, lines and well-finished rims.

B C

Many Roman Empire vessels are described as flagons, including a splendid Nubian pot illustrated in C.WC (see Booklist). Savage (S.DA) confuses the issue by equating the flagon with the elongated **tankard** or **schnelle.** This usage has given rise to the expression "to take a flagon of ale." The flagon for serving wine or other drink is not widely made by craft potters today, but a study of historical forms can be very rewarding.

FLAN DISH

This is a simple flat-bottomed and straight, often vertical-sided dish, which is a very useful addition to the modern kitchen. On commercial flan dishes the sides are often wavy or fluted. Unless there is some such emphasis of the rim, the dish can be formally rather uninteresting.

FLANGE

A flange is a projecting collar or rim. The word is used in ceramics to describe an external ledge or collar around a pot, the horizontal section of the rim, or, occasionally, the outer horizontal section of the lid itself. See **lid seating.**

Decorative flanges are found on Chinese and other pottery, breaking and giving interest to a

A. Small flanges on the rim of this large early Broze-Age Cypriot bowl probably served the practical purpose of separating the cords which passed through the lugs.

A

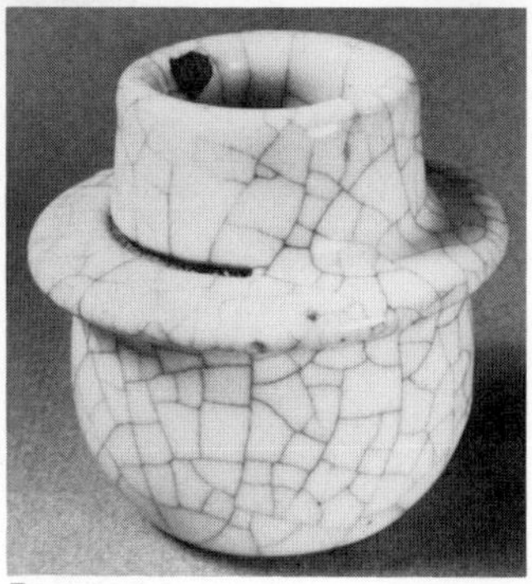

B. Here the flange dominates a simple shape from Sung China.

B

C

C. Also from Sung China is this unusual partial flange/handle on a very smoothly formed bowl. (Barlow Collection.)
D/E/F. Three variations on a basic form in which a flange separates the bowl from the stem of a gobletlike vessel. The first, a curiously leaning stemmed cup from 14th century Sultanband; the second, a more dramatic version of the form by Hans Coper; the third, a fairly restrained goblet by Mick Casson.

D

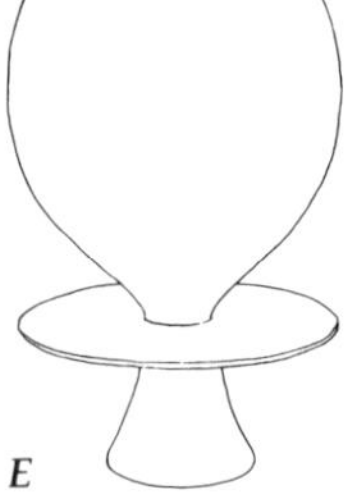

E

F

smooth form; they are sometimes worked up and down to give a scalloped-edge effect, a technique also used on Tudor pots (see CR50 in Booklist) and on the **planters** and pots of folk potters nearer our own day. Roman pottery was often flanged. A fine example is illustrated in J.ASP (see Booklist). See also **carination.** Hans Coper and others today have used flanged forms.

FLASK

The word comes from Middle French *flasque* and many other similar words meaning "a bottle." In general, this was a traveller's bottle for wine, spirits, or (more occasionally!) water. It may be small enough to go into a pocket, somewhat larger and

A

A. The well-articulated silhouette of a Cretan flask of about 1450 B.C.

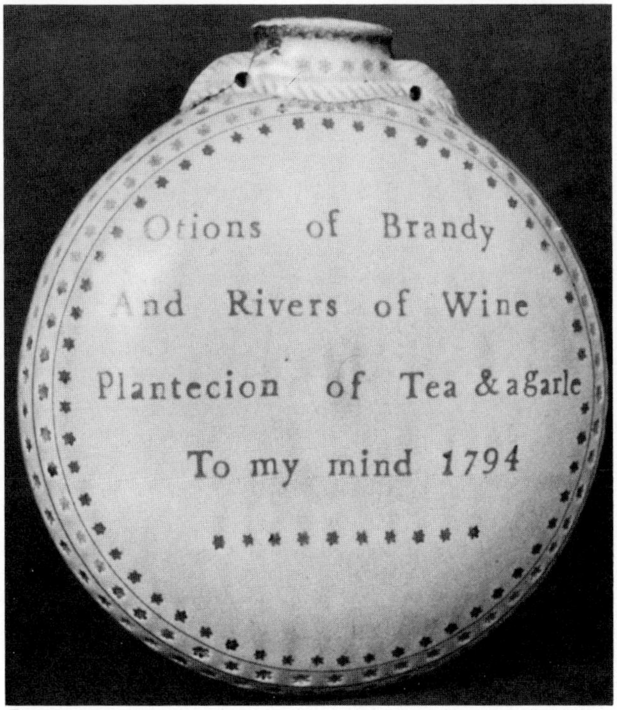

B

D

suspended from the waist (as **costrel, pilgrim bottle, flagon**), or up to 12 inches/300mm across for hanging from a horse's trappings or beneath a cart or carriage.

The form is normally more or less circular in one plane and flattened on the other, with suspension lugs near a short, narrow neck. The shape goes back to at least the 2nd millenium B.C. from Crete and elsewhere. The Greek **alabastros** and **aryballos** were types of flasks, and the vessel has taken on many shapes over the centuries. Sometimes it has a **button base** like a small **amphora;** in Italy it is the wickered wine and oil bottle; and it appears in various distinct types from areas of Crete up to the present day.

Flasks were common in Medieval England and

C

B. An 18th century flask with type-impressed inlay.
C. The very simple outline of an English harvest flask. A throng would have been threaded through the holes on each side of the neck.

D. This 20th century Cretan flask, 9 inches/230mm in diameter, has the flat back and rounded face typical of this vessel. It has obviously been well used.

there are many charming 17th century and 18th century flasks in salt-glaze and other materials. The Ming Chinese made elegant flasks in enamelled porcelain, while, at the other extreme, the term is used in a loose way for any small vessel designed to hold spirits, sometimes in the form of a **barrel,** or in the traditional bottle/jug form, as in the folk pottery of 19th century America. In 19th century England, fanciful shapes included a railway clock (Brighton Museum) and imitation potatoes. Today, glass has taken over from pottery, and with spirits available every few hundred yards, the traveller has less need to fortify himself from a flask. This is a pity, as it was a most attractive form.

FLATTENED FORM

Since the earliest times, potters have felt the need to vary the circular plan of thrown or built ware, although the greater number were left as full, round

A

forms befitting containers. Flattening the walls of a pot results in a different contour from every point of view, and this can offer considerable aesthetic satisfaction. There are practical reasons for flattening such shapes as **flasks,** but one wonders why the Egyptian potters who produced the splendid "black top" pottery of the 3rd millenium B.C. decided on the flattened version to be seen at the Downing College Museum at Cambridge.

The modern potter avails himself of this shape, the author and others basing shapes on "skimmer" **pebbles.** The majority of Hans Coper's pots are of the flattened type, some almost mere **envelopes** of clay, as is much of Val Barry's elegant porcelain. The list is endless. See also **beaten form, slab building.**

FLATWARE

In traditional English, and especially Stoke-on-Trent usage, flatware means plates, saucers, shallow dishes, etc., as opposed to **holloware.** In the United States, however, the term is used for cutlery, although, according to *Webster's Dictionary,* it also includes "tableware more or less flat and usually formed or cast in a single piece," which could also include plates, etc., as above.

FLOWER BRICK

An oblong box, about the size and proportions of a standard brick or a little larger, with holes of various sizes in the top designed to take the stems

B

of flowers. They were turned out in considerable numbers at Delft and in the various tin-glaze potteries in England through the 18th century, possibly in imitation of Chinese imports. Some very similar pieces with larger apertures, as well as small circular holes, are considered to have been **inkwells.**

A powerful modern realization of the same idea is that by Otto Natzler illustrated in CMmay78 (see Booklist), while in England, Peter Smith makes an almost Japanese rough-cut version (see illustration B). See also **flower holder.**

FLOWER FORM

See **plant form.**

A. One of the many brick-shaped containers made in Bristol in the 18th century. This one may have been an inkwell. (Bristol Museum.)
B. A directly made and beaten modern version by Peter Smith. It is difficult to imagine two almost identical forms farther apart in style.

FLOWER HOLDER

The flower holder may be differentiated from the **vase,** or flowerpot, in that it incorporates some means of holding individual stems upright; e.g., the holes in a flower brick. A simple clay dome can be pierced vertically with holes and used to support

An ingenious series of supports to hold stems in an 11th century Sung bowl. Flower arranging is obviously a very ancient art. (Barlow Collection.)

An attractive variation on the basic flowerpot shape. This pot holder was thrown by Stella Goorney.

flower stems in a bowl or open form. One can see such an arrangement in the illustration. A group of small pottery cylinders will serve the same purpose and will look more decorative. Many potters have rung the changes on the flower holder theme, using forms like stones, etc. The illustration shows an historical version, and there are many fanciful designs, such as the French 18th century cow with holes in its back (slightly macabre) and the many types of **finger vase** so popular in the 19th century. An asymmetric holder by Eileen Lewenstein is shown in CR9 (see Booklist).

FLOWERPOT

Since the early 17th century, potters have made straight-sided red earthenware unglazed horticultural or household pots for growing plants in soil. The walls typically taper towards the base and there is a hole in the base center. The rim is thickened into a collar of ½ to ¾ inch deep. A skilled flowerpot thrower, with an assistant to weigh the balls of clay and remove finished pots, could complete 1,500 in a day. In the film *Isaac Button* we see such a thrower at work.

More elaborate containers for houseplants are also fairly common: the Chinese pots in opalescent Chun glazes, ribbed and with an everted rim, for instance. Flowerpots in the traditional Western form, but decorated in various ways, were a significant part of a potter's output from the mid-16th century onwards. Some were paired with saucers. The early ones were rather expensive for the times: 2¼d (2 cents) each in 1754. Brears, in B.CECP (see Booklist), quotes a Wattisfield (Suffolk, England) 19th century catalog: "Lovers of anything pretty and artistic for ferns [the great craze at the time] should write for specimens." These were 1/3d (12 cents) a dozen. Even more ambitious flowerpots were set on pedestals with snakelike coils set vertically in tiers, while some squatter shapes had handles over them, like **buckets.** Surprisingly, the manufacture of plain flowerpots in great quantities for horticulture did not start until after World War I.

The humbler potters waved, fluted, or set points on the rims of their flowerpots; they added **bail** handles or set the pots on stands. Mr. Curtis, of Yorkshire, England, for instance, pinches a coil onto the wall of a pot in imitation of European styles. He discourses on flowerpots in his own fashion: "The idea was, how plastic pots got going, was that you could put . . . a small plant into a pot and it was nice and handy for slipping into a lady's shopping bag with a bit of tissue round it. You see it was more or less waterproof, and a clay pot isn't . . . but that's the pot you want, that ISN'T waterproof, for gardening."

Elizabeth David (see D.EBYC in Booklist) suggests a very different use for the plain flowerpot. It can be utilized either the right way up or inverted for baking bread. She gives details of flowerpot loaves on page 310. This opens possibilities for unglazed earthenware baking pots. A modern flowerpot holder, glazed inside, but of similar basic shape, is shown in the illustration.

FLUTE

Simple flutes or pipes with more than one note are among the oldest of musical instruments and were very early made in pottery. See more details under **whistle** and **ocarina.**

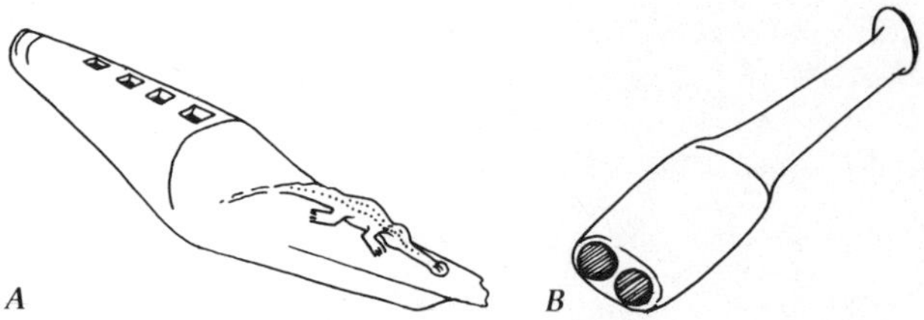

A. An ancient American (Colombian) flute with an alligator on the stem.
B. A "double flute," from 2nd to 5th century Nazca.

A. An ancient American (Colombian) flute with an alligator on the stem.
B. A "double flute," from 2nd to 5th century Nazca.

FLUTE DE PAN

A type of **lug** found on certain Neolithic pots and consisting of a number of small tubes set side by side, presumably to take multiple cords. The lug resembles the panpipes; hence, its name.

FLUTING

A channel or furrow resembling half of a flute or a pipe split lengthwise, as in Classic pillars. Although originally a curved channel, any long, adjacent series of cuts made in the surface of a bowl or pot; e.g., the well-known Chinese fluted porcelain, or David Leach's teapots and bowls, is known as "fluting." Fundamentally, it is a decorative, rather than a formal, technique.

Spaced-out fluting on this Sung Chinese bowl forms lobes, *and has more influence on the form than the shallower, close cuts of most modern fluting. (Barlow Collection.)*

FOLDED FORM

An attractive Romano-British form from the New Forest and other kiln sites, in which the walls of a full-formed thrown pot are pressed inwards, usually on four faces, is known as a "folded pot."

The technique can be used for practical flasks or flagons, depressing two faces to give an easy grip on the body of the vessel and obviating the necessity for a handle. Today clay is folded in very different styles: from the wild deformations of some U.S. work, to the more gentle curves of the work of Mary Rogers and others. See also **envelope form, slab building, indented form.**

A. Perhaps the best known of ancient folded forms. From the New Forest, 2nd to 4th century. This is an excellent example of this almost unique technique, rarely used by modern potters, even with their propensity for altering thrown forms.

A

B. A much more elaborately and irregularly folded clay bowl by Mary Rogers.
C. At the other extreme is this simple, lifted rim on a sawdust- fired dish by Sheila Fournier.
D. A nicely folded pot or deep bowl by Stuart Taylor, 1973.

B

C

D

FOOD WARMER

Quite handsome designs from the 17th and 18th centuries were used to keep drinks warm at night (see **possett, caudle,** etc.) and also to keep tea hot. They have an opening in the lower wall for the heating equipment—candle or spirit lamp—and decorative ventilation holes above. Earlier examples are found from the Korean Silla period, for example, or a pedestal jug with holes in the base from the Japanese Yayoi period. See also **brazier, chafing dish.**

Food warmers are still useful for coffee or even casseroles. In CMdec78 (see Booklist) a ''samovar'' by Ron Troughear is illustrated. It has a cylindrical base with a pierced ogee-shaped door and a standard type teapot on top.

A

B

A. A charming and stylish food or drink warmer in Creamware, possibly Wedgwood, circa 1800. Some similar designs have been made by modern potters. (Bristol Museum.)
B. A candle heater designed to take a casserole. By the author.

FOOT

"It is interesting to see an Oriental pick up a pot for examination and . . . turn it over to look at the form and cutting of the foot. He inspects it as carefully as a banker with a doubtful check—in fact he is looking for the bona-fides of the author. There in the most naked but hidden part of the work he expects to come into closest touch with the character and perception of the maker." (See L.PB in Booklist.)

A distinction can be made between **base** and foot. By the former, we usually mean the flat surface beneath a pot. The foot, however, is a distinct termination of the form; it is that part of the pot on which the main shape stands. Often it involves a **foot ring,** the clay being cut away from the inside of the base, as well as forming a change of profile on the outside.

Pots with well-defined feet are less common in primitive and early pottery, but the more developed cultures have splayed-out or even horizontal feet on some pots, a style nearer to metal forms and one taken up in some degree by modern industrial pottery. The Greek foot especially is very pronounced and rigid. In Chinese wares the foot is generally more subtle, and there is sometimes the merest suggestion of an outward turn, which,

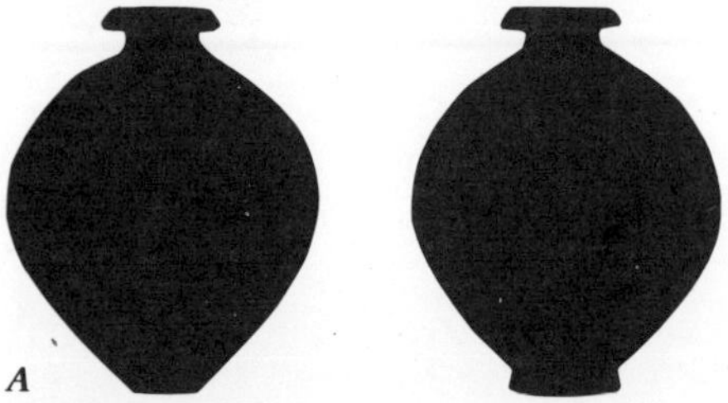

A

B

A. Two identical forms, the second with a short outward-turning foot, which greatly alters its character.
B. A curve, rather than a sharp angle, at the foot gives a smooth grace to this bowl by Lucie Rie.

C. In contrast, a much more aggressive foot or stem on a strictly decorative porcelain form (it would be something of a puzzle jug *if used as a goblet), by Victor Margrie.*

C

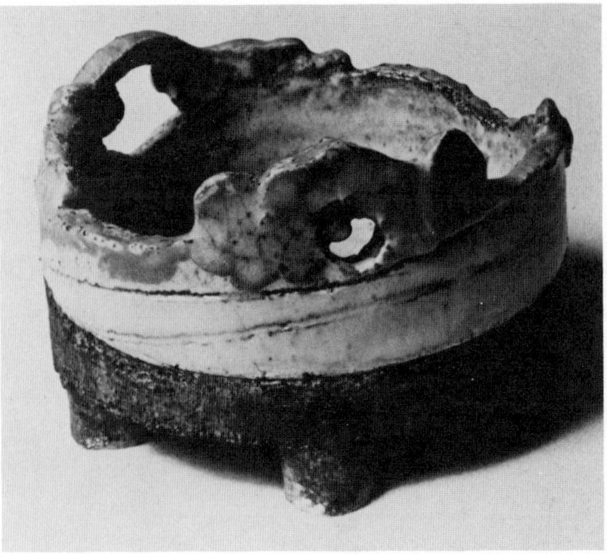

D

D. Here the foot is a projection from the base of a raku-fired bowl. Raku, by Emmanuel Cooper. (Photograph: Eileen Lewenstein, Emmanuel Cooper).

nevertheless, satisfactorily completes the shape. Medieval pots were nearly always finished with an outward turn of the profile, often elaborately thumbed down.

A pot with a low belly frequently needs a definite foot, or even a foot ring; a high-shouldered shape, more rarely so. The foot is as important as the rim and should be as carefully considered. Apart from the early round-based pots, which, of course, have no foot, some modern potters also consider the foot unnecessary. Elizabeth Fritsch, for instance, in discussing her work says: "Foot is conspicuous by its absence . . . let the pot rest comfortably in the hands and look air-borne, curving against gravity" (see C10 in Booklist).

E

E. Three very unusual coil feet on a 7th century B.C. Cypriot vessel.

In another sense a pot or bowl can have separate feet or supports, which may be cut from the thrown or built shape, or added as blocks or coils, etc. Some amusing human and animal feet have been applied to pots throughout history, and there is a wide field for invention in this area, which is not often explored by the craft potter.

FOOT RASP

See **bath rasp.**

FOOT RING

Normally, when throwing the base of a bowl, or, less frequently, a pot, a sufficient thickness of clay is left from which to cut a foot on which the main form will stand. This may be a simple straight-side ring, but the most subtle alteration of direction or proportion will influence the overall character of the vessel. An outward-turning foot ring tends to give an impression of stability; an inward slope, of elegance. The ring can flow from the main form or represent a fresh plane.

Cardew (see C.PP in Booklist) recommends throwing a foot ring onto an inverted leather-hard bowl, thereby avoiding "the unpleasant contrast

A B C

D

A/B/C. The slope of the ring affects the character of the whole. Here 3 identical bowls are shown with similarly sized, but differently sloping feet.
D. A foot ring typical of the hand wheel and the resultant rugged approach of certain Japanese potters. Akahada, circa 1850.

between the thrown contour of the bowl itself and the machined character of a turned foot." But this is, perhaps, a somewhat purist attitude and is certainly not often practiced. Leach, in L.PB (see Booklist) and others illustrate a wide variety of foot ring types, especially those found on Oriental pots. A plate will sometimes be given a foot ring, and in CR53 (see Booklist) David Lloyd Jones illustrates a very handsome plate with an outer and a central supporting ring.

FOUNTAIN

There appears to be little evidence of early ceramic fountains, apart from lavishly tiled examples which abound. The true fountain could only exist in an urban civilization with piped water or near the site

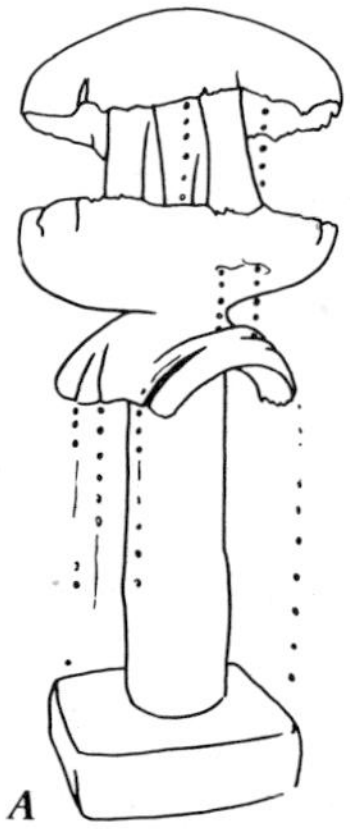

A

B

A/B. Two contrasting solutions to the running-water type of fountain; the right one by Gordon Baldwin, the left one, more fungilike form by Berésford Pealing.

of a spring. Water running from one container to another over glazed surfaces is perennially fascinating, and many modern potters have used ingenuity and imagination in fountain design. Jerome Abbo, Gordon Baldwin, and others have constructed very different forms for this purpose. (See CR7 and CR18 in Booklist.)

FRAME

The most famous pottery frames are probably the Della Robbia blue and white examples, but they have also been made for pictures, **plaques,** and

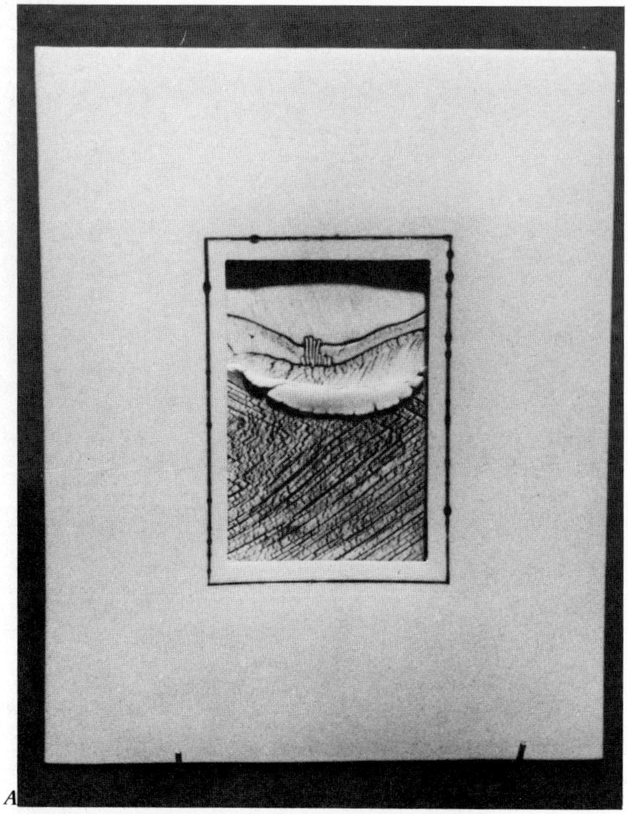

A

B

A. A porcelain frame and image by Gordon Cooke.
B. A frame as part of a piece of furniture, by Margaret Hall.

mirrors over the last 300 years. A typical country potter's attempt, from Denholme, Yorkshire, is in the York County Museum. A number of modern potters in England set mirrors, etc. in "landscapes" and model furniture, while John Maltby sets picture-frame style rims on his very decorative wall plates.

FROG MUG

These were **mugs** or **tankards** with a realistically modelled frog in the bottom, which came into view as the drinker drained his beer. This is an example of 18th century tavern humor, but the joke must have worn thin very quickly, since many thousands of them were made. In some early mugs the frog was hollow and it gurgled as the liquid was drunk. Snakes and newts were also done, but less often. Specimens are found all over England; Sunderland and Leeds potteries produced a great number. According to B.CECP (see Booklist), the frog mug was first made in the factories in 1775–80 and was later copied by country potters. It is still made occasionally by studio potters in England and America.

A 19th century English frog mug.

A sharply modelled and carinated fruit stand by Robin Welch, recalling, in its massive character, the Etruscan patera.

FRUIT DISH/STAND

The typical industrial form is a shallow bowl or plate on a high stem and foot, probably derived from the Greek forms (7th century B.C. onwards), which are confidently described by historians as "fruit stands." There is an early Minoan dish on a tall stem called a "fruit stand" in L.GPBA (see Booklist). See also **p'an.**

Robin Welch has made massive dishes of this type, rigid and carinated, while Paul Philip tends to an irregular, more plastic approach. They are not common among modern craft pottery.

FRUIT FORM

See **plant form.**

FRYING PAN

In America this is called a **skillet.** Shallow dishes with handles, made some 4500 years ago in the Aegean area of the Mediterranean are called "frying pans" by archaeologists, though this was not their use, and the "pan" part was probably a foot for the batlike utensil to stand on.

Modern heat-proof pans are available, but the thermal strains would tax any normal clay beyond its endurance. The industrial types are glazed all over, but appear to have a light, loose body without a ring when struck. They have concentric, slightly

The so-called "frying pan" from a very early Aegean culture. It is given by some authorities as a womb-shaped fertility symbol. It is, in any case, a very attractive shape.

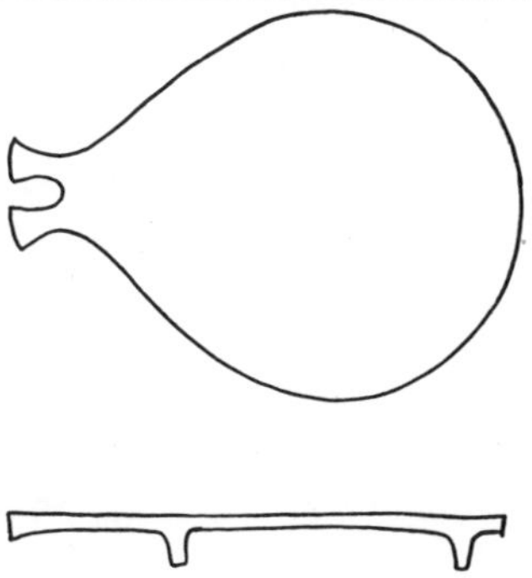

raised rings underneath. The Portuguese flame-resistant pans are low-fired and have a shallowly curving base in common with all early **cooking pots.** (See F.DPP in Booklist.) See also **pipkin.**

FUDDLING CUP

In Germany this is called a *drillingsbecher.* The word comes from *fuddle,* a "tipple" or "drinking bout." Several (up to ten) cups or beakers are joined together in such a way that, when they are all filled, the liquid can, with skill, be drunk from any one of them. They are interconnected by tubes or holes, but the operation must have demanded patience and skill, neither of which would have been in evidence later on in an evening's "fuddle." It is called "Jolly Boys" in Somerset, England.

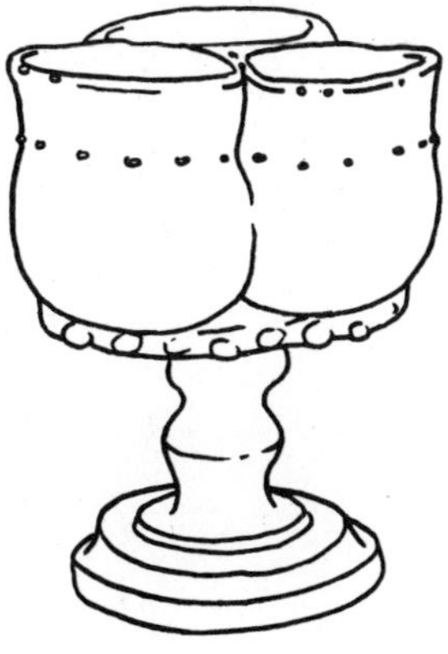

A threesome fuddling cup (Burslem, 17th century) designed like a multiple goblet. Other types had no stem.

FUNCTION AND FORM

The emphasis in this book is on pottery for use, even though that use may be for decoration or pleasure. We cannot separate the function of a useful pot from its shape; they are reflections one of the other. "In utilitarian pieces the form should be exactly appropriate for its use. If the vessel does not function properly it loses a great deal of its *aesthetic* quality [my italics]," says Guilland in G.EAFP (see Booklist). This may sound rather "Bauhaus," but it is more fundamental than that sometimes misapplied style in that it does not say that all things made for use are automatically pleasing, but that an inefficient utilitarian pot can never be pleasing in the fullest sense.

Wildenhain (see W.PFE in Booklist) stresses that form and function are closely related, but also that "something is needed that transcends technique and function and carries over into the realm of form." She then refers to the problem of a lid on a cylindrical coffeepot. If it overhangs the width of the pot, it is not only top-heavy in appearance and in fact, but will easily fall if the pot is tilted very far. If, however, it is set within the pot, on a flange, it will be lighter and smaller and less likely to fall out. Improvement in utility has been paralleled by an improvement in form.

Arthur Lane (see L.SiP in Booklist) also deals with the subject: "Pottery can be perfectly adapted for use and at the same time hideous to look at. Before the Second World War there was much talk of "Functionalism" in the useful arts. Its promoters used this catchword to discredit the fripperies of their predecessors and open the way for new fripperies of their own. But many simple people were deceived; at last, they thought, this incomprehensible nonsense called art can be explained away; usefulness and beauty are the same thing. Years of shabby living have taught us to think again. Usefulness is no more than a condition to be fulfilled. Grace in fulfillment is an extra, properly called art."

But it was not only simple people who were deceived; the sophisticated art theoreticians and teachers fooled themselves, while the "simple" country potter continued to make sound, practical, but instinctively pleasing, things in clay. The present-day ceramic art teacher has still another view. Bob Rogers (see CR32 in Booklist) says: "Ultimately, it is, of course, the work itself that counts and it will be judged much as a work of art is judged. To think the main thing about a really good handmade, functional pot is that one can put milk into it or pour tea from it is like thinking that the main thing about a painting is that it fills a blank on the dining room wall." Apart from the fact that he may be shocked at how often this last phrase is true, we can see that all these views are varying emphases on a central truth, that form and function in pottery are inseparable. For the craftsman, says Rhodes, "function is a balance wheel" and "throughout the years the potter will build up a whole store of efficient and beautiful solutions to functional problems" (Wildenhain in W.PFE).

On this practical level we will let a famous potter have the last word: "If I make a teapot, an article hedged about with functional aspects, I am still left with a vast opportunity to experiment with form and relationship which can serve function without being part of it. Most often my thinking concerns relationship, because I have studied and learned the drill of function so that I don't have to think about it any more; it does not occupy my conscious mind which is on qualitative things—shape, glaze, and decoration." (David Leach in F.DL—see Booklist.)

FUNERARY JAR/URN

Perhaps because they were buried with the dead (or contained their remains) funerary vessels are frequently found undamaged, or nearly so. We, therefore, have more of this than any other sort of pottery from some early cultures, although one dies only once, but one eats daily!

The superb Pan Shan Neolithic Chinese jars, with which we have become familiar, are described as funerary jars, and there are countless other shapes from the last 7000 years. The Egyptian Canopic jars from the 2nd millenium B.C. in Egypt with their human, bird, and dogs' heads representing the various gods modelled on the lids, each contained its particular organ from the body of the mummified corpse—liver, intestines, lungs, etc.—a somewhat macabre operation. Medley (see M.CP in Booklist) illustrates a proto-Yueh urn with many figures and houses modelled on the lid, a type which has become popular with some modern potters. See also **casket, larnax, cinerary urn.**

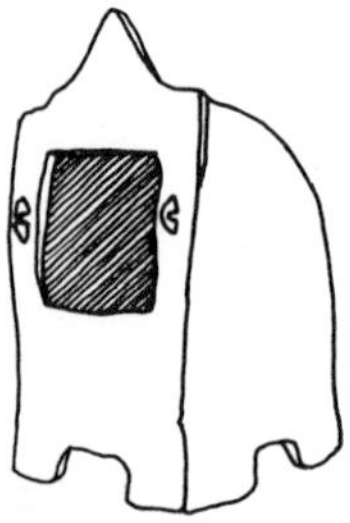

A large (21 inches/525mm high) Palestine urn (4th millenium B.C.) for the bones of the dead.

FUNGI FORM

Apart from occasional **knobs** on 18th century and later jar and pot lids (see illustration under **teapot**), the fungus has not been generally considered an appropriate subject for pottery form. The modern craft potter, however, has used these strange and varied forms in connection with pots and semi-sculptural pieces. The frilled, growing shapes of Ruth Duckworth's earlier porcelain are strongly reminiscent of fungi, although she appeared surprised when this was mentioned to her. More overt

A. The movement of unsupported porcelain during firing has produced this attractive mushroomlike form from a simple everted *cone. By Sheila Fournier.*

B. A glimpse into the magic, frozen world of a Mary Keepax split sphere *with fungilike growths. (Photograph: John Anderson.)*

C. A Ruth Duckworth 1962 porcelain pot with close affinities to the Shaggy Inkcap mushroom, but see text.

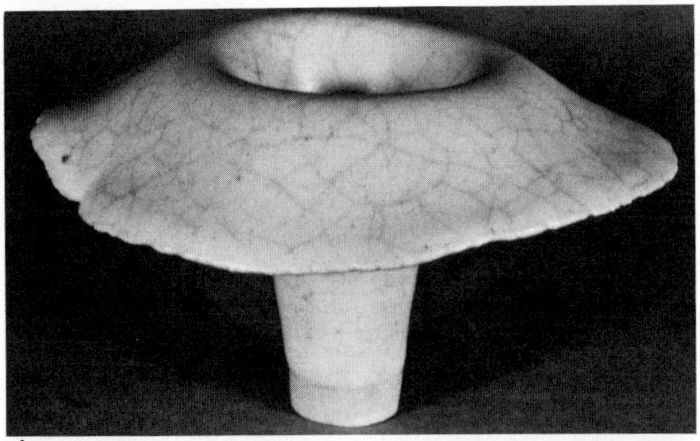

A

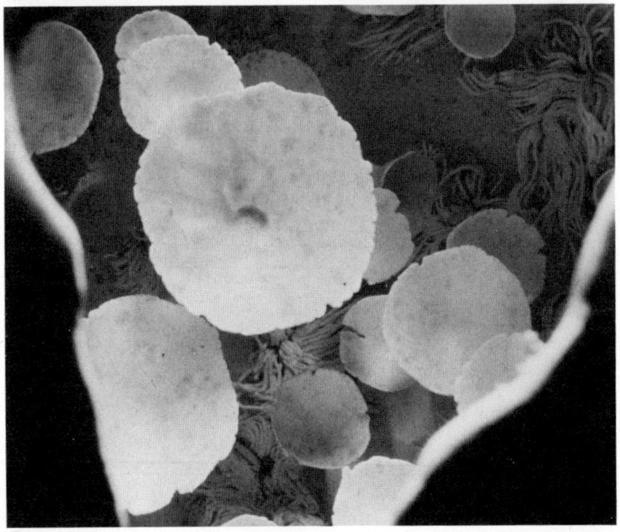

B

C

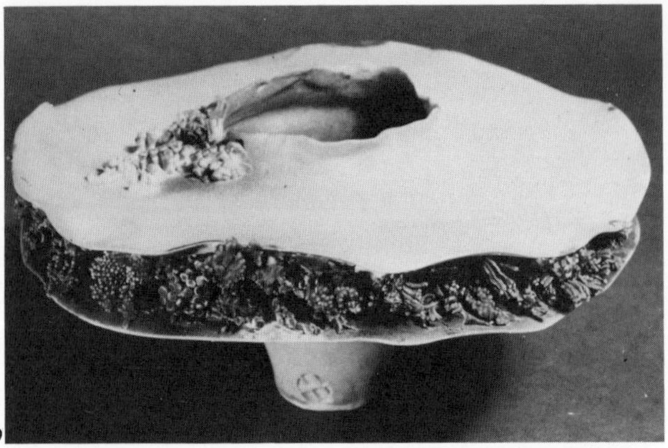
D

D. A spreading growth in porcelain by Peter Simpson.

forms are common—groups of small flaring pots on stems by Graham Newing (see CR14 in Booklist), for instance, or details may be selected as in the mushroom gills of Peter Simpson. Small fungi sprout from sometimes unlikely articles in some profusion, as if the craft had been suddenly attacked by dry rot. The author's **water gardens** share the preoccupation, but in these damp surroundings they at least have a certain logic.

FUNNEL

Stoneware cookery funnels were common in the 19th century. G.EAFP (see Booklist) illustrates a funnel set wide end down in a mixing bowl to form a **cake mold.** The Greek and Mycenaean pointed-based pots discussed under **filter** are a form of funnel.

FUNNEL BEAKER

A beaker shape with a flaring neck from early Neolithic cultures of Northern Europe.

One of the categories of beaker shape made by the Beaker Folk in Northern Europe, circa 3000 B.C.

FURNITURE

Clay models of furniture are rare from early times. We know from inventories that there was little furniture anyhow. Archaic Greek "goddesses" sitting precariously on rudimentary chairs or thrones and a few objects from tombs are among the infrequent suggestions of furnishings. The Eygyptian "soul houses" (see **building**) contain a few tables and there are Cypriot and Roman models of chairs. The Han tombs include little furniture in the profusion of models.

Model furniture became much more common in the 17th century. In Northern England, especially, rocking chairs and cradles, chests with sliding drawers, etc. were made at Halifax, Newcastle, etc. In the Brighton Museum there are models from Staffordshire (1800) of children in chairs. In F.EC (see Booklist) is illustrated a remarkable dovecote with a bird in all thirty or so openings, set on a chest of drawers on paw feet, as if it were all a piece of furniture. This, from circa 1780, is as strange and willful as any modern piece, and very decorative, as well.

Today we have a spate of chests, Welsh dressers, tables, even the kitchen sink (Paul Gandy), some making a rather obscure comment, drawers spilling strange objects (Neo-Dali?), and often with distorted proportions. Many are simple little totems,

A/B. The type of crude table which was probably all a family possessed in early times (6th century B.C. Cyprus) and a slightly more sophisticated and decorated chair from Sumeria. The herringbone pattern on the seat may suggest a woven covering.
C. A mother goddess figure in a primitive chair. Circa 1400 B.C. from Cyprus or Mycenae.

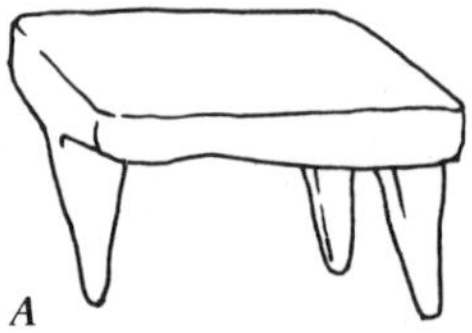
A

B

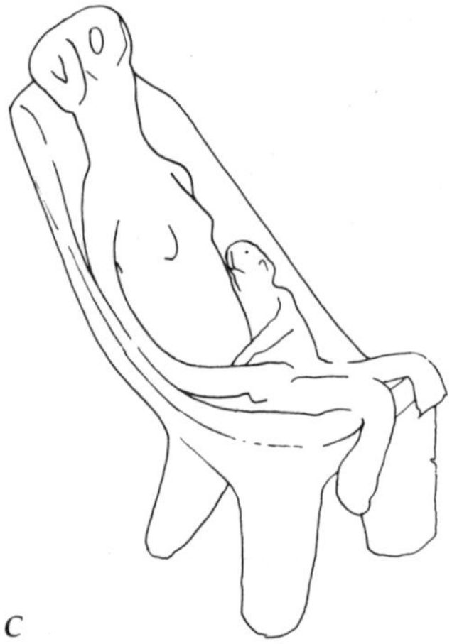
C

D

E

D. A solidly built kitchen table with pots, food, and a sliding drawer. By Margaret Hall. (See page 109.)
E. Not exactly a piece of furniture, but with uncannily realistic tools. By Margaret Hall.
F. A miniature by Ian Gregory. Like many of these pieces (see buildings) the salt-glaze finish retains the necessary crispness of outline.

F

replacing in an amusing way the knickknacks of yesterday. Salt-glaze (John Maltby, Ian Gregory, etc.) is a favorite finish. It retains the precision of detail important to these models. For a piece of full-size furniture see **garden seat.** See also **cradle, stove.**

FURNITURE INSET

Wedgwood made pieces of inlay for furniture in great quantities, mostly in Jasper ware. This form of decoration has almost disappeared, but is another area for possible cooperation among craftsmen today.

FUTAOKI

A ladle rest used in the Japanese Tea Ceremony.

G

GALLERY

The lid seating or flange, or the angle between it and the vertical rim, is sometimes called the "gallery."

GALLIPOT, Gallypot, Gallyware

There is some doubt as to the origin of this term and to precisely what sort of pot it describes. It has been suggested that the word is derived from the galley ships which brought tin-glazed ware from Italy and Spain. The earliest record seems to be from 1465. *Webster's New Collegiate Dictionary* gives as one meaning, "an archaic word for druggist" and, in fact, the importations were generally pharmaceutical: drug jars and storage pots for various medicines and ointments. The *Concise Oxford Dictionary* gives specifically as the meaning, "a small earthen glazed ointment pot." In D.EBYC (see Booklist) Cobbett, who obviously equates gallipots with medicines, is quoted: "If a young woman bake a bushel a week, she will do very well without phials and gallipots."

The term is often used as a general term for "painted earthenware" (tin-glazed ware), especially the earthenware introduced into England from Delft. "Gallipot makers" are referred to in mid-17th century England, and Dwight (of Fulham Pottery) at the end of the century still referred to "Galley ware or Whiteware." A large number of Bristol potters are listed as "Gally pot makers" or "white potters" (see P.OBP in Booklist). In his book describing his life as a potter in the early days of the 20th century Fishley Holland mentions quite another use: "The Gallipots, like a wide breakfast cup, had handles and were used by coach builders for paint."

Historians of Chinese pottery have their own use of the term, referring to a tall form with a wide shoulder, a short neck, and a small mouth (K'ang Hsi period). It is used and illustrated in this sense in B.DA (see Booklist). The shape is more generally known as **mei-p'ing.**

GAMES

See **chess, checkers, dominos, jigsaw puzzle, carpet bowls, solitaire.**

GARDEN SEAT

Pottery seats, usually more or less barrel shaped, were made in China from Sung times. Those from the Ming and Ch'ing dynasties are highly decorated. The top is often made slightly concave for comfort. They are also found in Africa and elsewhere. Construction must necessarily be sturdy, but the walls are often perforated to lighten the effect. In CR40 (see Booklist) a "stool" by Cardew

A. A seat or stool made in Africa by Michael Cardew. A great deal of the wall has been cut away. (Photograph: Eileen Lewenstein, Emmanuel Cooper.)

A

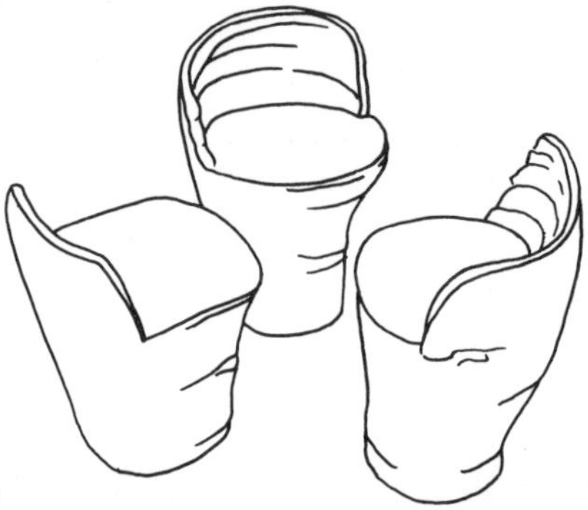

B

C

B. Three pot seats complete with backs. These were built in thick coils, the evidence of which is part of the design. By Karen Karnes.
C. A bowllike seat with a shaped top by Arthur Griffiths.

is illustrated. It was made at Wenford Bridge, but shows African influence. Karen Karnes (see CR50 in Booklist) coiled garden seats, complete with backrests, in flowing, potlike forms.

GARLIC VASE

A name given to a type of Chinese bottle with a rounded body and a long neck which swells and contracts near the top. It is so called because of its likeness to a garlic bulb, a similarity sometimes enhanced by vertical ribbing.

GINGER BEER BOTTLE

These are mundane, but sturdy, vessels, necessarily

A Chinese Sung garlic vase. This particular example has no ribbing. (Barlow Collection.)

A traditional Yorkshire stoneware ginger beer bottle. The cork would have been tied down, utilizing the undercut rim.

strong to take the gas pressure, and with a pronounced, generally rounded collar at the neck. Occasionally, a more sensitive potter would produce a more elegant neck and rim as seen in H.LCB (see Booklist). Most of the bottles are cylindrical. Fishley Holland (see H.FYP in Booklist) tells us: "It was at this pottery [Price Powell's, Bristol, destroyed by bombing in 1941] that I saw a man throwing ginger beer bottles at the rate of six hundred a day. Since they were inserted in a mechanical filler, great accuracy was necessary and the tops had to be uniform for sealing."

GINGER JAR

A distinctive Chinese form with a wide mouth and a globular body. It is fitted with a cover, often over a short vertical neck. The shape is well known as a container for imported ginger in syrup. In China it would be filled with various sweetmeats and given as a present on New Year's Day.

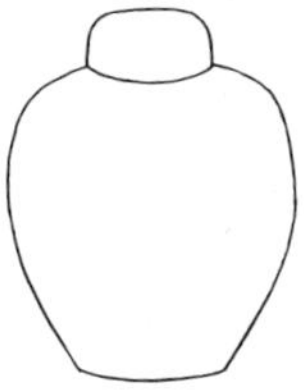

The typical blue and white K'ang Hsi profile (of the ginger jar), the lid fitting over a short neck.

GIN MEASURE

See **measure.**

GOAT AND BEE JUG

A molded **jug/pitcher** made at Chelsea circa 1745. The design is self-explanatory from its title, and it is remarkable more for its rarity than for its beauty.

GOBLET

Although its etymology is given as a diminutive of *gobel*, "a cup," a goblet is defined as "a large drinking vessel, properly without handles" (see CTCD in Booklist) and as a "large bowl-shaped drinking cup" (see EB in Booklist). *Webster's New Collegiate Dictionary* mentions a "foot and stem," and the word is usually associated today with a deep bowl set on a stem with a splayed foot. In *The Concise Oxford Dictionary* it says that the word is archaic, but this is only true of its meaning as a deep cup.

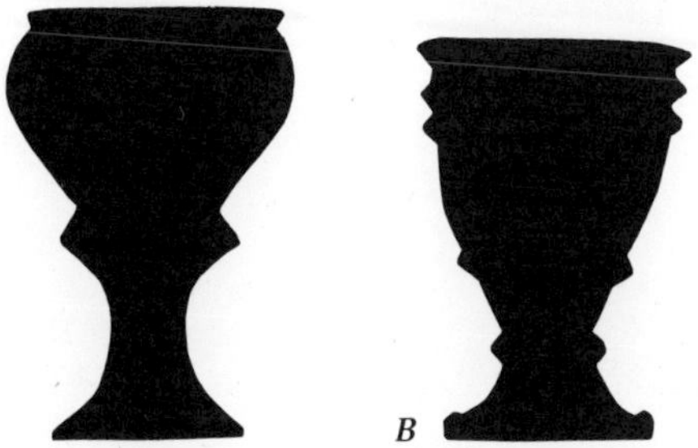

A B

A/B. Two heavily carinated *goblet forms separated by 3000 years, the first, from Jordon, 1500* B.C.*; the second, from Rennaissance Italy.*

Splendid examples are found as early as 1500 B.C. from Jordon, Crete, Mycenae, and other cultures, while many subtle variations come from the Near East and from Ming and Ch'ing China. In the Brighton Museum is shown an enormous "goblet" some 10 inches/250mm tall, in salt-glaze, from the Fulham Pottery, 1840.

There are problems in translating the stemmed form into ceramic (it is more often of glass), and goblets are perhaps more common in earthenware, which, although less strong, is also less subject to sagging in the kiln. In England, Alan Caiger Smith

C

C. Wine goblets in porcelain by David Leach. The stems are fairly sturdy to avoid falling out of true in the kiln. It is near in form to the stem cup.

is the best known designer of fine goblets. **Stem cups** are a compromise form better suited to stoneware and porcelain. In CR52 (see Booklist) there is an article by Fr. Harris on throwing goblets in one piece. Here the form is associated with the **chalice.**

D

GODET

A late Medieval shallow cup. The term is also applied to a 17th century beaker with no handle.

GOGLET, Gorgelet

According to some authorities, a goglet is a porous Portuguese earthenware water cooler with a long neck. Haggar (see H.CECP in Booklist) defines a gorgelet as an "Oriental round-bodied drinking vessel with a fairly long neck, used so that the lips do not touch the vessel." "Oriental" here may refer to the Near East. The fact that the liquid is poured as a stream into the mouth, probably for hygienic reasons, since several people would partake, is common to all definitions. A form with a similar use is found throughout the Mediterranean countries; it is a closed-in globular body with a handle over the top, a filling neck on one side of the shoulder, and a drinking spout opposite. Other names for this general type of vessel are **alcarraza,** or **cantaros,** and the goglet is almost identical with one type of English **harvest jug.**

GOTCH

An East Anglian **jug/pitcher.**

GOURD SHAPE

Various types of gourds have provided source material for pot shapes in many cultures—African, ancient American, Far Eastern, and modern—either as a single, generally asymmetric, form or as what is known as the **double-gourd vase.** See also **calabash form.**

B. A subtle little pot by the Martin Brothers (early 20th century), probably inspired by the gourd form.

B

GRANARY JAR/URN

An essential storage vessel in earlier cultures, the best known and perhaps the most handsome being those made in Crete from Minoan times up till this century. Much smaller (approximately 10 inches/250mm high), simple shapes with a cover, from 3rd century China, are called "granary or grain jars." The most remarkable clay granaries are those illustrated in C.PP (see Booklist). Some 8 to 10 feet/3m high, these fine pot-shapes are in, presumably, unfired clay. Modern China still produces large storage vessels of some 784 pounds/350 kilos capacity for grain. (See CMjun78 in Booklist.)

"Granary urn" is a term applied to a cylindrical pottery vessel from Han China, set on three feet modelled as bears. The top is shaped like a tiled roof with a hole in the center. The whole thing looks like a rather splendid trash can or dustbin.

Models of granaries are found throughout Chinese pottery. An ornate form on three legs comes from Han times; much later, a typical little Chinese building, on three legs and, with a removable door, was made in the Lung Ch'uan period and is very pretty.

D. Closer to the glass goblet form is this earthenware, tin-glaze example by Alan Caiger Smith. (See facing page.)

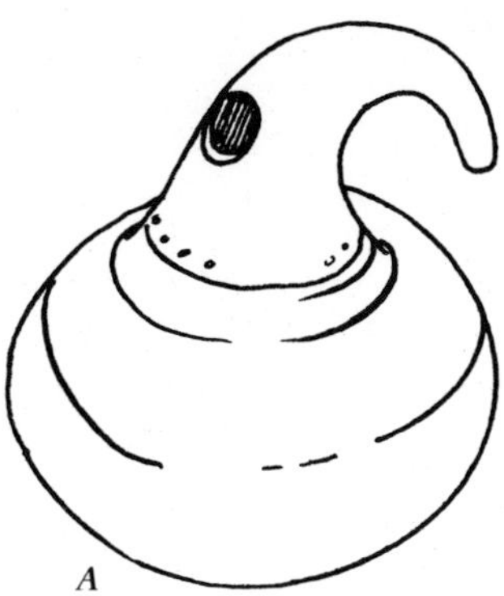

A. Directly inspired by a gourd or calabash is this curious little pot from 11th century Columbia.

A

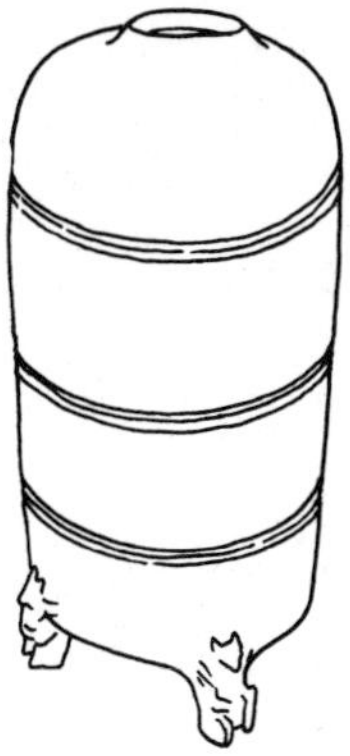

The rather splendid Han granary urn.

GRAPE CUP

A name given to small **incense burners** from Early Bronze Age Britain. They were covered with regularly applied balls of clay with a hole between each hump, or **boss.**

GRAPEN

A German tripod pot.

GRATIN DISH

A wide, shallow dish for cooking meals topped with cheese in the oven.

GREEK FORM

The classic Greek pots were, to a considerable degree, designed as vehicles for painted decoration, although they were also in general practical use (the word "vase" then meant a useful everyday pot). The surfaces were wholly smoothed over for the same reason, so little clay feeling comes through. Although they have the sharp, hard finish reminiscent of metal shapes, Arthur Lane (see L.GP in Booklist) denies direct influence (see **metal form**), but admits that "the form of Greek vases are drawn from a world of vitalized geometry." The many shapes, the principle names of which are included in this dictionary, are intellectually conceived profiles or silhouettes. Leach and Cardew have little time for the Greek ceramic ideals (see L.PB): "the middle and late Greeks were bad potters. . . . [The pots] were conceived coldly and without reference to the material and to the organic growth of spinning clay shaped by human hands." Nevertheless, early Chinese pots were often adapted and assimilated Greek forms.

GREYBEARD

An alternative name for the **bellarmine,** possibly that of a lighter fabric and glaze? Some were made at Fulham Pottery by Dwight.

GUTTIS, Guttus

A Roman pot not unlike a flat teapot, with a side handle and a spout opposite.

H

HAM PAN

See **salter.**

HAND

Models of hands were popular in Victorian England and were possibly associated with the cult of spiritualism. Some were in the form of a hand holding a small vase; others had splayed fingers for use as ring holders. See also **finger vase.**

HANDLE

In *Webster's New Collegiate Dictionary* "a part that is designed especially to be grasped in the hand." The pierced **lug** found on many early pots developed into a handle as soon as the hole became large enough to put a finger through. It then took on a more visually important role, one that can enhance or spoil a form. For a midway type see **lug handle.**

A. A hooked handle shaped like a bird's head on a Bavarian scoop *or ladle.*

A

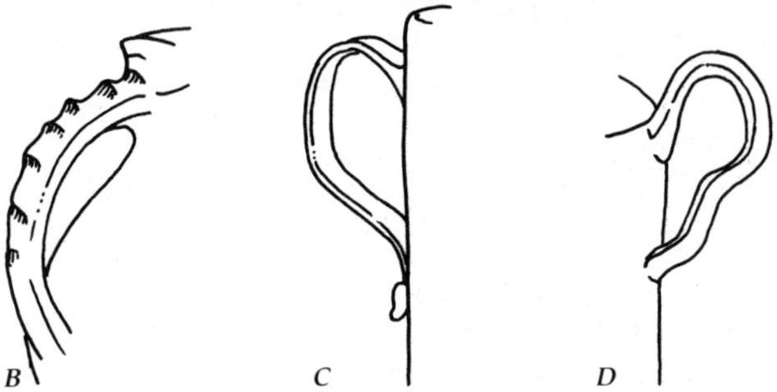

B C D

B/C/D. A decorated Medieval handle with "stops" all the way up; the slightly squared Stoke handle of the 18th century, which has been adapted by Geoffrey Whiting and others, and a triple curve from 18th/19th century Creamware, also back in favor in 1979 (see egg stand*).*

The handle was well developed by the 3rd millennium B.C. in the more sophisticated civilizations such as the Cretan. By the time of the Greeks it had become a dominant accessory to a pot. Greek handles are usually paired opposite to one another,

E. Many curious and intricate handles were invented in the 18th/19th centuries. The twisted double handle was common, as were handles in plant and animal shape (see hound-handled pitcher*).*

suggesting a draftsman's rather than a potter's approach, and, to modern eyes, they often seem exagerrated to an unacceptable degree. They have their champions, however. In L.GP (see Booklist) it refers to: "big handles, apt to the hand and so strong that they could not be knocked off without taking a large part of the vessel with them. It is a delight to observe how, by bold tapering and contrapuntal curve, the handle was often made to appear an inseparable organic part of the whole form." Whether the rigid intellectual concept of Greek pottery can be called "organic" is a moot point. Lane contrasts the Greek and Chinese: "Chinese potters of all dates have disliked handles on their pots, because paired handles unpleasantly punctuate in a two-dimensional plane the three-dimensional ovoid or globular volume that is, for them, the ideal ceramic form. The Greeks, like later

F

F. This strange serpent with a human head is on an octagonal 19th century cast jug. (Salisbury Museum.)

G

G. The somewhat tortuous crabstock handle. *Some examples are smoother than this rather extreme sample.*

Europeans, were not prepared to sacrifice practical convenience to aesthetic purism." To a modern potter's eyes a single handle can be balanced by a lip or spout and certainly need not "unpleasantly

H

H. A ribbed handle on a jug/pitcher by Richard Batterham with a lively, directly "wiped" lower junction.
I. Thrown handles on a creamer *and a* coffeepot *by David Leach.*

I

punctuate" the form of the pot. In the Middle Ages, and especially in England, the handle, usually on a jug/pitcher, assumed a great variety of bold and varied styles, many of which have become patterns for today's craft tableware. The terminals are of a special interest.

A handle can be formed by "pulling," which is the most commonly used technique among craft potters of all ages. "The actual gesture used in producing the form is almost identical to the gesture involved in its use." (See R.PF in Booklist.) It can also be made by cutting with a shaped wire hoop (see L.PB); by extruding through a die; by pressing or slip-casting in a mold, as practiced almost exclusively by the industry; or, as Rhodes says Greek handles were made, by rolling like a coil. Purely modelled handles are uncommon, but see also **winged form.** Each method impresses its own character. Today the most common type of handle is the springing side handle, but there are others, such as the arched-over handle (called a **bail** by Rhodes), which may be of clay or bamboo. (See also **spout and bridge.**

There are five factors to be considered when designing a handle. The first is the handle itself, its width and thickness, the degree of taper, the finger and thumb grooves made in the pulling. All are considered in relation to the pot and particularly to its weight. If the handle is visually strong enough to take the weight of the vessel full of liquid, this may be considered the minimum size. Circular section handles are occasionally used, but normally the width is considerably greater than the thickness. Geoffrey Whiting maintains the same width, top to bottom, of his handles, but tapers them slightly in the thinner section. Taper is inherent in a pulled handle, but, if extreme, results in a weak lower terminal. To quote Leach, a thin or overtapered handle is "an offence against the implicit plastic demand of any generous shape . . . and takes away from the breadth of form in a quite peculiar manner." (See L.PB in Booklist.) The ridges and grooves in the length of a handle are of great value in giving character and interest, but the inner surface is best left smooth and slightly rounded to give a comfortable grip.

The second factor is the upper termination. This takes all the weight of the vessel and needs to be strong and well attached. Normally, the handle is a good deal thicker at the point of junction where it is smoothed into the pot wall. Uncleanable crevices, especially under the top junction, are to be

J

J. A rather unusually curved handle, which leaves an oval space between body and handle.

K

K. The placing of a handle is crucial to the overall effect. Here 3 identical mugs and handles are assembled centrally, high, and low on the wall, each position giving its own character to the vessel.

avoided. The top termination can give the impression of the handle growing from the pot in an organic way, its character often enhanced by crisp thumb grooves where the stub is smoothed into the body. Where extruded or even-thickness handles are used, it is difficult to avoid an appearance of weakness at the top termination. A longer joint area can be achieved by turning the handle over so that the outer face is luted to the pot.

L

M

L. The handle as a major extension of the form, cut from a flat slab. By Jennifer Wright.
M. Another dominant flat handle on a porcelain cup by Nick Homoky.

The third factor is the lower terminal. The stress here is one of compression through most of the action of lifting and pouring with slight tension at the end of the movement. It need not, therefore, have the same weight as the top join. A number of lively and decorative types of finger wipes are possible as the clay is fastened down.

The relationship of the curve of the pot to that of the handle is the fourth factor. The line of the handle should be such that the grip is neither so close to the body that the knuckles touch it, nor so far away that unnecessary leverage need be exerted. A handle standing far from the pot will also be vulnerable to breakage. A slightly concave profile at the section of the wall that is spanned by the handle will give greater freedom and tolerance to the shaping of the handle. The space between handle and pot is of primary importance and should be considered as part of the form itself. On a traditional jug/pitcher shape this often resembles a fish. It is difficult to span a fully convex form satisfactorily. The handles of Geoffrey Whiting's teapots involve two changes of direction in place of the more usual steadily flowing curve, so that the gripping section reflects the shoulder of the pot in a subtle and satisfying way.

The fifth factor is the placing of the handle. A normal handle spans roughly the top two-thirds of a pot, but a case can be made for a lower placing, especially on smaller pieces such as beakers. Pitchers and mugs are frequently less than full of liquid, so that the weight is often in the lower section; thus, a beaker handle placed relatively low on the wall can be justified on practical, as well as aesthetic, grounds. Apart from its general position the handle must accommodate enough fingers to lift the pot comfortably and to be far enough from the base not to involve tipping the pot in order to get a grip.

These remarks refer mainly to side handles. Fishley Holland calls the attachment of handles "bowing," an excellent word, for a fine handle is as taut and lively as a drawn bow. Regarding Fishley's "bowing," Bernard Leach wrote in a letter after a meeting of the two men: "I piqued my crew when I told them that you had handled two hundred mugs in a little over an hour, meanwhile carrying on an interesting conversation."

Apart from the bow, handles attached only at one end have been used from early times, sometimes modelled as stylized animal heads and the like. Probably because of the low firing, the handles of many Medieval **skillets** had bracing strips below the handle for added strength. On modern bowls and dishes a thrown or flat, pulled handle stands out at a slightly upward angle from the side. Hooked handles are found on **ladles.**

Handles in a figure eight are found on Minoan pots; in a number of vertical loops on 18th century

loving cups; plaited; twisted; modelled as twigs or bamboo (**crabstock handle**); and generally disguised in fanciful ways. Many from Stoke-on-Trent have a charming and subtle double bend; others are curlicued with great joie de vivre. A few potters have used flat, cut-out handles. Decorated with thumbed bosses, modelled or carved, stabbed or engraved, the world of handles demonstrates the potter's imagination and ingenuity, embellishing and varying the basic design. But beneath all this the principles discussed above are needed to give a basis of practicality and grace to the form.

See also **wishbone handle, bell ringers' jug,** and the many handled forms such as **jug/pitcher, teapot,** etc.

HANDLE STOP

Many ingenious and decorative additions have been made to the tops of **handles** in order to give the thumb a steadier grip when the vessel is lifted. The simplest is a small roll, perhaps wiped into the handle curve, so that it looks like a bud on a branch, or simply a pellet of clay flattened on. "Handles [of harvest jugs] are topped with an applied pad or 'thumb bit' of clay which makes them more comfortable to grip." (See B.CECP in Booklist.) The two-handled Greek vessels needed no stops, but we find them on 18th century B.C. Cypriot handles, molded into the form, and some 1st century Par-

B

A. A Parthian 2nd/3rd century jug handle with earlike stops.

A

B. A spirited handle stop on a modern pitcher.

C

C. "backwards" handle stop, more of a thumb rest, by Jim Malone.

thian handles have a raised stop on a squared handle, the stop being pierced as if for hanging. Modelled animal head stops occur widely. A 13th century Kashan "tankard" has a round handle to the shoulder with a large, flat stop joined to the neck, making it a major item in the formal arrangement. For a built-in stop on a cut handle see the illustration under **measure.** Other handle stops are discussed under **teapot** and other entries, but the majority of pots, both historical and modern, do not avail themselves of this useful addition.

HAND WARMER

See **hot-water bottle**. The illustration shows a fairly elaborate hand warmer or **brazier** from 16th century London, possibly Richard Dyer's kiln outside Moorgate. It burned charcoal.

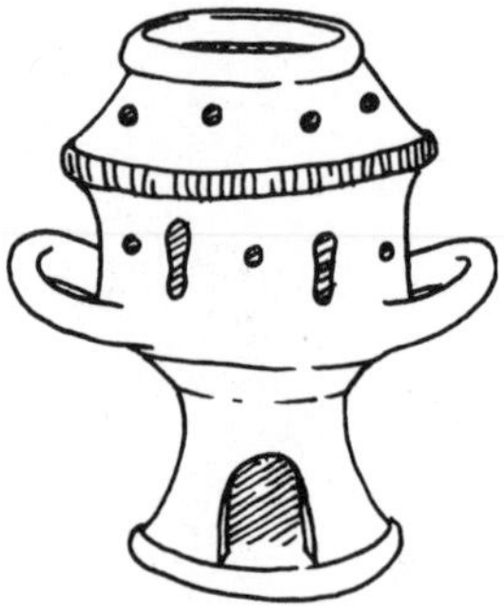

A 16th century hand warmer as described in the text.

HARE TUREEN

As mentioned under **bird tureen/casserole** modelled tureen/casseroles were made in the form of hare and other game. They are occasionally made by studio potters in a more stylized form. See also **tureen.**

HARVEST DISH

Some very large slipware dishes, up to 2 feet/625mm across, are known as "harvest dishes." They were probably used for taking food to the workers in the fields or for celebrating afterwards.

HARVEST JUG

Guilland (see G.EAFP in Booklist) shows a slightly tapering, enclosed vessel with a filling spout on one side of the shoulder and a spout on the other.

A really sizeable slipware harvest dish.

The liquid would be poured into the mouth from the spout without the lips actually touching it. This is almost identical to some versions of the **alcarraza** or **goglet.**

In England the term harvest jug would most likely indicate a large pitcher of traditional shape with appropriate emblems, often in relief. "Many of these pots epitomised the concept of good design flowing from functional necessity alone, bold spherical forms . . . and strong applied details." (See B.CECP in Booklist.) Spherical **flasks** with little scalloped lugs or handles on the shoulders have been called "owls," and are mentioned by Fishley Holland. Other types of flasks would have been used as harvest jugs or bottles. A harvest jug from Stoke has the inscription: "Here's to thee my honest friend/ wishing these hard times to mend," reminding us of the hardness of the country life. See also **ring bottle, flagon.**

HEADREST, Pillow

These were made in pottery in ancient Egypt and many other parts of the world and are especially numerous and varied in the Far East. Known as *chen* in Chinese, they were often a boxlike shape with an in-curved top, and may have been used filled with hot or cold water, as appropriate to the season, or with scented leaves. T'ao Shou (see B.DA in Booklist) tells us that they were "most efficacious in keeping the eyes clear and preserving the sight, so that even in old age fine writing can be read." Headrests were widely made in China and Korea, with later models in porcelain. There is a Sung

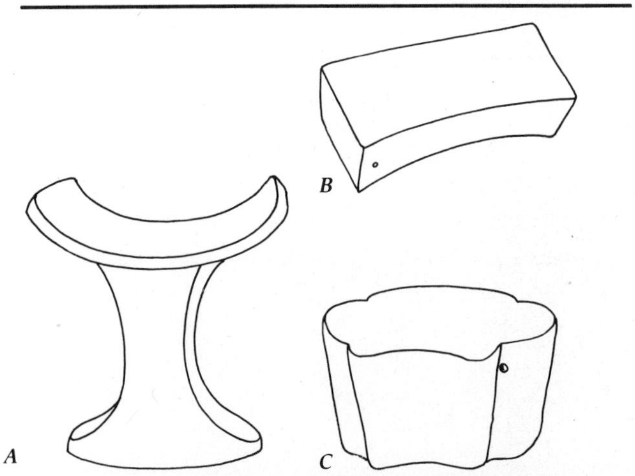

A. A tall and stately headrest from 3rd millennium B.C. *Egypt, blue glazed, about 8 inches/200mm tall, made "for a high official."*
B/C/D. Three types of Chinese headrests which were in use from T'ang to Ming times. There are many more fine, strong forms which deserve studying. (Crafts Study Centre, Bath.)

example modelled as a sleeping boy supporting a curved headrest.

Though unlikely to find a wide market today, the shapes are very attractive and could well be adapted to boxes and other items.

HEATER

See **brazier, food warmer, hot-water bottle, chafing dish, barbecue.**

HILL JAR, Hill-censer

A box or squat jar set on three feet, which are sometimes modelled in the form of bears, found

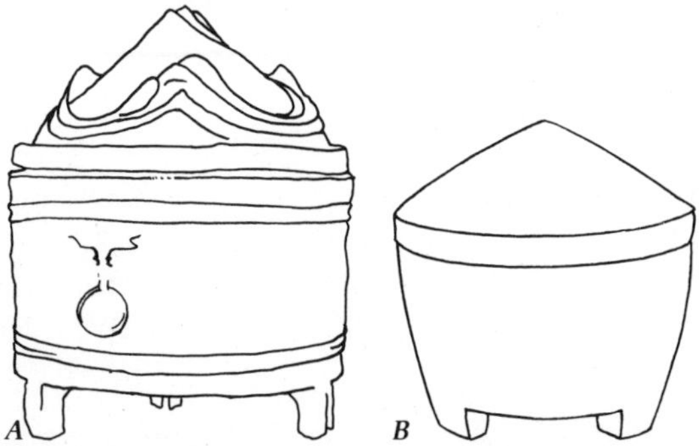

A. A Han hill jar in green glazed earthenware, about 10 inches/250mm high.
B. A porcelain box by Bernard Leach, 4 inches/100mm high, 1957. It is a very simplified version of the hill jar.

in many Han Chinese tombs. The name derives from the conical lid in the shape of a stylized mountain with waves round the base: The Isle of the Blessed in the Eastern Seas. The Chinese name is *po-shan-lu.* These boxes were much admired by Bernard Leach and were probably the inspiration for his charming conical lidded boxes.

HOLLOWARE

The term for industrial cups, bowls, etc., as distinguished from **flatware,** using this term in the English sense; see **flatware.** Holloware is normally made within a mold; flatware, over a hump-mold.

HOLY-WATER HOLDER

A flat-backed wall slab with a rough crucified figure and a small bowl beneath it is in the York County Museum. Similar, more sophisticated, versions have been made.

HONEY JAR/POT

B.CECP (see Booklist) refers to a specific form, somewhat barrel-shaped, with a firm slightly splayed rim, as a honey jar. A modern honey pot is usually of a similar form, but smaller and with an inset lid.

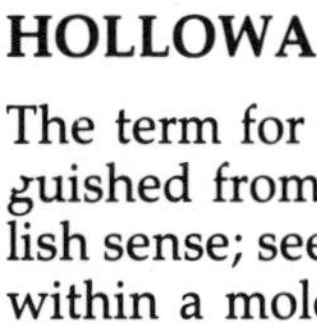

A 1st century Romano-British honey pot with very flat lug handles.

HONEYMOON POT

The enormous wine jars, reputedly up to 7 feet/2m high, made in Cyprus, were jokingly called "honeymoon pots" for they'd make a good place for a newly married couple to be. In fact, it is said, the pots were often built and fired on the spot and the house erected round them. First things first!

HORN

Quite a resonant sound can be produced from a pottery horn. In the Ashmolean Museum there is a 15th century English horn with a single curve. Guilland (see G.EAFP in Booklist) illustrates a horn actually used to call field workers at the Zoarite Community in Ohio around 1818. This horn consists of two and a half turns. Horns can be made by throwing closed rings of clay, which are then cut and joined.

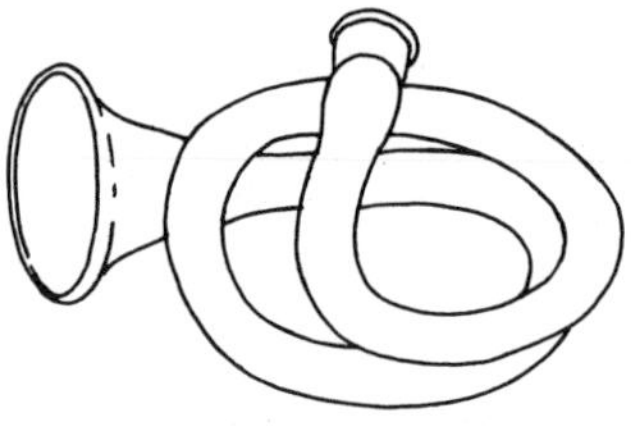

A terra-cotta horn or trumpet from North Portugal.

In the somewhat different sense of a cornucopia, the form has been used for wall pockets and vases for the last three hundred years.

HORS D'OEUVRES DISH

In LG (see Booklist) this is shown as flat-based, oblong, and with nearly straight vertical sides, sometimes fluted. It is very similar to a **gratin dish.**

HOT-WATER BOTTLE

When winters were colder and heating inefficient, many types of hot-water containers were made, mostly in stoneware. The standard shape has a flat base with a curved top and a screw stopper, like a cylindrical pot on its side. Small ones were made for muffs, and a flat variety with two foot-shaped depressions were used in carriages and elsewhere. Many fanciful shapes were made in the 19th century—a handbag, for instance. **Boot**-shaped bottles were made to slip into footware to warm the inside before wearing.

A

A. A common standard type of 19th/20th century hot-water bottle, provided with an effective screw stopper, made watertight with a rubber ring. Many other shapes were made.

B/C. This charming little flattened bottle, no more than 4 inches/100mm across, was probably used inside a muff to warm the hands.

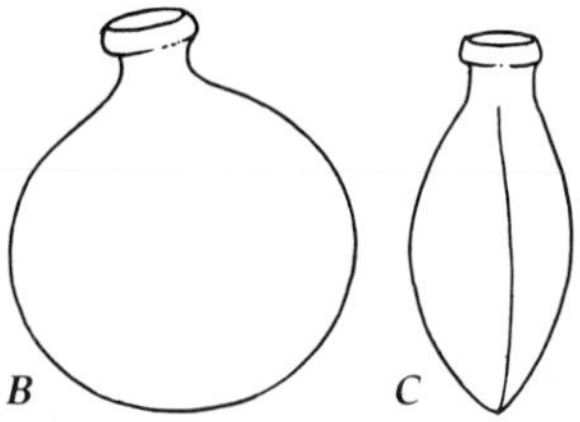

B C

D. A comfortable modern hot-water bottle by Ray Finch, 1979. The shape also doubles as a lampbase.

HOUND-HANDLED PITCHER

Originating in Hungary and also made in England, this type of jug/pitcher takes its name from the

D

handle, which is modelled as a greyhoundlike dog. It traveled to the United States where it was made by the Bennet Pottery in Baltimore in the early 19th century and later in Vermont and other places in the Eastern U.S.

HOUSE

See **building.**

HU

A Chinese form with a wide belly narrowing to a neck, derived from bronzes. Medley in M.CP (see Booklist) calls it "A wine vase in the broadest sense." It is from 1st millennium B.C.

This curious fancy, probably connected with hunting, was common both in Europe and 19th century U.S.A. The animal is, in fact, quite pleasantly accommodated into the handle.

HUMAN FORM

The representation of the human form in pottery appears to have almost-predated pots themselves, and has varied from the subtle schematized prehistoric bottles, through the more naturalistic, but

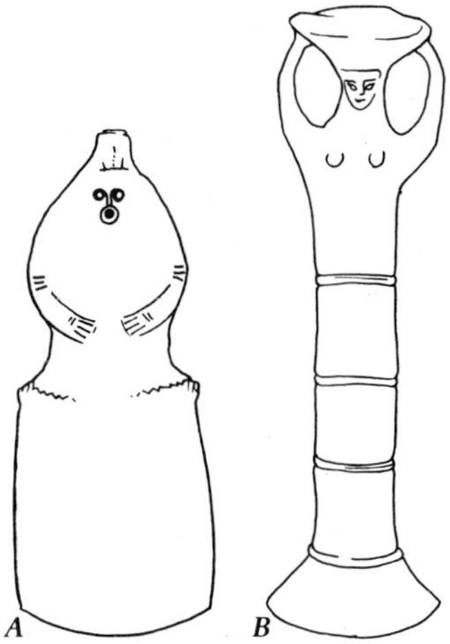

A. A very potlike schematized female figure from Bronze Age Romania, 8 inches/200mm high.
B. Another early (archaic Greek) figure pot, the arms serving as handles. The body is probably an abstract indication of the clothing fashion of the time.

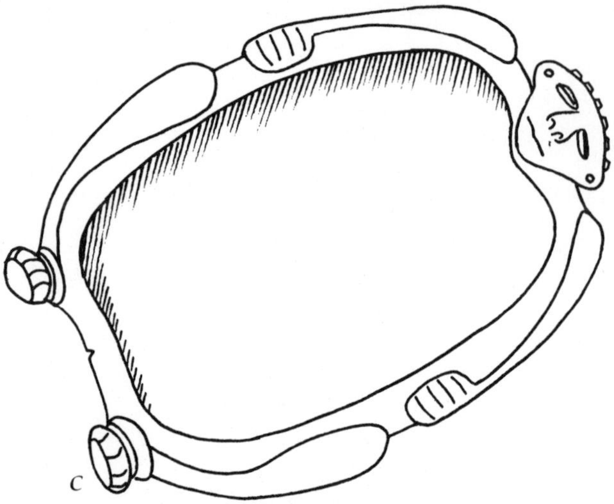

C. *A stylized modelled dish from ancient Colombia.*

still stylized Medieval pitchers, to the crudities of the **Toby Jug** of recent times. Splendid bowls on human **feet** in early Moravian pottery and jars modelled as female idols in even earlier neolithic Romania are found. Masks and simplified, often flat figures allied with pot forms are common to all cultures. Ancient America abounded in anthropomorphic pots, finely modelled, but usually more realistic. The Far East produced a great deal of figure modelling in clay, but usually kept pot and model separate.

Potters today use the undoubted parallels between pot and human shape to suggest the latter, often assisted by decoration.

See also **alabastron, arbor group, boggle, face pot, finial, foot, maiden's legs, mammiform, toy, pew group, doll.**

HUMPEN

A rather squat German **tankard** or **mug** with a slightly flaring base.

HYDRIA, Vyka or Byka

Pronounced "ithria." An ancient Greek three-handled water pot, a pair of handles being horizontally opposed, with a third loop handle for carrying.

The vyka is a modern country simplification of the hydria, the smaller version having one handle and a pouring lip, more like a pitcher; the larger type has two handles and a solid rounded rim. The latter would be used for storage and cooling. All may be equipped with a wooden stopper.

I

ICE BUCKET

Usually a simple open pot, sometimes equipped with double walls as in the **psykter.**

ICE CREAM WAFER MOLD

It took a long time to decide on the function of the curious white-glazed (probably 19th century) item illustrated. A wafer is placed in the oblong, the thickness of the ice cream is determined by the depth of the "mold," and another wafer slapped on top. It is removed by pressing through the hole with a finger—very hygienic!

See description of function in text.

IDO

A type of Korean bowl with a wide mouth and a high foot (see F.SOC in Booklist).

INCENSE BURNER/CUP/BOX

From the early Bronze Age onwards we find a great

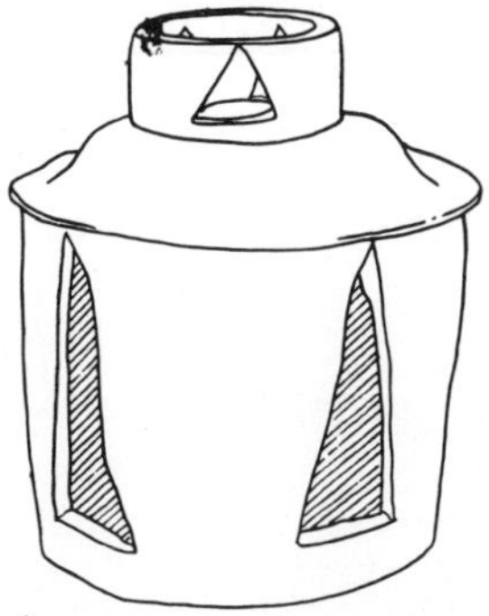
A

B

variety of vessels used for burning "incense" of fragrant herbs. They are usually perforated with cut openings or have a perforated lid. Small straight-sided bowls with bosses known as "pygmy cups" or **grape cups** are found in prehistoric England. Even earlier examples with chimneylike lids were made in the ancient Near East.

China has the word *ko* for incense ware, their forms being rather more sophisticated in glazed stoneware. A Ting example has a pierced, flattened globular top on a stem, and there are squat **kinuta**-type burners on three legs. There is a charming incense box in the form of a sparrow in Japanese Kioto ware (raku) illustrated in H.PPFE (see Booklist), and also swans and cockerels with removable heads. The Shino School of Incense was founded around 1550.

Boxes modelled as ducks and cows are also known of and there is a remarkable Nigerian burner which has the appearance of a growth of fungi on long stalks, each with a shallow cup on top. Hamada has made incense boxes, and in C23 (see Booklist) a modern holder by Laurie Short is shown. The form is open to countless variations. A distinct type is the incense or joss-stick holder, which needs only small holes in which to stand the stick upright. The French example shown in the illustration has a saucer built in to take the ash.

INDENTED FORM

The indentation of the wall of a pot done with the finger or a tool is largely a decorative technique,

A. Stated to have been an incense burner, this curious pot was made in the Near East some 6000 years ago.
B. A more sophisticated carved and pierced lid on a Sung Chinese incense burner. (Barlow Collection.)
C. A modern French incense or joss-stick burner by a craftsman potter.

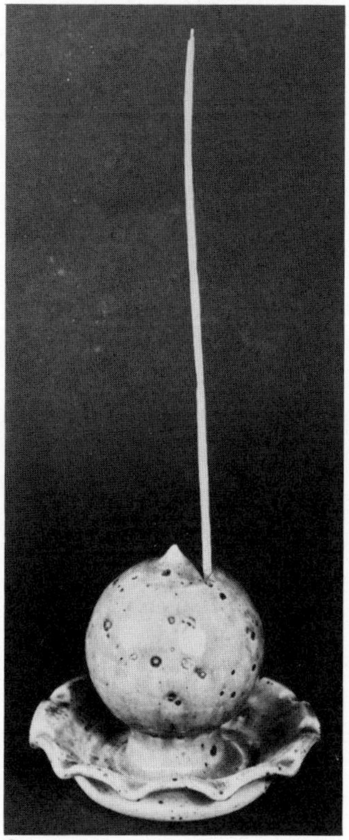
C

A. A freely indented pot by David Leach. (Photograph: Eileen Lewenstein, Emmanuel Cooper.)

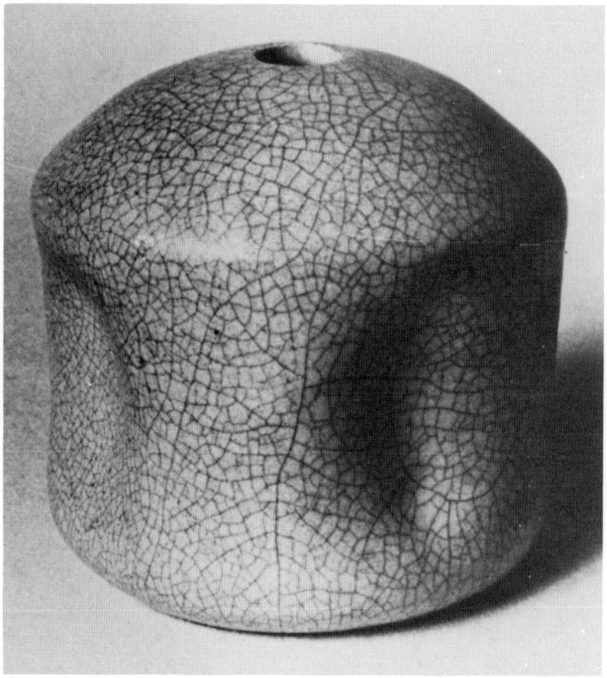
A

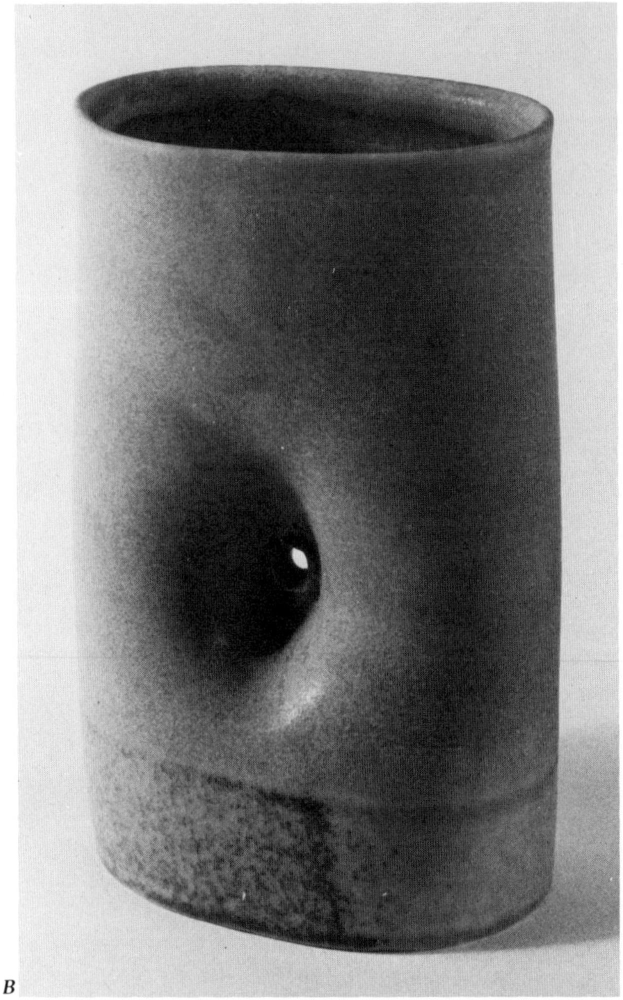

B

B. An indentation taken to the point where the pot is pierced, by Eileen Lewenstein.

but it can also alter and affect the form in subtle ways. The Romano-British **folded** pot is an extreme example and one which appears to be almost unique in pottery history. A 10th century Islamic water pot shows indentations around the belly, but the technique was not widely practiced. Eileen Lewenstein's finger-indented porcelain cylinder shown in COQ78 (see Booklist) illustrates how subtly the character of a shape can be modified. See also **saki bottle/cup.**

INHALER

Various types of inhalers for chest complaints, etc. were made, often in salt-glaze, through the 18th to 20th centuries. The body of the pot would contain the medicant in hot water. While these were essentially practical and medical, the ingenious forms were often very attractive.

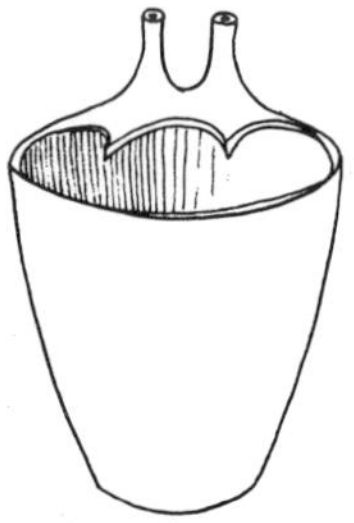

A rather extreme example: a 2-nostril inhaler inscribed "Sibden Hall, Halifax." The curious double point, reflecting the spouts, appears to be purely decorative and certainly gives interest to the form.

INKWELL/INK, Water Pot/Ink palette

In the East, ink would be mixed as it was used, and for this purpose a water pot and palette would be required. The palettes were objects of decorative value; they were little platforms on sturdy corner feet cut from the walls. The Western inkwell and ink pot were more humble containers, generally cylindrical.

In the British Museum BM (see Booklist) a tiny double container from ancient Egypt, each half a shallow, square bowl, is described as an inkwell for writing on papyrus and is called a *tes.* In the London Museum a simple 1st century Roman pot with a recessed top and a central hole is labelled "ink pot." Some later European ink pots have a certain charm. Extreme fancifulness took over in a number of inkwell designs. A Swiss example, for instance, in

A. A writing set from 18th century Bristol, complete with pounce pot or sander. (Bristol Museum.)

A

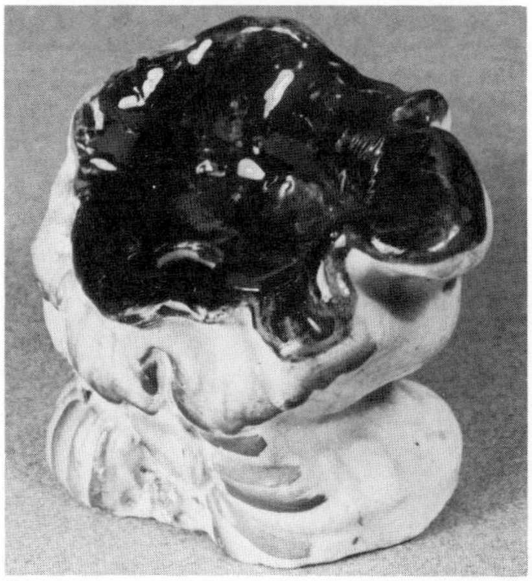

B. A very curious (what would now be called "funky") 19th century inkwell in rococo style. (Bristol Museum.)

B

the Fitzwilliam Museum, is in the shape of a temple complete with figures. Less ambitious shapes are more general: in the form of books (folk pottery of the Eastern U.S.); as pleasant square pots and "bricks" (see **flower brick**); as flat, circular drums with several holes for quill pens; and as more humorous models such as an 1840 salt-glazed head, resting face up, with the mouth open to receive the pens. The Martin Brothers made simple truncated pyramids. In C19 (see Booklist) a Hausa ink pot from North Nigeria is shown, with two dipping spouts branching from the side of the pot.

There is no reason why the range should not be expanded. Although calligraphers are, perhaps, the only ones who now use ink from a bottle, imaginative pieces could be devised as pen holders, even for the ubiquitous ball-point pen, and there are still specialists who might like a fine holder on their worktables in the same spirit as the earlier Chinese.

J

JAKOBAKANNE JUG

A tall, very handsome German jug/pitcher, more or less **baluster** shaped, but with a break in the profile above the shoulder, a high handle, and a spreading thumbed-down base. Lane calls it a **tankard,** and describes it as "wheel-made pottery in its most elementary form, a petrified record of the potter's first motions in throwing a lump of clay." (See L.SiP in Booklist.)

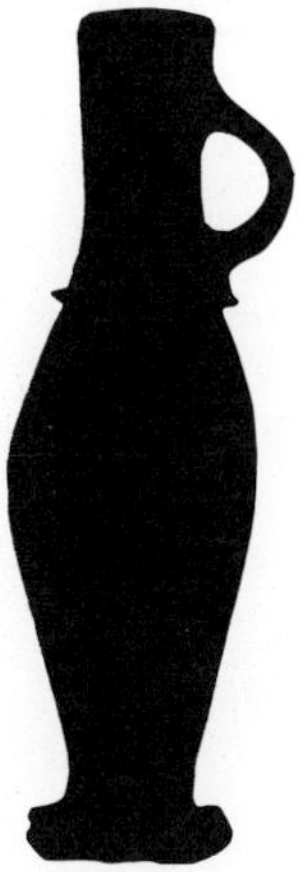

The silhouette of the jakobakanne.

JAM JAR

Jam jars were made in salt-glaze and specialist jam makers still use stoneware pots. They are normally simple cylinders with a groove just below the rim, but cast jars in hexagonal and octagonal shapes are also found.

JAM POT

This is usually a rounded jar with a lid, which may be cut with a circular notch to take the spoon, but

The classic Leach jam pot, made in quantity at the St. Ives Pottery, especially in the forties and fifties. This one was probably painted by Bernard.

A

there is no reason why the potter should limit himself to this form.

JAR

From the Arabic word *jara.* According to the *Shorter Oxford English Dictionary,* a jar is a vessel "without a spout or handle (or two-handled), usually cylindrical." In normal usage a jar is a wide-mouthed pot, sometimes with a lid and **lug handles,** used for the storage of food, etc. Many of the large pots from the Bronze and Iron ages must have been **storage jars.** A frequent deep groove below the rim suggests the use of skin or other material for covering. Rhodes (see R.PF in Booklist) calls the jar "the elemental pottery form" the basic elements of which are "a sturdy base, swelling mid-section, and an open but somewhat constricted neck."

The most noble of storage jars are found at Knossos: tall with slightly curving walls and a mouth a little wider than the foot. The line of the profile is broken by ropelike reliefs, which covered the join between the large rolled and thrown coils from which they were constructed, and by **lugs,** often in profusion, some of which may have been used to stretch a cover over the top; others which were repeated from rim to base were rope guides used when lifting, moving, or tilting. The jars were often set a foot or more into the ground. Hand-built storage jars up to 5 feet/1.6m high are found in Romano-British and later Saxon wares, the latter often described as **cinerary urns,** though similar designs probably served for both purposes. See also **granary jar/urn, honeymoon pot,** etc.

Jars do not figure quite so widely in the Far East, where the general form is known as the *lei,* but there are some very fine examples and they are still being made (see cover picture of CR54). The most ubiquitous small jar is the **albarello.** The modern potter usually fits a jar with a lid.

See also illustration under **lug, crock.**

A. Storage jars up to 6 feet high at Knossos, Crete. From 1500 B.C.
B. A monumental lidded jar by Louise Hannsen. The slightly concave walls give an easy grip (see albarello*), but with both hands in this case.*

B

JARDINIERE

A garden vase or trough; according to *The Concise Oxford Dictionary,* "an ornamental pot or stand for the display of growing flowers in a room, on the windowsill, etc." The common boat-shaped jardiniere is mock-classic and rather florid, but it is only one possible form among many. In books on Far Eastern pottery the name is likely to be applied to almost any shape that can be used as a **flowerpot,** or even to the cover of such a piece. Lobed and squared shapes and semicircular containers set on four little legs are found (from Staffordshire, etc.). Simple slab troughs are often made by students.

JELLY MOLD

These have been made in quantity since the 18th century, often in stoneware. They were usually smooth on the outside, but with an elaborately modelled interior, so designed that there are no undercuts, which would prevent the jelly from dropping out. G.EAFP (see Booklist) shows a pleasantly simple scalloped gelatin mold, quite small—about 1½ by 4½ inches—from 19th century New England. M.K (see Booklist) illustrates some ambitious jelly molds shaped as pyramids and obelisks and used as follows: an outer case contained liquid jelly, the inner form was inserted, the whole reversed when the jelly was set, and the outer case

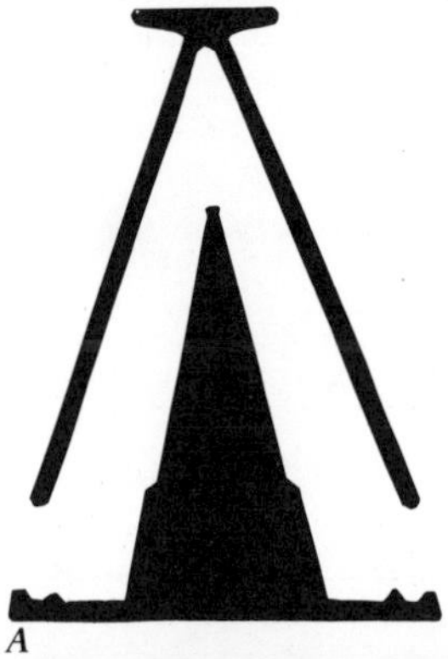

A

A. An "obelisk" mold or core of the type made by Wedgwood in the 18th/19th centuries. The outer cover is conjectural.
B. A typical 19th century jelly mold. Food decorated in this way is now rare and a loss to our dinner tables. Other foods—chicken in aspic, custards, etc.—could be made very decorative through the use of these molds.

B

removed. The inner shape acted as a support, with the design on it showing through the jelly coating. It is rare to find a complete support and case. Jellies were generally confined to the wealthier classes in the late 18th and early 19th centuries and few molds have survived. After about 1875, however, packet jellies became commonly available and the interior modelled mold was almost universally used.

JIGGER AND JOLLEY WARE

Most industrial pottery is made in or over revolving molds, the thickness of the wall being controlled by a metal arm and profile. This technique imposes limits on the forms it produces. Bulbous or "returned" profiles, for instance, are unsuitable, as are more than vestigial foot rings.

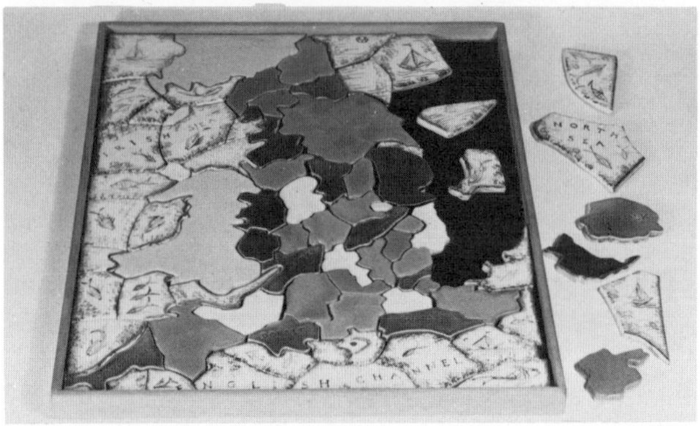

The English Counties and the sea around form the pieces of this pottery jigsaw puzzle in colored earthenware glazes and painted tin-glaze. By Mary Ball, it is a test of geography for all ages.

JIGSAW PUZZLE

These games, made in the manner of tesserae for mosaic, do not, strictly speaking, have "form," unless we consider each piece separately. They do, however, make pleasant toys "for all ages," especially if applied to such timeless subjects as maps, etc.

JOINT DISH

A large, flat ended, oval dish with gravy runnels is shown in L.PB (see Booklist) and called a "joint dish." It is press-molded with added feet. See also **charger, platter, meat dish.** A large, oblong dish with an out-standing handle and pouring lips, often called a "joint dish," is similar to a **fish dish** (see illustration).

JOLLY BOYS

A Somerset and North Devon name for a **fuddling cup.**

JUG/PITCHER

The etymology of "jug" is, surprisingly, very vague. Most dictionaries suggest a nickname for Joan or Jenny (perhaps they preferred their ladies pitcher shaped!), and *The Shorter Oxford Dictionary* quotes from King Lear: "Whoop Jug I love thee." Both definitions are rather unsatisfactory. The first recorded use of the term is given as 1596, the end of the great period of pitcher forms. It is a fairly

A

B

deep vessel with a wide mouth for holding and pouring liquids. Usually, it has a swelling body and a lip or spout, but it is not covered. In the U.S. this vessel would be called a "pitcher," the word "jug" often indicating a more closed-over, full-shouldered pot, which, in England, would be called a "bottle." *Webster's* gives jug as "a deep earthenware container with a narrow mouth and a handle." In this book we have resolved the quandary by referring to the shape under discussion here as a **jug/pitcher.** It has existed in one form or another wherever it was required to pour liquids into drinking vessels. Occasionally, a jug would serve both purposes (see **drinking jug/pitcher,** and also **ewer, harvest jug.**)

The vessel was known as an **oenochoe** in ancient Greece. Mediterranean jugs from 3000 B.C. with modelled or cut-away, spoutlike lips are common, often with narrower necks than the modern jug/pitcher. Jug types from the Near East are generally lipless. The typical form was not evident in the Far East (but see "chueh" below) until it was introduced from the West; pouring vessels were in ewer form, or had short spouts from the shoulder. However, a Shang pot from 1500 B.C. called a *chueh* is rather juglike with a wide mouth and set on three feet, and Medley (see M.CP in Booklist) describes some Yan Shao (5th millennium B.C.) vessels as "jugs with straight necks and simple strap handles." The pitcher attained its greatest glory in Medieval times when it appeared to occupy most of the creative energy of the potters. Its various forms are dealt with in detail in Rackham's *Medieval English Pottery* and other books. In the 19th century the jug/pitcher appeared in countless often deformed and grossly over-decorated shapes of little or no aesthetic value. Various "spirit jugs" approximated the American idea of a jug, having a small neck which could be corked. Today jugs are made by all tableware potters and, perhaps more than any other form, reflect the character of the maker.

Because it is used essentially for holding and pouring liquids, the pitcher should be balanced and comfortable in the hand. Some concavity of profile

A. An early type of pouring vessel, full formed and with dignity and style, from Bronze Age Cyprus. Note the vestigial lugs, *now merely decorative, and the twisted handle which was to be so popular 4000 years later in Stoke-on-Trent!*

B. Again from Cyprus circa 800 B.C., *still very rounded, but nearer to the modern form, this jug is assured and wholly satisfactory. (Victoria and Albert Museum.)*

C

C/D/E. Three examples from the wide and imaginative range of English Medieval pitchers, two without lips. The tall baluster *shape shows continental influence; the large wide-based line drawing is of a type sometimes called a* cistern.

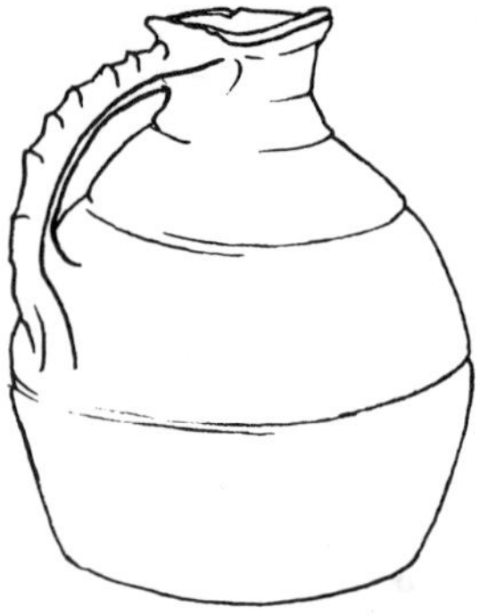

D

E

F

F. Another lipless jug, more sophisticated in outline, from 16th century Turkey.

G. A small, but well-articulated, pitcher by Michael Casson.

H. It would be difficult to imagine a more apt and satisfactory jug/pitcher than this fine example by Geoffrey Whiting.

G

H

makes handle design easier. The range from squat and round to tall and elegant is greater than that for any other useful vessel. The outline can be smooth or angular, and the throwing spiral is a frequent decorative feature. The **lip** offers a subtle balance to the handle and varies from a mere suggestion (none at all on some Medieval and Near East forms) to the exaggerated deformation of the rim which is characteristic of much Italian ware. A lip which starts as a bulge well down the wall can give variety and interest to the form. R.PF (see Booklist) discusses the throwing of pitchers in some detail (and see also under **pitcher** for further discussion).

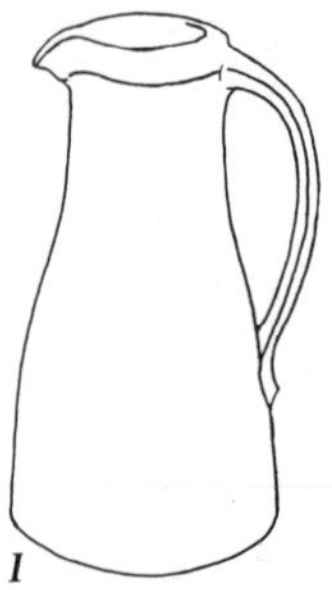

I

I. One of Bernard Leach's most attractive shapes, combining strength with style.

J. A remarkable and uncompromisingly direct treatment of the jug form by Peter Smith, sculptural rather than practical and probably without its like from any past or present potter.

J

Today there are many fine jug/pitcher makers. Some of Bernard Leach's finest pots have been in this form, while his grandson, John Leach, together with Cardew, Michael Casson (who had an exhibition entitled *One Hundred Jugs*), Batterham, and many others, follow in the Medieval tradition of strong, virile shapes. See also illustrations under **bell-ringers' jug, cylinder, handle, lip, jakobakanne jug, creamer.**

K

KALIAN

A hubble-bubble **pipe.** See **water pipe.**

KALYX

See **kylix.**

KANAKI

Minoan and Mycenaean inverted-cone pots, sometimes called **sprinklers.** See under **filter.**

KANTHAROS, Akathi

A small Greek drinking goblet or cup on a stem with high, springing handles set opposite to one another. They are quite dramatic to drink from and easy to break. The same word is used for the thistle flower and thus refers to the flowerlike form of the cup (see under **cup** for a modern thistle shape). Called *akathi* in modern Greece.

KEBAB POT

While "kebab" is often thought of as meat, etc., braised on a skewer, in Cyprus and the Mediterranean countries it is more often a stew of meat and vegetables cooked in their own juices. For this purpose a kebab pot is a typically rounded **cooking pot** with a lid, frequently coiled and hand-formed by women potters. Kebab pots were made at Kornos in Cyprus at least until the latest "troubles" in 1976. The pots were wood-fired and unglazed. See illustrations in F.DPP (in Booklist).

KENDI

Used for pouring water onto the hands (in the

manner of an **aquamanile**), this vessel assumed a number of shapes. It appears as a long-necked bottle with a **mammiform** spout, from Islam (Persia, etc.) circa 1600, and also from Japan, and as water bottles from China made in "peculiar form" (see M.CP in Booklist) made for the Indonesian market and modelled as horses, squatting animals, or toads, etc.

KENSUI, KOBISHA

Waste-water bowls used in the Japanese Tea Ceremony.

KERNOS

Also called a "cluster vase," this took on several forms in Greece and Rome. Essentially, it was a number of small pots or bowls attached to a larger base form. See also **fuddling cup, composite pot, multiple pots.** *Kerno* means "to pour," so this action is likely to have been connected with the kernos although its precise function is obscure.

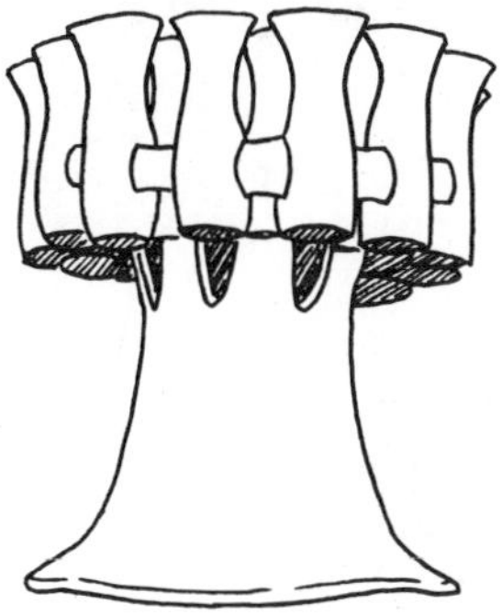

A kernos from the Cyclades circa 1500 B.C.

KESKUL

An Islamic rose-water sprinkler, perforated at the end of a spout for flavoring sweetmeats.

KILN

Unfortunately, potters have seldom left behind models of their kilns to show what they were like, although one such is known from T'ang China, which also shows wares inside. The bottle kilns of Stoke-on-Trent were among the finest shapes they produced. Leach made a model of his kiln and workshop in 1917 when he was working at Abiko. One or two potters today have made kiln models,

A

B

A. The Leach model of his Japanese raku kiln mentioned in text. (Crafts Study Centre, Bath.)
B. Ian Gregory's slat-glaze kiln in salt-glaze, complete with pots, 1979.

A model at Bristol, of a large pottery factory from early 20th century, with ten kilns is a valuable, but rare, record.

KINUTA

A Japanese mallet-shaped vessel. See **mallet shape.**

KNEE BOWLS

Shallow bowls formed over the knee in Japan. See **elbow dish.**

KNIFE REST

For use at the table, these were often made in metal and occasionally in ceramic. The illustration shows a very simple example.

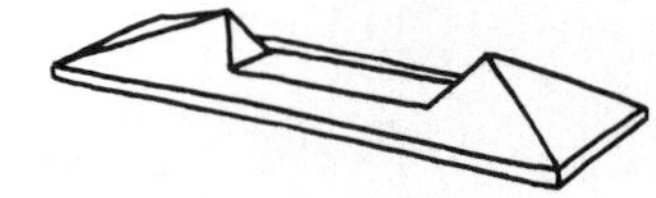

A 19th century knife rest for the table.

KNOB

From the Middle English *knobbe,* meaning "a knob" or "bud." The knob, usually associated with a **lid,** can vary from a simple ball on a short stem, or a slightly undercut **boss,** to elaborate thrown, turned, or modelled shapes. In this context the term is widened from its dictionary definition of "a rounded protuberance" to include any addition to a lid, short of an open **handle,** that is designed to lift it by.

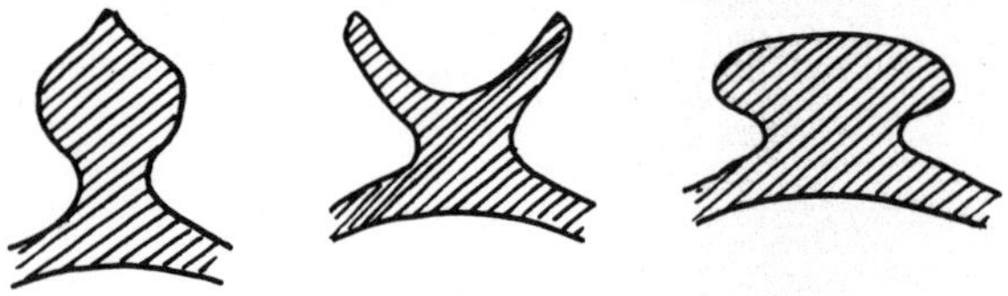

A

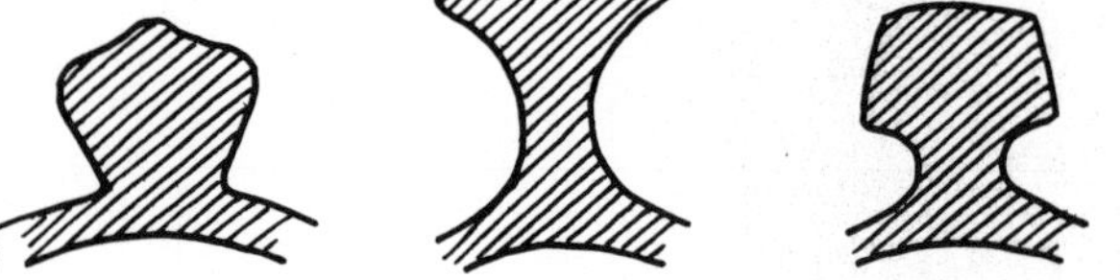

B

A/B. Six varieties of thrown knobs commonly found on lids both historical and modern.

C. A box by Sheila Fournier in which the form of the knob reflects the wide, curving rim of the box itself.

D. Two decorative knobs on stoppered *bottles, providing a very satisfactory completion of the main form. By Turrell.*

E. A curious mixture of rigid turning, slab-building, and modelling from Japan, which includes an effective fungi-form *knob.*

C

D

E

Potters from all ages have let their fancy run free. There are charming kissing birds on a proto-Yueh pot from 3rd century China; more realistic bird models off center on 14th century Sultanabad lids; the massive stylized horses on Greek boxes; dragons and flowers; and the opening seed pod by Karen Karnes illustrated in CR50 (see Booklist). Coils and spirals figure on many modern pots and

F

F. *An ingenious knob formed by pinching a thrown ring, by Ian Hinchcliffe, 1975.*

G

G. *String through a lug used in place of a conventional knob, by John Maltby.*

H

H. *The lid of an Ian Godfrey jar, crowded with creatures, the largest of which acts as a knob.*
I. *A bold coil knob by Jane Hampton.*

the illustrations show something of the very wide range of forms possible.

The only essential practical aspects are that the fingers or hand should be able easily to grip the knob (i.e., it should be wider at the top or the center than it is at the base) and that it should be convenient in use (e.g., too high a knob on a casserole will soon become a casualty in the oven). Of course, any modelling should not be easily breakable when gripping the knob. The shape, size, and proportion compared to the whole pot is of paramount importance. A small, weak knob on the most handsome jar or teapot will effectively spoil it, while, on the other hand, a big, clumsy knob can overwhelm any form.

See also **teapot, butter dish, food warmer,** etc.

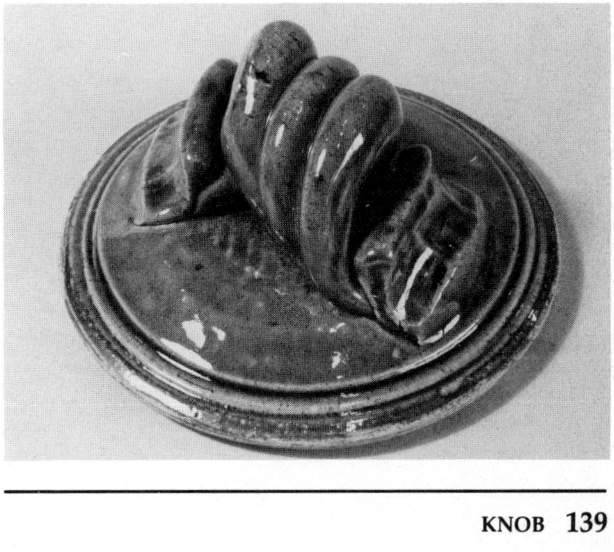

I

J. Almost a completion of the main form, this convoluted knob is by Mary White.
K. An original variation, dominating the box, by Sheila Casson.

J

K

L

L. An impressive double handle/knob by Andrew and Johana Young.

KOUTALA

In modern Greece the koutala is a **ladle,** and the koutali a smaller ladle or **spoon.**

KRATER

From the Greek verb meaning "to mix," and so, a mixing bowl for wine and water. It is found in various forms, but is always large and full bodied with opposed loop handles. The bell-krater is fuller in shape than the "volute" and other styles.

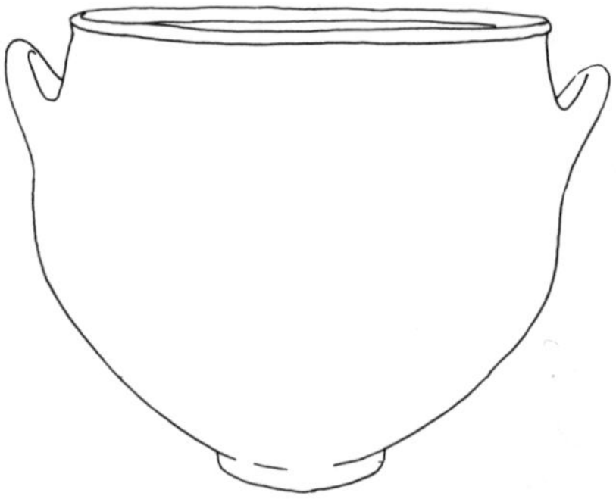

This generous open jar or mixing bowl is from 1300 B.C. Mycenae.

It is among the simplest and currently acceptable of the Greek shapes. Those from Mycenae are especially satisfying. The **stamnos** or wine jar is somewhat similar. See also illustration under **wishbone handle.**

A Sung Chinese ku. (Barlow Collection.)

KU

A stately Chinese form, which has simplifed a bronze original and adapted it to clay and glaze.

KUAN JAR

A massive Chinese wine jar with high shoulders and a rather wide mouth. These are mostly 14th century and early Ming. (See M.HCA in Booklist.)

KUEI

A wide-based, low-bellied bowl with two fairly large modelled vertical handles. They were made in China from Sung to Lung Ch'uan and later.

The kuei form exhibited quite a wide range of proportion and different types of handle. The drawing is based on a typical heavily glazed Lung Ch'uan celadon example.

KUGELHOPF

See **ring mold, cake mold.**

KUNDIKA

A Chinese water pot associated with India and Buddhism. A rounded body with a filler on the shoulder is surmounted by a long neck, which spreads and then contracts sharply to a spout at the top.

KYATHOS, Kyanthion

A Greek wine **ladle** in the form of a small-based cup with a high handle. In modern Greece the kyanthion is a shallow bowl or deep plate.

KYLIX

A shallow, wide **goblet** or **stem cup** with spreading horizontal handles, similar to a **tazza.** Some were modelled; there is one known that has a monkey's face.

A/B. A deep and shallower version of the Greek kylix, circa 500 B.C. Although rigid, and, to modern eyes, unclaylike, these cups have a certain dramatic appeal and forthrightness. The horizontal handles are open ones, not lugs, as the silhouettes could suggest.

A

B

L

LABORATORY VESSEL

A number of containers used in chemistry are made of heat-resistant porcelain. They are not craft pieces, but their design is often an object lesson in simplicity and fitness for purpose.

LADING POT

A half-gallon pot with a large handle used for bailing water from the boiler to the washtub. They are usually cylindrical.

LADLE

A large **spoon** in the form of a small bowl on a stem. Many modern ladles imitate metal styles, and the stem is often too slender to sustain a long life. The early potters did better, and there are ladles from as far back as Neolithic cultures which show considerable design ability and fitness for purpose.

A

A. A beautifully integrated ladle/spoon from Czechoslovakia, 3000 B.C.
B. A delicate and rather vulnerable early 19th century sifter ladle in Creamware. (Salisbury Museum.)

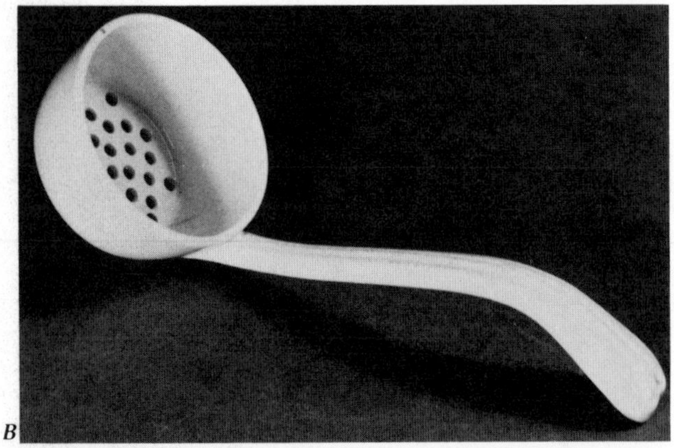

B

C

C. A slightly sturdier ladle in slipware by Michael Cardew, 1938. It is about 8 inches/200mm long. (Crafts Study Centre, Bath.)

Common to most ladles is a hook or backward curve at the end, which rests over the rim of a bowl or pot and prevents it from falling into the liquid. In many early forms the handle and bowl are integrated and merge one into the other. The modern Chinese soup spoon is of this type. In others a bowl with a slightly constricted neck is given a stem with a hook, sometimes modelled as a bird or animal head. See also **milk ladle, stacking pots.**

LAMP

According to *Webster's New Collegiate Dictionary*, "a vessel with a wick burning inflammable liquid (e.g., oil) to produce light." An essential item of household equipment throughout the ages, the lamp has taken on many and varied forms. The simplest is the Japanese **elbow dish.** One stage more elaborate is a shallow dish or plate folded inwards to accommodate the wick, the so-called "cocked-hat" design, which gives very satisfying shapes. More sophisticated lamps separated the burning end of the wick from the oil container in various ways, as in the ubiquitous and often highly modelled Roman hand or altar lamp, which could accommodate several

A. Lively and amusing, this triple lamp was made in Nigeria.

B. A simply folded "cocked hat" lamp. Possibly from Nineveh or similar origin, circa 700 B.C.

A

B

wicks (nine are known) in very attractive designs. Larger Near Eastern vessels had high, long open-topped **spouts.** Roman lamps were frequently given as birthday presents with suitable devices and good wishes incorporated in the pattern. From Saxon/Norman times a shape is found resembling a large, traditional U.K. **eggcup.** The wide-necked Islamic mosque lamps had three lugs for hanging from chains and may have been fitted with a fat candle. A globular pot on a stem, with a spreading base and a spout and lid, burned grease or oil in 19th century America and was called a "slut lamp."

Lanterns or "lanthorns," open-fronted pots resembling house models, were made in 18th century Bristol tin-glazed ware, and also in lead-glaze of which a dated example "1712 Isa Wood" is known. These probably held candles. A triple lamp from Nigeria is an interesting shape, which could be a starting point for modern forms (see illustration B). Today the flame has been replaced by the filament of an electric lamp, and it is for this type that potters have designed some imaginative ceramics, often in porcelain, which is shown in its full attraction when light is shining through it. Eva Anderson's "trees" on hills are of this type. (See CR29 in Booklist.) See also **lamp base, light shade, night-light holder, chills, candlestick.**

LAMP BASE

Although with electric light we no longer need a reservoir to hold fuel, lights are still perched up on pots and other pedestals, which are used to raise them from the floor or table, but which are otherwise purely decorative. Many Chinese and other pots have been barbarously drilled to take flex and other fittings. Almost any pot can be utilized, but many are made for the purpose. These may be aesthetically incomplete until fully fitted with lamp and shade. The unresolved form, however, is anathema to many potters and prevents them venturing into the field, so that one of the most common modern household requirements is left to the often garish industrial object.

A

A. An interesting flanged form by Gordon Baldwin, which would give highlights and shadowed areas. The shade would represent a completion of the form.

B

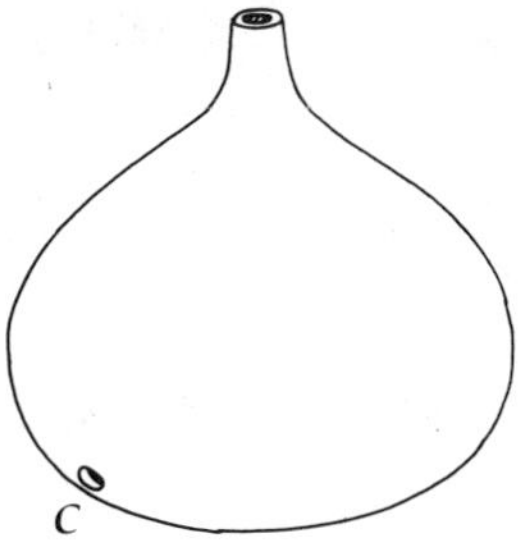

C

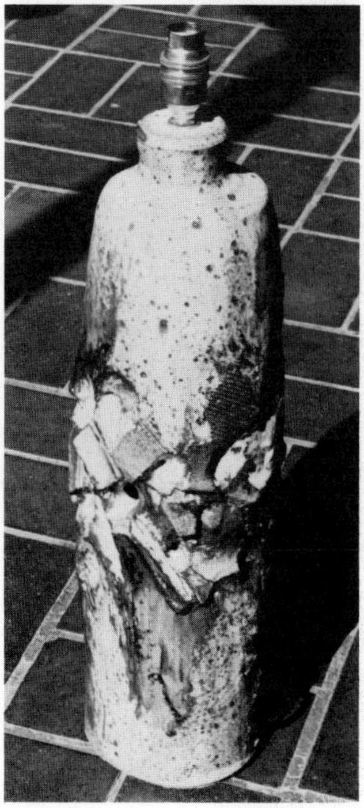

D

B/C. Two contrasting lamp bases—one built up in rings, rigid, and angular; the second of the type made by Derek Davies, very stable and full formed.
D. A hand-built, hacked cylinder lamp base by Colin Kellam.
E. Two dramatic slab-built lamp bases by Sheila Fournier. (Photograph: John Anderson.) See next page.

The bottle is the most common form, sometimes with a longish neck, but squat, square shapes also occur. The latter may need a brass tube to raise the lamp and shade. A tall form with good stability is normally the best solution.

LAMP FILLER

Small jars from ancient times, with narrow necks and a small "teat" on the side from which oil was poured. They have also been called "baby feeders," but this function is now in doubt.

E

LAMP POST

In CMjun78 (see Booklist), a full-sized ceramic lamp post from modern Canton, China, is illustrated.

LANDSCAPE

Chinese **hill jars** and **brush rests** (see under **brush jar/rest**) with their stylized mountains are evocations of landscape, but examples are rare in the history of pottery. The landscape has, however, been widely exploited in recent years by the studio potter. Among the early examples were Ian Godfrey's "dishes with objects" in which he managed to suggest wide vistas by means of proportion and texture—landscapes each with its petrified story or incident. Richard Dunning in CR5 (see Booklist) says "These delectable objects satisfy the vision, the tactile sense, and the imagination." Bryan Newman builds **towns** and landscapes set on often boat-shaped base forms, with stylized trees, birds, and fungi. Peter Lane discusses "My hills" in CR34 (see Booklist): "The smooth round blandness of the Downs is cut away to encourage curiosity and tempt imagination. I would not pretend they have any deep artistic significance. They are objects for enjoyment; reality and fantasy—a kind of peep-show."

In Santa Fe in June, 1978, an entire exhibition was given over to the landscape theme. See also **alcarraza, cut rim.**

A. An almost two-dimensional "garden landscape with urn" by John Maltby.

A

B

C

B. By subtle proportions, glaze effects, and minimal modelling, this dish, about 13 inches/330mm square, is transformed into a landscape large enough to get lost in. By Ian Godfrey.
C. In contrast, a fairly crowded little farmstead by Rosemary Wren, 1979.

LARNAX, Larnaca

A terra-cotta chest from Minoan and Mycenaean times, used for the burial of the dead. See also **bath.** In the modern Greek National Anthem there is a phrase which, roughly translated, goes: "Greece

A very curious, slipper-shaped pottery Parthian coffin complete with cover, glazed and decorated. The larnax was the standard form of burial in this area from 200 B.C. to 200 A.D.

has been the larnaca of many brave men." The chests were often highly decorated and decorative in form. There is a rich collection in the Hania Museum in Crete. Strange, half-closed clay coffins were in use in Parthia from 200 B.C. to 200 A.D.

LAWS OF POTTERY FORM

Leach, in *A Potter's Book,* lists some of these "laws," but warns that they should be considered only as generalizations based on sense experience. No formula, however accurate, can take the place of direct perception. The following statements sum up his understanding of pottery form:

1. Ends of lines are important; the middles take care of themselves.
2. Lines are forces and the points at which they change or cross are significant and call for emphasis.
3. Vertical lines are of growth, horizontal lines are of rest, diagonals are of change.
4. Straight line and curve, square and circle, cube and sphere are the polarities which [the potter] works into a rhythm of form under one clear concept.
5. Curves for beauty; angles for strength.
6. A small foot for grace; a broad one for stability.
7. Enduring forms are full of quiet assurance. Overstatement is worse than understatement.

The last "law" would not find much echo in the work of many modern potters, especially in America, but it is a fact that one gets tired soonest of pots which shout too loudly. See also **analysis of form.**

LEAF DISHES

Dishes in the form of leaves were made in the 18th century and onwards for sauces, pickles, etc. on the table. They are often made today by impressing a leaf onto a slab of clay, cutting round the shape, and then lifting the edges to form a dish—not a very creative exercise. They may also be formed over a mold. They require a degree of simplification and conscious design if they are to have any value.

Characteristic of the type of leaf dish very common from the 18th century onwards. Possibly Wedgwood, circa 1775. (Bristol Museum.)

LEATHER FORM

Leather flasks and other typical forms have been copied by potters throughout history. Sometimes the results are rather slack, baggy shapes as in the German *beutelflasche,* but they can also be much more taut and attractive. Witness the T'ang and

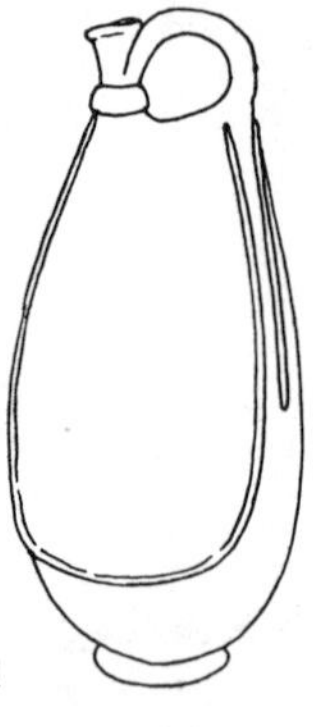

A

A. A fluent Liao period (10th/11th century) Chinese leather-form bottle, the original stitching of which was transformed into a raised linear decoration.

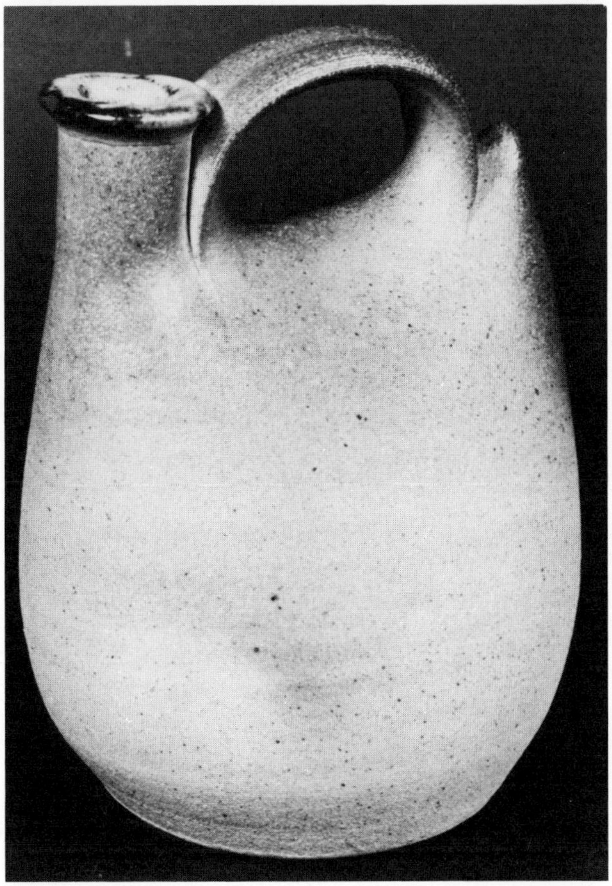

B

B. The same technique, a closed-in pot with added neck, by John Leach.

Liao Chinese bottles, forms which have been adapted in the present century by craft potters by closing in the top of a thrown shape. Leather black-jacks were made by Doulton.

LEBES

In ancient Greece, a ceremonial pedestal bowl.

LEI

A Chinese jar shape derived from bronze; a tall wine vessel with a short neck and wide shoulders, circular or rectangular in plan.

LEKANOS

See **plate.**

LEKYTHOS

A Greek oil bottle/jug with a narrow neck for slow pouring (the word is associated with the Greek verb meaning "to pour"), and a simple, but strong handle. Reputedly used chiefly for funerary rites.

A typical late-classic-period Greek Lekythos.

LEMON SQUEEZER, Juicer

The traditional British form is a fluted mound surrounded by a well with a pouring lip. Modern potters have made them by throwing the form and carving the flutes. In CMdec78 (see Booklist), Ron Bower shows a citrus fruit squeezer set in a wooden handle, the fruit being held in the hand while dejuicing.

The basic form of the lemon squeezer. The top section would lift from the lower container, which often has a lip for pouring the juice.

LENTICULAR

Shaped like a lentil; a double convex. See, for instance, **pilgrim bottle, hot-water bottle.**

An early European (La Tene) lenticular bodied pot.

LEYS JAR

An historian's name for a squat Chinese jar shape with a wide flaring mouth.

LID

According to *The Concise Oxford Dictionary*, "a detachable cover for an aperture, especially for the opening at the top of a vessel." Few lids of very early vessels have survived; either they have been broken and lost or else most of the pots were open. The general absence of **flanges** or **galleries** suggests the latter. There are splendid Greek lidded boxes and some amphoras and pitchers had lids, but a majority of wares, up to and including those of Medieval times, appear to have been open.

A

A. This lid, on a powerfully designed Iranian "faience" box, from 1st millennium B.C., *was apparently tied on through the corner lobes or lugs.*

B

B. A strong flanged lid on a deep Sung bowl, the curve of the lid reflecting the lower curve and following through the main form. (Barlow Collection.)

Lids are more common, but are still comparatively rare on Far Eastern pots and jars. There are vessels from the Silla period of Korea, where pot and lid have an equal role in the design. They are, says Rhodes (see R.PF in Booklist), some of the world's greatest lidded pots. The Eastern Chou tou (350 B.C.) had a reversible lid, which could be stood down on its flat spreading knob and possibly used as a cup, and there are also bold lidded pots of quite remarkable form from the 500 B.C. Jomon period of Japan.

In the West, a Roman circular **divided dish** in the Colchester Museum has a flanged rim which suggests a lid; a Roman grave jar has a lid, but no seating to keep it steady; while another large banded and **carinated** pot has a tall, equally carinated lid and knob which continues and completes the silhouette, making the whole piece look like a bottle. A small cup again has a lid but no flange, but an attractive Roman box or jar, about 10 inches in diameter, has a lid fitting over an upright short neck on the pot (see diagram under **lid seating**). A 16th century chamber pot has a flanged rim which would be pointless without a lid, though none has survived.

These examples are, however, the exceptions rather than the rule. Many bread crocks had (and have) turned wooden lids, and some older pots may

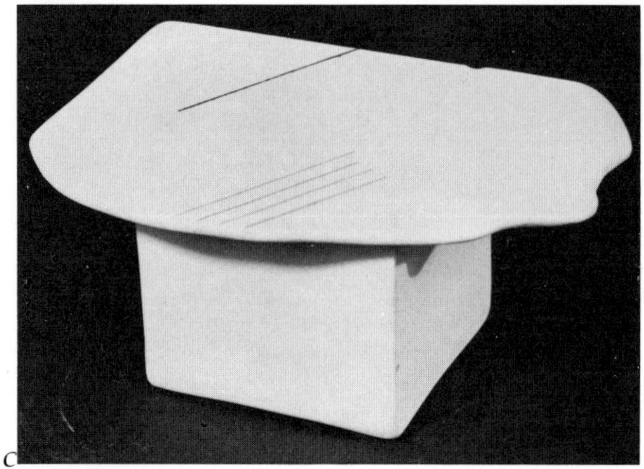

C

C. A sculptured lid for which the box is merely a stand, by Gordon Baldwin.

have been fitted in the same way; but in general it appears that some sort of material was stretched across the top and this is even true of most of the **albarelli.** See also **lid seating, box, knob, sliding lid.**

Lids are normally thrown either upside down in the form of a shallow bowl on a stem, which is later reversed and turned to shape, or flat on the wheel head, complete with knob. Under **lid seating** the entry shows a number of basic types. A method of throwing a convex lid and knob in one piece was illustrated in PQ44 (see Booklist) by Ian Hinchcliffe. "The snug fit of lids is a matter which deserves special attention, for it gives particular satisfaction to the user," says Leach in L.PB (see Booklist). See also many other examples of lids under **knob, box, slip-cast, tea pot, casserole,** etc.

LID SEATING

The seating of a lid is simply a method of ensuring that it will not fall off during the normal use of a pot. A tea or coffeepot lid will, therefore, demand a firmer seating than that of a purely decorative **box.** A close, firm fit between lid and pot gives great satisfaction to the user, both from a practical and aesthetic point of view. The diagrams here (taken from F.DPP) show the main types of seating and the appropriate lid forms. See F.DPP (Booklist) for a discussion of these fittings. See also under **building.**

A

A. As mentioned in text, the lid seatings on many ancient pots are nonexistent or, as on the slight recess in the lid of this Romano-British bowl, rather ineffective. (Devizes Museum.)

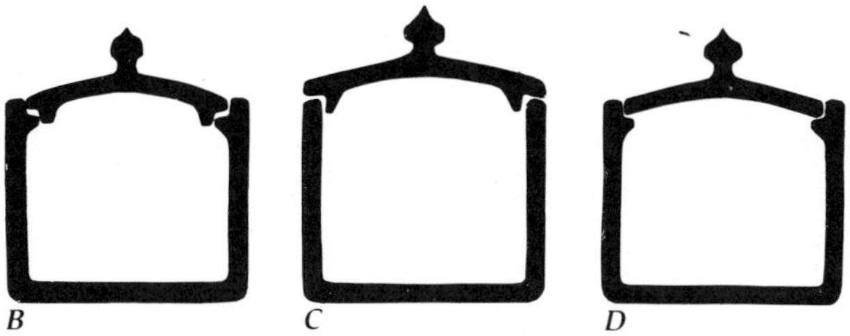

B *C* *D*

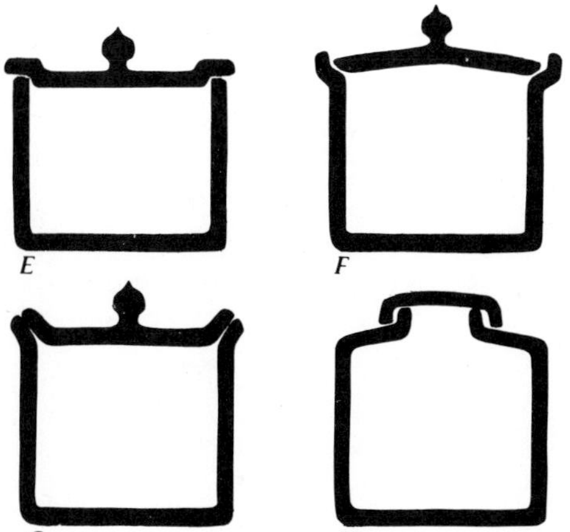

E *F* *G* *H*

B–H. These diagrams sum up the main types of lids and seatings. See F.DPP (Booklist) for fuller discussion.

I/J. A number of potters today use an irregular junction between lid and body to hold the lid in place, as shown in these boxes by Sheila Fournier and Eileen Lewenstein.

I

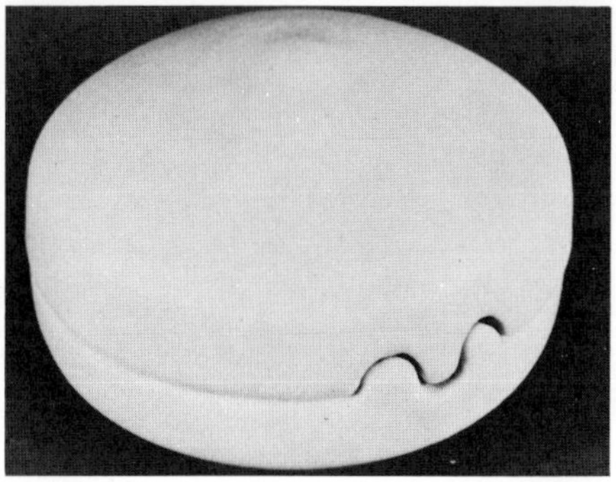

J

LIGHT PULL

See **pull handle.**

LIGHT SHADE

The advent of electricity has made the light shade an almost universal necessity, but few potters have attempted the rather unlikely medium of ceramics for this purpose. Use has been made of perforations

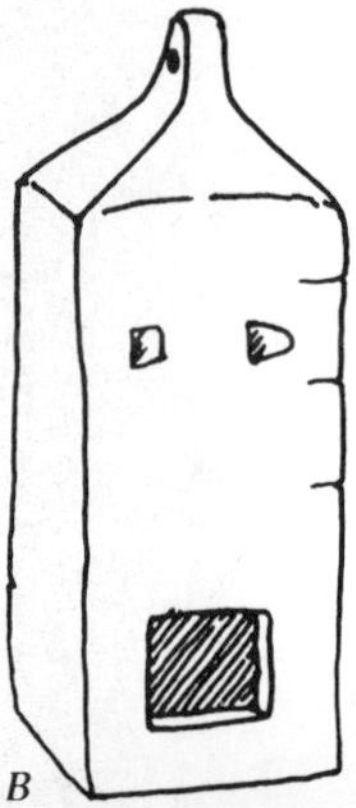
B

B/C. A lamp-holder "shade" in the form of a house from 150 B.C. Alexandria, and a modern "block of flats" variation on the same idea by Molly Watkins.

A. The perforated type of ceramic light shade, in this case described as a night-light cover, but the principle is similar. By Ian Godfrey.

A

C

through opaque material or by exploiting the translucence of porcelain.

In a sense the old lanterns (see **lamp**) were shades, protecting and directing the light, but here it was feeble and the eyes needed no protection from it.

The hanging cylinder will direct the light downwards over a limited area when this is needed, especially if the inside is glazed a light color; it can also be perforated with holes or designs. More ingenious systems for standing lights have been evolved.

LIP

The *Concise Oxford Dictionary* gives "lip" as "the edge of a vessel," but in this book we have called this the **rim.** *Webster's* gives "a projecting edge: a short spout as on a pitcher," which is nearer to our definition; i.e., the pouring area of a jug, mixing bowl, etc. A lip is necessarily open; if closed over, it becomes a **spout.**

The pouring lip is not common in primitive or Far Eastern ceramics, where a spout is more often added to control the flow of liquid. In ancient Greece the simple deformation of a flaring rim forms a lip, a style which has continued in Italy and the Mediterranean to the present day. The lips of Medieval pitchers, while not always beautiful, are very varied and generally well defined.

Craft potters often "pull" a lip from a generous rim, a section of which is thereby thinned and

A. This rather excessively formed lip derived from early Greek originals. This is from 17th century Teruel, Spain, and the type is known as "trefoil."

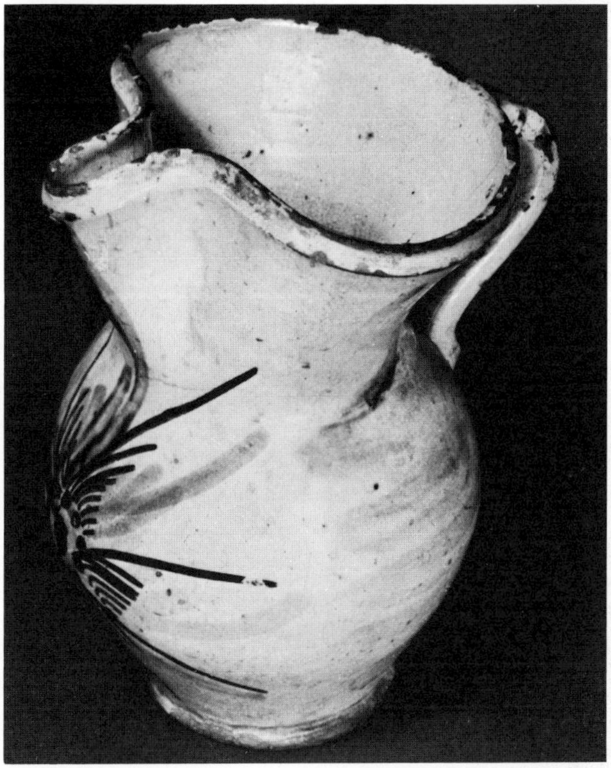

A

B

C

B. A standard, fully rounded lip on a mixing bowl by the author, its form emphasized by the glaze.
C. A lip given prominence by stretching and raising it as it was formed. By David Morris.

stretched so that the lip becomes a distinct aspect of the form. It may also be started well down the neck of a vessel, altering its silhouette and giving extra interest. At the other extreme, the lip can be simple, perhaps a cut depression in the thick rim of a mixing bowl or **mortar,** although on many Roman and early mortars the lip is a thing of great interest and beauty. Lips can also be cut from the rim itself, as on many Minoan, Cretan, and Near Eastern pots, or added as a separate entity, either modelled or from a small thrown shape. See an extreme example under **jug/pitcher.**

LOBE

From the Greek *lobos,* "a pod." In *The Shorter Oxford Dictionary* lobes are given as "rounded, projecting parts, separated by a fissure."

There are fine pieces from China, where a five-lobed bowl or dish is called a **mei-hua p'an,** and a bowl with flat lobes is known as a **sunflower bowl.** Lobed bowls were made in Tudor England. Subtle, modified lobes sometimes surround Turkish and Japanese plates and Delft dishes. The original inspiration was probably a petal or flower. The style is rarely practiced in modern pottery, where, if the rim is touched at all, it is **cut** or **slashed** in a bolder and more irregular manner.

A

B

A. A lobed dish from Sung China. (Barlow Collection.)

B. There is no halfheartedness about this sharply lobed 17th century cup or bleeding bowl found at Cornhill, London.

LOOM WEIGHT

Various shapes of loom weights have been found from Bronze Age Britain and other places. They are generally flat and often triangular with two holes through the thinner section. There are also circular, doughnutlike Saxon weights up to 6 inches/150mm across.

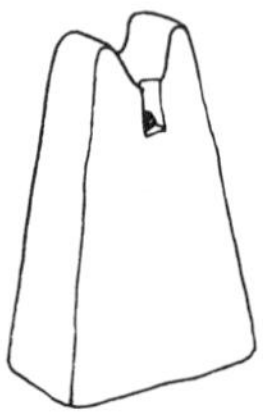

A formally interesting 2nd century loom weight.

LOTUS CUP

A Chinese bowl with lobed wall and a fluted top, resembling the lotus flower.

LOVING CUP

A large drinking cup, the later types often shaped like a sporting trophy or urn, with two (sometimes double-curved) handles to enable it to be passed from one person to another at the close of a banquet. Such shared drinks gave rise to the phrase "hob-nobbing," i.e., from hob to nob, or give and take, in Northern and Midland England (see OBPP in Booklist). Hot toddy or similar liquors would be taken from a loving cup. Especially in its simpler forms it is quite a handsome vessel. The ancestor of the loving cup was the **tyg** and early forms of the loving cup resemble the tyg, although they are often more bulbous and with a neck like squat pitcher. It is surprising how long the unhygienic habit of sharing drinking vessels continued. The form was still being made in Devon in 1930, with four multiple handles, but by then it was probably purely decorative.

LOZENGE POT

A small 18th century drug pot.

LUG

The word comes from "ear," and hence, it is an ear-shaped projection, normally pierced to take a

A

A. A finely designed and potted 1750 Nottingham salt-glazed loving cup. Note the interesting shapes left between the handles and body and the detail at the lower junction. (Bristol Museum.)

rope or cord, and situated on the sides of a pot for carrying and tilting. A pierced lug can be said to become a **handle** when one can get one's finger through it.

The lug probably preceded the handle and appears on the earliest pottery. It is found on pre-Dynastic Egyptian pots, prehistoric Chinese wares,

B. A later "trophy"-type of loving cup.

B

A

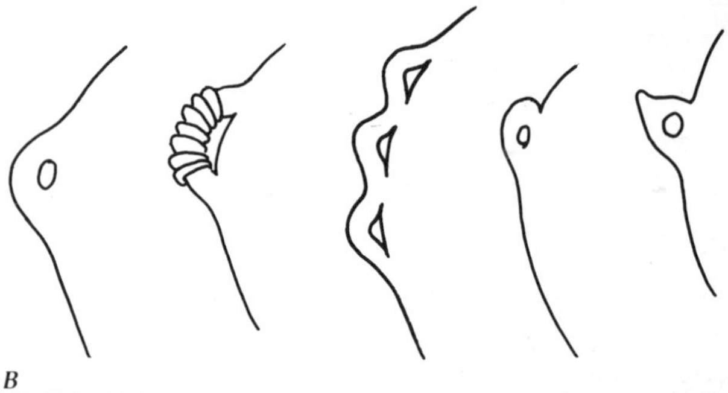

B

A. Like the ancient box under lid, *small lugs are used here with string. By Byron Temple.*
B. A variety of lug forms found on early pots. The first three may be horizontal or vertical.

ancient American pottery, on Minoan jars in great profusion, on Indian pots, etc. Even when its practical use declined, it often remained as a vestigial or decorative element. Lugs on T'ang and Sung pots are often purely ornamental and are frequently modelled in the form of masks, fishes, animals, lizards, etc. Lugs do not appear so often on Medieval pottery, which saw the great development of the handle.

The simplest and most common lugs consist of a pierced boss or a coil of clay hooped over and pressed home at each end. These and more elaborate and imaginative designs are found on modern pots. They are used for holding cane handles on **teapots,** for the strings on hanging planters, etc., and occasionally for less practical and more decorative purposes.

LUG HANDLE

This still retains the earlike form of the **lug,** but is usually larger as it is used for getting a grip on a **crock, casserole,** etc. when lifting with both hands. The horizontal lug handle is normally solid and slightly curved, though hooped types are also found.

The solid lug handle can be formed by applying a wet coil and working it into the wall with a back and forth movement of the fingers which shape it at the same time. It is finished off with a quick wipe of the thumb at either end. (See films *Isaac*

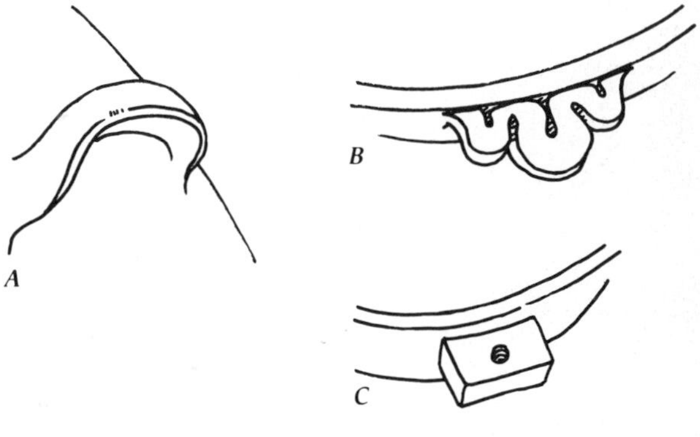

A/B/C. Three types of lug handle—the traditional crock handle, as described above; a modern coil handle (B¹); and a sharply cut block suitable for an angular or carinated *form.*

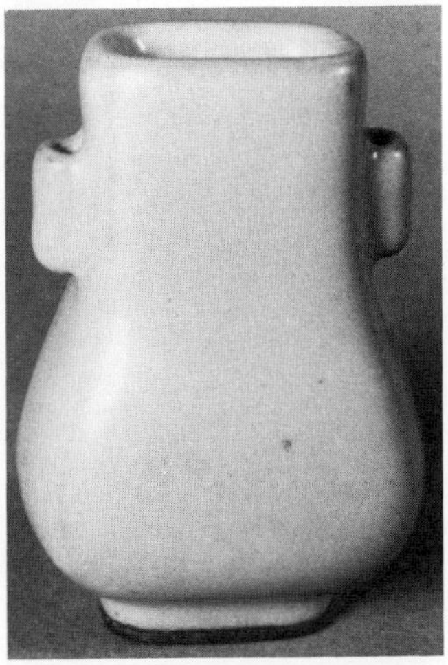

C

C. A pair of deep, vertical lugs on a Sung Chinese pot, now more decorative than useful, and blending with the general nature of the piece. (Barlow Collection.)

D

D. The flat lugs on this French salt-glazed jar help one to grip the pot and, as such, are really lug handles, *but they are also pierced for tying down the lid. Like the Sung pot, they are well integrated with the main form.*

E

E. Again, something between a lug and a lug handle are these fairly dominant additions to a jar. By David Morris.

D

D. A strong lug handle with decorative studs on a bowl, by David Winkley.

Button and *Big Ware*). The lug handle can also be cut from a slab, from a section of a pulled handle, or it can be modelled.

LUTROPHOROUS

An ancient Greek vessel with a long neck and two handles. It sometimes has a hole in the base for sprinkling libations over a grave.

The Sung version of the mallet or kinuta form, its severity modified by the tapering body, decorative handles, and thick glaze. (Barlow Collection.)

M

MAIDEN'S LEGS

Needle cases, tobacco stoppers, etc., were made in the form of shapely legs at Meissen and other potteries in the 18th century. Later examples became more plump!

MALLET SHAPE

A fairly straight-sided vessel with a sharp shoulder and a longish neck. The Japanese call the shape **kinuta.** It originated in Sung China (where it is called *chih-ch'ui ping*) as a celadon pot, often with pronounced opposed handles and a well-articulated contour well suited to the rich glaze which covered it. It was a popular form in Lung-ch'uan celadons.

See also **rouleau vase.** It is much admired in Japan and some Bizen pots resemble the form.

Although it is fundamentally a bottle, a favorite shape with modern potters, the kinuta is not often thrown and would be a pleasant addition to the repertoire of forms. It would also lend itself to beating and cutting. See **bud vase** for a version by Rosemary Wren.

MAMMIFORM

The term spelled this way does not appear in the Oxford or Webster dictionaries where the preference is for "mamilliform," although the spelling is often used in books, especially on archaeology. CTCD (see Booklist) gives the definition as "a nipple-shaped protuberance," but, in general use, a **costrel** for instance, has been described as flat on one side with a mammiform convexity on the other, and it is in this sense of a breast and only sometimes with a nipple that it is normally used in ceramics. The term has been used to describe the bases of certain early Cypriot pots or the feet of some Salvador bowls. See also **votive.**

MARBLE

Children's marbles have been made in pottery from at least ancient Egyptian times. Sixteenth century examples are shown in the Horniman Museum. They may be variegated or decorated. See **solitaire.**

MARMITE

From the French word meaning "stockpot" or "saucepan," but also applied to a rather smaller

A

A. Two sturdy lidded cooking pots, which might be called marmites, from the Leach Pottery.
B. A modern stewpot *in traditional form.*

B

casserole-type vessel. LG (see Booklist) points out that it may be with or without feet, depending on whether it is used on a hearth fire or a stove.

MASK

Pottery masks or **faces** used decoratively on pots, such as those on **bellarmines,** are not uncommon in ceramics, but the true, independent form is rare. There is a circular mask of some ferocity from early

A

A. A Capo San Marco mask of circa 500 B.C. *in which various features—the eyes, the mouth, the line of the skull, etc.—reflect and complement one another, building up a unified character.*
B. Another tragic mask with an overall formal unity, by Ruth Duckworth.

B

Jomon times in Japan, circa 1000 B.C., and an early European mask is illustrated here. There are "sun" masks from preColumbian America. Among modern potters, Ruth Duckworth has produced mask-like models.

MEASURE

Various simple, usually cylindrical, pots have been made through the ages for measuring quantities of grain, spirits, etc. While they must have been in very wide and common use, they rarely figure in museum collections. The most handsome are the Islamic grain measures, often labelled as **tankards,** with their excellent proportions and fine, angular handles. Roughly made and glazed small cylinders,

A. The general form of the Islamic grain measure. Isnik 1560–80.
B. Roughly thrown little pots from 14th century London, which are found in "sets" of different sizes and which may have been measuring pots.

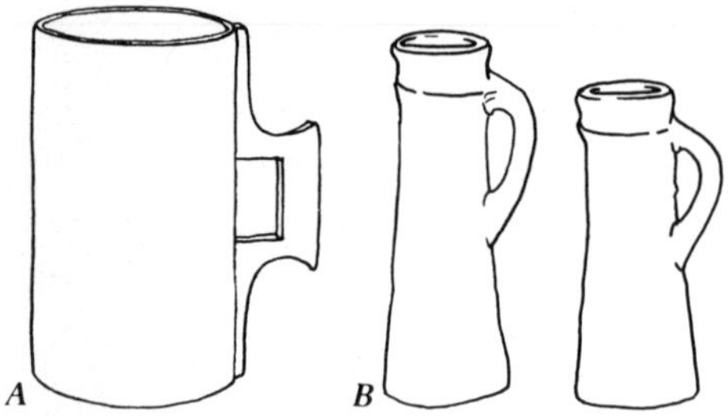

with a handle, about 2½ inches high and dating from the 17th century are labelled as "gin measures." These simple objects are more evocative of a way of life than are many more elaborate pieces.

MEAT DISH

Apart from the oval industrial dish potters have made a number of large, often rectangular dishes or trays for meat joints. From the 16th century rectangular dishes, some 18 by 13 inches/460 by 330mm with a thick flat handle and a sort of lip at each corner, were made at Bristol and elsewhere. A butcher's meat dish from Stockton-on-Tees in the 19th century was known as a **Welsh Tray.** (See B.CECP in Booklist.) See also **joint dish.**

MEDICINE TAKER

See **spoon.**

MEI-HUA P'AN

The word means "prunus blossom dish." It is a five-**lobed** dish or bowl from China.

MEI-P'ING

A Chinese pot form, known from the 10th century onwards, with a high shoulder and a small neck and mouth. Although tall versions are common, C.PPGT (see Booklist) mentions "a squat body," while Boger (see B.DA in Booklist) stipulates a "small" vase or **gallipot,** used to hold a flowering plum-blossom branch. There is a T'zu Chou truncated type (a wide bottle shape) and a Lung Ch'uan mei p'ing with six facets on the body and a straight neck. (See below and facing page.)

A/B. Tall and squat versions of the mei p'ing shape.

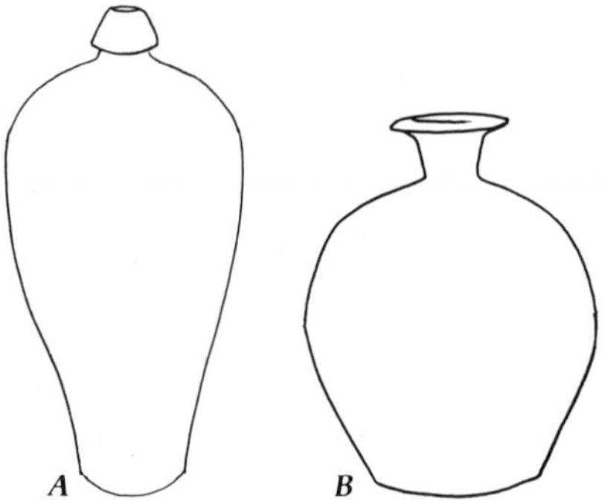

MEMO PAD

The memo pad illustrated is the only ceramic example I have ever seen. It is in a smoothly glazed

C

C. *A splendid T'zu Chou Sung Chinese painted mei p'ing. As is true with most of this type, there is a slight flare at the base. (Barlow Collection.)*

D

D. *A modern version by Bernard Leach, 1960, 13½ inches/345mm high.*

The memorandum block mentioned in the text, probably 19th century.

stoneware and probably needs a special crayon. In a modest way it shows the infinite variety of the potter's work.

MERCURY POT

Small stoneware corked pots of the type illustrated were reputed to have held mercury and were made as recently as the 1950s. The forms are unpretentious, but sturdy and satisfying.

Stoneware mercury pots.

METAL FORM

Most historians of ceramics confidently trace a number of pottery forms from metal originals, and there is good evidence for certain **bronze forms,** although pottery was made in vast quantities before metals came into general use. Were the metal workers so imaginative, or the potters so poorly equipped? The evidence often denies the latter and there are examples of influence both ways. Medley (see M.CP in Booklist) tells of a very silverlike goblet from 2500 B.C. China although no metal has ever been found on the Lung-shan sites. The rigid and unclaylike classic Greek pottery often suggest metal forms, but Arthur Lane, in an uncharacteristically fervent denial, writes in L.GP (see Booklist): "A loose generalization is sometimes made, to the effect that Greek potters habitually derived their shapes from metal vases. In a broad sense this is absurd; if at a certain time well-established workshops for pottery and metal-work exist, and a given form could be equally well expressed in either medium, we are quite unjustified in assuming without specific evidence that the form took concrete shape in this or that material. Form can be arrived at by empirical methods, as a happy accident supervening on the experimental manipulation of a material; or it may be a concept in the mind that struggles into tangible shape through whatever channels it can. Their literature, philosophy, and art show that the conceptual attitude to form was more deeply ingrained in the Greeks than in any other people of whom we know."

MILK COOLER

See **cooler.**

MILK LADLE

Rounded hand-built bowls with **wishbone handles** from the Bronze Age of Mediterranean countries are called "milk ladles" by dealers and archaeologists, though one would have thought that continuous soaking in milk might have left discoloration or other marking, which is not evident in the examples I have seen. They are very comfortable in the hand, with the thumb laid over the handle, and, therefore, make good **scoops** whether for milk or other materials. They are quite incredibly thin-walled and, like so many other soft earthenware early vessels, seem too fragile for general use. (Photograph: facing page.)

MILK PAN

This was usually a fairly shallow pan with straight, outward-sloping walls and a strong rim, used for separating cream from milk. It is about 12 inches/300mm across and 3 to 4 inches/75 to 100mm deep, but others are known which are much larger. It is very similar to a **pancheon.** Milk pans were fired on edge in rows at the top of the kiln. Vessels for the same purpose must have been in common use in ancient times but no typical pot is described as serving the specific function of separating cream from milk. The shape described above was found in the country districts of 18th and 19th century Europe and America. Cardew, in his book *Pioneer Pottery*, mentions milk pans in connection with a lip "which pours well and does not distort the circle" of the rim. A fine milk pan is illustrated in G.EAFP (see Booklist).

An amusing Cypriot scoop, often known as a "milk ladle," with the wishbone handle modelled as a face; possibly 1500 B.C.

MILK SKIMMER

A small bowl on a handle, like a **ladle,** but perforated like a colander. (See C.PPGT in Booklist.) Used for clotted cream?

MINGEI WARE

A Japanese peasant pottery of often bold and lively form.

MIRROR FRAME

See **frame.**

MIXING BOWL

A **pancheon** was a mixing bowl, but this had virtually straight sides, while the modern preference is for some curvature to contain the material being mixed. A smallish base, a sturdy rim, and perhaps a flat area on one side near the base so that the bowl can be tipped and still hold firm are the characteristics. Elizabeth David always champions earthenware for this purpose, but stoneware is equally acceptable so long as it is not too heavy and the glaze is a smooth one. Many mixing bowls do not have a lip.

MOLDED DISH

See **pressed dish/bowl.**

MOLDED FORM

Leach states both the dangers and advantages of the plaster mold in L.PB (see Booklist): "There is no question as to the convenience of . . . plaster . . . but it is debatable whether from the point of view of beauty, plaster is to be welcomed, not so much because of any inherent evil in the material as of the fatal facility with which it has been used to multiply florid forms." About industrial molded shapes, however, he writes: "Practical domestic crockery . . . though seldom beautiful has nevertheless brought a large measure of physical refinement into millions of homes."

Molded forms have been with us for thousands of years—the Egyptians made them in a small way; the Romans very widely. Hard-setting plaster is a very ancient material. The Chinese used molds very circumspectly, usually made of pottery biscuit. Today Leach has himself used two- and three-piece molds for noncircular shapes, and there has been a widespread return to molded shapes, often used as elements in a larger composition, in schools of art.

As mentioned under **jigger and jolley ware,** the molding of pottery imposes its own limitations, but the "fatal facility," especially of multipiece *slip* molds, has often lead to the breakdown of aesthetic discipline. There is not the space here to discuss the complex considerations involved, but it seems clear that the identity of the individual craft potter is intimately connected with his hands, as well as his imagination and invention, and, if this prime characteristic is removed, it would be more honest of him to move into the factories. Others would argue that it is possible to be truly creative with the use of molds. See also under **slip-cast form, cheese dish, tobacco jar, cup,** etc., and illustrations under **press molding.**

A press-molded bowl from Roman Gaul. It is very sharp and industrial in concept. (British Museum.)

MONEY BOX, Money bank, Penny bank, Piggy bank

Money boxes in pottery have been made at least since the Middle Ages, but, because they usually had to be broken to retrieve the savings, few survive whole. While many were in the shape of a conventional pot, closed in at the top and finished with a little knob, they were also modelled as chickens, cottages, beehives, cats, and the like. Several pots may have been luted onto one another, forming **double gourds** or even triple ones, and covered with small birds and figures, etc., or made in other extravagant forms such as bird cages. They were also made as chests of drawers (see **furniture**), or as dressers in Yorkshire. The inscription "George Fisher, 12 Jan 1862" appears on a round thatched cottage model. As coins became larger in the 19th century, so money boxes followed suit. The best-known box in England is the Sussex Piggy Bank (imitated elsewhere), which originally was decorated with run slip.

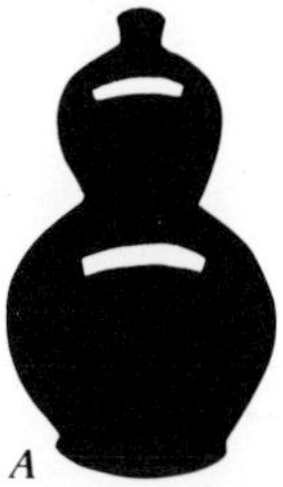

A

A. A typical 18th/19th century double money box form.

B

B. *A late 18th century Worcestershire money box with a bird whistle on top.*
C. *A thrown 19th century country pottery money box with modelling and additions to represent a chicken. Quickly made and lively.*
D. *Made from two pinch pots by a twelve-year-old, this hippo money box manages to suggest some of the monumental weightiness of the animal.*

C

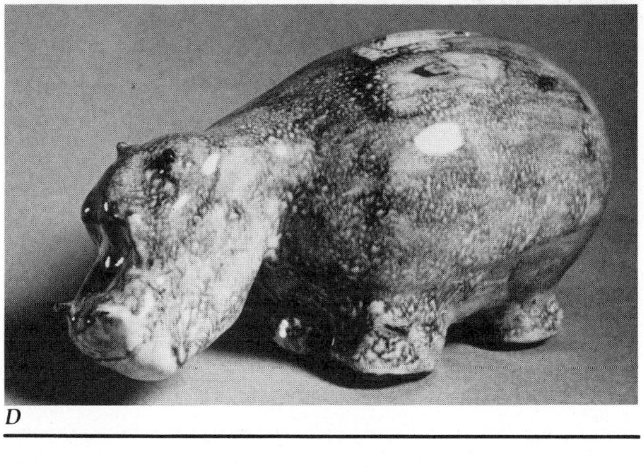

D

MONTEITH

A large **punch bowl** with a scalloped rim, the word deriving from the name of a 17th century eccentric who wore a cloak with a scalloped hem. See *Webster's New Collegiate Dictionary*. In some examples two-thirds of a circle is cut at intervals from around the rim. Small cups may have been hung in these embrasures, or glasses held in the grooves by their stems, the heads being kept cool in water in the bowl. Some 18th century monteiths are rather graceless, though others are more successful, and the idea could well be adapted today for practical or ornamental use.

MORTAR, Mortarium

In early times this was a large, heavy, usually shallow bowl with embedded grit or an otherwise roughened interior surface, used for grinding food into paste. These humble utensils rarely find much space in the histories of ceramics, but they must have been an indispensable item in most kitchens, where they were used for grinding or crushing a variety of foods. They usually had a pronounced rounded rim for strength and a lip (more rarely an added open spout). The lip is often magnificently strong and positive and deserves study by any potter. The Chinese had their own mortar forms—a shallow form with splayed sides in porcelain and a Tingware hexagonal mortar have been quoted. Their functions must have been somewhat different from the thick, bold Roman and other types.

A. These Roman mortaria are truly splendid pottery shapes and the formation of the lip is often more powerful and elaborate than on this example. (Devizes Museum.)

A

B

B. In a totally different style and without any lip at all is this charming mortar and pestle by David Eeles.

The modern mortar is a smooth hemispherical bowl of thick porcelain or fine stoneware with a firm, slightly splayed or **rolled** foot and a blunt, cut lip. It is used by chemists etc. for grinding small quantities of rocks, oxides, etc. Except for experimental work, most grinding is now done in ball or vibratory mills. The mortar is still sometimes used in the kitchen by devoted cooks, and a few craft potters cater to this need. The mortar is always used with a **pestle,** a smooth stone or pottery implement which is worked round and round with the hand.

MUFFIN DISH

A flat dish or plate with a high cover, either hemispherical or more or less cylindrical.

MUG

Probably of Scandinavian origin, e.g., *mugge* (Norwegian), meaning "a pitcher with a handle." The term is now generally applied to a drinking vessel with more or less vertical walls. It is often looked upon as a somewhat plebeian term for a **beaker,** but it suggests a thicker fabric and a less elegant style. It nearly always has a handle. It has also been described as similar to a **tankard,** but with no cover and smaller. In a Nottinghamshire stoneware potter's catalog of 1700, it is listed (and naively illustrated) as "A Mogg." T.L. Peacocke mentions its use in the early 19th century (quoted in D.EBYC—see Booklist): "The Rev. Dr. Gaster found himself rather queasy in the morning, therefore preferred breakfast in bed on a mug of buttered ale and an anchovy toast." One wonders what his breakfast might have been had he felt well!

According to B.CECP (see Booklist), the mug attained some importance in the early 18th century after numerous stages of development during the preceding hundred years, and was used for soups, stews, porridge, etc., sometimes holding a pint and a half. The meeas (mease) mug was round-bodied and used for soup with oatcake in the 18th/19th centuries. It had a single-finger loop handle, a style common to many mugs from Roman times onwards. In the Annual Register for 1775 there is an "Ode on the Breaking of a China Quart Mug belonging to the Buttery of Lincoln College, Oxford." To quote a few lines from this timeless verse, the

This typical 18th century mug has strength in the body and style in the sharp rise of the handle. (Bristol Museum.)

author points out that it might not have broken "Had'st thou been formed of coarser earth / Had Nottingham but given thee birth," a reference to Nottingham salt-glaze. The rest of the pots bemoan its fate: "in guggling tone / Decanters pour out their moan / and sympathising Tankards drop't a tear."

Rhodes in R.PF (see Booklist), remarks that the mug "suggests a more hearty and uninhibited way of life than the cup and saucer" and adds that "old Staffordshire mugs are best" and "for some mysterious reason beer tastes better in a pottery mug than from glass or from the can."

The mug is at once the most common and often the least considered shape in the potter's output. Because variation is limited, proportion and balance should be carefully considered. A squat barrel shape too often eventuates, especially from the amateur potter. The simpler the form the more precise should be its definition and design. It is a form in which early industrial potters had the edge on their craft colleagues.

MUKOZUKI

A small dish or deep bowl for a light meal taken before the Japanese Tea Ceremony. They were made in a great variety of styles and shapes often richly decorated. See under **bail** for illustration of one unusual type.

MULTIPLE POTS

The joining of individual pots into more complex forms has always been part of the potter's stock-in-trade. Usually described as "ritual" pots, they often display a great *jeu d'esprit* and are technically very capable; e.g., four joined bowls with a very tall stylized figure rising from the center made at Lapithos, Cyprus, 2000 B.C. There is also the **kernos,** consisting of little bowls or pots set on a hollow ring. In 18th century England **fuddling cups** were built up of many separate pieces. See also **composite pots.**

Today the technique is widely practiced, the pots usually being cut into sections and the result more sculptural than the historic examples mentioned. Chris Jenkins in CR45 (see Booklist), shows a very satisfactory lobed complex built up from cut bowls.

A. Three bell-shaped pots are joined at the belly and set up on stems. From the 1st millennium B.C. Iran, possibly used for libations.

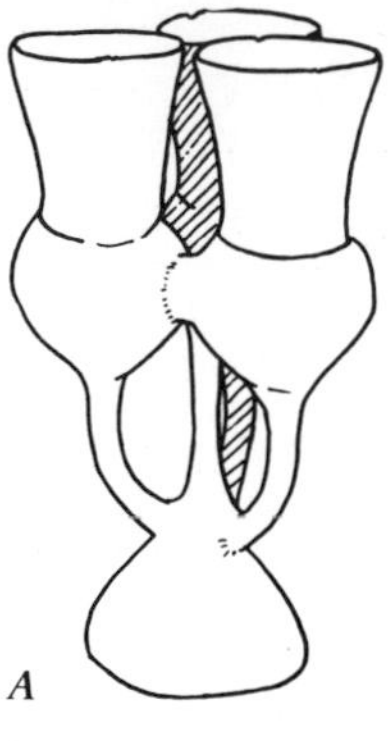

A

B. A little twin-cup cosmetic pot from ancient Egypt.

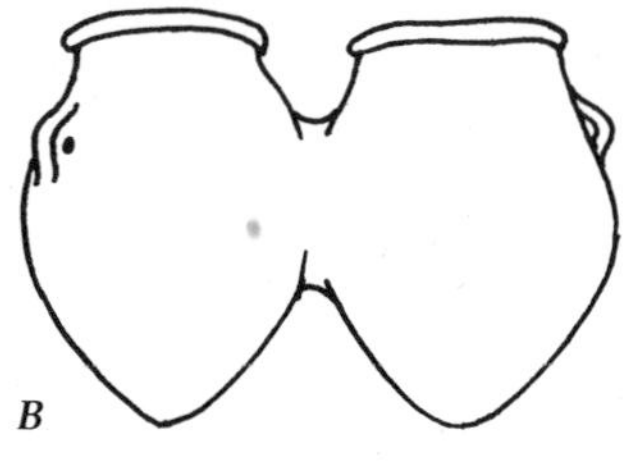

B

MURDERERS' HOUSES

Favorite subjects in 19th century pottery were model houses or cottages that had been the sites of famous or particulary gruesome murders or other crimes. Sometimes they were complete with an out-of-scale figure of the criminal, taking the place of the "popular" press of today.

MUSICAL INSTRUMENTS

Many musical instruments are possible in pottery. **Horns** have been made in many parts of the world, including America ancient and modern; **whistles** and **flutes** go back almost as far as pottery itself. In CMapr78 (see Booklist) two Chinese "lutes" are illustrated. In addition many percussion instruments, such as tubular and other types of **bell,** a kazoo, **drums,** glockenspiel bars, etc., are possible. CR49 (see Booklist) contained an article by M.J. French with many ideas for making musical pottery in schools. In India the "jaltarung" consists of porcelain cups struck like a xylophone. See also **ocarina.**

MUSTACHE CUP

These were fairly large cups or mugs with a bridge across the drinking side of the rim to keep a droopy mustache dry. Although mustaches have recently become stylish again, they now, apparently, just

The typical late 19th century mustache cup with its decorative inset flange.

get wet. Rhodes, in *Pottery Form*, however, tells us that the cups have had a revival in the sixties in the United States.

MUSTARD POT

In the 18th century handled, often cylindrical lidded pots were made especially for serving mustard at the table. The pot is now usually part of the **cruet** set and is designed to blend with salt and pepper **shakers.**

A charming salt-glaze pot, reputedly French, in which mustard was sold. A central hole in the top is for the spoon.

N

NARGHILE

See **water pipe.**

NECK

The part of a pot between shoulder and rim. Some pots are like fish and have no neck; others are like swans, where the neck is a focus of attention. A basic body form will change character when fitted with different necks. The precise curve and width of a neck involves great subtlety and a few fractions of an inch can make or break a form. See also **bottle, garlic vase, thrown shape, wine bottle, bud vase, double-necked pot.**

A

A. A variety of necks applied to identical bodies.

B. A hand-built form with 3 necks, by Peter Wright. Although an integrated form, the carved decoration gives even more point to the multiple neck.

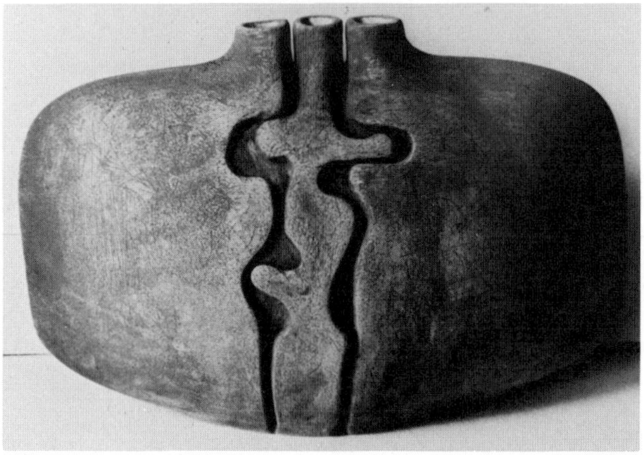

B

NIGHT-LIGHT HOLDER

Lanterns were made in the 19th century to hold a short candle or night-light. They were typically cylindrical with a conical roof and a handle at the top or on the side. An opening was cut in the wall to take the candle and to direct and protect the light. See also **candlestick.**

Today several potters make night-light holders either for illumination or for keeping food or drink warm. See **food warmer.** A simple form is a slab-built cube with varied openings for the light, but they can be thrown and very decorative.

This slab-built night-light holder has sufficient ventilation, a requirement sometimes not adequately taken care of.

NOAH'S ARK

A perennial subject for childrens' toys. It has been used in a sophisticated way by several potters, including Ian Godfrey's ark in several pieces, Lorraine McGuinness's tiny porcelain model with a tortoise, and Alan Heap's ark with ladder and willfully disproportionate creatures.

A simple and sculptural coiled version, albeit singularly unpopulated, of Noah's Ark, floating in its own sea. By Elizabeth Fritsch, 1974.

NOGGIN

A term used in England since the early 17th century for a small cup or mug of about one gill, or a quarter of a pint, in capacity. It is now sometimes used for a glass of beer, but on this rating a "noggin of ale" would be a meager portion. All is not lost however, as C.PPGT (see Booklist) gives it as a 17th century term for "possibly a **tankard"** in German salt-glaze.

O

OCARINA

An elongated ovoid toy musical pipe resembling a goose or goose's egg from the Italian *oca,* meaning "a goose." It normally has eight or ten holes and the pitch is controlled by the number of holes left open. It may have come from Italy into the rest of Europe, although there is also a Chinese ocarina, the *hsuan.* Charming examples are found, especially in porcelain. Simple so-called ocarinas are found in ancient America in shell and other forms.

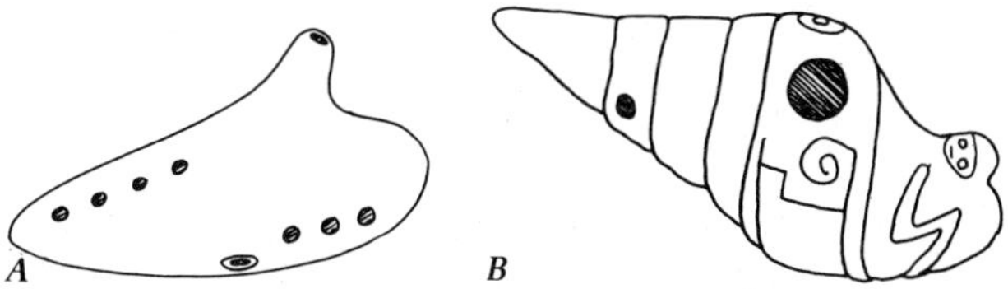

A. The traditional form of the octave ocarina.
B. An ocarina/whistle from Colombia. The shell form is not so different from the European ovoid.

OENOCHOE

From the Greek word *oneo,* meaning "wine," and *ochoe,* meaning "a spout or pouring lip" (in modern Greece, a "drain"); hence, a jug/pitcher sometimes close to the traditional modern pitcher in form, but

One of the many types of oenochoe, this one from Cyprus, circa 700 B.C.

also found in a low-bellied pear-shaped form, or with a higher shoulder and quite a narrow, longish neck with a spreading rim and lip.

OFFERING DISH

The well-known T'ang Chinese run-glaze plates set on three feet are said to have been offering dishes; they may be up to 17 inches/430mm across. There is in existence a slipware dish with the single cryptic word "Money" scrawled across it.

A typical T'ang Chinese offering dish. (Barlow Collection.)

OIL FLASK

Almost any small pot with a very small neck may have been used for the oils which were once essential for cleaning the body, especially in ancient Greek times. There is a quite large, very **depressed** shape with a small filling neck and a tiny spout in the Ipswich Museum labelled "oil flask." The specific Greek forms were the **askos, aryballos,** and **alabastron.**

OINTMENT JAR/POT

These were found in abundance in Europe and England from the 17th century. They are small, cylindrical pots or flatter, thick-walled, and sometimes lidded jars which were vertical outside, but curved inside. Some very attractive pieces were made at Lambeth.

All face creams and medicants are more efficacious if taken from an imaginatively designed jar, as cosmetic manufacturers know.

OLLA

A Roman storage jar. The name also applies to a **cinerary urn.** *Olla* in modern Greek means "all or everything," so perhaps the vessel is a holdall or general storage pot.

OLPE

An ancient Greek jug/pitcher with a short neck.

Cretan pots (and potter) drying in the sun. See text on facing page.

OMPHALOS

Literally, a "navel" from the Greek. The term is generally applied to dented or concave-based bowls from the Hallstat Iron Age in Europe, but in the illustration we can see the similar small, round indentations in the centers of the bases of Cretan pots being made today.

OPIUM BOX

A series of 18th/19th century simple boxes were said to have been used for this then widespread drug. They were very small and cylindrical, like modern pillboxes, but decorated with colors.

OVEN

According to *Webster's New Collegiate Dictionary*, "a chamber for baking, heating, or drying." Simple brick ovens, often of an attractive beehive shape, have always been built in Mediterranean and Near Eastern countries. Elaborately tiled stoves are found throughout Europe and especially in Germany and Holland. Portable ovens, or "cooking bells" (which indicates their shape), are known from early times, from 5th century B.C. Athens for instance, or a more elaborate form from Dardanus illustrated in D.EBYC (see Booklist). Hump-shaped ovens about 16 inches/400mm high, with a front opening and a fitting door, called "Tudor Welsh," were produced in Barnstaple and Fremington and exported to America. Elizabeth David has a soft spot for them: "Heavy and crude, with their bulging heads, small openings and roughly fashioned loose doors, the old West Country ovens have an ancient and moving beauty of their own." Dr. Richard Pococke, in 1750, remarked: "They make great use round here of Cloume Ovens, which are earthenware of different sizes, like an oven, and being heated they stop 'em up and cover 'em with embers to keep in the heat." Fire inside an oven, which is raked out when the fabric is hot has been the method the world over, and was used by bakers until quite recently. Fishley Holland describes the making of an oven (see H.FYP in Booklist): "The oven was made by hand, first treading the clay on a wood floor and shaping with an iron frame like a horseshoe. Then the back portion was trodden out, raised on end, and the board trigged up until the front has been made. This too was raised and the two ends joined, forming a ring. This was manipulated to the correct shape and domed until it could be closed over," sometimes with coils. He adds "I question if anybody now living could make and fire an oven."

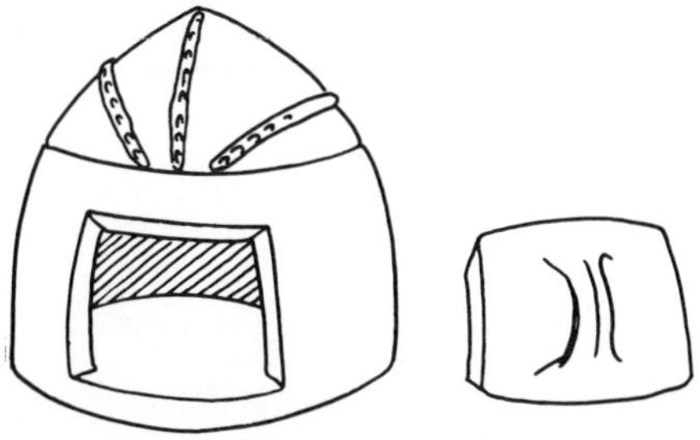

One of the helmetlike hump ovens admired by Elizabeth David. Made in the West Country, this example is in the Welsh St. Fagan's Folk Museum.

Barbecues are the nearest thing to an oven made by the modern potter. See also **brazier, stove.**

OVENWARE

The technical problem of heat-resistance does not concern us here, but, in fact, the form is significant in this connection. A rounded profile will more readily accommodate the strains of uneven heating, as early potters knew instinctively.

Ovenware consists mainly of **casseroles** and **baking dishes.** Obviously, only the former can have a rounded contour, although baking dishes should also avoid sharp angles. A large, flat plate is the most vulnerable form for oven cooking. These considerations do not apply to microwave cooking ovens where, so long as the vessel is quite dry *within the fabric,* the dish itself will not get hot except where it is in contact with the food. Earthenware, if at all crazed, is, therefore, at great risk in these ovens and could shatter as the moisture in the body turns to steam. Well-vitrified stoneware is recommended.

OVIFORM

Egg-shaped. The basic form of many pots and a term often invoked in attempts at pot **analysis.**

OWL JUG/POT

A jug/pitcher shaped like an owl, often with a removable head, used as a cup. Examples were made

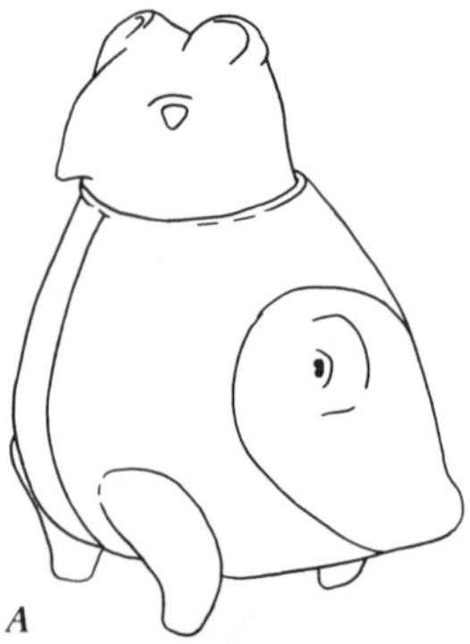

A

C

B

A. Lidded pot in the form of an owl from Chou China, a forerunner of countless variations on the cup and jug.
B. An owl harvest flask, the lugs serrated to suggest the bird's eyes (or ears?).
C. A. Peruvian Mochica tribe bottle about 8 inches/200mm high. (University Museum of Archeology and Anthropology, Cambridge.)

as early as the Chou Dynasty (1st millennium B.C.) in China, while in mid-16th century Nuremburg and in the Tyrol they were given as archery prizes, with a coat of arms on the breast. They are also found in Rhenish ware. Those from Sieburg around the year 1600 are sometimes simply and well designed. Later they appeared in England, made at Staffordshire and other centers.

Fishley Holland in *Fifty Years a Potter* mentions "owlsheads" although he does not say what they were used for but that they were so called "because of their resemblance to an owl." But Brears (see B.CECP in Booklist) says that they were full-bodied pots used in Devon and Cornwall for preparing whiting (the fish not the mineral). An "owl" also referred to a **costrel**-type bottle with two serrated lugs on the shoulders like an owl's ears. The illustrations show three adaptations of the owl form over the last 3000 years.

P

PACCHA

A Peruvian drinking vessel resembling a **rhyton.** An example in C.APP (see Booklist) shows a strange simplified animal's head with a pot on top.

PAGODA VASE

An elaborate construction from 17th/18th century Delft in pagoda form. Each roof served as a water tray with a spout above, which held a bulb, the roots of which reached down into the tray. Some of these "vases" were very large.

PAIL

This shape, like a **flowerpot** with a handle over it, has been adapted to pottery; e.g., in the Tamba example shown. A simple pail body, with more or less straight sides sloping in slightly towards the base, is known, especially among archaeologists as a **situla.** It was used by many potters through the Neolithic, Bronze, and Iron Ages. English examples are shown in B.PiE (see Booklist). It occurs in Japanese pottery and in large Chinese pots. Today Ian Auld and Helen Wilmer have shown pots in this form with a handle over them. See also **basket, well.**

PAN

The word (probably deriving from *patina,* an ancient Roman vessel) is sometimes used in a very general sense for any open utensil, as in "pots and pans," but more specifically is usually circular, a little deeper than a **plate,** and without the plate's broad rim. One of the most common pottery pans was the **milk pan,** used for separating cream from milk.

To confuse the issue, however, "bread pans" and "saucepans" are much deeper and have a lid. The common denominators are probably the wide mouth, flat bottom, and generally straight sides.

D.EBYC (see Booklist) discusses pans (also called **pancheons**) for making bread: large, round "earthenware pots, preferably glazed and of suitable shape yield a more flavoury loaf." The Greeks baked bread in earthenware at Athens; and hence, the later Roman "pan bread." She also dismisses stoneware pans: "A studio potter . . . will . . .

often be pleased to attempt a shape specially ordered, but the earthenware pans best for baking are of crude unglazed terra-cotta . . . rather than the weighty, heavily glazed stoneware usually turned out by 'art' potters." Her types of pan, though probably glazed inside, were cheap and plentiful in the past. Fremington pans for Devonshire cream started at 15 inches/380mm in diameter costing 3½d (1½p in England today, 3 cents in the U.S.) and went up from there: "Widebottoms," (with more vertical sides) were twice the price; larger still came: "Cawderns," "Bigpans," and finally "Washing Pans" at 18d (the startling equivalent of 7½p or 15 cents today). The last was too big for one man to get his arms round. (See H.FYP in Booklist.)

P'AN

A plate or basin on a high foot or pedestal, similar to a **fruit dish** or **comport,** from 3rd to 2nd millennium B.C. China. It had a sharp and carinated outline.

PANCHEON

A large, and according to CTCD (see Booklist) "coarse," shallow earthenware **pan,** with outward sloping straight walls and a bold everted rim, usu-

A. A corner of Isaac Button's showroom in Yorkshire showing large finished pancheons and flowerpots.

A

B

B. Slipware Welsh pancheons were made in sizes from 6 inches/150mm to 20 inches/500mm across.

A slab-cube paperweight by Marianne de Trey.

ally used for mixing pastry, bread, and other foods. A shallow form was the **milk pan.** The pancheon was probably also used for temporary storage. Although the term is considered archaic, it is still used by country or folk potters where they exist and is a much more evocative and fine-sounding word than **mixing bowl,** which has more or less taken its place. But then the pancheon was a noble article and in size far outstripped a mere mixing bowl. Strangely enough, the word does not appear in *Webster's* although they were turned out in vast quantities throughout the last two centuries in America. The pancheon was usually of red clay, slipped creamy-white inside, and glazed inside to the rim. See the film *Isaac Button* for the making and finishing of these fine pots.

PAO-YUEH P'ING

A Chinese **flask,** all but circular in one section and with two short handles to the neck.

PAPERWEIGHT

The traditional shape for a paperweight is a flattened sphere. The majority are of glass, but pottery examples do occur, and, in this form, they make a useful end product for centering exercises on the wheel in schools. Any heavy, flat-based form, however, can be suitable. The Bow Pottery in 1760 produced gaudy and "funky" paperweights in the shapes of grotesque dolphins and the like. The field is wide open to invention. The normal size is 3 to 5 inches/75 to 130mm across. The design should be such that the weight can be easily gripped and lifted.

PASTILLE BURNER

Also known as a **cassolette,** this was a little perforated container used for burning pastilles, or pastils, which were small blocks of aromatic paste. Burners were made in many fanciful shapes: a little house with twisted pillars and a perforated roof in English "Delph," 1691; a hare model from St. Cloud, 1750; and so on.

PATELLA, Piatella

A Roman fish dish. The word is also used for a dish for offering first fruits to the gods. In Spain it is a rice dish, and in modern Greece a piatella is a large open dish or platter, usually for meat.

PATERA

An Etruscan pedestal dish of very powerful design.

A Faliscan patera, from 4th century B.C.

PATH EDGER

Sturdy tiles with one decorated edge—domed, hooped, scalloped, perforated, etc.—used set upright in the ground for edging paths and lawns.

PEAR BOTTLE

Sometimes used to describe a low-bellied, narrow-necked pot, especially in Chinese forms. See also **bottle vase.**

PEBBLE FORM

Although the Rococo style was based on rock and shell fantasies, the idea of a polished pebble as a starting point for a pottery form does not appear to have been used until comparatively recently. Alan Wallwork, Tina Forrester, and the author, among others, have exploited these subtle shapes. The flattened, irregular sphere, which characterizes many flint pebbles found on beaches, especially those known as "skimmers," is the form most often used. The shape can be horizontal or vertical; can have a neck or necks added; or can be opened up into a sort of dish. See also **bottle, asymmetry, double-necked pot, water garden.**

A flattened hand-built "pebble" by the author. One of the problems with this type of shape is to give the impression of virtually circular silhouette, while retaining an adequately firm base.

PEDESTAL DISH

The wide, shallow bowl set on a stem with a spreading foot is a common form in many cultures, and especially in the West. It is frequently of earthenware. See also **comport, fruit dish, kylix, patera, p'an.**

PEDESTAL URN/JUG

Applied to an Iron Age (Belgic) and Romano-British form, with a wide; fairly sharp, shoulder tapering to a concave lower section and a splayed foot; a very "turned" shape.

Pedestal jugs, set up on perforated bases, possibly used with some sort of fuel to keep liquid warm (see also **food warmer, chafing dish**) are also known; e.g., from 3rd century Japan.

A typical Romano-British pedestal urn and the prototype of all decorative garden "urns" to the present day.

PEEP POT

A pottery toy developed by Ian Godfrey from very early Cypriot and other decorated **rims,** with flat modelled creatures set around.

PELIKE

A small, flat-based **amphora,** with a low belly.

One of Ian Godfrey's "peep pots," in which the small creature can be isolated by viewing it through the little hole in the wall opposite.

PEN/BRUSH REST

The best known of this form is the "five mountain" Chinese **brush rest.** See under this heading for illustration. There are also Islamic pen boxes, and, of course the Western **inkwell.**

PERFUME BOTTLE

See **scent bottle.**

PESTLE

The moving part of the hand-grinding process. See **mortar.** Its form depends on its use, which has varied through the ages. It can be flat-bottomed, with a large knob handle for food grinding, a form also used today for grinding enamel colors on a flat bed. Or it can be longer, round-ended, and of porcelain for hard materials, edible or not. Sanders (see S.WJC in Booklist) illustrates a Japanese square pestle.

PEW GROUP

The name given to a series of simple, stylized models made in Staffordshire over a comparatively short period, roughly 1735 to '45, but nevertheless well known. They were slab and coil figures seated

A Staffordshire pew group, very nicely observed and modelled (see fingers and slightly open jackets) and with the lady slightly favoring one of the gentlemen. (British Museum.)

either on a pew or settle, sometimes with musical instruments. The fabric was salt-glazed stoneware, grayish white with black details. The characters are usually in country attire. Many attractive figure groups have been made in a similar way since, but without ever quite recapturing their innocent charm. Some modern potters have reinterpreted the style in a modern fashion.

PHAILE

See **plate.**

PHARMACY VASE

See **drug jar, albarello.**

PICKLING JAR

In R.PF (see Booklist) Rhodes mentions fine *kinchi*, or pickling jars, from the Far East, especially Korea. Most families would have several sizes of vessels for vegetables, as this was the principal method of providing for the winter food supply. Lead-glazed vessels are now very suspect for this purpose, but in earlier times were often used. In the West pickling jars were more mundane. They were usually simple cylinders, often in salt-glaze. **Amphoras** are reputed to have been used to store and transport "fish pickle sauce" and probably other winter supplies.

PICTURE FRAME

See **frame.**

PIECRUST WARE

During the Napoleonic wars, flour became very expensive in England. The great pies known as "standing pies," which were common in many households, largely disappeared, to be replaced (by Wedgwood and others) by replicas in pottery, presumably to cover casseroled meat and vegetables. They are reputed to have been supplied in great quantities to universities! They might be a good idea to help with the voluntary slimming diets of today. The piecrust or "crock pie" developed into the **casserole** of today.

PIE DISH

See baking dish.

PIE FUNNEL

A small pottery support for piecrust during baking. It is often now in the form of a blackbird, but can be in any decorative form so long as it fulfills its function. It is apparently a mid-19th century invention.

PIE PLATE

A very simple form, somewhere between a plate and a dish in depth. An 1808 example from the U.S. is shown in G.EAFP (see Booklist). It has curved sides and a flattened rim.

PIERCED FORM

Except for **colanders** and the occasional **incense burner, cheese press,** or **brazier,** the early potters saw little reason for cutting away a wall which they had laboriously built up. Later pierced work is largely decorative: the 12th century Rayy openwork on the outer cases of ewers; the Seljuk approxi-

A certain intangible influence on the form is achieved by the piercing on this restrained porcelain piece.

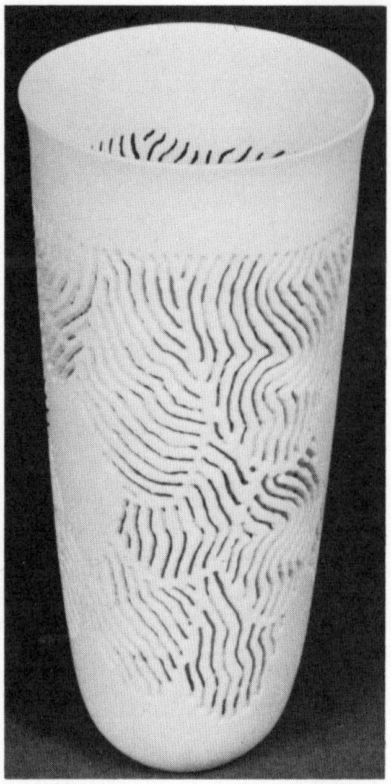

mations to porcelain; and the 16th century Gombron wares, all from the Near East; the extensively cut Italian Comendians plates; and English Leeds ware are examples.

Today, cutting through the wall is commonly done to alter the formal appearance, to increase the feeling of transluscency in porcelain, for **light shades,** or simply as a surface decoration. Ian Godfrey cuts the rims of plates in Leeds fashion; Peter Lane's bowls have almost as much space as wall; and there are many more. See **cut rim.**

PIG

The humble pig has been featured in many pottery forms: jugs with pig-head cups, **money boxes, rattles,** etc., as well as straight modelling from the Han tomb figures to the present day. See also **Sussex Pig.**

A charming model of a pigsty, with a ramp and enclosure, again from a Han tomb, was shown in CMapr78 (see Booklist). Fishley Holland mentions terra-cotta pig troughs made in the 19th and early 20th centuries. (See H.FYP in Booklist.)

PIGGIN

The origin of this term is apparently unknown. *Webster's New Collegiate Dictionary* mentions a wooden

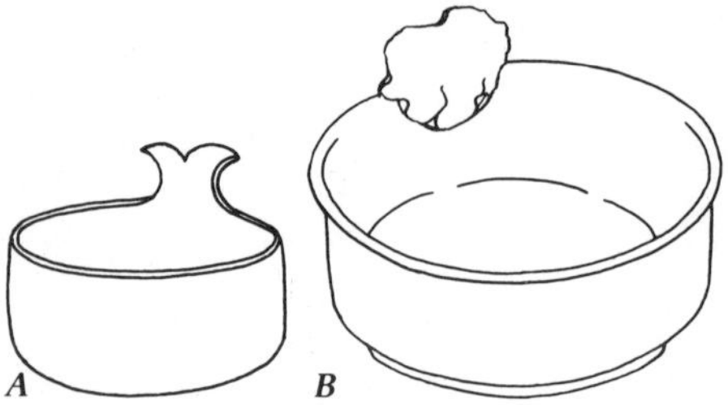

A. An 18th century Staffordshire piggin in slip-decorated buff earthenware. The little handle is integrated into the form of the pot.
B. A modern version of the piggin, with landscape handle.

pail with one stave extended as a handle, and this corresponds with the little pot illustrated, with a section of the rim extended to form a handle. Other authorities give a rather confusing picture: a shallow pot with a long handle used as a ladle which Charles (see C.PPGT in Booklist) mentions in connection with **posset pots** and **tygs;** *The Shorter Oxford Dictionary* defines it as "a vessel to drink out of"; while H.LCB (see Booklist) illustrates a paillike vessel with a **bail** handle and a ladle, which the author calls a "cream piggin."

PILGRIM BOTTLE

A type of **flask** or **costrel** to contain water or liquor when travelling. In Germany, it is called a *Beutelflasche.* In China the **pao-yueh p'ing** was a 15th century porcelain flask or pilgrim bottle. The general form is known from the earliest times: a large early Egyptian example is in the Ashmolean Museum; there are 6th century flasks of roughly made earthenware with relief decoration; etc. Some forms derived from **leather** originals. There are barrel-shaped pilgrim bottles with a neck or short spout in the long axis (Delft, U.S. folk pottery, etc.), but most are of a flattened or **lenticular** shape. They were a necessity in every culture up to the 19th century, and numerous variations on the basic form are found in the East, as well as the West. Most have two **lugs** for a strap or cord, these often modelled as goats' heads, masks, etc. See also **askos.** (Photograph: facing page.)

PILL

The Dorset pill or **owl** was a bottle/jug with serrated lugs, looking, to some like owl's ears.

Lugs and a groove around the perimeter take a throng or string by which this harvest or pilgrim bottle was carried. (Salisbury Museum.)

PILLOW

See **headrest.**

PILL SLAB

Flat pottery slabs, usually of tin-glazed earthenware, which take the place of a **mortar** for grinding and mixing the ingredients of medicines and pills. They were common in 16th to 18th century Europe and the Mediterranean countries. The plan varies. They can be oblong, octagonal, heart-shaped, etc., seldom circular, but their main attraction lies in the decoration. More mundane slabs, usually of glass, are used today for the grinding of colors, especially enamels.

PINAX

See **plate.**

PINCHED POT FORM

While this book does not deal with technique, the point can be made that the various forms of pinched pot (or thumb pot) have a distinctive formal char-

A

A. The archetype pinched pot, round-based and full-formed, from Colombia, circa 1400. (University Museum of Archeology and Anthropology, Cambridge.)

B. An interesting combination of a simple pinched bowl and slabs. The ancient pots we admire were sometimes partly pinched, but most were formed by a mixture of techniques, including stroking, coiling, etc.

B

acter, although I would not go as far as Rhodes (in *Pottery Form*) when he says that "pinch pots tend to look alike no matter who does them." The thinning and shaping of the wall of a pot by this method is a useful and direct way of making comparatively simple shapes (but see illustration under **composite pot**). To quote Rhodes again: "the intimate relationship of fingers and clay . . . is an intensely human thing, and to hold a pinched pot is to communicate quite directly with its maker." Forms can vary from the rough and primitive to the fine, smooth, and sophisticated; and it can be cut, beaten, or modelled. Larger compositions can be made by joining two or more pots together (see F.DPP in Booklist).

In Japan the method is called *trebineri* and is used especially for **tea bowls** onto which a small coil is often added as a **foot ring.** The method is quite widely used today by student and professional potters, notably in porcelain. At the time of this writing, a book on pinched pot forms by Mary Rogers is in the making.

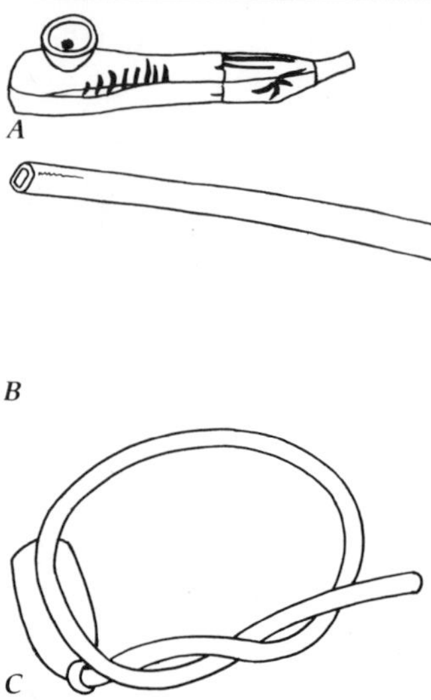
A
B
C

A. A strange, crude, but interesting, pipe from Japan (Oribe).
B. West Marshall's pipe, as mentioned in text, in clay pipe tradition, but with a crisp modern finish.
C. An extravagantly twisted Gauda (Dutch) clay pipe.

PINTE

Also called a *schnelle,* this is a handsome, tall German **tankard** (Rhenish 16/17th century), tapering towards the top and with a roll molding at foot and rim. See illustration under **tankard.**

PIPE

Apart from the ubiquitous white pipe-clay type, smoking pipe bowls were made at Meissen, some in the form of a head, later "somewhat vulgarized in the Biedermeier period . . . such masculine pleasures as hunting . . . and naked women." (See H.CECP in Booklist.) Guilland (see G.EAFP in Booklist) illustrates two American settler types, one with the bowl only in pottery, the other a large clay pipe, called a "John Bunyon" (1862). Clay pipes were used for tobacco from the last quarter of the 16th century on and are so various in detail that they form a study in themselves. They were pressed in metal and wood molds, and in the Leeds Abbey House Museum there is an actual pipe-maker's workshop with all its equipment and a small kiln. Many were made in Staffordshire in fanciful forms such as coiled snakes. West Marshall in PQ40 (see Booklist) shows stoneware pipes with thrown bowls and extruded stems.

PIPKIN

A small earthenware pot used in 16th century England and elsewhere and which continued to be made until fairly recent times. Earlier types were generally raised on three legs, often quite long ones, and all were equipped with a straight handle also of some length. Guilland (see G.EAFP in Booklist), however, shows pipkins from 19th century America without legs. Charles (C.PPGT) gives "small ovenware cooking dishes suitable for sauces, usually with two **lug handles**" as well as the long-handled variety mentioned above as the definition, but I have not found any lugged pots labelled as pipkins. The American pipkins were about 6 inches/150mm wide and with well-defined pouring lips. Vessels called "pipkins" were also made in the early years of the 20th century at Fremington in Devon, but whether they resembled the original type, I have been unable to discover.

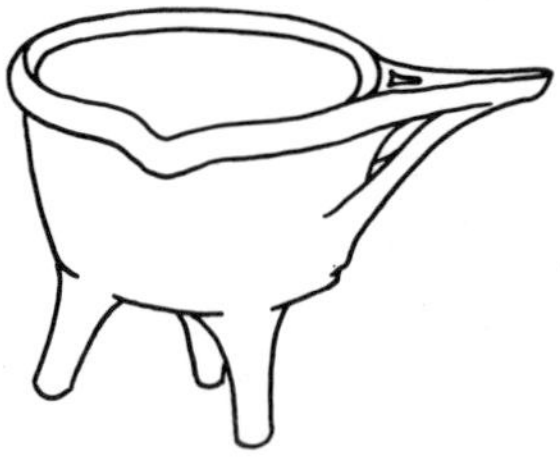

An early English pipkin, with a crude, but elaborate, handle strengthened with a brace underneath.

PITCHER

The word comes from the Greek *bikos* and the old French *pichier* and means "an earthen jug for holding and pouring liquid." It has the same root as the word **beaker.** In England the word is considered archaic (more's the pity), and is only occasionally used for large vessels. But in the United States, the

A

A. A vessel often called a pitcher *by ceramic historians. This example is a 12th century Oxford type. Note the spout in place of a lip and the tripod feet. The whole form is monumental in effect.*

word is still in current use for any size of the vessel which, in England, would be called a **jug.** To resolve this difference of usage, in this book the vessel is referred to as a **jug/pitcher.** "Pitcher" originally described a large water pot, often with a single handle, but also, apparently, with two—a type which gave rise to the expression "little pitchers have big ears," meaning that children overhear things. This type is rare, but it is said that certain Scottish jug/pitchers had two lug handles for lifting with both hands. Cardew uses the word for any large, full-formed jug and says: "a good pitcher is the most lively and athletic of all pots, realizing the conjunction of grace and strength, ready and apt for action and yet majestic in repose." (See C.PP in Booklist.) He goes on to analyze the making and form of a good pitcher.

The Greek pitcher was the **oenochoe.** In England it is possible to trace an evolution of the splendid Medieval shapes from Saxon pot forms as well as from Continental imports. Ceramic historians often use "pitcher" and "jug" in a confusing way (e.g., Rackham in R.MEP), reserving the latter for taller shapes with handles and the former for wider, squatter shapes, some with tripod feet and even with spouts. **Cistern** is also applied to similar forms. Fishley Holland uses pitcher, but he also calls the pint size "penny joogs." Others on his list are worth a mention, their vivid names indicative of their shapes: the four-pint "Pinchgut"; a larger "Gallymouth" (selling at about 3 cents retail!); a two-gallon "Long Tom"; and "Thirtytales"; this last title indicating that there were thirty to the "tale" or "long dozen," a somewhat confusing system of counting!

A few simple sentences by Guilland (see G.EAFP in Booklist) sum up the necessary qualities of a pitcher: "The form should be not only pleasant to look at, but also light because of the added weight of the contents. The handle should be placed to balance the weight of the pitcher and contents while it is being carried and poured. The spout . . . adequate for pouring . . . should not drip. The mouth must be large enough for easy cleaning and the foot broad and stable. . . . Should any of these qualities be lacking in the pitcher, it will not be used, for objects meant for use which do not

B. A more familiar Medieval pitcher with a neck and lip, but still with 3 stubby feet. (Salisbury Museum.)

B

function are extremely frustrating." Rhodes in R.PF (see Booklist) also deals in detail with the pitcher form.

See more illustrations under **jug/pitcher, creamer, handle, lip.**

PITHOS, Pithari

A large jar with a narrow base and a short, wide neck. Although a Greek form, the early Cretan pots similar to it are called by the same name. The Cretan pithos had lugs or hoops for lifting with a cord, and was often partly buried in the soil to keep the contents cool. See **storage jar.** *Pithari* is a modern Greek term for storage jars in general, large or small.

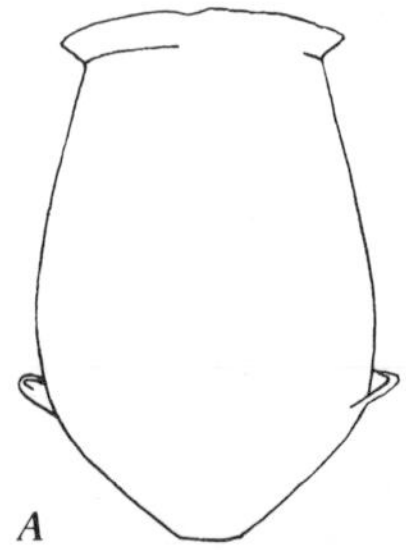
A

A. With curiously low-set handles, this fine jar, about 36 inches/1m tall, was made in about 1700 B.C. in Crete.

B. A typical small-based storage jar or pithos from circa 700 B.C. Cyprus.

B

PI T'UNG

A Chinese brush pot. A flat-based cylindrical jar (see M.HCA in Booklist). See also **coupe.**

PLANT FORM

There are fewer examples than might be expected of the overt use of plant forms in very early pottery, and, even in the ceramics nearer our own time, the inspiration has been evident in the decoration rather than the body shape. In keeping with their general character, the Far Eastern potter's exploitation of plant form is usually oblique; e.g., in the suggestion of petals on **lobed** bowls. The **gourd** and **calabash** have been sources of invention. In the 18th century Fukien produced overlapping leaf forms. See also **leaf dish.** Wedgwood and other 19th century potteries produced tableware and vases inspired by such unlikely vegetables as the cauliflower and celery. The sinuous shapes of some Art Nouveau pots reflect plant growth, which is reinforced by petallike rims. Fruits and flowers have been used to a much greater extent in designing **knobs** and **handles** than they have in the pot itself.

Many teachers today emphasize the role of plant study for potters, although, as we see, this has little

A. This Sung cosmetic box manages to be truly ceramic and, at the same time, beautifully evocative of the melon form from which it is derived.

A

B

B. A hand-built bowl by Sheila Fournier resembling the opening sheaf of a flower. Black and gold stoneware, 1979.

C

C. A carved flower foot on a little bowl by Ian Godfrey. This care and invention devoted to a part of a pot normally hidden is a pleasant bonus to the viewer, but one that is too rarely practiced.

traditional backing. Potters today occasionally exploit plant shapes although the growth of a pot on the wheel obeys laws different from those of a plant. Mike Dodd in PQ43 (see Booklist) gives a wise warning, which can be applied to this subject: "We should be careful . . . not to intellectually misinterpret Aristotle. 'Art imitates nature' does not mean that art imitates the *appearance* of nature, but the *nature* of nature."

PLANTER

In the United States this is a pot or bowl for growing plants in, especially those of the hanging type. See also **flowerpot, bonsai bowl.** Watkins (see W.ENEP in Booklist) mentions 19th century American planters as being shallow pots with "ruffled rims." The hanging planter, being viewed from below, transfers its area of greatest interest to the lower wall and base, the form often being brought to a point or to a modelled boss or terminal. The formal possibilities of standing planters are endless and have been widely exploited, although, apart from **bulb bowls,** they are a comparatively modern development.

A. By Madelaine Causfield, this hanging planter emphasizes the rim and harness.

A

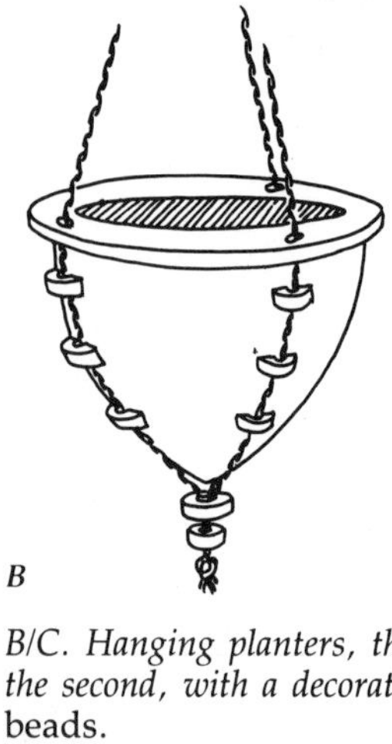

B

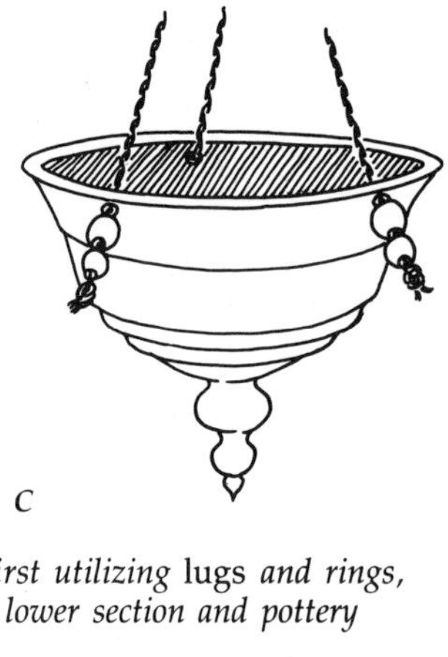

C

B/C. Hanging planters, the first utilizing lugs *and rings, the second, with a decorative lower section and pottery* beads.

Rhodes, in R.PF (see Booklist), discusses planters and stresses that the forms are incomplete without their plants (see a parallel under **lamp base.**) Since plants like to breathe, earthenware has the advantage; they like the moisture which is absorbed by the body; the drainage; and the coolness that comes from evaporation. Stoneware, on the other hand, has the advantage that it does not discolor from soluble salts. The great popularity of planters in the U.S. spurred Art Siederbaum, in CR43 (see Booklist), to comment: "There is no reason to make each green thing hang in a bowl like Babylon."

PLAQUE

See **wall plaque.**

PLATE

A shallow, one might say very shallow, vessel from which food is eaten. The derivation is, in fact, from the Latin word *plattus,* "a flat sheet." It is usually circular, but can be oval or even square. A plate may have a foot ring or may be left as cut from the wheel. Industrial plates have a vestigial foot. The true ceramic plate has a fairly wide rim, which is a continuation of the section. A plate without a wide rim, large in size and with a low **coup,** has been called a **platter.** If the well of a plate is deepened, it can then be described as a **dish.**

Rhodes is rather dismissive on plates: "its form can be almost overlooked . . . [in use] the form is felt rather than seen." (See R.PF in Booklist.) This is, however, contradicted by his illustration of a very strong shape, while the plates illustrated in CR53 (see Booklist) by David Lloyd Lones could hardly be "overlooked."

Plates appear to have been scarce in early communities and even among the remains of Medieval pottery; most were probably of wood or pewter. Several sharply molded Roman types and some very smoothly potted shallow dishes from Neolithic Britain are known. The Classic Greek plate types were known variously as the "phaile," "pinax," and "lekanos." Deepish plates with a horizontal rim resembling modern Western types were made in China from T'ang times onwards, although the well

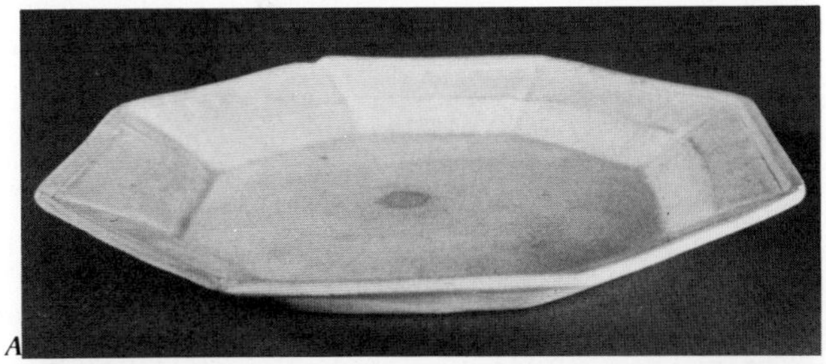

A

B

A. An octagonal, sharply defined plate from Sung China. (Barlow Collection.)
B. On the borderline between plate and dish, the thick glaze softens the edges and angles of this substantially thrown Chinese piece. (Barlow Collection.)

or central section is often more curved. The T'ang plates were often set on three modelled feet (see **offering dish**). Flat vessels with small, deepish wells and sometimes a bossed center are a feature of Spanish and Italian pottery of the 16th century onwards. It has been stated that the central boss separated the portions of food when more than one person ate from the same dish. The modern standard shape and proportions became common in Europe only in the latter part of the 17th century. Although the form is not complicated, proportion and detail need careful consideration in relation both to use and to survival at high temperatures during firing. Plates should stack easily without chipping or unduly wearing one another.

PLATTER

Usually a large, very shallow vessel with a simple profile. *Webster's New Collegiate Dictionary* calls it "a large plate especially for serving meat." It was originally a scooped-out slab of wood. See also **trencher.** Barton (see B.PiE in Booklist) suggests a rather curious progression: "The dish [in] . . . England in the late 15th century had become a platter by the end of the 16th century and a plate by the middle of the 17th century by which time it was in general use."

The term is more or less archaic in Britain, though it has been revived in the titles of some restaurants, but is still in use in the U.S. to describe a large plate or dish for serving food. Elizabeth David (see D.EBYC in Booklist) tells us that "on a 12-inch flat oven platter of rough or glazed earthenware it is easy to make a pizza large enough for 7 to 10 ample helpings."

PLUNGE POT

Here the form arises directly from the method (see R.EDP in Booklist for description), usually resulting in a thick-walled and rough-cut pot with a square external plan and a circular cavity, although both can be varied. It is almost certainly a modern technique. See illustration under **beaten shape.**

A small, squared plunge pot, the sides impressed with a block of wood, by Sybil Houldsworth. Other examples are often much less restrained.

POACHER

See **egg baker, apala.**

POLYPOD

Bowls standing on several feet are found quite widely in early European and preColumbian American pottery. These are often connected with cooking over an open fire, though several are associated with ceremony. Tripod feet are found on round-bottomed pots throughout the world and on **pipkins,** etc. from Medieval England; there were even tripod **pitchers** in the 13th century. In the 18th century milk jugs, etc. were sometimes set on three cabriole feet. Pots or bowls on separate feet are more rare in modern pottery. Leach in his *Pottery Book* shows a **joint dish** on four studs, and a deep **foot ring** is sometimes cut away to form feet. Colin Kellam has made a series of pots on three short legs, but, in general, pots today stand firmly on their own bases.

POMANDER

From the French word meaning "apple of amber," this is a perforated ball or box filled with aromatic herbs, petals, etc. It was originally worn as a guard against infection (or the less pleasant odors). The simplest pottery arrangement would be two hemispherical bowls, one with a **flange** like a **box.** As pomanders were usually hung, the parts could be strung together in decorative ways. See also **potpourri.**

PORRINGER

From the Middle French *potager,* indicating a vessel for *pottage* (a thick soup), and the Middle English *potinger.* The word is applied in pottery to two distinct forms—a small soup or porridge bowl, especially for use by children; and a two-handled, cuplike vessel with vertical sides and a cover. Both were for serving food to be eaten with a spoon. Benjamin Franklin in the mid-18th century wrote: "My breakfast was a long time bread and milk . . . and I ate out of a two-penny earthen porringer with a pewter spoon," which seems to suggest that it was a poor man's utensil. However, there were more sophisticated porringers, and one illustrated in G.EAFP (see Booklist) resembles a large, shallow cup with a handle, and a saucer or plate: the shape is a handsome one. "Small porringers" appear in 18th and 19th century potters' accounts and pattern books, especially in the U.S.

A charming porringer of the open-bowl type with a decorative lug handle, 18th century tin-glaze. (On loan to Bristol Museum and Art Gallery.)

Larousse Gastronomique translates porringer as *ecuelle,* meaning "a deep dish to hold an individual portion of food." In the Middle Ages it was usual for two people to share a porringer; hence, the expression "manger a la meme ecuelle," which now translates into colloquial English as "to live in one another's pockets." A 16th century porringer with two flat lug handles was called a "Bagyne Cup."

The modern equivalent is the cereal or soup bowl, the design of which could be made more varied and interesting by reference back to some of the fine old porringers.

PO-SHAN-LU

See **hill jar.**

POSSET POT

"Posset" was a drink of warm ale or wine, hot curdled milk, sugar, spices, and oatcake fragments. LG (see Booklist) defines it as "a hot drink of milk and white wine or beer." The posset pot was a two-handled lidded vessel. In the 17th century it was a full, handsome shape with a low-set curving spout, through which the posset may have been sucked, as B.CECP puts it, from beneath "a thick, glutinous froth." Some held as much as 2 gallons and would have been passed around the company. Posset pots are mentioned by Pepys. Many were made at Wrotham and Staffordshire, but production declined at the end of the 18th century. Lids

A/B. Lidded and open types of posset pot silhouettes, the first from the late 17th century, the second from 1700, and about 7 inches/180mm high.

C. *A very thickly glazed circa 1650 Lambeth Pottery posset pot showing the curious low spout.*

were sometimes decorated with figures, and we even find a "puzzle" posset pot (see **puzzle jug**). The variation in shape was wide: some were simply large cups with a spreading rim and, generally, two low handles; others were elaborate and fanciful. Later examples have no spout and finally became similar to **punch bowls,** too large to hand around. See also **caudle cup, loving cup.**

POSY RING

This rather coy-sounding flower holder is interesting to throw and is capable of some variation in proportions and in the curvature or straightness of the walls. It is very suitable for short-stemmed garden or wild flowers.

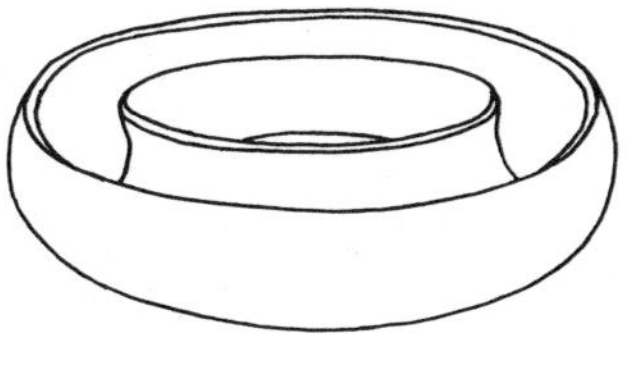

The typical posy ring. A slightly in-turned rim is normal.

POT

At a Leach lecture in the sixties, he was presented with a large, involved ceramic form in bright colors for comment. He inspected it quizzically until he found a tiny hole in the top, "Ah," he said, "that makes it a pot."

A "pot" was also a 17th century gin **measure.** See **pottle size.**

POTICHE

A Chinese pot shape, usually with a high, rounded shoulder, a lid set over a short neck, and an animal model knob.

POTPOURRI

Literally a "rotten pot." A potpourri is a covered jar or box, usually with perforations, to hold scented herbs, petals, or spices. Today the contents consist mainly of dried flowers. PQ42 (see Booklist) illustrates Mildred Slatter's complex of hanging potpourri boxes in pierced porcelain.

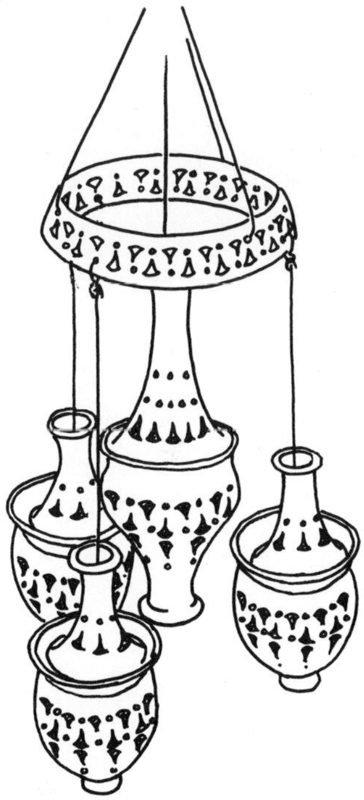

Very decorative hanging potpourri containers, by Mildred Slatter.

POTTER'S WHEEL

There are two pottery models of throwers in the Brighton Museum. One is of a potter and his assistant operating Wedgwood's hand-turned wheel; the other, in white porcelain, is of a lively thrower spinning a Continental-type wheel with his bare feet. The Martin Brothers also made models of potters throwing.

Of wheels themselves it appears that bearings were made in porcelain in the Far East and an example is shown on the next page.

POTTLE SIZE

A pottle sized mug in 19th century America held 2 quarts—a man's mug! A pottle was also 17th/18th century measure in England: a pottle pot, half a gallon; a pot, one quart; a little pot, one pint.

The lower bearing from an early Korean wheel. (Shown at the Leach Exhibition at the Crafts Study Center, Bath, 1979.)

P'OU

Described by Medley (see M.CP in Booklist) as "a large subspherical vessel with a straight plain mouth rim, on a slightly splayed high foot." It dates back to 2nd millennium B.C. China.

POUNCE POT

See **sander, inkwell.**

PRESSED DISH/BOWL

Dishes and bowls have been formed by pressing clay into biscuit or plaster molds at least since Roman times. This made possible the mass repetition of relief designs on the outside walls. Both Roman and the later Sung Chinese wares were mainly circular and were probably formed in a way not unlike the modern **jigger and jolley;** the insides are very smooth. The well-known oblong pie dish, often divided down the middle, was made in great quantity in England, but, according to Brears (see B.CECP in Booklist), between 1700 and 1900, almost all were made in Staffordshire and Northern England: "Throughout Southern England the technique of making pressed flatware was almost entirely unknown, the dishes or plates being either thrown or formed from basic thrown shapes."

Today the press-mold is used mainly to reproduce noncircular dishes in plaster molds. The very fact that almost any shape is possible leads to some very mean and poor ones. Clay most readily responds to comparatively gentle changes of plane and this should be borne in mind both in the plan and elevation of the mold, to avoid sharp angles. See also **press-molding.**

A

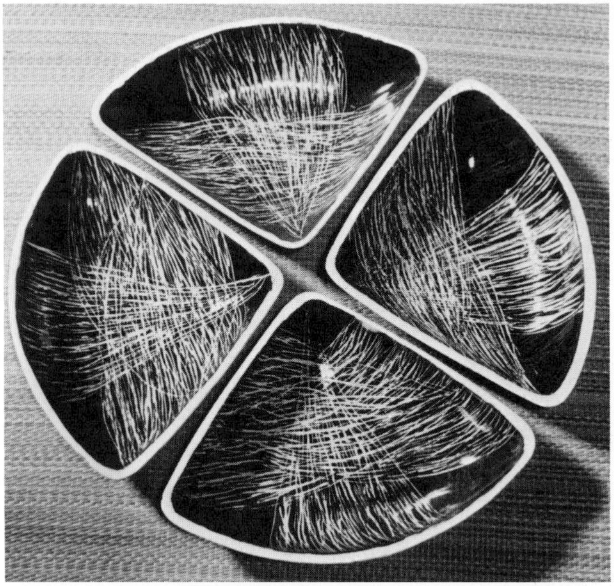

B

A. A set of 4 pressed dishes by a 12-year-old. All curves smooth and corners rounded.
B. More shaply designed but still lively is this dish by David Morris.
C. A very plastic, directly made dish with unusual integrated flat handles. See facing page.

PRESS-MOLDING

Apart from **pressed dishes,** any hollow form can be made in this way, most requiring two or more

C

sections of mold. Many Chinese pots, as early as Han, but especially in the T'ang dynasty, were pressed in molds. Simple press-molds were in use in ancient Egypt. Masks for bellarmines and other decorative "sprigs" were taken from press-molds. They were common in Rome.

A. A pressed shape by Hamada, one difficult to form in any other way.

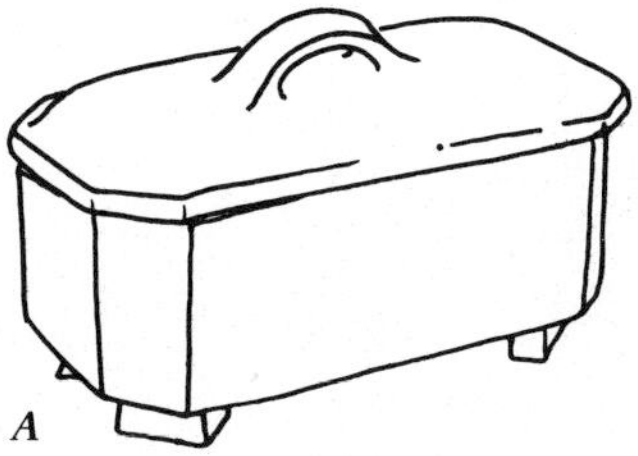

A

Press-molds are used by craft potters today to shape the main body of noncircular pots; e.g., a flat-sided oblong form, the neck, foot, etc. being added, thrown, or coiled. Leach, Hamada, Kawai, etc. used press-molds for oblong bottles, etc. For pressing very large pots, Fishley Holland used to beat the clay into the shape (usually large garden

B. A noble press-molded bottle by Bernard Leach. (Photograph: John Anderson.)

B

pots, etc.) with an old sock tightly filled with rag, "pressure by hand being insufficient to fill the grooves in the mold." (See H.FYP in Booklist.) For hand-building, rough shapes are often pressed out in large bowls simply in order to get a series of hollow forms. These can then be joined and beaten, planed, and added to until the final piece has little resemblance to the original. This maintains the essential creative contact between the object and the hands of the craftsman.

PSYKTER

An ancient Greek double-walled wine cooler. From the word *psychos,* meaning "cold." According to some authorities, it was filled with ice and lowered into a wine **krater.**

The low-bellied Attic psykter, one of the Greek forms which is less rigid and more acceptable to modern craftsmen.

PUDDING PAN

Guilland in *Early American Folk Pottery* shows a pudding pan looking like a shallow mixing bowl or **pancheon.** It is almost indistinguishable from a **milk pan,** but only about 7 inches/180mm across.

PULL HANDLE

Handles for bell pulls, lavatory cisterns, and, later, light switches have been made in the millions through the 19th and 20th centuries. The shape varied, but was always designed to give a good grip. There is a wide field of invention here for the modern potter.

A. The standard type of bell/lavatory pull usually in stoneware or the semiporcelains of the 19th century. This outline could be used for an interesting pot shape.

B. A nicely stylized "owl" pull by Sybil Houldsworth.

B

PUNCH BOWL

"Punch" was originally a Hindu drink of five ingredients, which included fermented coconut milk and tea! It is now generally a spiced mixture of wine, brandy, and fruit or fruit juice, drunk hot or cold. A punch bowl is a large, deep bowl, the upper area of the walls often vertical or nearly so, usually accompanied by a **ladle** and often by a set of goblets or small cups. See also **monteith.** Boger (see B.DA—Booklist) says that the shape was inspired by Chinese export porcelain. Tin-glazed examples from Bristol etc. ofter bear inscriptions, the favorite being: "One bowl and then." Burton (see B.GAH in Booklist) quotes an inventory of a Widow Ha-

A

ward in the 18th century whose effects were few but included two punch bowls. Punch bowls of the 18th/19th centuries were sometimes raised on a stem and fitted with a lid which was cut away to accommodate a ladle. Wedgwood creamware examples had perforated lids. **Posset pots** resembled punch bowls after the late 18th century. Today punch sets are often made by craft potters, but the bowl is rarely provided with a lid.

B

C

A. A capacious punch bowl from the mid-18th century, possibly London, the walls were normally more vertical than is shown in this example. (Bristol Museum.)
B. Punch bowl and cups by Colin Pearson. The in-turned walls would help to keep punch warm. It could serve equally well as soup bowls and server.
C. A more rigidly upright wall designed to take hanging cups, by the author.

PUNCH POT/KETTLE

A punch (see **punch bowl**) pot looked like an outsize teapot, but had no strainer at the base of the spout. It was probably used to serve punch or to transport it from an inn. The "kettles" stood on a spirit heater or **brazier** and had arched-over handles. A very large 19th century punch pot in the Fitzwilliam Museum looks like a vast, and one must say ugly, teapot.

PUNSAI

See **bonsai.**

PUZZLE JUG

These were joke jug/pitchers pierced with a design at the neck so that the liquid could not be poured from them. A hollow rim, with two or more small spouts standing horizontally from it, is connected through a hollow handle to a hole in the body of the jug. The idea was to suck liquid up through the operative spout (some were dummies), and this could only be done when other spouts and often

A. A fairly standard design of puzzle made by Isaac Button in 1958, the pattern covering some 250 years.

A

B. An elaborate and much rarer type of puzzle jug or fuddling cup, *which also bears a formal relation to the ancient* kernos.

B

a hole in the handle were covered by the fingers. Very popular in bucolic circles and very unhygienic!

Puzzle jugs are known from Medieval times onwards, but especially from the 17th/18th centuries, which was the highpoint in their manufacture, although Isaac Button was still making them in 1960. They were not always noted for their beauty, ingenuity being the chief criterion, but some, especially those in tin-glaze, are charming. Brears warns that early-dated puzzle jugs (there is one instance of a 1571 one) may be fakes. Most had a rhyme on the front, typically (see B.CECP in Booklist): "Within this jug there be good liquor/ Fit for Parson or for Vicar/ But to drink and not to spill/ Will try the Utmost of yr. skill." Or rather more profoundly: "From Mother Earth I claim my birth/ I'm made a joke for Man!"

PYRIFORM

The term refers to pear-shaped pots with a low belly. The aryballos is often pyriform, as are some Chinese bottles.

PYTHAKION

A classic Greek plate. In modern Greek, a piato.

PYXIS

From the Greek *puxis*, "a box tree." A small Greek **box** or casket to hold trinkets, usually with a flat shoulder and a lid. There were also taller forms for **cosmetics** (equivalent to the powder bowl of today). The walls are often concave or diabolo shaped. "They show an astonishing precision of shape and delicacy of ornament." (See L.GP in Booklist.) An attractive variant is the tripod pyxis with the base cut to three square feet.

A/B. Two very different types of pyxis. The first is the more typical concave or upright wall form cut into 3 legs, but, in this case, it consists of an outer wall round a curved bowl; circa 600 B.C.. The second is earlier by about 100 years and illustrates a splendid type of modelled knob or handle. In this case a turned knob has been rather incongruously left between the horses legs.

A

B

R

RAMEKIN, Ramequin

From the Low German *ramken*, which is a diminutive of *ram*, meaning "cream." The term, therefore, derived from the word for the food cooked in it, which has been described as a mixture of cheese, breadcrumbs, and egg, or, as LG (see Booklist) puts it, "a tartlet with cream cheese." The word "ramekin" is also used to describe a small, deepish dish for cooking and serving an individual helping of food.

RATTLE

Pots, often in the shape of stylized birds, pigs, etc., containing balls of clay or pebbles, have been made since Neolithic times. The feet of many Peruvian and other ancient American tripod bowls were hollow, and they rattle when shaken. See illustration

A. A bird-shaped rattle from Switzerland, Hallstat period, circa 750 B.C. The small holes may have been for the attachment of clappers. This was probably used in connection with a magic ritual to impress the worshippers, rather than as a toy.

A

B

B. A modern rocking toy rattle (for adults?) from the inexhaustible imagination of Ian Godfrey.

under **tripod pot/bowl.** The early rattles rarely had their modern use as children's toys. See caption for illustration A.

RELIQUARY

In the Ipswich Museum there is a Coptic terra-cotta circular plaque with a depression for a piece of glass in the center "for protection" (similar amulets with pieces of inset, colored glass come from the Middle East). On it is drawn a saint, with one hand resting on a large pot, the other holding what looks like a large wrench!

RHUBARB POT

This is basically a tall pot, open at both ends, used in forcing rhubarb, sea kale, or Swiss chard. In shape it may be a simple cylinder or may be domed to a smaller top opening and equipped with a lid. It is approximately 8 inches/200mm wide by 14 inches/350mm high.

RHYTON

From the Greek verb, meaning "to pour." It is a tall Minoan and Greek pointed-based vessel, with a single handle, for pouring libations to the gods. The Mycenaean rhyton resembles an inverted cone with up-standing handles. Other characteristic forms are modelled as horns, or bulls' heads. A Chinese horn-shaped vessel in the Bristol Museum is labelled as a "rhyton." Some types of rhyton are similar to a **stirrup cup** in that they cannot be set down until empty; the pointed bases may have been set in a **stand;** others have a firm base. See also under **boot.**

A handsome rhyton from late Minoan times.

RIBBED FORM

Guilland (see G.EAFP—Booklist) uses the term "ribbed foot" to describe a foot ring in which grooves have been turned. Ribbing, both vertical and horizontal, occurs on pots from all ages as a formal decoration; e.g., the vertical ribs on certain powerful Bronze Age European forms, through to the assertive lines of the Delaherche Art Nouveau pot of 1891, shown in C.WC (see Booklist). It is a comparatively neglected addition to pot form today, except where it is associated with **fluting.**

Horizontal ribs on a large modern hand-built pot from Crete; about 30 inches/775mm tall.

RIDGE TILE

See **roof tile.**

RIM

The dictionary definition of "rim" is "the edge, border, or margin of an object, usually circular." It is applied to the top edge of a pot or bowl, and can include the outer flat surface of a **plate** or dish. Leach, in *A Potter's Book,* states that: "The ends of lines are important." Most pottery shapes need some accent, subtle or bold, which will terminate the curve or line of the wall. It is useful when throwing to retain a slight extra thickness of wall at the top in order to be able to form a satisfactory

A. A raku bowl bowl by Martin Smith in which the sharply angled cut-away rim reflects the character of the pot and its decoration.

A

B

rim. There are practical, as well as aesthetic, considerations: a rounded rim on a mixing bowl for chip resistance; the most comfortable shape and width of a rim for drinking; and so on. In *Ceramic Art of China* Honey mentions "certain cups . . . reveal to advantage the physical charm of the material and the potter's skill in shaping the edges." A nicely rounded rim is known to archaeologists as a **bead rim.**

Rims may be fluted or otherwise decoratively treated: a 15th century B.C. pot from Anatolia has a rim modelled as a castle wall; the rims of certain 3rd millennium B.C. Cypriot stemmed bowls are mounted with animal models, a style which Ian Godfrey has developed in his **peep pots** and other pieces. The rims of early Medieval pots were often thickened by being folded inwards. The emphatic, carinated rims of many Hispano-Morseque bowls warrant careful study.

The term "rim" is sometimes replaced by "lip," which we have confined in this book to a pouring lip on a jug or bowl. H. Hamm, writing in *Crafts* (issue No. 14) has said of Staite Murray: "He dis-

B. David Leach carefully finishing and sharpening the rim of one of his tall bottles. (Photograph: John Anderson.)
C. An "interrupted" rim by Wally Keeler—2 simple, but very effective, pinches in the plastic clay.

C

D. An ancient Cypriot stemmed bowl set with animals, tiny pots etc.

liked pots with thin lips and would ask if we liked kissing girls with thin lips?" Leach, in *A Potter's Book,* illustrates a variety of rim contours (which he also calls "lips"). Rhodes rightly calls the rim "the final accent, and the thickening of the clay here is a kind of punctuation mark." (See R.PF in Booklist.)

For a multirimmed vessel see **bowl,** and look for examples of rims in many of the other pictures in this book.

RIM PAN

A fairly straight-sided tapering bowl with a very pronounced, carinated rim to facilitate holding and carrying, made by country potters, especially in America. There are Roman pans with similar rims.

RING BOTTLE/VASE

A circular, tubular container with a neck at the top and sometimes a foot at the bottom. They are found in the ancient world as far apart as Mycenae, where the ring is horizontal and the neck and handle stand out at an upward angle, to the upright ring pots from Recuay, Peru, which have a foot and a figure at the top. More modern types, known as "Harvest" or "Mower's" bottles, are featured especially in 19th century folk pottery. Guilland (see G.EAFP in Booklist) shows an old photograph of a pottery with a ring bottle of quite large proportions hanging on the wall. They were probably adapted from the ring vase or flask of Rhenish stoneware, imported by German immigrants. This type was more ornate and had a longer neck.

A few potters have used the form today: Waistel Cooper in the 1960s and Ian Godfrey, surmounted by his inevitable creatures.

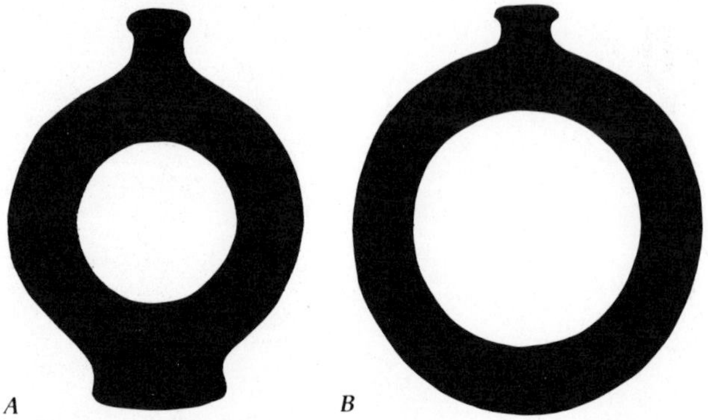

A/B. Two 18th/19th century American ring bottles, the one on the right with a foot for standing down (Connecticut), the other probably for carrying over the arm or shoulder on long horse or carriage rides, when it could be used without dismounting.

RING MOLD

See also **cake mold.** A similar form is mentioned by Elizabeth David (see D.EBYC in Booklist). It is made in earthenware and known as a "kugelhopf," glazed inside, biscuit outside. LG (see Booklist) specifies a special kind of ring mold for a Savarin cake, which is a cross between a ring doughnut and a rum baba.

RING TREE

A small, branching construction on a base, for use on a dressing table (a dresser in the United States) to hold finger rings.

ROACH TRAP

See **cockroach trap.**

ROASTER

A curved, open-fronted utensil for cooking in front of an open fire. There may be earlier examples, but roasters were certainly made by the Wedgwood family in 1712, and examples are known from Staffordshire and Yorkshire. Some were modified for apples with small cups built in, and the wall is sometimes perforated. Various types are illustrated

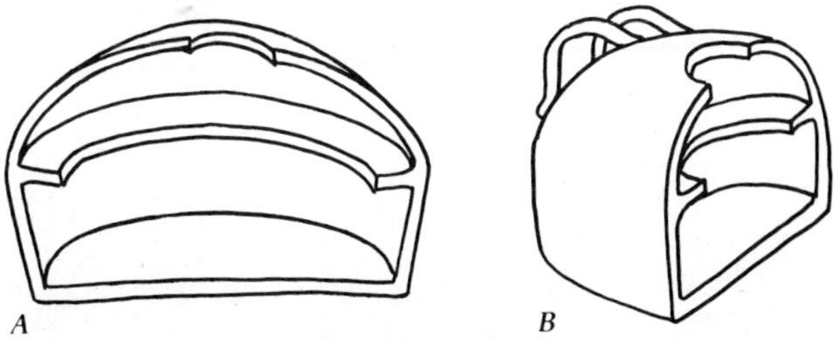

A/B. Two views of the roaster or Dutch oven on exhibition in the St. Fagans Folk Museum, Wales. Glazed earthenware, 19th century.

in B.CECP (see Booklist). Some were simple trays with one straight edge; others semicircular, a squat cylindrical pot cut in two; still another form had a curved-over hood with a handle at the top. It is called a "Dutch oven" at St. Fagans Folk Museum, Wales.

ROLLED RIM/FOOT

A term for a very rounded rim or base, like an added coil. Sometimes the curve is repeated, one above the other. It is found on many pots, but more especially the Greek, Roman, some folk pottery, and on modern industrial designs.

ROLLING PIN

This kitchen utensil was often made in pottery. Sometimes the roller would be fitted with a wooden shaft and handles, others were made in one piece, usually in a porcellaneous body, and could be filled with water.

A typical rolling pin with a cork in one end. This enabled the pin to be filled with water, which added to the weight and which also kept the pastry cool during rolling. These rolling pins sometimes had flour advertisements printed on them.

ROOF TILE

Roofs, from Paris to Peking, have always presented rich patterns of form and texture, which have in-

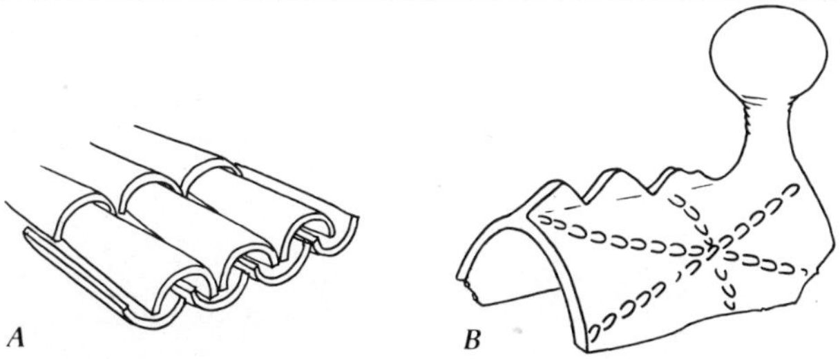

A. Thrown cylinders cut in half and used as roof tiles.
B. Just one example from the 13th century Salisbury, of the great multitude of ridge tiles.

spired painters and photographers alike. The variety of ways in which men have solved the simple business of running water from the ridge to the eaves is astonishing, and the potter has contributed very extensively to this. Norman Davey, in D.HBM (see Booklist), deals with the history and development of pottery tiles starting with Olympia in 640 B.C. The simplest consisted of halves of thrown cylinders or slightly tapering pots, one reversed over the join between two others. Similar shapes set over

C. Very decorative heads like this one would close the ends of the tiles at the eaves and, in a long row, must have looked magnificent.

A

flatter and wider base, S-shaped tiles that look, in sections, like the waves of the sea, pear-shaped flat tiles, and others, have persisted until modern times.

The ridges and eaves have frequently been treated to a great deal of modelling, which must have made the roof a fitting climax to a house. Chinese ridge tiles are especially imaginative and ornate, but the more modest efforts of the Medieval potter are also of great interest and are often nearer to their pot origins. All can be a revelation to potters today.

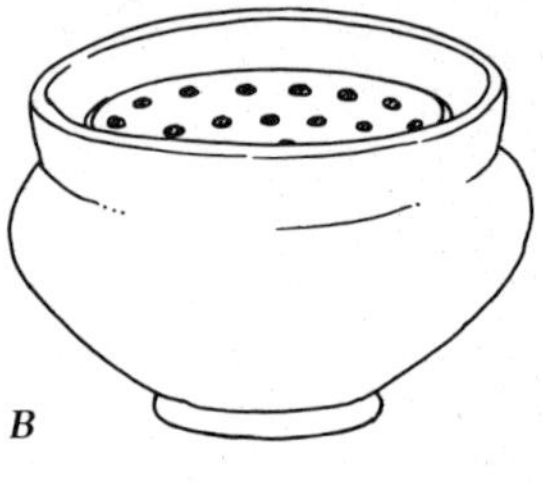

B

A. The open type of rose or flower bowl, in which short stems would allow the flowers to lie on the wide rim, or support might be placed in the well. By the author. (Photograph: John Anderson.)
B. A rose bowl with a grid in the top to hold flower stems.

ROSE BOWL

There is some difference of opinion as to what constitutes a rose bowl, but there seem to be two main types—a fairly shallow bowl with slightly in-turned walls and either a flower grid in the center or a perforated cover over, or a flattish vessel with a wide rim and a narrow, fairly deep central well. The aim in each case is to enable roses with fairly short stems to be shown to advantage.

ROUGE POT

See **cosmetic pot.**

ROULEAU VASE

A 17th century Chinese shape resembling a **mallet** or **kinuta,** but less defined and more attenuated with a comparatively taller body.

RUFFLED RIM

The name given to a scalloped rim by Watkins (see W.ENEP in Booklist). "The ruffled [flowerpot] was often made to hang and was provided with holes for strings or wires"; a **planter,** in fact.

S

SAKI BOTTLE/CUP

A modern saki cup by Tenryu Kaeda (see CMoct78 in Booklist) resembles a **goblet** or **stem cup,** but with a smaller bowl. The base is irregularly cut into facets. Simple and attractive small bottles for saki have been made for centuries in Japan. Two are illustrated: one fairly sharply defined, from Higo Province; the second, with a tiny lid, is indented to give a grip (Awata).

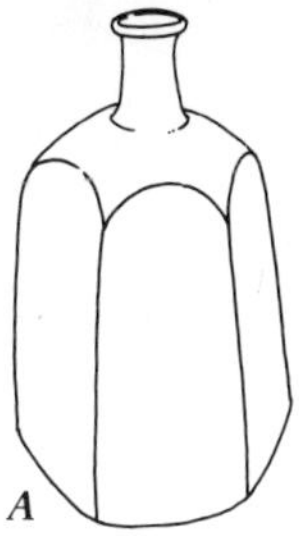

A

A/B. Two contrasting saki bottles from Japan (see text).

B

SALLIBUBE CUP

Possibly "syllabub" cup, similar to a **caudle** or **posset pot.**

SALT CELLAR

The "cellar" is derived from *salier,* meaning "a box." It should, therefore, presumably have a lid. Generally, it is a small container for salt to be used at the table. Historically, salt cellars are of silver or other metals, but pottery examples are known from as early as the 15th century in Italian majolica.

There are certain dangers in using earthenware, if it is at all crazed. Nevertheless, many thousands have been made. Many decorative forms have been made, such as the one illustrated here and a 1770 scallop shell, etc. The modern salt cellar is the **shaker** or **cruet.** See also **salt pot.**

A

A. A late 18th century German salt cellar in tin-glaze.
B. A double salt pot, rather crudely made and painted. Moustiers, mid-18th century. (Bristol Museum.)

B

SALTER/Salting pan/Ham pan

A large, usually oval trough for salting meat. The walls were thrown and the oval base beaten out on

A fine big ham pan, shaped to take a Yorkshire ham, with the usual decoration of thumbed-down strips of clay round the side, circa 1800.

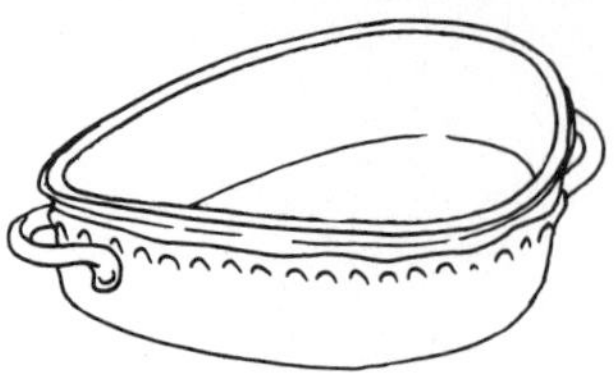

a large board. It was a four-man job. See also **stein, brine pan, bussa.**

A salting pan, according to B.CECP (see Booklist) was more shallow but still very large, up to 30 inches/850mm by 12 inches/300mm deep. It was pear-shaped in Yorkshire to take the famous whole hams.

SALT POT/KIT

Traditionally, a container with a large vertical mouth big enough to insert the hand. Strangely, it is not mentioned in G.EAFP (see Booklist), which suggests that it was not common at the time in the settlement of America. In fact, most examples date from the late 18th or 19th centuries, although a 1749 Nottingham salt-glazed kit is in the Fitzwilliam Museum.

A very similar form, called a "suspension pot," is known from 11th century B.C. Mycenae; a charming shape is illustrated in L.GPBA (see Booklist). The 19th century English examples include a closed-over bottle shape with the shoulder cut out and a bottomless bowl fitted into the aperture. This splendid shape was made notably at the Northern England pottery of Wetheriggs. A very different type, more like an English letter box with a very large slot, came from Kitson's Pottery in Halifax; it is a straight-sided pot tapering slightly towards the base, the closed-over top surmounted by a broad round knob, or a hen model. It is illustrated in

A/B. Two salt kits by modern potters: the first by Andrew Young, probably built from 2 sections of one thrown pot; the second, more traditional, with a ring set on a closed shape.

A

B

B.CECP (see Booklist). Some were highly decorated with strips and little figures all over and with very flamboyant knobs. The name "salt kit" derives from the word for a small wooden tub.

Many potters make salt pots today, usually simple in form, with a flange around the aperture, but the vessel is capable of considerable variation.

SANDER, Pounce pot

This was an essential item at the desk or writing table for absorbing ink. See **inkwell** illustration. An 1829 U.S. example is shown in G.EAFP (see Booklist).

SARCOPHAGUS

A very decorative example with a curved top from ancient Japan is shown in E.ACJ (see Booklist).

SAUCE POT/BOAT

An early Greek example with a long horizontal, spoutlike lip is called a "sauce boat" in L.GPBA (see Booklist), but, whether there is proof of this use, or whether it merely resembles the modern type, is not clear. Certainly sauces have been made for thousands of years and some **amphoras** are reputed to have contained "fish pickle sauce." A Sung Chinese teapotlike vessel with a small neck is labelled as a "sauce pot" in the Clarke Collection catalog. The modern sauce boat form is described by its name and is largely an industrial product.

SAUCER

Originally a shallow dish for sauces, it became a similar vessel first for drinking tea and later as a stand to catch spillings from the cup. Historically, it is a comparatively recent innovation in the second sense.

The profile can vary from the simplest small, shallow dish to a more involved form with a well and foot ring. See **cup and saucer.** (Photo: top.)

A series of saucer sections, the top type doubles as a small plate.

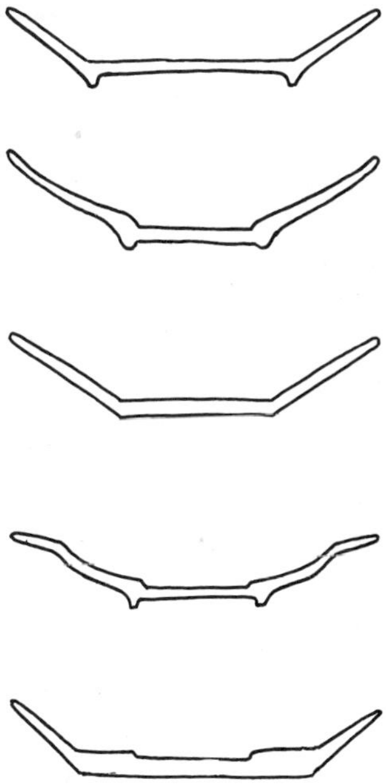

SCALLOP

"A radially ribbed shell with the edge undulating," according to *Webster's New Collegiate Dictionary*. "An . . . outline cut into a series of [convex] segments of circles" (*The Shorter Oxford English Dictionary*). In C.PPGT (see Booklist) however, scallops are referred to as "small semicircular indentations cut at regular intervals around the rim of a vessel." The convex form is more general. It was used especially on rococo shapes.

SCALLOP DISH

A shallow dish in the form of a scallop shell and used for serving the fish.

A scallop shell dish from the Chelsea factory circa 1775. The decoration almost destroys the form. (Bristol Museum.)

SCENT BOTTLE

Several of the small Greek bottles may have been used for aromatic liquids, as well as oil. The **alabastron, aryballos,** and **askos,** for instance, and small bottles from other times must have been used for perfume, although this is rarely mentioned in histories of ceramics, except in F.SB (see Booklist), which shows a number of Corinthian and other examples. A 6th century B.C. Greek bottle is in the apt form of a siren. The Egyptians used aromatic herbs or perfume both in their temples and for personal use. Containers in very pretty forms in terra-cotta and "Egyptian paste" or "faience" are well known. One cannot imagine the Egyptian or Chinese lady without her perfume. Perfume became something of an obsession in Ancient Greece, where the scent shops became a meeting place for fashionable society. It was also considered, as were many scented plants, to be a guard against disease, a belief which has persisted. The Romans, typically enough, were interested in its aphrodisiac effects. Greek bottles from 600 to 500 B.C. were common in a wide variety of shapes; many were from Rhodes. With Christianity, scent containers became rare, though we must not forget the importance attached to "frankincense and myrrh."

A

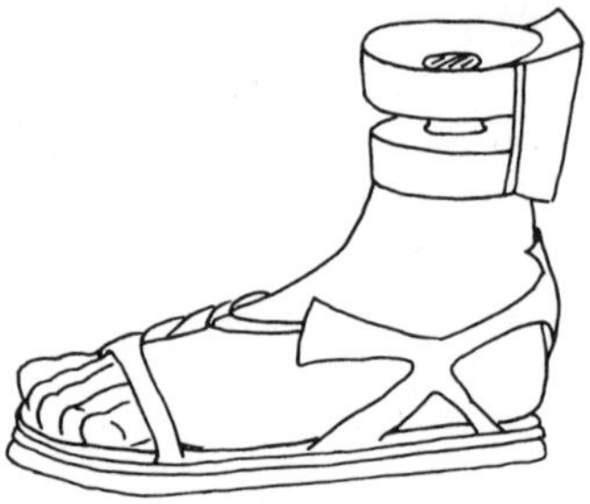
B

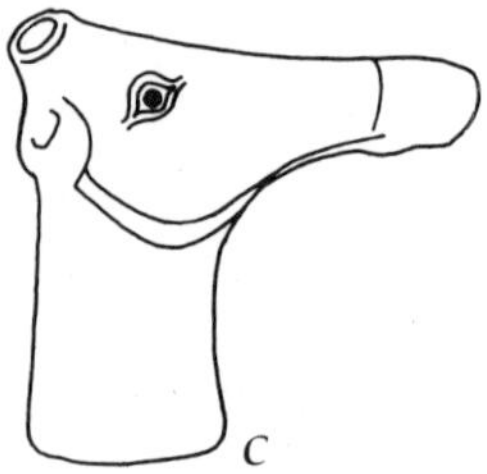
C

A/B/C. Three modelled scent bottles from 6th century B.C. Greece. Compared with the often severe pot shapes of the time, the imagination of the potter was obviously allowed to run free in this field. One wonders what kind of perfume went into a sandalled foot!

At the soft-paste factories of Chelsea, etc. scent bottles or "smelling bottles" were made in quantity, and in every conceivable shape; human, animal, fruit, flowers, even whole stories and allegories were modelled in. Wedgwood made more sober **flask**like bottles in Jasper ware, often with metal screw caps. The plainer bottles were usually pear shaped. Kate Foster, to whom we are indebted for most of the information on the subject, quotes Madame de Pompadour as spending 500,000 francs a year on perfume, only a minority of whose containers, of course, would have been in ceramic. Often a grill in "smelling bottles" held a sponge steeped in smelling salts, aromatic vinegar, etc.

A curious form of scented red pottery, originating in Central America, was also made in Portugal and Spain. It was known as "boccaro," and in the early 18th century women are reputed to have eaten it "causing obstructions and often [proving] very dangerous."

To be effective, of course, scent bottles must have air-tight stoppers and this has limited the number made by craft potters.

SCHNABELKRUG

A Rhenish (16th/17th century Sieberg) stoneware jug/pitcher with a long beaklike spout.

SCHNELLE

See also **pinte.** A tall tapering **tankard** (see illustration A under **tankard**) from 16th century Germany.

SCOOP

A number of early pots are distorted in such a way that it seems probable that they were intended for scooping up grain, etc. or water. The so-called **milk ladles** from Cyprus, etc. make excellent scoops. A few are made by craft potters today, but there is much less use for them than there once was.

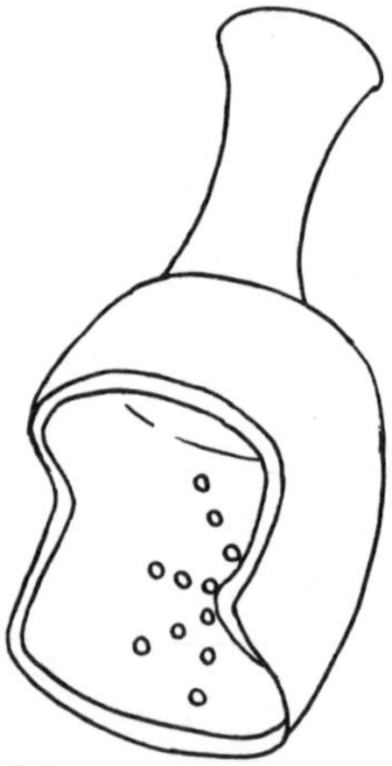
A

A. A charming sugar or flour sifter scoop by Michael Casson. B. This hand-built Bronze Age spouted bowl has been deformed in a way which suggests its use as a large scoop perhaps for water. (Photo: facing page.)

B

SCREW STOPPER/LID

Piccolpasso describes the making of a screw stopper (in *The Three Books of the Potter's Art*, written circa 1565) to fit into a thread on a thrown pot neck.

A. Michael Cardew's teapot with a screw-on lid. (Crafts Study Centre, Bath.)
B. A modern hot-water bottle, 1979, by Ray Finch, with a very professional screw-in stopper.

A

B

Bristol and other jars were often fitted with screw tops. Cardew, in C.PP (see Booklist) gives details for making his now famous screw stoppers and screw-on lids, the latter illustrated in PQ46. See also the illustration of the **hot-water bottle** by Ray Finch.

SCUTELLA

A Roman drinking cup.

SEAT

See **garden seat.**

SERVING DISH

A three-legged dish with an out-standing handle is specifically labelled "serving dish" in G.EAFP (see Booklist). Modern oven-to-table ware has reduced the necessity for serving dishes, but a number are still made, often with a thrown handle.

A serving dish by the author. It can be held without putting a finger in the food. It is also wide enough to easily spoon vegetables, etc., but has a slight return to the rim to help prevent them from spilling over, and it is oven-proof to keep them hot.

SHAKER

U.S. term for the English **salt cellar;** see at **cruet.** At one time, sugar shakers were made, but they are now quite rare in England.

SHAVING MUG

Large mugs, the mouth partly covered with a perforated soap dish, or with a half dish luted on, were made from the 1840s on.

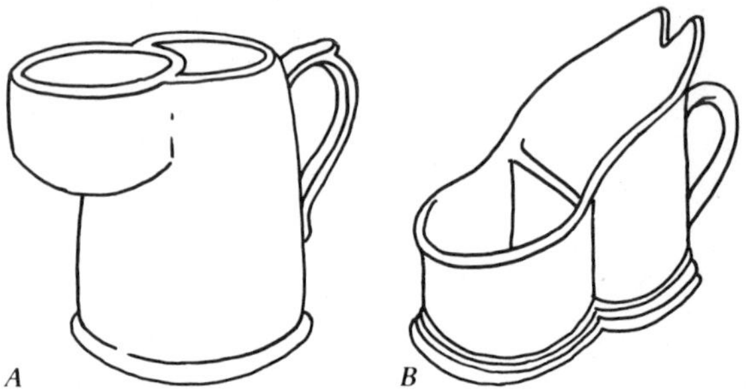

A/B. Two types of shaving mug—one American, the other English, both 19th century.

SHELL FORM

Early uses of the shell form in ceramics are the Cretan "argonaut" shell illustrated, and a much more vigorous, but still realistic, form from the Japanese Jomon period shown in E.ACJ (see Booklist). Shells, however, are not commonly used as a basis for pots. Some crude ones appear on Minoan wall

A. An argonaut shell in "faience" from 15th century B.C. *Crete.*

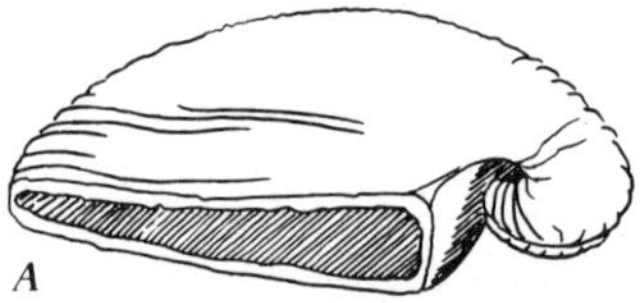

B. A more potlike shell in Chinese porcelain, much imitated by the soft-paste potters of the West. (Barlow Collection.)

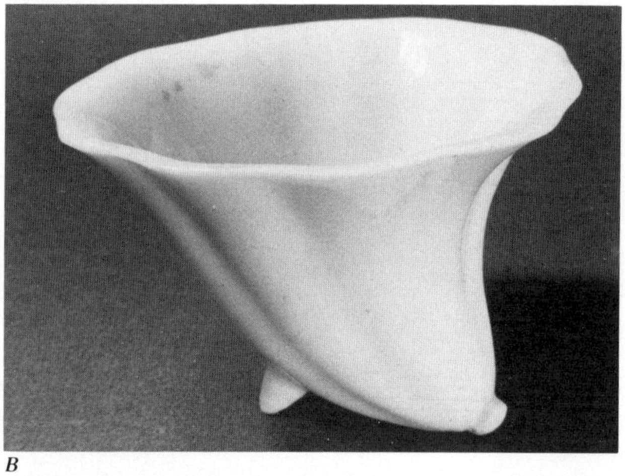

B

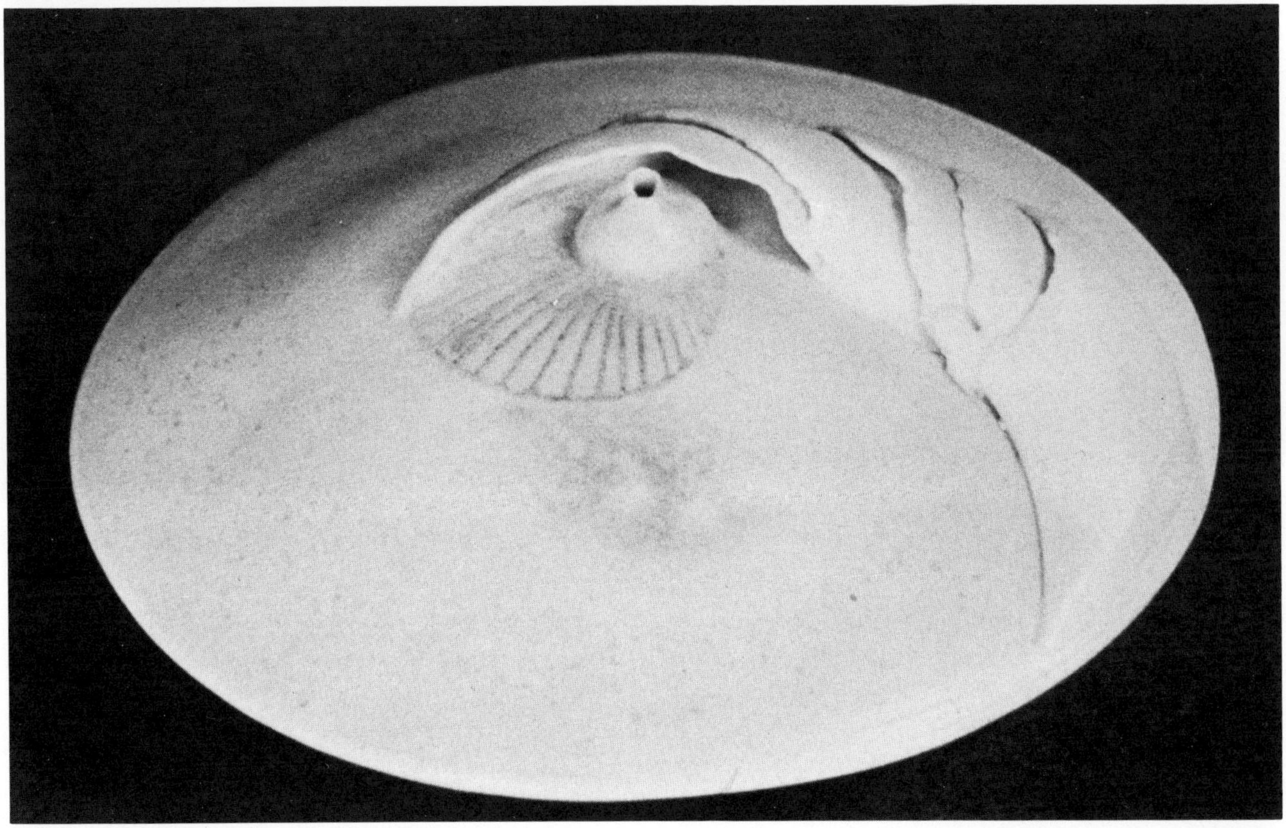

C

decorations and on superbly potted flower holders from the later Chinese dynasties. See also **scallop dish.** Today the shell is translated into ceramics in a more abstract fashion.

C. A modern adaptation of the shell form by Geoffrey Swindell, simplified and "abstracted."
D. A simpler, but more overt, shell form by James Tower, 1953. See boat. *(Photograph:* Pottery Quarterly.*)*

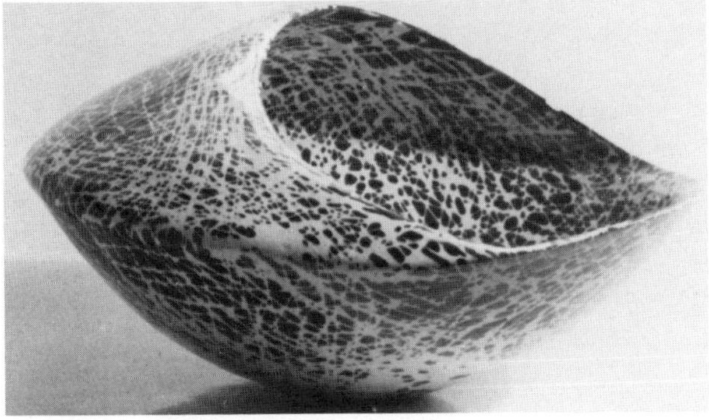

D

SHIP

See **boat.**

SHOULDER

The upper part of the curved wall of a pot; that part immediately below the neck.

SIEVE

See **colander, scoop.**

SILVER FORM

T'ang pottery is said to have been influenced in some degree by contemporary Chinese and Persian silverware. Small ring handles and certain straight-sided cups are cited. In later times (Ming and Ch'ing), silver objects were certainly sent from the West to China as models for porcelain orders. The Derby factory made **sugar bowls** with ring handles, which would normally only appear on silver pots.

These influences, however, are fairly slight, and certain ranges of form are common to several materials within a given culture. The folk potters have always imitated their more wealthy contemporaries' tastes, but the results quickly assume a purely ceramic style. See under **metal form** for Arthur Lane's analysis of this subject. Among craft potters today, influences from other materials are negligible.

SITULA, Situlate

The word is used, especially by archaeologists, to describe shapes whose main form is rather flowerpot or bucketlike; i.e., straight sides tapering downwards. There may also be a shoulder and a neck above this main form. There are many examples from late Neolithic and Bronze Age England. See also under **pail.** C.PPGT (see Booklist) also gives "situla" as a small Greek wine container; a small **stamnos.**

A hand-built situlate urn, reputedly derived from bronze forms. Early Iron Age Britain, 7th century B.C. (Devizes Museum.)

SKEUOMORPH

From *skya,* meaning "shadow," and *morph,* "form." Fagg, in F.PAA (see Booklist), describes the meaning as a representation of utensils in other materials complete with details which were necessary features of construction in the original, but which are carried over as decoration, for instance, **leather forms** in pottery complete with studs, **calabash** copies in clay with representations of the harness, etc. See also illustration A under **jug/pitcher.**

SKILLET

Possibly from the Old French *escuelete,* "a small platter." The word has disappeared from English usage, but in the United States, it denotes a frying pan. Long-handled pans, similar to **pipkins,** often with three feet, are called "skillets" in books on archaeology. Charleston (see C.WC in Booklist) calls the German *grapen,* which is a tripod cooking pot, a "skillet." There are very pleasant 16th/17th century frying pan shapes about 10 inches/255mm wide, with pulled, flat, straight handles.

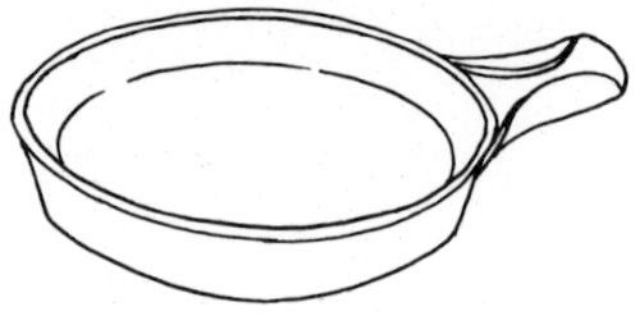

Called a skillet in York County Museum, this 17th century shallow pan (about 9 inches/230mm diameter) has a very unusual handle in which a rounded slab of clay has been folded inwards, possibly for extra strength, possibly for insulation.

SKINKER

Similar to a **caudle cup** or **posset pot.** According to H.LCB (see Booklist), "Spout pots were originally called skinkers."

SKYPHOS, Scyphus

A deep Greek drinking bowl or cup with two handles, which may be horizontal or diagonal, and a small, spreading foot. See illustration B under **cup** for general silhouette. There are variations in the width of foot and angle of handle.

SLAB BUILDING

Pots built of clay slabs can be very diverse in character. They may have the sharp, clean lines which result from building with leather-hard clay, or they

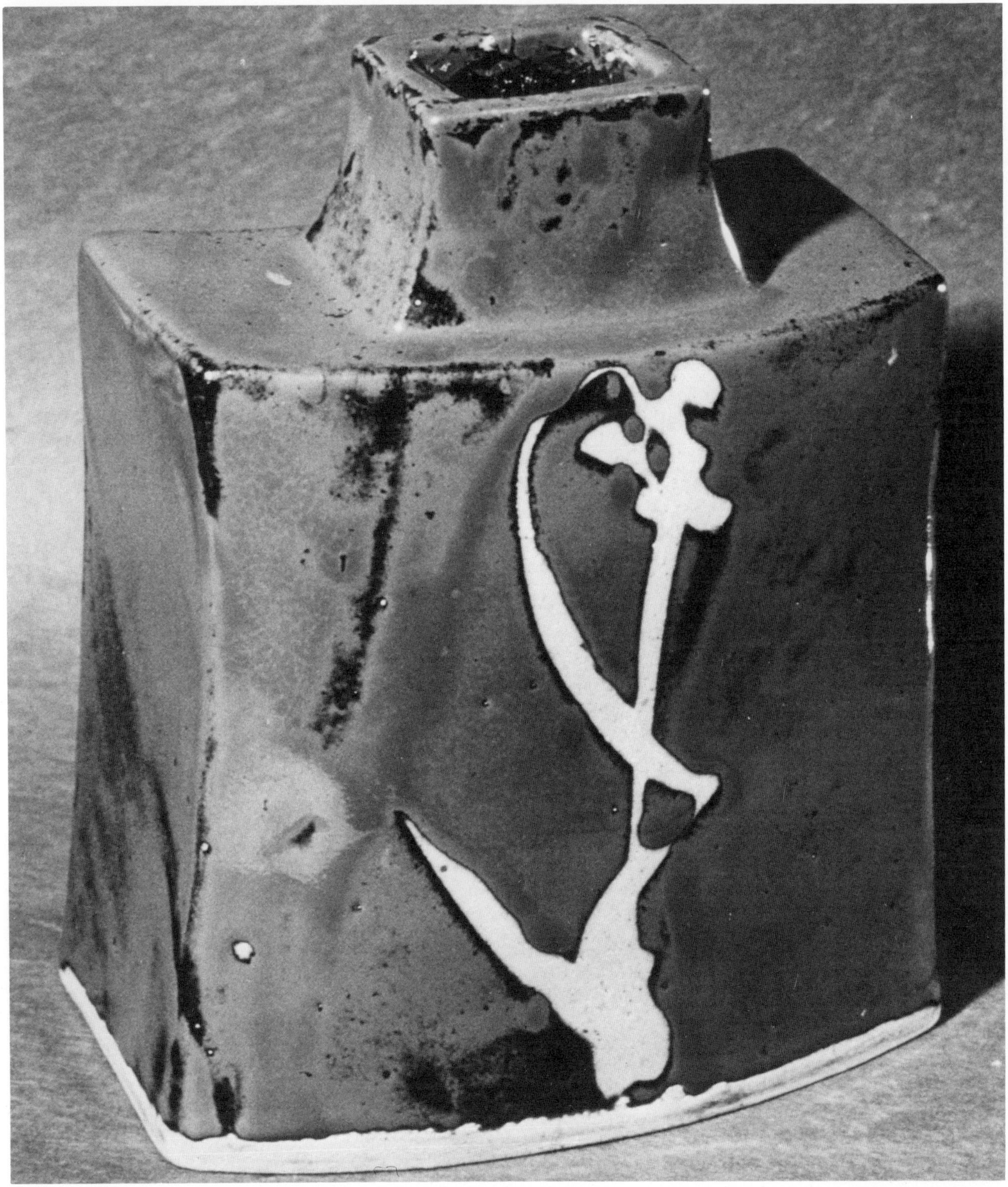

A

B

A. A mighty slab pot by Hamada, the curves on all faces softening the overall severity of form. (See page 205.)
B. A "castle" by Ian Auld, varying the usual rectangular plan.

C

C. Much looser in feeling and combined with some representational modelling is this slab construction by Gillian Lowndes. (Photograph: Design Council, London.)
D. Still further from the angular is this "standing form" flower holder by Sheila Fournier (on facing page), its holes and irregularities giving light and space to what would otherwise be a rather blank wall of clay. (Photograph: John Anderson.)
E. Slab building around a core can be rigid, or it can be more "slack" and plastic, as in these pots (on facing page) by Dan Arbeid.

may be more lively and "squashy" when clay is used in its plastic state. Rhodes (see R.PF in Booklist) suggests that "building with slabs is architectonic rather than growth-organic" and that it "introduces a needed counterpoint in pottery to the otherwise all prevailing curves." He also warns that there is a tendency in slab work for the forms to become stiff and mechanical.

In older pieces it is difficult to distinguish between slab and molded, flat-sided pots. The Japanese especially made a number of boxes, incense burners, jars, etc. which could have been slab-built, and they have names for the technique—*sashimono* (cabinet work) in Tokyo; *hariawase* (pasting together) in Kyoto. From earlier cultures, votive figures, model **houses,** etc. are slab built, and there are occasional slab additions to **composite pots,** but the vast majority of wares were made by other means.

Today, however, slab building is used by potters the world over. Rules cannot be laid down, but an oblong plan tends to be more interesting than a square one. Curved walls and large, composite forms can be built up. The wide range can be illustrated by comparing the elegant, gentle curving **envelopes** of clay by Val Barry, with the rigid rectangles of Sarah Perry, or the massive constructions of Colin Kellam.

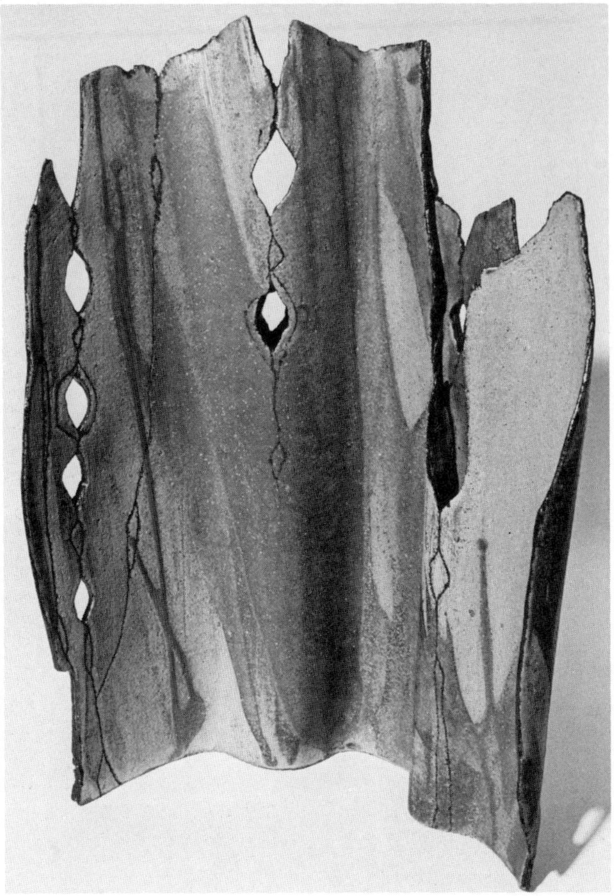

D

SLAB PLATE/DISH

A very simple form may be achieved by merely lifting the edges of a flat slab of clay. This is very suitable for raku (see the film *Raku, English Style*). The technique is practiced in Japan.

A

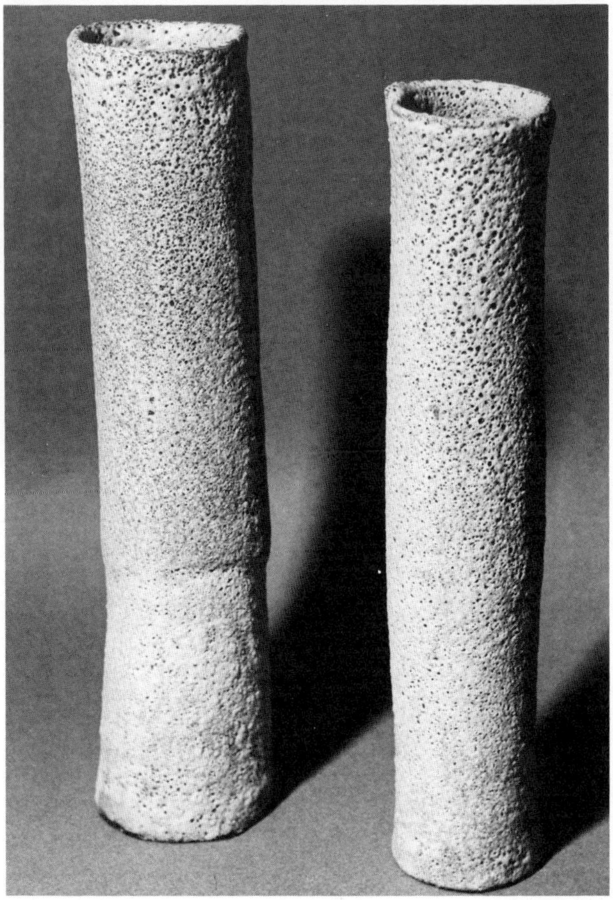

E

A flat platter or tray can also be made by throwing a wall onto a circular slab of clay by way of a thick coil.

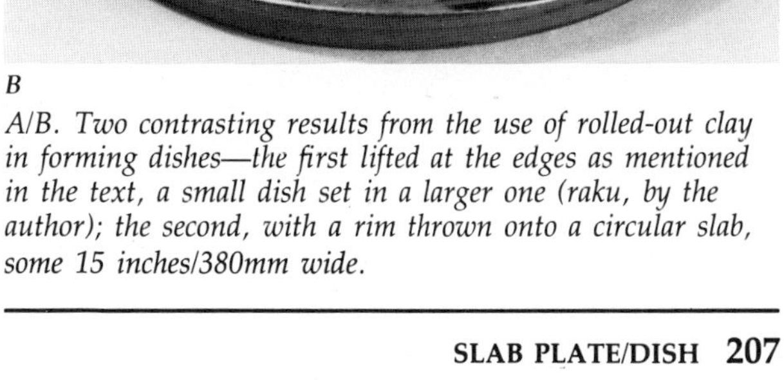

B

A/B. Two contrasting results from the use of rolled-out clay in forming dishes—the first lifted at the edges as mentioned in the text, a small dish set in a larger one (raku, by the author); the second, with a rim thrown onto a circular slab, some 15 inches/380mm wide.

A sliding lid on a compartmented box in the Bristol Museum. It tends to stick a bit halfway! (Bristol Museum.)

SLIDING LID

These are very rare, and the only example the author has found is in Bristol tin-glaze, as illustrated.

SLING STONES

Special nut-shaped sling stones were made in the British Iron Age, (examples in the Salisbury Museum), and this must have been repeated elsewhere.

SLIP-CAST FORM

This is more an industrial than a creative technique, but a number of potters are exploring its possibilities—its precision, its ability to reproduce crisply intricate surface modelling or texture, and it usefulness in making a number of identical forms which can then be built into sculptural constructions.

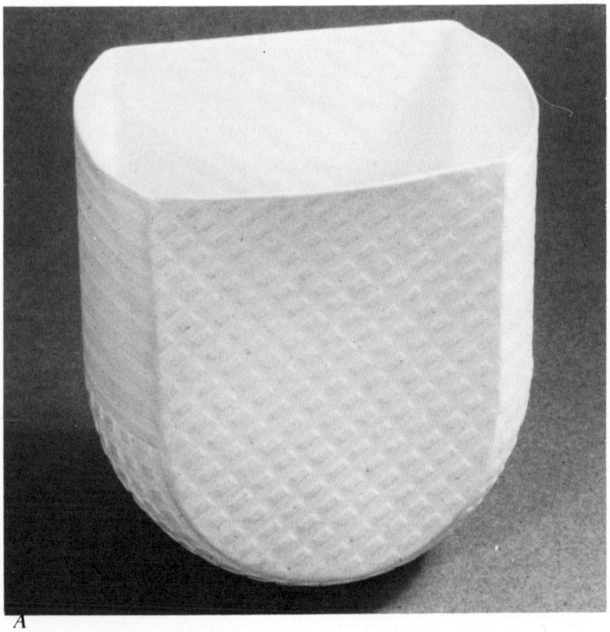

A

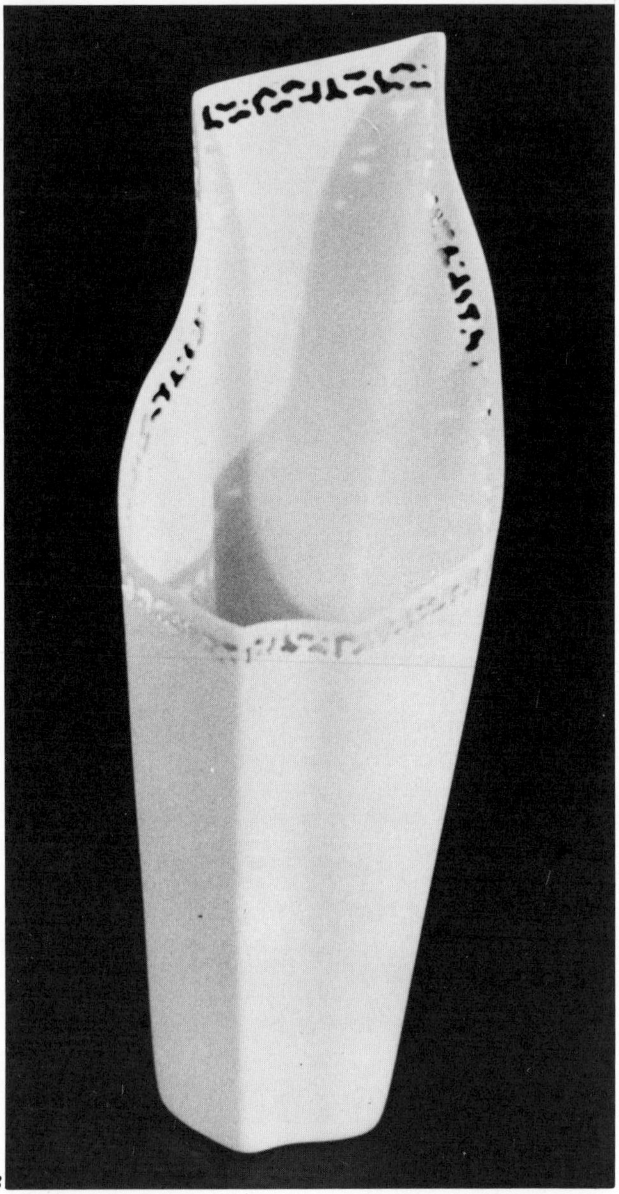

B

A/B. Some of the advantages of slip-casting for certain effects are summed up in these porcelain (bone china) pieces by Jaqueline Poncelet and Angela Verdon—wafer thinness for maximum transluscency, reproduction of an intricate surface texture, and a shape difficult to form by any other means.

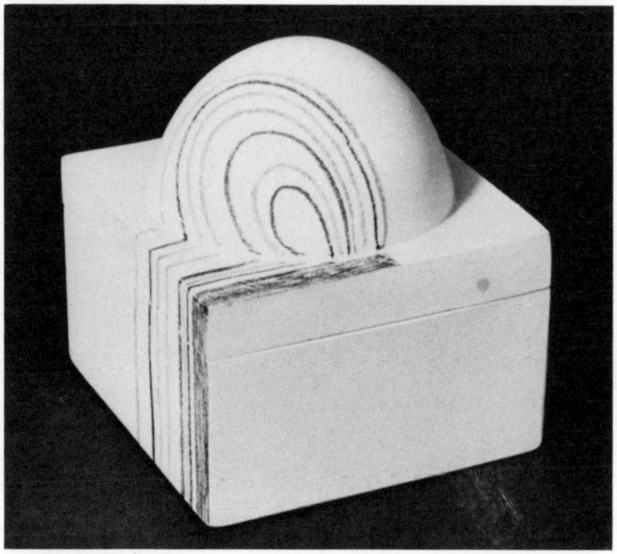

C

C. Slip-casting here gives a more solid, but very sharp and precise result. By Pat Schilston.

SLIP CUP/TRAILER

Most of the early slip-trailing was done using pottery trailers. These may have had a single spout or an inserted hollow quill, sometimes a number side by side of which as many as seven have been reported. Various designs are found, all aiming at a maximum charge of slip combined with ease of use. Guilland (see G.EAFP in Booklist) shows a squat, squarish, open-topped vessel, about tea-cup size, and with depressions on the sides to fit the fingers. There is no obvious way of controlling the flow of slip in this design, as there is in many other types which are closed, except for a hole which the thumb can cover. Potters should make their own trailers and should not rely on the rubber contraptions currently supplied.

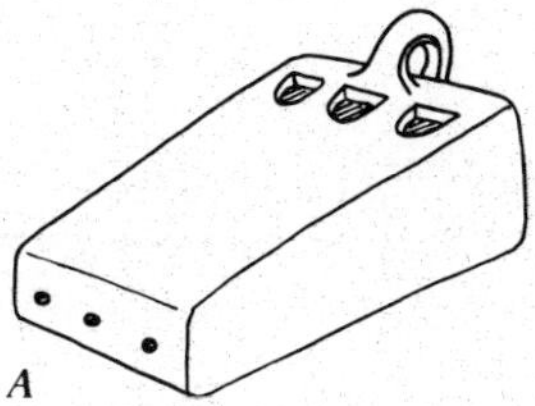

A

A. A three-section slip trailer from 18th century England. Quills would have been inserted in the holes in the front end.

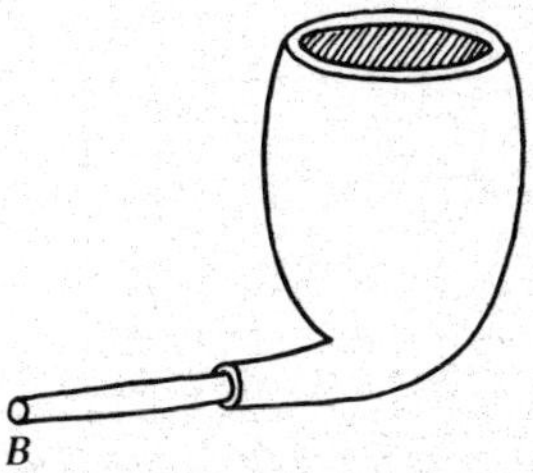

B

B. An English slip cup very like the bowl of a tobacco pipe but, of course, considerably larger. Used with an inset quill.

SNAIL DISH

A dish with a number of small depressions for serving snails.

SNUFF BOX, Snuffing pipe

These were made in quantity, especially in Germany and France, either as plain rectangular or oval boxes, or modelled as animals, miniature chests of drawers, shells, etc. They were sometimes fitted with a silver mount. A small Chinese vessel about 4 inches high is called a "snuff bottle." The snuffing pipe was used in ancient Colombia, the snuff being taken through a spout.

A snuff pipe from PreColumbian American; the snuff would have been inhaled through the spout. The bowl has a suggestion of animal form.

SOAP DISH

So that the soap bar does not lie in water and disintegrate the main object of a soap dish, as opposed to any small bowl or dish which may be used, is

A soap dish in 3 parts (the saucerlike drainer lifts off), in Art Nouveau style, by Minton's Pottery.

the provision for drainage. G.EAFP (see Booklist) illustrates an 1850 soap dish as a covered-in bowl with a hole in the concave top. A grill is more often used, and there must be some way of swilling out the interior.

SOLITAIRE

A rare game to find in ceramic, but Laurel Keeley makes it look like a perfectly natural thing to do.

The game of solitaire in stoneware; see text.

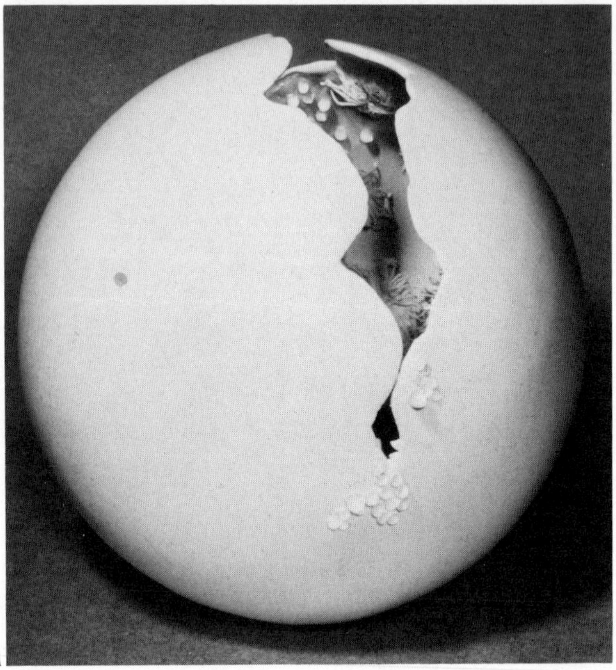

A

A. A broken sphere by Mary Keepax. The interior is shown in detail under fungi form.

SOUFFLÉ DISH

A vertically walled, flat-bottomed, fairly deep dish, usually in fire-proof ware. Industrial examples are often fluted on the outside, probably in order to absorb and distribute the heat. They have no lid. Similar dishes are known as **cocottes.**

SOUL HOUSE

See **building.**

SPHERE

One of the shapes "read" into pottery form in attempts at **analysis,** but seldom present in practice where curves are nearly always progressively sharpening or decreasing.

The sphere is occasionally used in its own right; decorated balls in Egyptian paste are known from the 2nd millennium B.C., although few seem to have been made between then and the 18th century when **carpet bowls** became a fashionable game. Today, purely decorative ceramics are made as spheres, usually pierced and slightly deformed, or with an opening to show miniature contents; e.g., the fungi forms of Mary Keepax. Spheres in variegated clays sometimes solid, or as spherical bottles, are made by Michael Bayley and others.

SPIGOT

A plug, tap, or faucet. Used in **cider bottles** and other pottery; see **bunghole.**

SPINDLE WHORL

These have been made in pottery since very early times. There are examples from 13th century England, for instance.

SPIRIT/CORDIAL BOTTLE

See **flask, costrel, pilgrim bottle, barrel.** More specifically, it is a tall, straight-sided spirit bottle made in vast numbers, especially in salt-glaze, over the last 500 years in Europe. Squared and other individual shapes appeared with the development of casting in the 19th century. (Photo: page 212.)

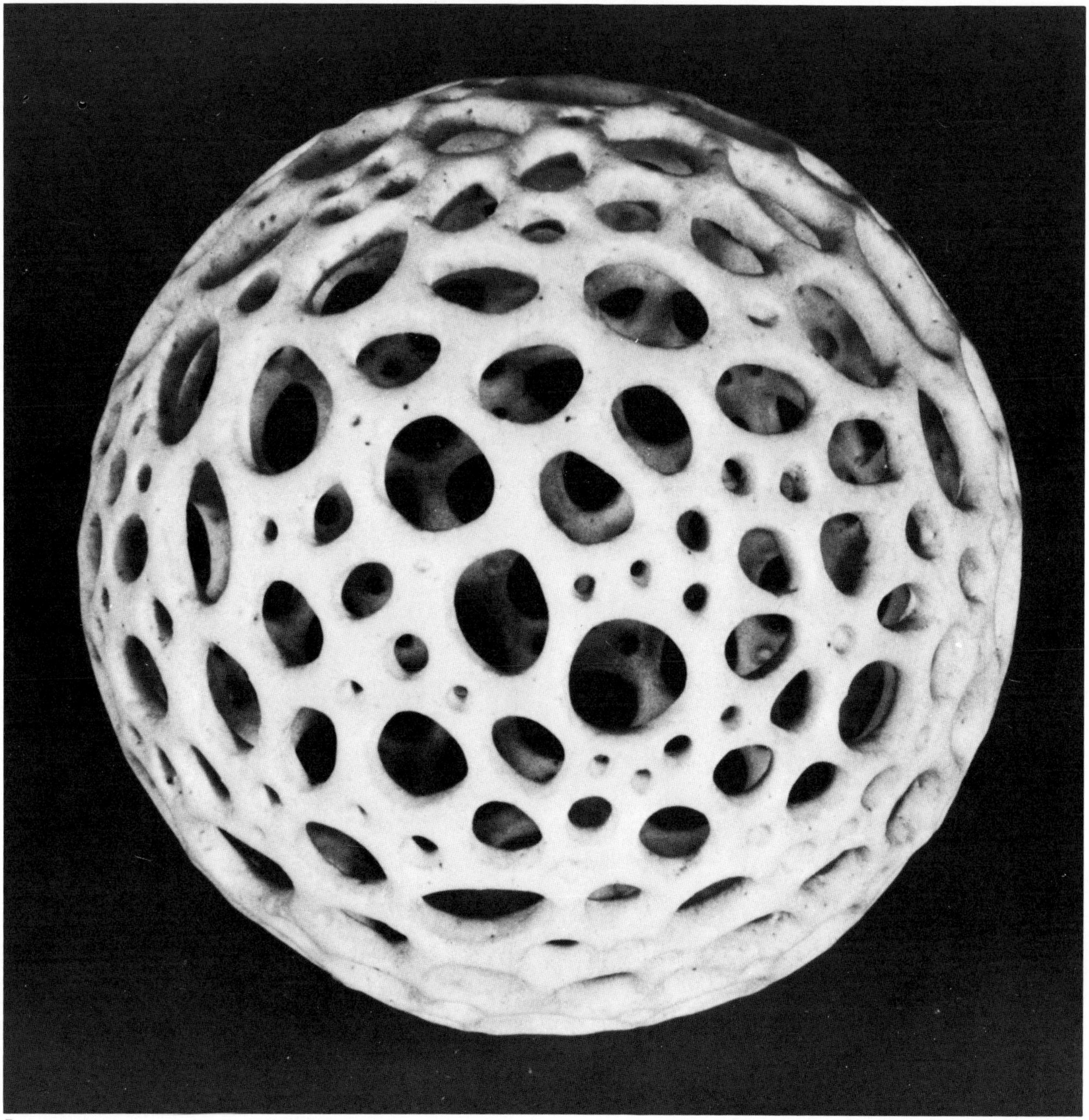

B

B. A finely and beautifully cut porcelain sphere, like a truly natural object. By Mary Rogers, circa 1971.

A spirit bottle (See page 210) by Doultons, modelled in the form of John Burns, a well-known social reformer of the late 19th century. He would not, perhaps, have been ideally pleased at the fact that his memory is being linked with alcohol, although there are other rather larger figures labelled "Cordial"!

SPITTOON

Also called a "cuspidor." Some rather splendid examples come from the Sung Sui period and later in Blanc-de-Chine. In G.EAFP (see Booklist) Guilland shows a form like a large soap dish, with a concave, closed-in top and a hole in the center. There is also another in the side for emptying. How far our ideas about spitting have changed over the last 100 years can be gauged by the 19th century quotation he gives: "The large or first size, called professional, added dignity to law offices and barrooms [while smaller spitoons] graced the household."

SPLIT and SLASHED FORM

This very free style of broken and interrupted form is essentially modern. See also discussion under **distorted form.** The tearing of clay for formal excitement is a reflection of despair with established forms which occasionally can make its own statement, but, which often provides no more than a temporary frisson. Out of the welter of such work, especially in the United States, some additions to the aesthetics of pottery might arise, and there have undoubtedly been some fine pieces; but the hit-or-miss nature of the "technique" makes judgment on the mass of work difficult. As usual, time will sort it out, as it has the ceramics of every age.

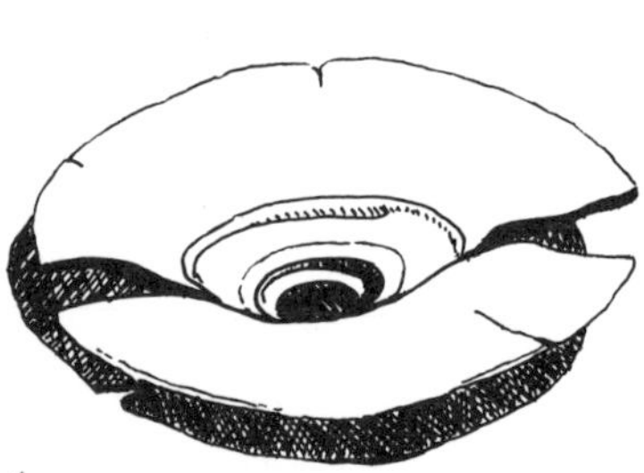

A

A. A double layer, split-rimmed, hand-built bowl by Ruth Duckworth. The break is carefully considered and the final form has its own logic, a feature missing from much of this type of pottery.

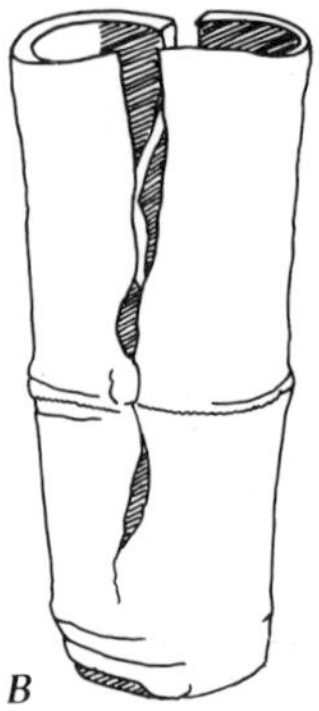

B

B. A Japanese "flower arrangement" pot, slashed almost in two.

C. A. layered bowl by Sheila Fournier. (Photo: facing page.)

SPOON

Spoons or small **ladles** in pottery have been made since Neolithic times, and there are some beautifully designed examples from early Europe and from Sussex, England, for instance, from around 2000 B.C. Very similar shapes, integrating bowl and spoon, are still made in their millions in the Far East, and many are exported. Porcelain teaspoons have been made at all the soft-paste factories since the 18th century, although European ceramic spoons

A. A charming spoon in Chinese style in Worcester porcelain, circa 1790. (Bristol Museum.)

A

C

B. Porcelain spoons or scoops, the taller about 5 inches/125mm high, in very original shapes. By Ruth Franklin, 1977.
C. The smooth and flowing shape of a 18th/19th century medicine spoon, very similar in form to a common type of lamp.

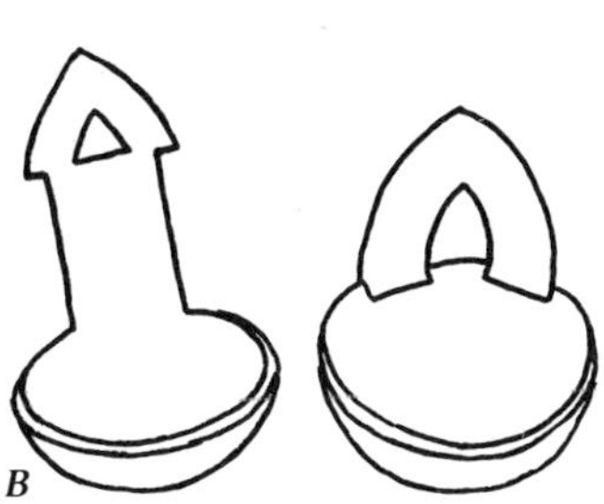

B

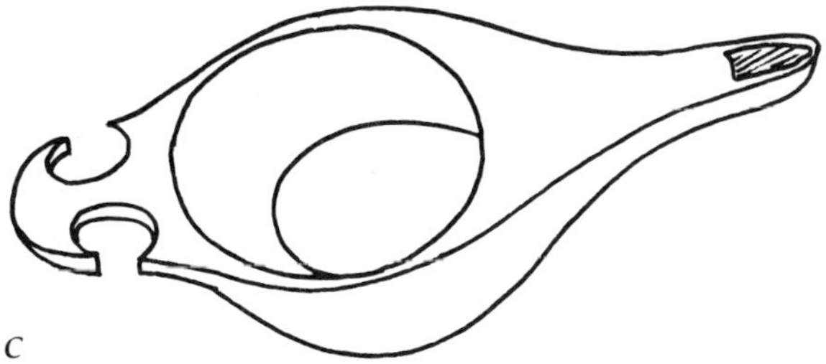

C

are not at all common now. A handle which is curved along its length is much stronger than a flat one. Various ingenious (and terrifying) medical "spoons" were devised for giving, often forcibly, medicines or pills to children. As with many very specialized ceramics, however, the shapes were often rather splendid. A few craft potters still make spoons today.

SPOUT

According to *Webster's New Collegiate Dictionary*, "a projecting tube or lip." A spout is normally tubular, but, as suggested in this definition, can also be an open trough for directing and pouring liquid from a vessel. In the case of certain designs of **lamp**, the spout held the wick. Where the **lip** of a jug/pitcher is luted onto the pot as a separate form, or is long and pronounced, it is sometimes called a "spout."

A. A long-spouted "jug" (or, more likely, a lamp) from 1st millennium B.C. Iran. An extreme example, but well-balanced and designed with great élan.

A

B. A multiple spout Chinese Sung pot. In some of this style, the hole in the spout does not go through into the pot. (Barlow Collection.)

B

Pitchers with short tube spouts were made from mid-Saxon times in England, and many interesting styles developed in preColumbian America (**stirrup spouts,** etc.). Spouts are often found on Chinese wares, not only on wine and teapots, but also springing from the shoulders of **ewers,** etc. They are usually straight and slightly tapering, but may be bent forward at the end or modelled in the shapes of dragons and other creatures. A late T'ang lidded pot is shown in M.CP (see Booklist) with five "false spouts"; even at this early date, they had come to be used decoratively. In Ancient Greece the spout is often in the form of an open-mouthed creature, a continuation of a much older tradition (see illustration A under **animal form**). A Roman bowl has a spout modelled as a wild boar. See also illustration for **scoop** for a spouted bowl. Near Eastern spouts, like some from China (see **wine bottle**), were often long and curving, precursors of the modern industrial coffeepot.

C. A lip extended to an open spout, the thrown rim still remaining as a bridge above it. By Ray Finch, 1979.

C

In modern craft pottery the spout is comparatively rare, except, of course, on teapots, where it is usually straight and tapering. An impression of the industrial double-curved teapot spout can be obtained by the judicious cutting of a thrown bottle-kiln shape (see F.DPP in Booklist). Occasional experiments, such as the pressed spout made by Harry Davis, have not been very successful. Multispouts are found on a few modern pieces—the teapots of Brian Newman and on an assembled slab-pot form by Tony Sterckx (illustrated in CR8). Elizabeth Fritsch goes back to the open-trough types of the Near East and other early pottery with her cut rims.

SPOUT and BRIDGE

A type of closed-over, double-spouted early South American pot, with a handle bridging the two spouts. Sometimes one spout is replaced by a model head or figure, which may also contain a whistle. See also **bridge handle, double-necked pot.**

SPOUTED BOWL

As mentioned under **spout,** a number of early bowls were fitted with a trough spout for pouring. This alters and gives interest to the form. Modern potters are usually content with a **lip.**

SPRINKLER

In the Ipswich Museum there is a very narrow-necked bottle, about 12 inches high, with two handles springing from the rim and a number of holes in the wide base. It is labelled "sprinkler," but how

This fine spouted bowl is from Early Bronze Age Cyprus. It was probably used as a scoop *and for pouring. The lug has 2 holes for hanging.*

it was used and for what purpose is not mentioned. Possibly it was used for damping rushes on the floor and to lay the dust. A slightly less elegant, but full and strongly formed example is illustrated here. Minoan and Mycenaean pots, with a small hole in a pointed base, were once considered to have been sprinklers, but are now thought to have been wine **filters.** See also **watering can/pot.**

An English 16th/17th century earthenware water sprinkler; 11 inches/250mm high.

SQUARE-MOUTHED BOWLS/POTS

Square plan bowls and pots occur very early in pottery history; e.g., in Neolithic Moravia. They were sometimes square-built, possibly of slabs, but

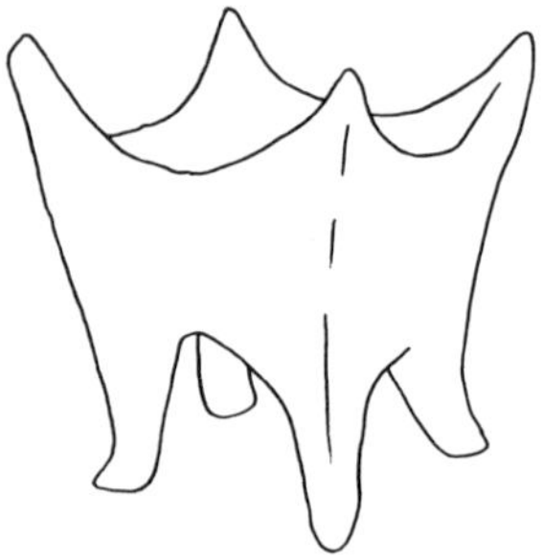

A bold square bowl from Neolithic Moravia. As so often in these early Central European vessels, it is slightly anthropomorphic in feeling.

were more often deformed circles. From several sites in Europe, pots or deep bowls were found whose rims had been pinched or pressed into a square, sometimes with standing knobs at the corners, rather like a **chafing dish.** These are known as "square-mouth bowls." A similar, but more rugged and serrated, top to a carinated bowl was made during the Japanese Jomon period, some 3000 B.C. See also **slab building.** All are bold and interesting and would repay study by the modern potter. See also the illustrations under **beaten shape, basket.**

STACKING POTS

In earlier times, when possesions were few and cupboards nonexistent, there was little demand for pottery designed to pack into the smallest possible space. Even today, when this is an increasing need, the design of pots that will sit comfortably and safely upon one another does not often enter into the reckoning of the average craft potter. Stacking is thought of as an industrial problem, but a little thought and minor alterations in design can sometimes greatly assist the owner of a small kitchen and a lot of pots.

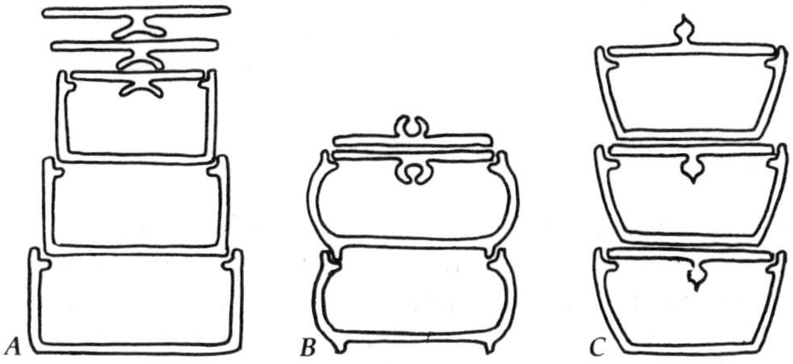

A/B/C. Some ideas for stacking designs: in diminishing sizes, (see also E); a foot in the rim of a flange below; a set on reversed lids.

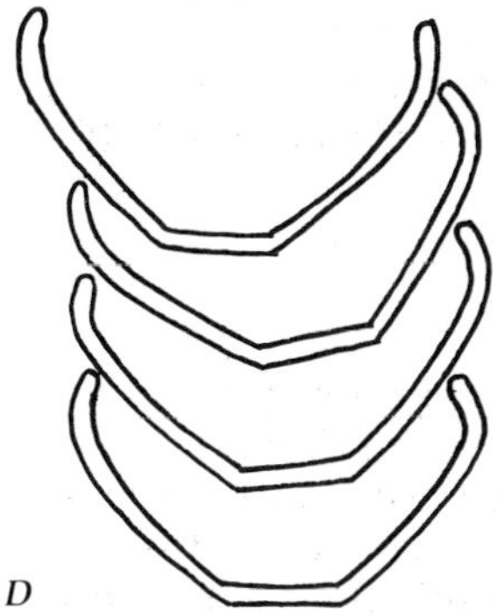

D. Rounded forms tend to slide about when stacked and can be unsteady and difficult to pick up.

E. A set of kitchen bowls, occupying the smallest possible space and with the ladle lying comfortably along the lined-up lips, by the author.

STAMNOS

A Greek storage vessel, not unlike a footed **amphora.** In modern Greece, stamna are glazed inside and used for storing olives, honey, etc.

STAND

The practicalities of the use of round-bottomed pots in comparatively sophisticated communities has always been difficult to envisage. In the British Museum two types of stands—tall diabolo shapes possibly for ritual vessels, and short, open-topped stands for domestic use—are displayed. These are very rarely shown or mentioned in books or mu-

A/B. The tall ritual and shorter domestic stands for roundbased pots mentioned in text. From Egypt, 3rd millennium B.C.

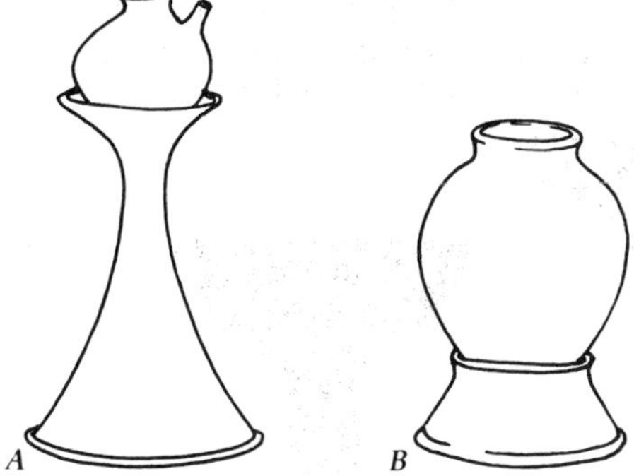

seums. Are they, in fact, very uncommon or do archaeologists and historians fail to recognize them when they appear? There is a subject for a thesis here, including inquiry into why round bases continued for so long.

STANDING BOWL

A term often used to describe a bowl, usually a large one, raised on a very deep, wide foot ring. There are a number of fine bowls of this type from 16th century Turkey (Isnik).

A typical outline of the type of sturdy bowl produced in 16th century Turkey.

STEIN

A large beer mug or **tankard** (see illustration under tankard), of earthenware or salt-glazed stoneware, from Germany, frequently with a hinged metal lid. According to *Webster's New Collegiate Dictionary,* it held a pint. Tall and tapering towards the top, it is a strong, handsome shape. To quote Rawson (see R.C in Booklist): "Some of the German 17th century beer tankards . . . convey a semihumorous and boastful extravagance."

Fishley Holland (H.FYP) uses "stein" to describe a very different vessel: a very large crock used for pickling pilchards in Cornwall, and which is also called a "greatnock" or "bussa."

STEM CUP

A bowl or cup set on a tall, slightly flaring foot or stem. Crete and Mycenae produced attractive early types, as did Crete, in a rather weightier way, be-

A

B

C

A. A form widely made in the Mediterranean countries over many centuries. This silhouette is typical. Late Mycenean, circa 8 inches/205mm high.
B. The type of stem cup from Ming and later periods of China. Proportions vary, but the bowl is always wide.
C. A modern variation with a shorter stem, by Stella Goorney. The small flange between bowl and stem gives interest to the outline.

fore them. But the most characteristic stem cups come from China, a few from the T'ang dynasty, the simplest and most graceful from Hsuan Te (circa 1430). Much earlier (pre4000 B.C., according to C.HRNC—see Booklist), China produced very involved stem cup shapes (or **goblets**), with a perforated bulb in the stem and a thistle-shaped top. Japan in the first centuries A.D. produced typically assertive carinated forms on a wide foot or stem, which also had a hole pierced through it.

Stem cups are produced today, often in porcelain, by David Leach and others. See also **saki bottle/cup, chalice.**

STEW POT/JAR

As understood by the 19th century folk potters, this was a fairly tall pot, often with a lid, used for the slow cooking of poor cuts of meat. In the north of England it was cylindrical; elsewhere, and on the Continent, it was more frequently rounded. A form

The traditional type of Yorkshire stew pot, by Isaac Button, circa 1958.

resembling a jug/pitcher, with no handle, but with a **lip,** is listed as a "stew pot" by John Safford, a U.S. potter, in 1845.

STILL

See **alembic.**

STIRRUP CUP

A cup for liquor, handed to a huntsman or horseman in the saddle, usually modelled as an animal's head—fox, deer, hare, etc.—or as a dog. It was designed so that it could not be set down until empty; i.e., only on its rim. In Ancient Greece a similar form was known as a **rhyton.** There is mention of stirrup cups in England as early as 1681.

STIRRUP JAR

The term is applied to certain types of Mediterranean water pots (Mycenae, etc.), which had a trefoil handle over a closed top or over a dummy (i.e., closed) neck. Those with a closed neck had a spout on the shoulder.

A

A. The typical ancient American stirrup spout bottle. Often they are a good deal more elaborate.

B. A clever modern adaptation of the stirrup spout, by George Rainer.

B

STIRRUP SPOUT

A hooped semicircular tube on an otherwise closed shape, with a further spout set at the apex of the curve. It is common in Peruvian and other early American pottery, and also occurs in ware from Etruria, Italy.

STONE FORM

From the Naquada area of Egypt (circa 3500 B.C.) has been found a direct copy in pottery of a carved stone original, even to the graining of the stone. Many rectangular Chinese pots are based on carved jade and other rocks. In some cases, however, the influence may have worked in reverse.

STOPPER

A plug for the neck of a vessel, usually a bottle. There are few stoppers reported from ancient sites: Some, of course, may have been lost, or they may have been made of some more perishable materials.

A

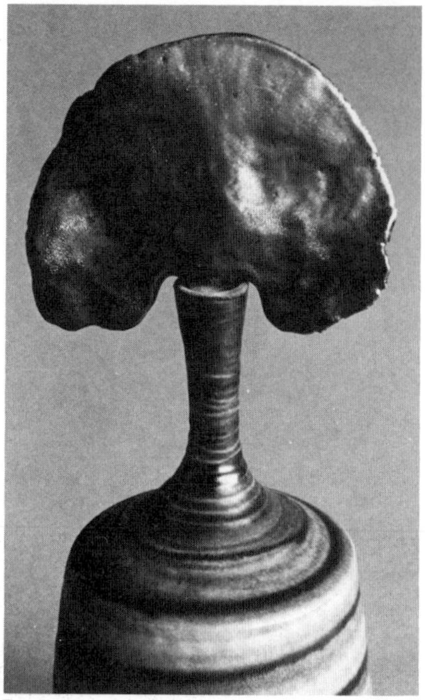

B

A. An interesting, hollow, thrown stopper on a small porcelain bottle, by Mary White. The stopper constitutes a major aspect of the form.
B. Another dominant, treelike stopper on a bottle by Mary Rich.

Like the **knob** on a lid, a stopper can crown and complete a pottery form. Invention and fantasy can have a place in its design. It is difficult to make a close-fitting ceramic stopper without resorting to a cork or rubber ring or sleeve. In theory, a tapered stopper should drop into a similar neck, but in practice, it is not easy. **Screw stoppers** are possible.

STORAGE JAR/Potting jar

This was one of the most common of pottery articles from the earliest times and right up to the early part of the 20th century in most parts of the world. They range from the vast **pithos** of Minoan Crete, to small lidded jars, such as the **barm jar.** The word "potted," for meat, etc., came from the use of pots for storing and preserving. These were known as "canisters" in Sussex. In the 18/19th centuries the sides were generally vertical, like jam jars, and they occasionally had lids, but were more often capped with some tied-on material for which a strong rim or groove was provided. Different shapes and sizes

A

A. This admirable large open pot is from 3rd millennium B.C. Iran. The sharp shoulder contrasts effectively with the rounded body.
B. A lidded and well-balanced store jar by Mick Casson.
C. One of the many vast (up to 7 feet/2m) and handsome storage jars from Minoan Crete (and still being made from arm-thick coils in 1976).

B

C

D

D. A firm-based, yet lively, jar in salt-glaze by Wally Keeler.
E. Two store jars by Vince Jackson. The flange on the taller jar renders handles unnecessary, but, if shorter, it would be too wide to span with the fingers; hence, the lug handles.

E

of jars have always been made for specific foods; e.g., a lid on a wide neck for sugar. See also **jar, albarello, ali baba, crock, granary jar, honeymoon pot, kuan jar, pickling jar,** etc.

Storage jars are still commonly made both by industrial and craft potters. A slightly rounded crock is the most usual shape for commercial jars, and others are made for the more expensive preserves. In England, Richard Batterham and Michael Casson are notable for their large storage jars and crocks.

STOVE

Earthenware boxes containing hot or burning fuel have been used as heaters at least since Pompeii (see **brazier**), but the true stove was of two types. There is the clay-built beehive shaped **oven,** found widely in the Mediterranean countries and in Europe, where the fuel was raked out before the food to be cooked was inserted (i.e., it had only a single chamber), and the more sophisticated type, with a hearth and a cooking chamber. In the latter form, famous in Germany and Holland, the ceramic element was confined largely to the elaborate tile work which covered them. Made from the 14th century onwards, the tiles were often heavily embossed with designs and figures and glazed in strong greens and other colors, the Hafner tiles being especially noteworthy. The single-chamber oven was used for bread until recently, and some are probably still working. Bread is reputed to be superior if cooked in a "falling" oven. Portable stoves were also made, such as those shown in the Museum of London, and were used for heating **posset,** etc. in the bed chamber. See also **food warmer, fire pot/bowl.**

Modern potters have made stoves but they are rare. A rather striking **barbecue** stove is illustrated in C.P&C (see Booklist). In CMsep74 an article by Zeljko Kujendzic describes the making of a pottery stove.

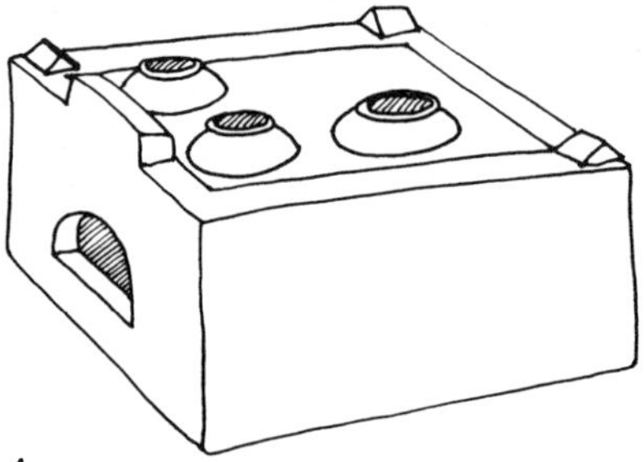

A

A. A Han Chinese model of a stove, about 11 inches/280mm square. No other period has given us so many three-dimensional glimpses of everyday life.

B

B. A simple country stove modelled in salt-glaze by Ian Gregory.

STRAINER

See **colander, drainer.**

STRAP HANDLE

The term describes a flat handle, like a leather strap in section. It is frequently found on Greek ware and on some ancient American pots, but also occurs throughout pottery history. The term is also sometimes used to indicate a handle springing over the top of a teapot or other vessel. See **bail.**

A strap handle in both senses of the word. Teapot by Sheila Fournier.

STRAWBERRY POT

A generally large, rounded crock in unglazed earthenware, the walls of which are cut through into semicircular holes over which half bowls are fixed. The whole pot is filled with soil, and plants are set in the cups and hang down as they grow. (Photo: page 224.)

STURZEBECHER

A German stoneware cup, the base of which was modelled as a man or a goblin. Like a stirrup cup, it could not be set down while containing liquid. When placed on its rim, the figure is the right way up.

The traditional strawberry pot. (See page 223.)

SUGAR BOWL/BOX

Sugar bowls, often with a high foot, were made in great numbers in the 18th/19th centuries. Highly ornate red earthenware covered pots were made by folk and country potters as special table pieces. Brears (see B.CECP in Booklist) quotes a rhyme on one: "If Some Shuger you have got/ Pray put it In this Little Pot."

A. A modern potter's very attractive variation on the covered sugar bowl, by Bernard Leach.
B. An early Derby sugar box circa 1780, probably imitating silver, even to the ring on the lid.

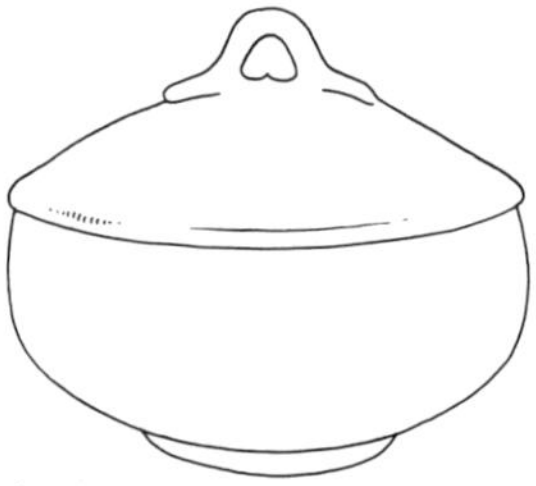

A

B

SUGAR LOAF MOLD

These large and handsome molds—up to 30 inches/ 760mm high—in unglazed earthenware, resemble the early Egyptian "black-top" pots, i.e., narrow, slightly curved inverted cones. They were made in the 18th/19th centuries for casting "sugar loaves." There are examples in the Museum of London and Bristol Museum.

SUNFLOWER BOWL

A deepish Chinese bowl shape, popular during the Sung dynasty, with five indentations in the rim, giving five flat **lobes.** This pleasant form has been imitated by modern potters.

SUSSEX PIG

There are two types of pottery Sussex Pig. One is the well-known **money box** in the form of a pig, curvaceous and usually decorated with run slip (engobe). The other is a vessel with a more or less cylindrical body, which is used as a jug/pitcher with a removable head as a cup (similar to the **bear jug, owl jug,** etc.). They were made near Rye and, in 1979, are still made at the Rye Pottery. B.CECP (see Booklist) quotes the phrase, possibly connected with these wares: "Drink a hogshead of wine to the health of the bride." There were various sizes, up to 11 inches/275mm long, and each was so designed that the jug could be set upright on its flat bottom and the cup on its ears and snout.

A Sussex Pig drinking vessel as described in text, the body a thrown cylinder.

SWEETMEAT (CANDY) TRAY

Flat-topped, covered bowls with five recesses around

a central one, used for sweetmeats, are found in Islamic pottery. A charming Ming box is illustrated in F.CBW (see Booklist) as being for sweetmeats. Trays were made extensively in tin-glaze and creamware. Often there were several trays fitted together, and this has become a favorite scheme with school and amateur potters today (see illustration under **pressed dish/bowl.** In PQ42 an attractive "sweet dish" by John Maltby has cut sides and a cane handle. See also at **confectionary mold.**

From the Near East, the home of sweetmeats of many delicious kinds, comes this Damascus 16th/17th century elaborately designed blue and white sectioned tray.

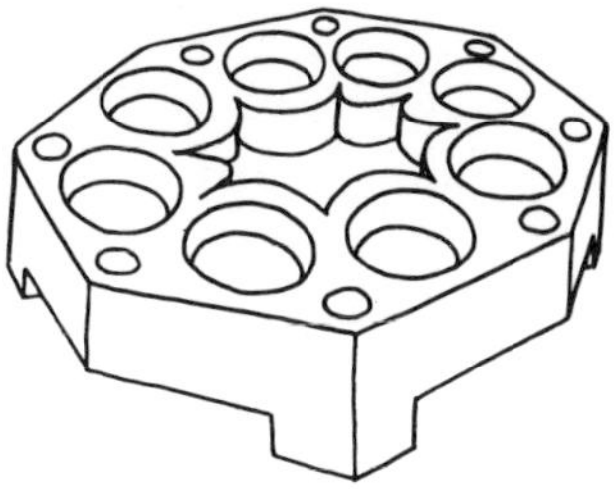

T

TABLE DECORATION

Porcelain replaced confectionary as centerpieces on the tables of 18th century fashionable society of Europe. "Harlequins, gondoliers, Turks, Chinese, and shepherdesses of Saxon china . . . whole meadows . . . Neptunes in cars of cockleshell triumph over oceans of looking glass." (Walpole, 1753.) Also described was a fountain "at least eight feet high . . . which ran with rosewater."

Imitation fruit, flowers, and food was reproduced to excess in the 19th century. Tables of pottery cakes and similar "fancies" have been made by Barbara Booth, Ernest Collyer, and others in the 1970s. Illustrations may be found in CR6 and 14 (see Booklist).

TANKARD

According to *Webster's New Collegiate Dictionary,* "a tall, one-handled drinking vessel." Originally, the word applied to hollow logs bound with iron and used as water pipes, and later it applied to metal-bound wooden drinking vessels; it came to mean a fairly tall pot, usually for ale or beer. Wordsworth speaks of "Tankards foaming from the tap." Described by CTCD (see Booklist) as a large muglike vessel, the tankard usually has a handle set just above midway. Some are fitted with a metal rim and lid.

Sturdy tankard shapes with angular handles were made in 16th century Turkey, but these are now considered to have been grain **measures** (see illustration). Splendid black-glazed examples were made in England where there was no such inhibition on the quaffing of spiritous liquors. Large drinking vessels from much earlier in history, e.g., 1400 B.C.

A

A. A real "power to your elbow" salt-glaze tankard or schnelle from Germany.

B. The typical 18th century English tankard from Bristol. (Bristol Museum.)

B

C

C. A squatter, but strongly thrown, tankard by Stella Goorney. The slight carinations of the profile add interest and provide natural junction points for the handle.

Mycenae, are called "tankards" by archaeologists. Some Roman "tankards" are more like large cups. Arthur Lane calls a **jakobakanne** a "tankard." A very large, squat German tankard with a metal lid is called a *humpen,* while at the other extreme, the **schnelle** is a fine tall shape. Another tall tankard, some 11 inches/280mm high, was made at Lambeth in 1660 and is fitted with a pottery lid. In France the tankard is called a *bock* and holds half a liter. Surprisingly few really stately tankards are made today in spite of the return to "real ale" in Britain.

TAWS

The Scots name for **carpet bowls.**

TAZZA

From the Arabic *tasa,* meaning "a basin." The tazza was an Italian type of **stem cup,** but the word is now often applied to any shallow, often ornamental, bowl or dish set on a stand, and Medley has even applied it to the prehistoric **tou.** In a country potter's catalog the term is applied simply to a cup.

TEA and COFFEE SET

In the 18th century the two sets were integrated, the same **saucer** serving for both tea cups or bowls and for coffee cups. **Coffeepots** or "cans" were usually straight sided. **Sugar** and cream containers were originally lidded. See also **cup, coffee cup, teapot, creamer, caddy,** etc. *Webster's New Collegiate Dictionary* defines a teapot, sugar bowl, creamer, cups and saucers, and plates as the components of a tea service, but in craft pottery, the plates are often omitted and a larger milk jug included.

A

A. A morning tea set by Geoffrey Whiting, 1963. The cup shape reverses that of the teapot, but the "match" is not wholly successful.
B. Part of a porcelain coffee service by David Leach. The basic cylinder form is easier to follow through and the decoration helps to unify the set. (See facing page.)

To achieve a formal harmony and balance between the disparate items in a set is one of the major challenges faced by the potter. Among the more extreme solutions was the one done by Clarice Cliff in the 1930s, in the angular designs of the aptly named "Bizarre" range in Art Deco style.

TEA BOWL

The use of tea became widespread in China in the T'ang period, and with it came the tea bowl, although there had been cups and bowls for wine, etc. previous to this. Many earlier drinking vessels were in **goblet** form, but the tea bowl is primarily designed to be cradled in both hands and is not, therefore, provided with a stem. Rhodes (see R.PF

B

in Booklist) tells us that the more earthy dark Ch'ien ware bowls were for green tea taken with the leaves; the porcellaneous bowls, for infused tea. The green or leaf-tea bowl was known as the *chatsubo;* another type was known as the *charwan* (see also **wan** and **bowl**). Tea drinking was introduced to Japan in the 12th century, the people eagerly embracing the habit and turning it into a nationwide contemplative ceremony. Two main varieties of bowls developed—the slightly in-turned rim denoting a "winter bowl," which helped to retain the heat, and the "summer" bowl, which was more open in form, allowing the tea to cool easily. Of the typical raku tea bowl Rhodes says: "The clay seems to grow hesitantly from foot to lip . . . of all the world's pots the Raku bowl is perhaps the most inviting to the touch." Rawson (R.C) expresses the same feelings: "During prolonged meditative sipping, bowls were nursed in the cupped palms; and so became a focus for tactile as well as visual contemplation." Tea is rarely drunk in the same way in the West (to our loss), but the tea bowl holds a perennial

A. An open "summer" tea bowl. Kyoto, mark of Mossu.

A

B

B. A more irregular and slightly closed-in raku Japanese tea bowl. (A and B Maidstone Museum.)

fascination for potters in its modesty and subtle variety. See also under **foot ring.**

TEA CADDY

See **caddy.**

TEAPOT

The early Chinese and Korean spouted pots, which we can easily equate with teapots, were probably wine pots. Similar shapes are known from 2000 B.C. Crete and are "teapots" by formal association. Tea, however, was drunk from T'ang times onwards in China (see also **tea bowl**) and a variety of teapots, including pots on three or four legs (Ch'ien Lung), had been developed in the East by the time that tea was exported in quantity to the West. Early imports were accompanied by teapots which had a burnished surface and a rather squat, but integrated and animated, shape (see **buccaro**).

In the 18th and 19th centuries the teapot took on a bewildering variety of forms, some very attractive, but others not infrequently willful, extreme, and lacking in both practical and aesthetic value. Haggar, in an article in *Pottery and Glass,* discusses teapots of the earlier industrial era: "[The] fundamental necessities [which give all teapots a basic similarity] were modified in line and visual appearance by the compulsions of period styles;

A

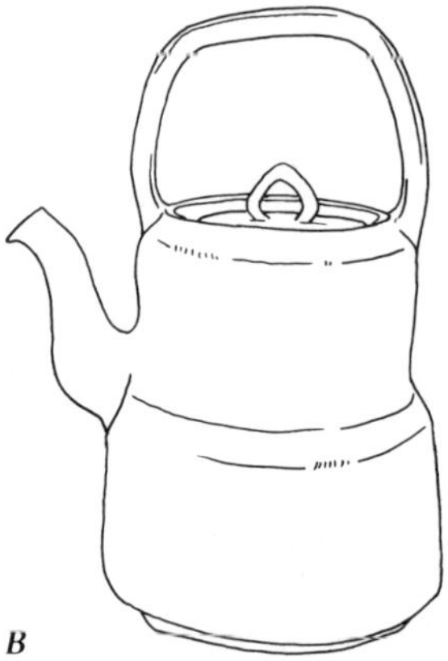

B

A. A form resembling the modern teapot from 2000 B.C. Crete.
B. This is, in fact, described as a Japanese ewer, *but in many respects it is similar to a teapot.*
C. A Yi-hsing type teapot, close in its rigidity of form to the Art Deco wares of the 1920s.

C

. . . the Baroque, bold, capacious . . . often subtly corresponding to objects in nature; rococo asymmetric balance, lively rhythms and flowing lines . . . the bulk of the shape nearer the shoulder . . . the spout perched high. Later forms became hard and severe, boatlike, square shoulders . . . also squat forms like Roman lamps."

Teapots were modelled as houses, cauliflowers, etc., in the 19th century and in the 20th century as cubes and other rather tortuous variations—motor

D

D. Bamboo handles are very popular on modern craft potters' teapots, as on this four-square example by David Leach.

cars, airplanes, etc. Many of the forms were made possible only by slip-casting. Other more standard pots were made throughout the 19th and 20th centuries often in porcelain, but in even greater quantity as straightforward, practical, often brown-glazed, capacious shapes with a double-curve spout and a comfortable handle. Large teapots were given a second handle in front of the lid. These unpretentious styles have been given a fresh aesthetic and tactile appeal by the craft potters of our own time. Eastern influence is evident in the ubiquitous **cane handle,** but the forms reflect individual character. Practical aspects must be considered, but must be subjugated to the design. David Leach in F.DL (see Booklist) states: "If I make a teapot, an article hedged about with functional aspects, I am still left with a vast opportunity to experiment with form and relationship, which can serve function without being part of it. Most of my thinking concerns relationship

E

E. A side-handled teapot by Michael Cardew, unusual because of its screw-on lid (see screw stopper*).*

F. Another cane handle on a handsome pot by Sheila Casson, which makes a feature of the lugs.

G

G. A miniature teapot by Mary Rich, the knob following the form through and becoming an important element in the design.

H

because I have studied and learned the drill of function so that I don't have to think about it any more: it does not occupy my conscious mind which is on qualitative things . . . shape, glaze, decoration."

There has been a reaction to this approach by a few potters who return to more fanciful teapot shapes, multispouted or covered with handles, even to the airplane. The teapot is perhaps the most challenging of all utilitarian forms. It is an assembly of disparate units—body, spout, handle, lid—which must finally not only please the eye with a sense of balance and cohesion, but must also be pleasant to hold and effective in pouring. Two of the basic approaches to the problem might be termed "the articulated" and "the integrated." In the first, there is no attempt made to suggest that the parts are other than put together; the junctions are visible and made a virtue, giving sharpness and angularity and a generally frank indication of the method of making. The second approach is to smooth the shapes into one another so that the whole takes on an appearance of physical unity. Most industrial teapots, of necessity (unless cast whole), belong to

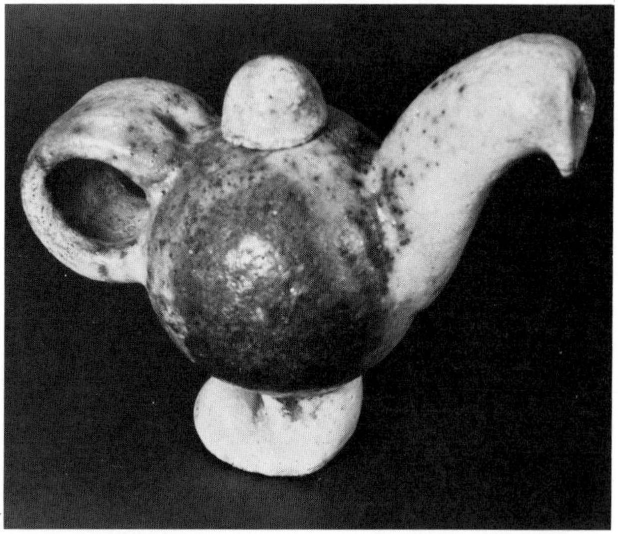

I

H. As well as bail *handles in cane, this type is also fairly common. A firm-standing little pot by Sheila Fournier.*
I. A reaction among some modern potters has led to multihandled, pornographic, and other "monstrous" teapots, such as this odd little item, by Jill Crowley, 1970.

the first category. The teapots of Geoffrey Whiting are, on the other hand, among the world's best smoothed-in forms. Many hand-made teapots come somewhere in between.

The body controls the general character to a great degree. A spherical shape is a difficult one on which to assemble the handle and spout; a sloping top section facilitates both placings. Cylindrical sides impart a third, quite distinct character. Rhodes says "The body, especially in view of the appendages it must carry, needs to be a strongly stated form, not meagre or hesitant."

Needless to say (though in practice often overlooked), the end of the spout should be as high or slightly higher than the flange of the opening, and neither it nor the handle should normally stand out more than about half the width of the body. A crisply cut or even slightly turned-over spout end will minimize drips. The total area of the grill holes should be greater than the area across the end of the spout (as Whiting was one of the first to point out in PQ—see Booklist) so that a "head" of liquid is built up when pouring which will force the tea out in a steady stream.

The four principal types of **handles** are—a clay handle on the side opposite to the spout, a clay handle arched over the lid, a cane handle threaded through lugs, and a tubular clay handle at right angles to the spout. Most of the **lid seatings** can be used on a teapot, the choice controlled by the overall character. A double seating (a flange on both lid and pot) offers greater security, as will an extension of about ½ inch on the vertical flange of the lid. Too small an aperture will prove a nuisance in use.

Rhodes (see R.PF in Booklist) makes the prediction that "the teapot may now be on the verge of obsolescence. Brewing tea in a pot has been largely replaced by the teabag. And gatherings of five or six people who are all inclined to take tea together seem to be becoming rarer." This seems less likely in England and, we hope, may never come true. There needs to be some focus of relaxation, even of meditation, if we are to preserve our sanity.

TEAR JAR

A small **aryballos** found with Greek burials and, according to some sources, used for the rather macabre purpose of holding the tears of the bereaved.

TEA STRAINER

A strainer, like a small **colander** with a handle, which sits in a splay-sided dish is illustrated in M.K (see Booklist), dated 1910. Tea strainers seldom appear in museums or books, but, like so many other everyday utensils, have their interest and appeal and must have been made in large numbers.

A typical 19th century porcelain strainer and bowl.

TERRACE VASE

An **urn**-shaped vase with applied flowers and leaves, raised on a rococo scroll base.

TERRINE

From the French *terre*, meaning "earth," suggesting an earthenware vessel. Used as a container, usually for the sale of food delicacies and pâtés. CTCD (see Booklist) describes it as a casserole, originally of earthenware; and *Webster's* connects it with **tureen,** although this normally has a somewhat different function. C.WC illustrates a vessel as illustrated described as a terrine for pâté. The word is not entered in *Webster's* and so is apparently not current in America. In LG a vaguely heart-shaped terrine is shown, used especially for cooking "hare a la Royale."

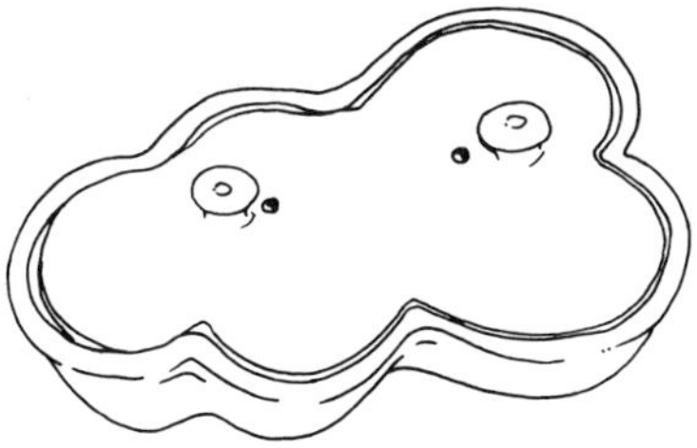

A lobed French terrine typical of many made in the 18th/19th centuries.

THIMBLE

A bell-shaped sheath worn on a finger to push the needle when sewing. A wide range of porcelain thimbles were made at Chelsea, Minton, etc. in the

18th and 19th centuries. They are still made at Worcester and highly decorated sets were still advertised in 1979.

THUMB POT

See **pinched pot.**

TIG

See **tyg.**

TILE

We are dealing here with outline, rather than form, as far as the flat wall tile is concerned. The ancient Egyptians made small wall tiles in the form of birds, animals, and plants, and also in shield shapes. The Fitzwilliam Museum calls them "inlays." Islamic tiles were made in variety, fitting cunningly together. Today the boring 6- by 6-inch ones have largely taken over.

Relief tiles were made as far back as Assyrian times and earlier. Shallow reliefs were rolled onto tiles with a 1¾-inch pastry roller in the 19th century at Wattisfield. A number of modern potters make sculptural reliefs on wall tiles or **wall plaques.** Hans Coper and Derek Davis, especially, have executed some quite large commissions, and remarkable work has been done in America by Ruth Duckworth and others.

In a wider sense the word "tile" is sometimes used to describe drainage and hollow items, such as those used as hot-air ducts in ancient Rome. These were often very handsome and can provide a starting point for ideas, especially for slab pots. They are very rarely illustrated, as being too mundane for mention, but examples can be seen in the archaeological sections of some museums, most often in small local ones. See also **roof tile.**

A. There is great potential in three-dimensional tile design for murals. The illustration shows one tile from a larger composition by Derek Davies.

A

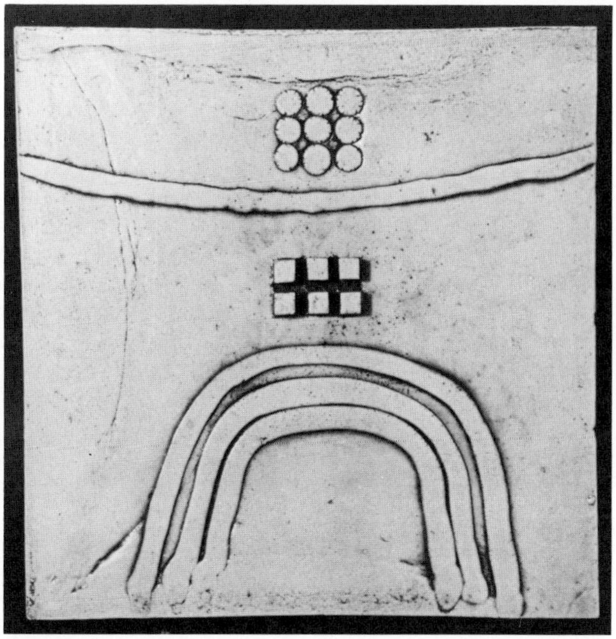

B

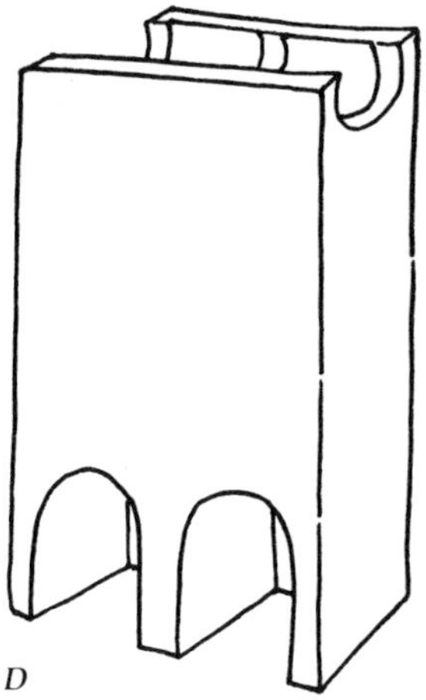

D

C

B. A (just) three-dimensional tile design by James Campbell. C/D. In the wider sense of pottery—flues, ducts, pipes, etc.—here are 2 forms, the first (Roman) probably for warm air circulation over an arch (hence, the slope on one face), and the second, a ducting "tile," which could easily be a construction by a modern potter. (Devizes Museum.)

E

E. Various types of hand-made tiles used decoratively in a garden (Photo: page 234).

TING

A tripod bowl common in both pottery and bronze in early China. It had straight legs, a deep bowl usually with a flat wide rim, and two up-standing handles like large lugs.

This curious Chinese Sung pot is derived from bronze originally. (Barlow Collection.)

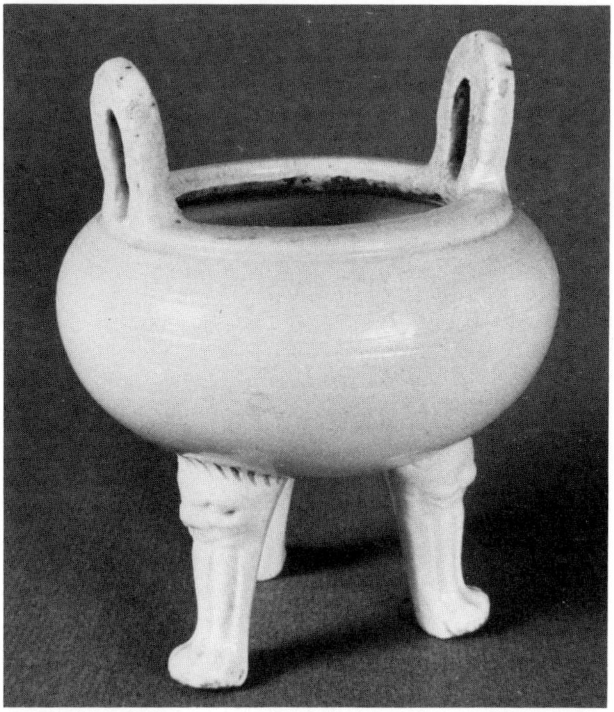

TOAST RACK

A comparatively modern form in pottery, consisting of a number of upright slabs of clay set on a base,

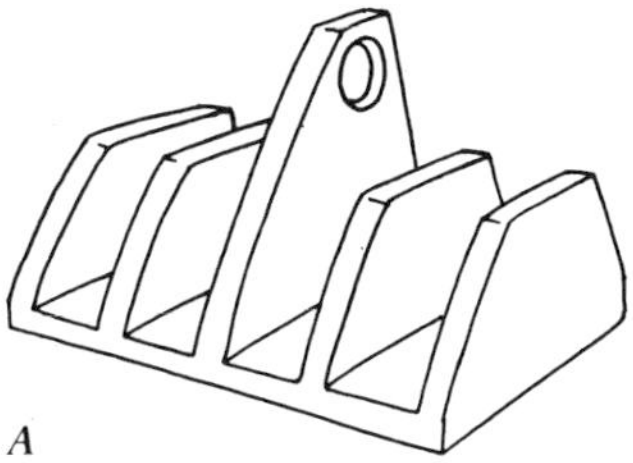

A

A/B/C. Three ideas for a toast rack design: the first two based on the standard form, the third could be cut from a thrown posey ring *form.*

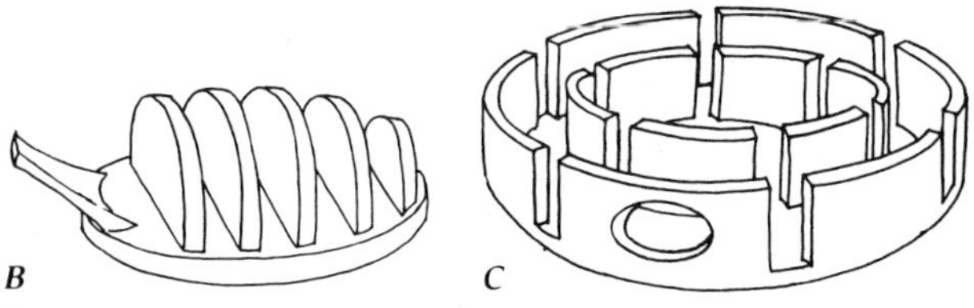

B C

forming slots for the toast. A handle or knob is also usually provided. Circular and other types are possible.

TOBACCO JAR

A number of styles were made in ceramic, some hexagonal (influenced by metal originals). CR24 (see Booklist) illustrates one of Doulton's elegant "Aesthetic Movement" cylindrical jars. G.EAFP shows

The Victorian craze for cottage models is here used as a design for a tobacco jar. Bristol, Powell's Pottery, 1880. (Bristol Museum.)

a carved, pierced outside cover to a tobacco bowl. A snug-fitting lid is essential, otherwise the shape can be anything that the imagination dictates. The usual size is about 5 inches/130mm high.

TOBY JUG

According to *Webster's New Collegiate Dictionary,* the plural of the term is "Tobies." The Toby Jug was a mid-18th century development by Ralph Wood of a long line of **anthropomorphic face pots.** Originally, the Toby Jug was a seated figure holding a mug of ale called "Toby Philpot" (a pun!). A three-cornered hat formed the rim and lip of a jug/pitcher, with the crown of the hat detachable for use as a cup. There have been countless and frequently tasteless variations on well-known figures through the 19th and 20th centuries but the cup element has tended to disappear. An early French equivalent is a man sitting on a barrel.

TOILET BOX

In ancient Greece this would have been the **pyxis.**

TONDINO

An Italian 15th/16th century dish with a wide rim and a deep, comparatively narrow well; like an inverted Cardinal's hat.

TOOTHBRUSH HOLDER

A barely useful item of bathroom equipment. A covered, shallow box, about 8 by 3 by 1½ inches with rests inside (to separate "his" and "hers"?) was made by Copelands in 1847.

TOU

A type of early **stem cup,** which Medley in M.CP (see Booklist) calls a **tazza.** In the very early (4000 B.C.) examples the stem is comparatively wide and pierced with holes. The Eastern Chou (circa 350 B.C.) tou is a rounded, lidded bowl on a shorter, flaring stem or foot. (Drawings: top, right.)

TOWN

Groups of dwellings are rare in historical pottery (but see **alcarraza**), but several modern potters make model towns. There are the closely integrated carv-

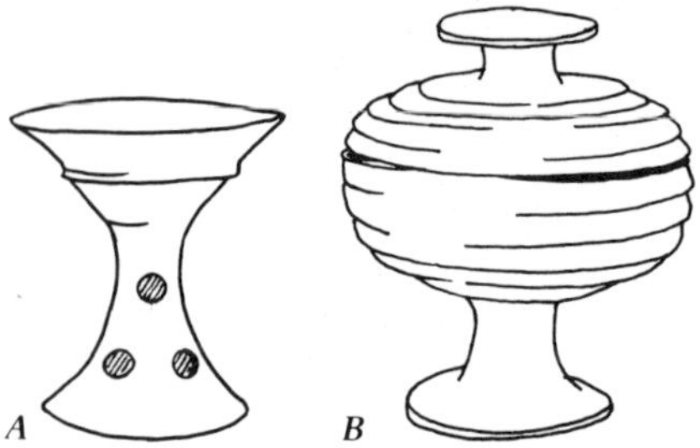

A. A brown earthenware tou form, Honan, circa 2500 B.C. The purpose of the holes in the base is uncertain, but they occur in a number of Far Eastern stemmed pots and bowls, including those from Japan.
B. A covered tou from 3rd century B.C. China. The lid would form another cup when reversed.

A. An Eastern type city-cum-box, suggested rather than realistically modelled by Brian Newman.

A

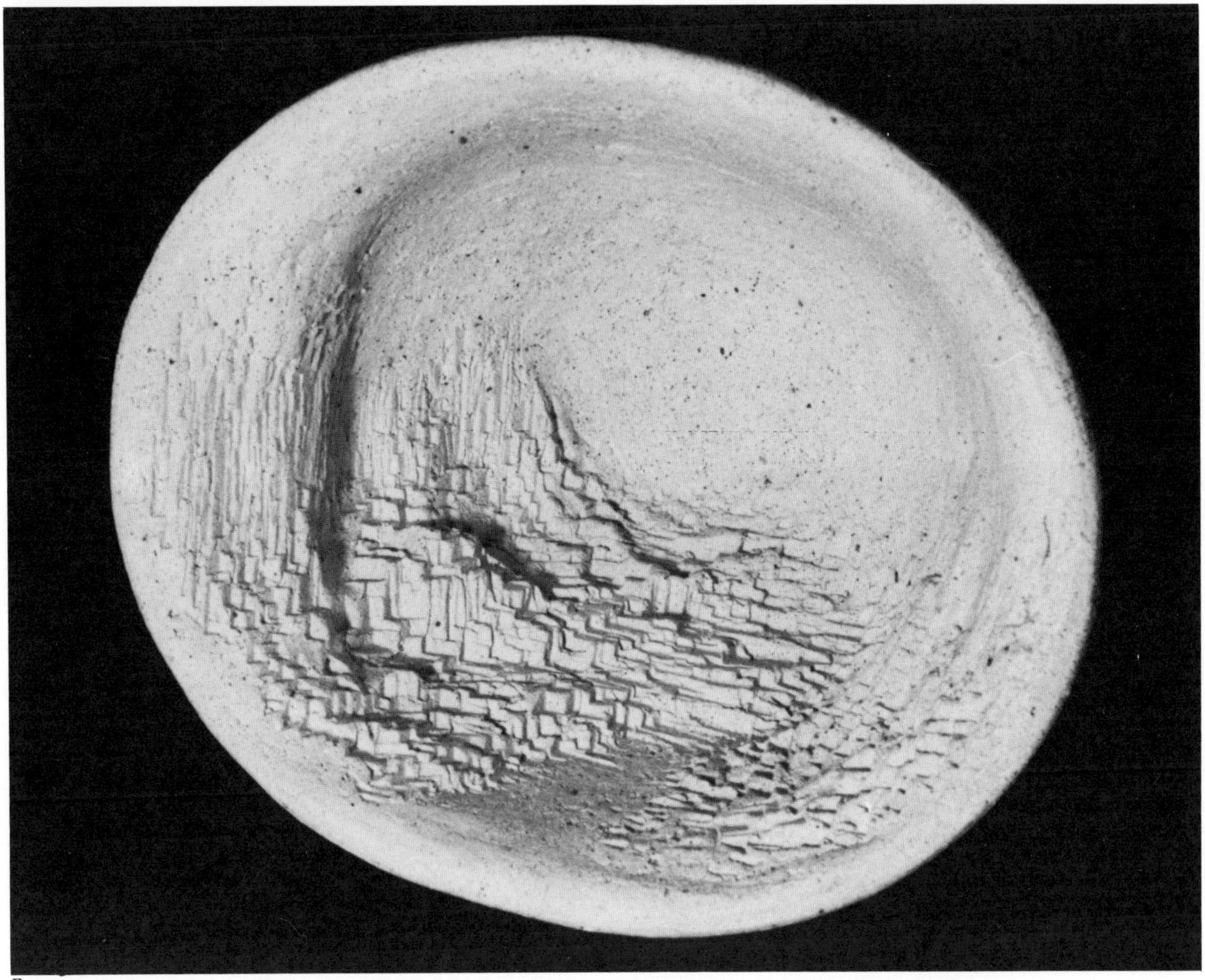

B

ings of Bob Rogers set on a sculptural block or within a bowl; Brian Newman's more disparate forms on undulating bases; Paul Gandy's villages complete with church, set on a thrown hemisphere; etc. These are all "ceramic sculpture." Towns and building integrated as part of a pot, have taken the form of cut or modelled rims, or pierced walls. See **landscape.**

B. A vast rock city "in a nutshell," brilliantly carved by Bob Rogers.

C. A street of houses by Brian Newman. A weakness here is the lack of interest in the large base form.
D. A somewhat constricted walled town by Andrew Richardson, with separate houses.

C

D

TOY

A knickknack; a diminutive representation; or a child's plaything. "Toys" in a 1754 Chelsea Pottery sale announcement included "Porcelain Toys . . . snuff boxes, smelling Bottles, Etwees and Trinkets for Watches . . . in various beautiful shapes . . . Porcelain Hafts for Table Dessert knives and forks." Burton (see B.GAH in Booklist) mentions a miniscule Cupid figure drumming on a pair of breasts, and, among other 18th century love tokens, a nun on a rock inscribed "Amour Spirituelle." In ancient times Egypt produced spinning tops, balls, etc. in "faience" (turquoise "paste"). Little model swings

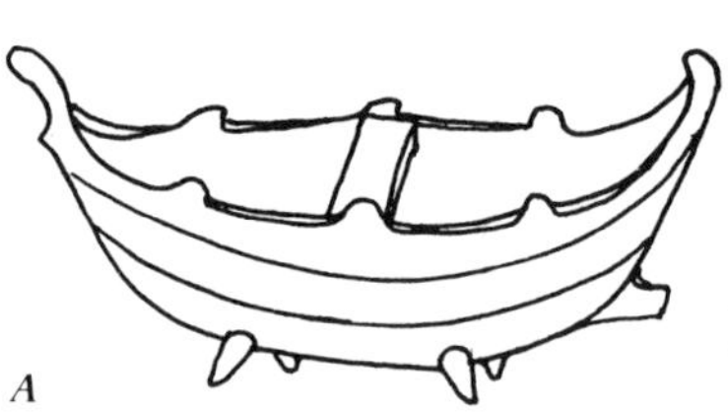

A

A. A charming toy boat on little feet, from 1st century Italy.

B. In one of the quirks of history this little creature has been given wheels in a civilization (ancient American) which did not use them on full-size vehicles.

B

C. Miniature pots for doll's houses were made in quantity especially in the 19th century, of which this is an example. Brigitta Appleby of Briglin Pottery has made a number of these tiny sets.

C

come from Ancient Greece and animals with moving heads from several sources including the Indus Valley. In European and American folk pottery, toys seldom appear, though roughly made objects to keep the children quiet must have been produced. See **doll.** "Miniatures" appear in late 19th century catalogs and have a perennial fascination (see **teapot** illustration G).

Some ceramic "fancies," such as John Maltby's "Lunch in a Garden" may be considered modern toys—but usually for grown-ups. See also under the various **games.**

TRASH/WASTE CAN

In CMjun78 (see Booklist) a modern pottery waste bin from People's Republic of China is illustrated. It appears to be about 3 feet/900mm tall, with an opening in the top half.

TRAY

A utensil with a completely flat base and a short, usually vertical wall. Lug handles or some system for gripping each side is useful. Examples are found

D

E

F

D/E/F. Ian Godfrey's fertile invention has given us many "toys." Here is a Noah's Ark type model (or is it a farmyard) with a number of pieces to play with and a fantasy bird-rocking see-saw.

from 17th century China in "famille verte," and there must be many more.

They may be made by rolling out a sheet of clay and throwing a wall onto it. They are more often decorative than useful. See also **slab plate/dish, Welsh tray.**

TRENCHER

From *trenchier,* meaning "to cut." Originally, the trencher was a thick slice of bread on which portions of meat were placed. After the meal, the bread was given to the poor! Later trenchers were made of wood and other materials. In the 18th century a narrow-rimmed earthenware plate was known as a trencher. LG (see Booklist) suggests that the trencher replaced individual plates in the Middle Ages, but what is meant here by plates is not quite certain; see under **platter** for a different progression.

TRICHTERBECHER

A type of German beaker with a rounded body, a neck and flaring mouth, and a thumbed-down base in the Medieval tradition from 16th century Sieberg.

TRIPOD POT/BOWL

Cooking pots on tripod legs or feet have been common to all cultures, worldwide, although they were greatly outnumbered by plain, round-based pots. In China, **incense burners,** the **ting,** and various lidded bowls among other forms were often set on three legs, as was the German **grapen,** and the **skillet.** There are many, often long-legged tripod pots from ancient America (Mixtec, etc).

They are not common today but Colin Kellam has made a series of covered tripod bowls. In CMdec78 (see Booklist), elaborate "pulled handle" legs are shown on a pot by James Dawson. See also illustration E under **foot.**

A tripod bowl from ancient Costa Rica, 12 inches/300mm wide. The feet contain rattles. (University Museum of Archeology and Anthropology, Cambridge.)

TROUGH SPOUT

A spout shaped by extending the **lip** of a vessel to form a narrow furrow, or by attaching a tube to the side of a vessel, from which the upper half of the tube is then cut away. Many early Near Eastern **lamps** had trough spouts to take the wick. See also **animal form,** and illustration A under spout.

TRULLA

A Roman basin or ladle.

TRUMPET

See **horn.**

TRYPS, Tryblion

Given in LG (see Booklist) as a large Greek plate, with tryblion as a smaller version.

TSOULAKA

A rounded, small-based Greek casserole dish, but rarely with a lid. It has two lug handles and, today, is glazed inside. It is mainly for use over an open fire.

T'SUNG, T'sun

A Chinese ritual vessel used in the worship of the earth, possibly for holding divining rods. It has a tall, rectangular body with a circular foot and rim and with molded reliefs or vertical ribs.

TUB

Chinese tubs or **baths** were made during the Ming period. A 1770 Portuguese tureen is in the form of a tub of fish. An earthenware tub, circa 1840, is shown in G.EAFP (see Booklist). The large **salting** and **pickling jars** are often tublike in shape.

TUBE PAN

See **cake mold.**

TUI

According to M.CP (see Booklist) this is a "roughly spherical vessel made in two indentical halves each with three projections which serve as feet. [It is] Middle Chou period bronze in origin."

The plan and evolution of the tunnel-handle type. In this case it is on the lid of a modern casserole.

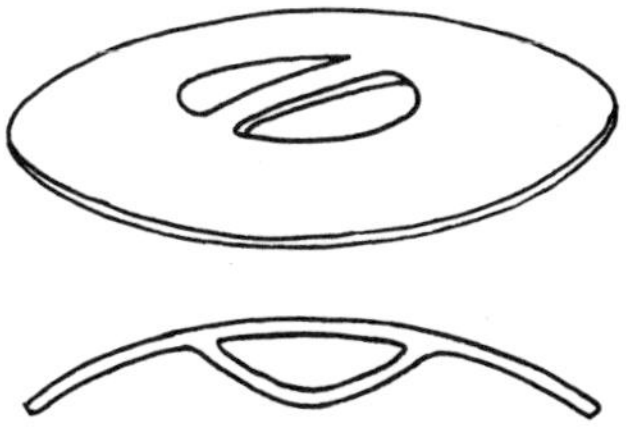

TUNNEL HANDLE

A term given by archaeologists to a handle flush with the surface of pot and bridging a hollow in the wall.

TUREEN

From **terrine,** it is an earthenware vessel for food, but which developed into a more "cultivated" form in creamware and bone china. The tureen was often used to serve gravy or soup and also other cooked foods.

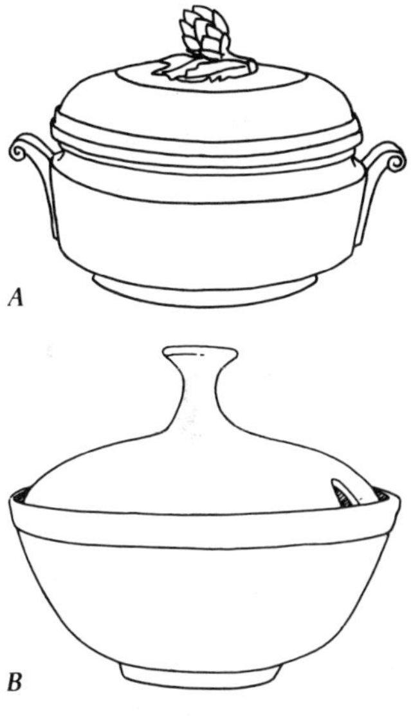

A. An 18th century tureen from Denmark.

B. An early (1949) Peter Voulkos tureen. The bowl is more open than a casserole, and there is a spoon aperture in the lid.

There are similar forms to the somewhat boat-shaped ("gravy boat") vessel generally thought of as a tureen. There is one from Helladic Greece, for instance; and there is a strange vessel called a "tureen" in the Museum of London, with four legs, two little handles, and a lid cut into the form; but the tureen is largely an 18th and 19th century industrial cast object. Usually oval in plan, the tureen has also taken on many animal and bird forms. See also under **bird tureen.** It usually had a lid and

C. Tureens have been made in every conceivable animal and vegetable form. Here is a modern example of a very appealing sheep, by Charles Imbert of Switzerland.

C

sometimes a plate or stand. In LG (see Booklist) it says that the term was first used in the 18th century. Wedgwood made a type of tureen nearer to our oven-to-table ware, which has largely taken its place. This consisted of a covered vessel with a removable inner lining in which pies, etc. were cooked and then served complete with the decorated outer cover. See also **piecrust ware, ecuelle, casserole.**

The term is more generally used in the United States than it is in the U.K., where it is largely obsolete. Its use is sensible as the vessel fulfills a specific function.

TWIFFLER

A small pudding plate in early 19th century industrial pottery in Stoke-on-Trent.

TWIN CUPS

Pottery vessels joined at the belly. Found in early and European folk pottery. See also **fuddling cup, multiple pot.**

TYG, Tig

A large 16th/17th century drinking vessel, with two or more handles and often a flaring rim, for passing liquor round a company of people. A fine double-handled black tyg is illustrated in C.WC (see Booklist). Later, they were often squatter and wider, and may have four double handles (i.e., one above the other). They also became very large, eventually developing into the **loving cup.** A 1612 Hedingham example in the Colchester Museum is about 10 inches/255mm high by 7 inches/180mm wide, an early example of the elephantine proportions

A. A two-handled black-glazed tyg from 17th century London, 8½ inches/220mm high.
B. A sprigged, four-handled tyg from Wrotham, Kent, dated 1621. (Victoria and Albert Museum.)

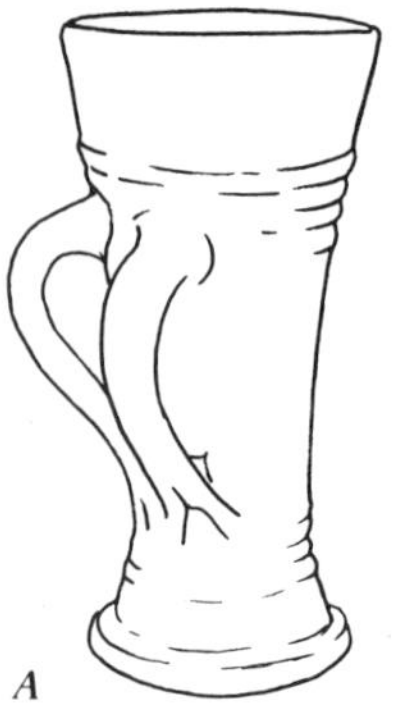

A

achieved. "Tygs" are mentioned by Fishley Holland (H.FYP) as still being made in Devon in the early 20th century. **Puzzle** tygs are known of.

Confusingly, according to Hughes (H.PBC), the name was given also by Staffordshire potters to **porringers.**

U

UMBRELLA STAND

Usually a simple, tall cylinder about 18 inches/450mm high.

URN/URNA

A term used specifically since the early 17th century for a "classical" pot with a rounded, often high-shouldered oviform body, a fairly narrow mouth, and often a slightly flaring foot. In a more general sense, the ancient urns were sometimes for water, but were more often **funerary** containers for the ashes or bones of the dead. "How small an urn contains a King," said the Elizabethan playwright Thomas Dekker. See also **cinerary urn.**

Often any large, full-shaped pot is called an "urn"; e.g., the fine decorated Yang Shao pots from China. Today urns are either decorative garden pots or grave decorations with, as mentioned above, a tendency towards Greek or Roman forms. In Roman times an "urna" was a water jar similar to a Greek **hydria.** See the illustration under **pedestal urn/jug.**

B

V

VASE

Often pronounced "varz" or "vauze" in England, but "vaaz" in the United States. In Ancient Greece the word indicated a useful household pot, but, in the 18th and 19th centuries, imitations of the later Classic pottery from Pompeii and elsewhere were purely ornamental, or were used for holding flowers. Now almost any decorative pot, or a pot for flowers, may be called a "vase," although the word is not commonly used among craft potters. The shape is often tall and circular in plan. See also **wall vase.**

Very unlike the popular notion of a vase, this example, however, was made to hold a flower at the Japanese Tea Ceremony.

VEGETABLE FORM

See **plant form.**

A

A. This handsome model chariot (Lohengrin?) is from prehistoric Serbia.

B

C

B. A very crisp model of a 6th century Chinese ox cart. There may have been another small wheel in front.
C. A Silla Korean 8th century or earlier double pot on wheels, the whole assembled on a pottery stand.
D. With that curious mixture of realism and phantasy so popular in the late seventies, this splendid tram that never was is by Charles Foster. It is a real ceramic tour de force. (See facing page.)
E A more stylized "Phaeton" by Steven Sykes, 1954. (See facing page.)

VEHICLE

In early Europe and the Mediterranean, and in the Far East (especially Han period China), potters have made many fine models of chariots and other vehicles, often to furnish tombs and graves. Isolated examples have been found all over the world, and they can be very exciting and lively. Most of them are chariots, but occasionally there are more peaceable vehicles. As illustration C shows, wheels and pots have been integrated into a very satisfactory whole. They feature much more rarely in later pottery. The 19th century, of course, saw sentimentalized wheelbarrows and such and a few larger representations of carriages, etc; and in the 20th century teapots and the like were transformed into cars, airplanes, and other unlikely and uncomfortable models. Modern potters have not exploited the subject to any degree, as they have with **landscapes** and **buildings** which seem even less likely subjects. See also under **boat.**

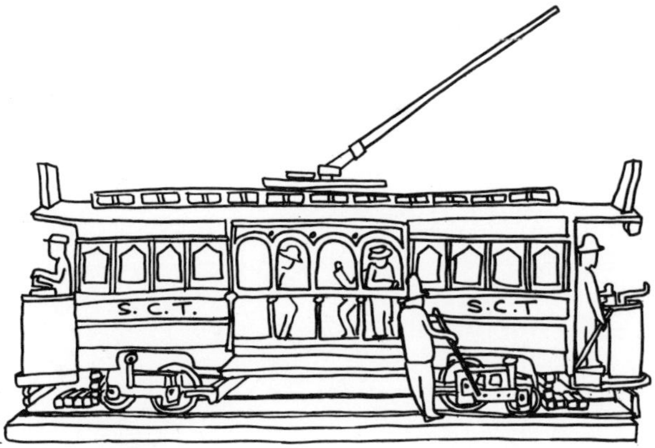

D

E

VINAIGRIER, Vinegar barrel

LG (see Booklist) defines "vinaigrier" as "a small barrel, sometimes of earthenware [i.e., pottery, probably salt-glaze] in which vinegar is made." It is also for storing vinegar in the house.

VIOLIN

Pottery violins, probably ornamental, are known to have been made at Delft. In the typical slightly surrealist manner of the 1970s, Tony Birks shows a broken violin model in COQ78 (see Booklist).

VOTIVE

Called "votives" in the British Museum are a number of terra-cotta models of different parts of the body. Ear, nose, breast, etc., were found in "sanctuaries of healing" in 3rd century B.C. Etruria. They are offerings either in thanks for healing or in hope of such. (Drawing: top, right.)

VYKA, Byka

See **hydria.**

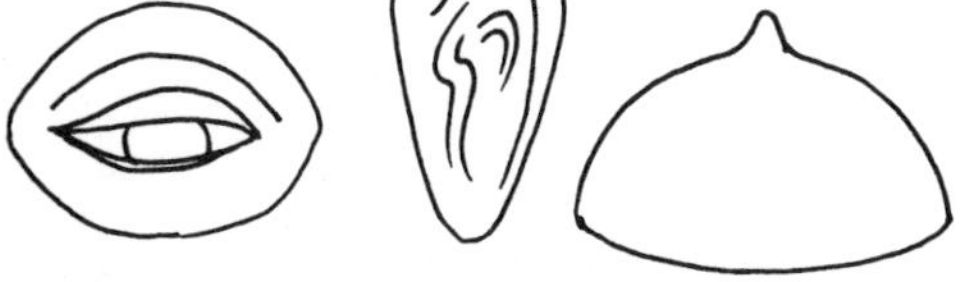

Three of the "votive" offerings described in the text.

W

WALL FOUNTAIN

A container for holding water, with a spigot near the base. A "lavabo" or wash basin was placed beneath it. In Spain the "fountain" was placed in a wall niche lined with colored tiles, often in the dining room. The French also sported colorful wall fountains, often rather florid. See also **water fountain.**

WALL PLAQUE, Wall decoration

Given by *Webster's New Collegiate Dictionary* as a commemorative or identifying inscribed tablet, but often used in a more general sense for any three-dimensional wall decoration. See also **bacini.** It is the ceramic answer to wall pictures, often in bas-relief, showing flowers, historical scenes, etc., and, today, more abstract compositions.

The Cretans, in around 1600 B.C., made realistic wall decorations showing sea creatures—flying fish, shells, etc.—in rather poor and unsatisfactory compositions. The Della Robbia factory in the 15th/16th centuries issued many well-designed plaques, including figures in ornamental surroundings. Blue Dash chargers, Hispano-Moresque, and many other plates were made specifically to hang on the wall. P.OBP (see Booklist) illustrates a large 18th century Bristol tin-glazed plaque (in the true sense of the word) painted with the words and music of a contemporary ballad "Topeing Jack," made to hang in the Trout Tavern.

Today the whole currency of plaques (hideous word) is debased by plaster of Paris and worthless modelling, but wall decoration is still an important part of a home and potters can do much to reinstate it with some artistic merit. See also discussion under **tile.** (Photograph: page 246.)

A

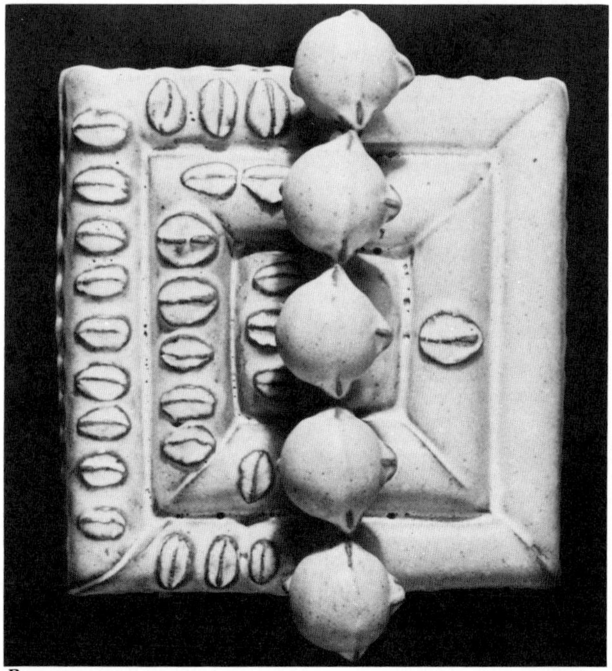

B

A. A black and gold stoneware wall decoration by Sheila Fournier. (See page 245.)
B. A wall decoration based on the cowrie shell by Gillian Lowndes.

WALL VASE, Wall pocket

A vase or container with a flat back to hang on a wall. They were made in China from the 16th century and highly elaborate examples abound in 18th/19th century England and Europe. They were made by country potters. "Wall pots" are listed at 3/9 (19p in England or 40 cents in the U.S.) a dozen from Harris's of Farnham, Surrey, in the late 19th century. A number of adaptations have been made by modern potters; e.g., by Nigel Wood as shown in PQ43 (see Booklist).

A typical 18th/19th century tin-glazed wall pocket, probably from London, 1730. (Bristol Museum.)

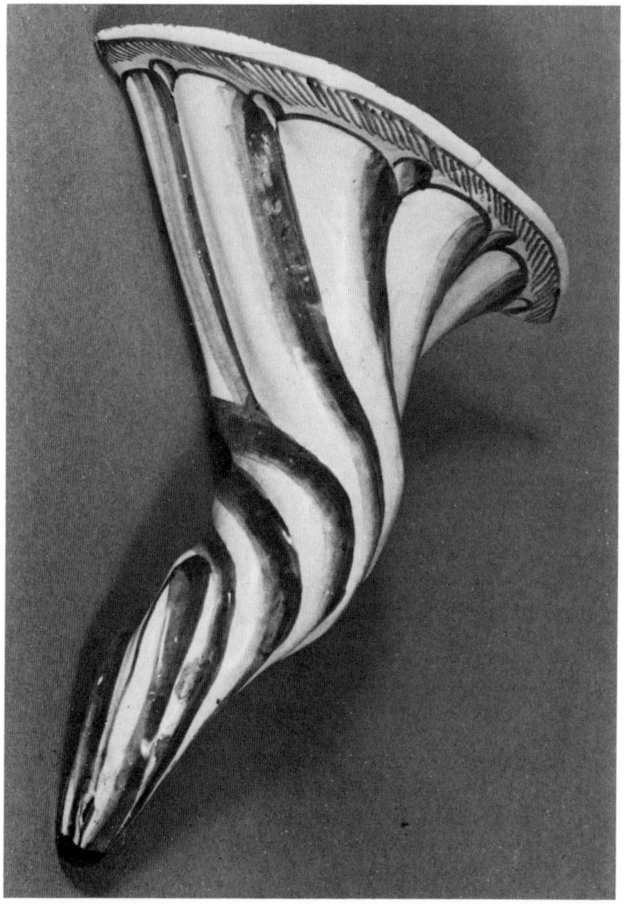

WAN

A Chinese word for "bowl." See under **bowl** for types and also under **tea bowl.**

WASHSTAND SET

An essential piece of bedroom equipment before the advent of running hot water. It is composed of a large **ewer** (which had a longish neck in the 18th century, but later developed into a curvaceous jug/pitcher), a deep bowl or dish, and usually a **soap dish.** The bowl was often set into a special piece of furniture.

WASSELL/WASSAIL CUP/BOWL

In the ceremony of "wassailing," offerings of cider and cider-soaked toast, with suitable incantations, were made to the apple trees on old Christmas Eve, which was the fifth of January. A wassail cup is illustrated in B.CECP (see Booklist) with more or less vertical sides, two handles, a lid, and a short spout, very similar to **caudle** or **posset** cups. Examples are known from 1692 (Bridgend) and Fremington in the 1840s, each about 9 inches/230mm high. But these pale into insignificance beside the extravagant lidded wassail bowl in the St. Fagans Folk Museum of Wales, with its 18 handles and conical lid crowded with birds, figures, and snake-like decorations. If the apples didn't grow after this offering the trees were in a bad way indeed.

WATCH POCKET

A construction (mainly 19th century) in which to hang a watch. An 1800 Fremington, Devon, example in B.CECP (see Booklist) shows a "classical" building of extreme naiveté with watchmen set around it. EB states that most watches (which were larger than modern ones) in the 16th century were enclosed in cases, but illustrations or even mention of pottery cases or "pockets" are hard to find. They were certainly made in the 18th and 19th centuries and industrially into the 20th. (Photograph: top.)

WATER COOLER

All early porous water containers tended to cool their contents by evaporation, and no special vessel was required. See **goglet.** Watkins in W.ENEP (see Booklist) mentions a "huge twelve gallon barrel-shaped water cooler in the National Museum [U.S.] . . . with three spigot openings at different levels."

The days of the fob watch are probably over, though one never knows how fashion will change. Here is a decorative and amusing "pocket" into which a watch would have been installed overnight or more permanently. A curious feature of the design is that, in the days of poor candle and rush lights, it must have been as difficult to see the time as it was to photograph this pocket. (Bristol Museum.)

WATER DROPPER

An item of Chinese calligraphic equipment in existence at least since Han times. They were often made in the form of fruit, toads, etc., sometimes with an extra little bowl at the mouth (for filling?). Charming gourd shapes and flattish pots also abound. (Photograph: page 248.)

WATER FOUNTAIN

Large water storage vessels with a bung or spigot, sometimes in the built-in form of **wall fountains,** or as tall, free-standing pots on a narrowed base and a splayed foot. They were used for dispensing water and not in the modern sense of moving water (see **fountain**) for decorative purposes. There is a Ch'ing example in the Ashmolean Museum. C.WC (see Booklist) illustrates a 1787 French water fountain made for a surgeon, with a portrait of himself on top and camels around!

A

C

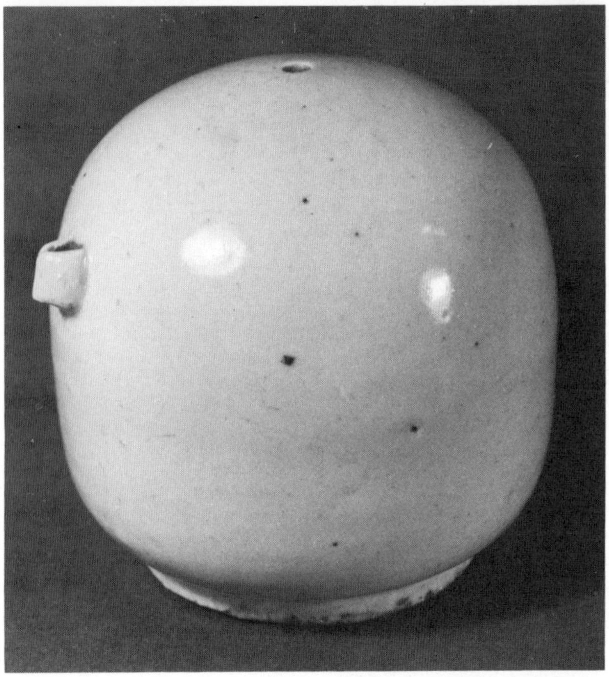

B

A. A nicely proportioned water dropper with cut feet. (See page 247.)
B. An unusual domed Chinese Sung pot with only the tiny luglike spout to break the line. The flow of water would have been controlled by the thumb over the hole in the top as is practiced in some slip-trailers.
C. A later Chinese water dropper of totally different design, but fulfilling the same purpose. (A, B, and C from Crafts Study Centre, Bath.)

WATER GARDEN

One would have thought that the decorative possibilities of pottery "ponds" or fish bowls would have been widely exploited, and probably flowers were floated on Japanese bowls filled with water, but this does not appear to be so, and a whole range of invention in this field is open to the potter. The author has developed a series of water gardens of the type shown in the illustration (facing).

WATERING CAN/POT

Watering cans or sprinklers in the shape of a pitcher with a very dominating nozzle or "rose" on the shoulder are known from the 16th/18th centuries. Like the **sprinkler,** they were often used to freshen rushes on the floor. There are also more elegant examples, very small, used by 18th century high society for sprinkling rosewater or lavender onto artificial flowers! See also **keskul.** Later purely decorative miniatures were made, but watering cans (*Webster's New Collegiate Dictionary* gives "watering pot") were also produced for the proper use of refreshing indoor plants. "Automatic" waterers are currently made to moisten plants. They operate through the slow seepage of water through an earthenware "spike" fed by a small reservoir. They are often made in the shape of a bird.

WATER PIPE

Called a "narghlie" in the Near East, this often took

A textured hand-built bowl, broken blue glaze inside, for use as a water garden with flowers, shells, etc., or for a candle centerpiece on a dining table.

This watering can is probably from the 17th century, but has the spreading thumbed base of earlier styles. Not, perhaps, to be recommended for its beauty, but a strong and uncompromising shape.

A

the form of a low-bellied bottle with a nozzle on one side, a narrow neck, and an arrangement on top for burning the tobacco. A tube and mouth piece would be attached to the spout and the smoke drawn through water in the bottle.

WATER POT

These essential items of household equipment before piped water have taken many forms, but they are mostly full-bodied and always capacious, generally with a fairly wide mouth, as the water was frequently bailed out with a scoop or ladle. They were used for the temporary storage of water. Of the Nigerian round-bottomed pots Cardew has said, "the Kwali village pots must rank as some of the finest pots being made anywhere in the world today." The large **pitchers** and **cisterns** of the Middle Ages are equally splendid and practical.

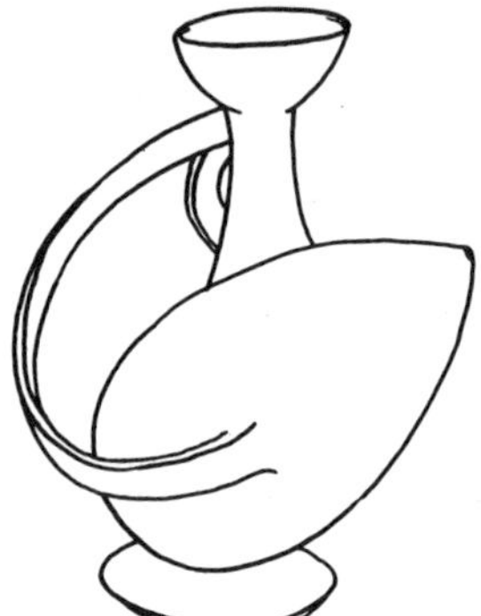

B

A. The magnificent water pots (used also for grain and other storage) from Nigeria. See text. (Photograph: Shan Bristow.)
B. At the other extreme are Picasso's willful and impractical excursion into ceramics produced this "horse and rider" water pitcher.

The modern jug/pitcher has occupied the creative talents of many potters, but the necessity for storing water no longer exists in most of the Western world, and so-called water pots have tended to be more decorative than practical. Picasso's "water

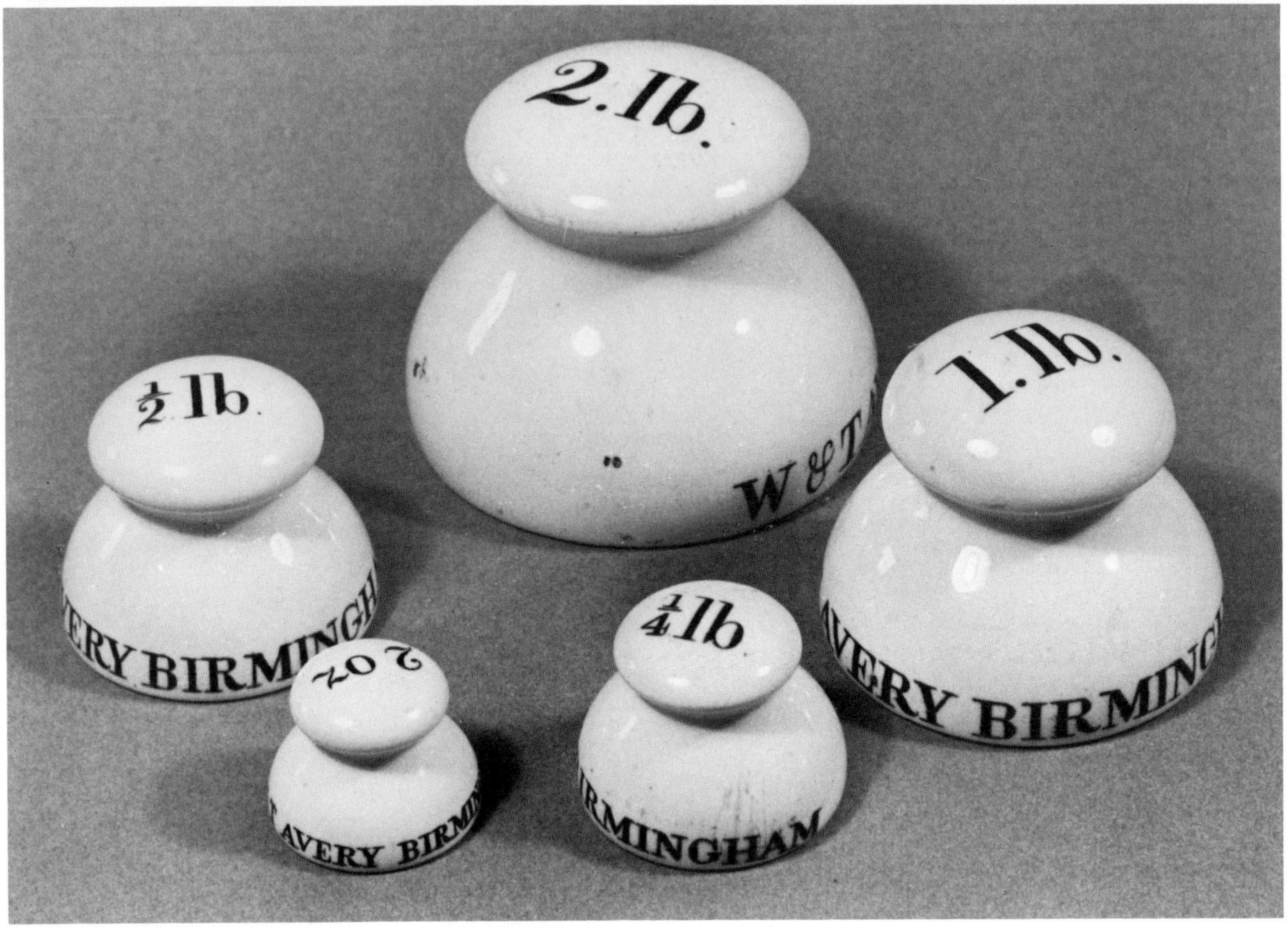

Nicely lettered weights, practical and satsifying in form, and with a good grip on the knobs.

pitcher,'' for example, could not have been more useless, though this is an extreme example.

WEED POT

A U.S. term for a smallish pot for flowers of which Art Seiderbaum has said: ''The time for zero pottery growth is surely here. I would remind the earthy people there's no need to have a weed pot for every weed in the universe.'' (See CR43 in Booklist.)

WEI CH'I

A white porcelain Chinese checkerboard with 20 squares each way.

WEIGHT

Scale weights were often made in pottery in the 19th/20th centuries. It was necessary to make a hollow in the base so that lead could be introduced to bring each piece to the exact weight. They can be attractive and decorative.

WELL

There are splendid Han models of wells complete with water pot. More sentimentalized models have been made in recent times, and the general form has been used as a basis for pottery by some modern craftsmen. (Drawings: page 252.)

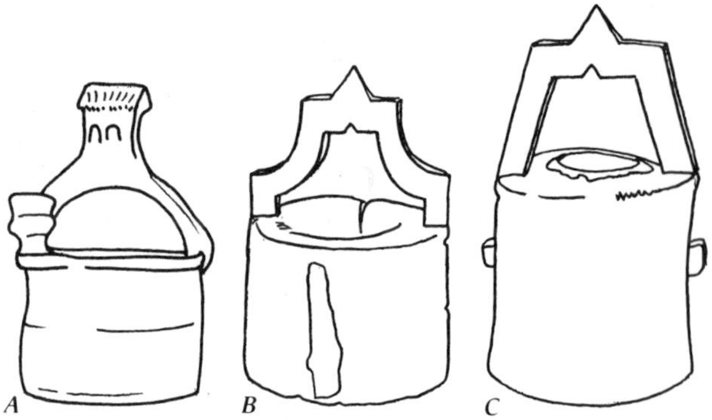

A. A Han Chinese model of a well head with water pot. There is a magnificent series of these models. (See page 251.)
B/C. Two "well forms" by Ian Auld, 1977, 12 inches/300mm high, of soft-slab construction. They could almost equally well be called pail form.

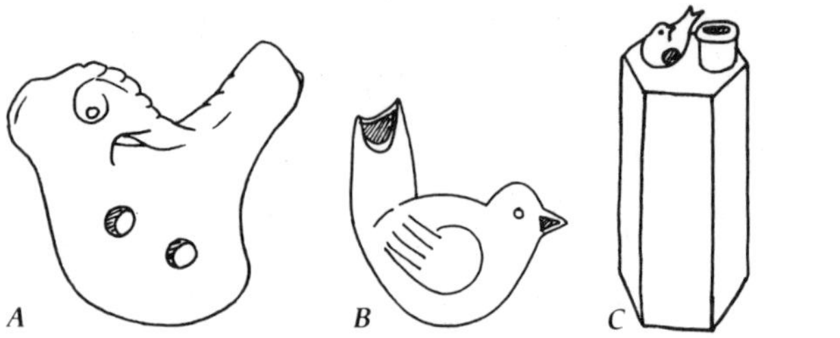

A. A whistle with 4 holes, in the form of a bird, from ancient Colombia. The head and beak are well integrated into the main form.
B/C. Two types of bird whistle, the first a very basic form from T'ang China, 3 inches/75mm long, and the second a more elaborate water whistle, which, "if blown gently when it is half full of water, sounds like a nightingale."
D. This example from Majorca is a common type of horse and rider whistle. It is a peasant piece, and the whistle is in the base.

D

WELSH TRAY

Large rectangular dishes for butchers in Stockton-on-Tees were called Welsh trays. (See B.CECP in Booklist.)

WHISTLE

Potters of all countries and all times have made whistles and **flutes,** sometimes as simple egglike forms (see **ocarina**), but also modelled as birds, animals, horsemen, etc. Modelled whistles were known as "blow-birds" in 19th century America.

Robert Fromme explores the history of whistles in CMapr77 (see Booklist), from the simplest "ductless aerophones" of 28,000 B.C. (?). He shows whistles with sliding pellets in the tube to produce glissando, double flutes (see illustration under **flute**), and other forms. He also gives advice on making them, as does Richard Dunning in PQ13 (see Booklist). Brears (see B.CECP in Booklist) discusses the whistles of 18/19th century England—small, plain types given in quantity to children to attract custom (could be self-defeating!); four birds on a base, each with a whistle in the tail; cuckoo calls with a single finger hole to change the note; highly ornamental whistles, more decorative than practical; whistles built into chimney pots to keep away evil spirits; etc. Many ancient American pots also incorporate whistles, sometimes as a human figure. See also illustration under **fish form.**

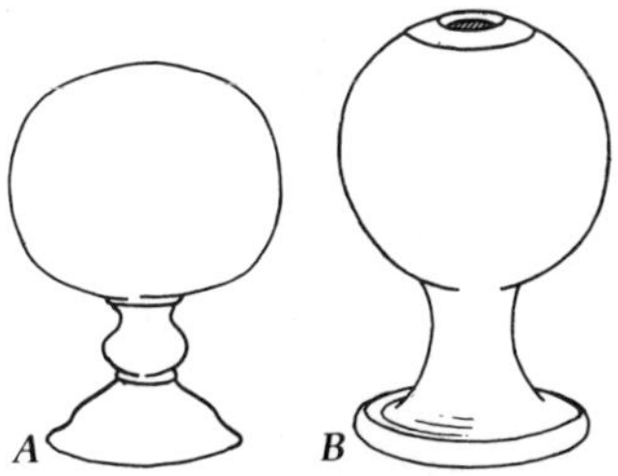

A. A late 18th century tin-glazed earthenware wig stand from Delft. B. A pot by Mo Jupp using a similar form.

WIG/CAP STAND

A sphere on a stem, made all over Europe at Rouen, Delft, etc. Similar cap stands are known to have existed from the 17th century.

WIND CHIMES

Small pieces of hard material strung on thin string, close to one another, so that they collide and give off a tinkling or chiming sound when moved by the wind. By their nature, they are unlikely to have survived (or be recognized) from far back in history, but they have been exported from the East for many years. The decorative possibilities are extensive, and stoneware and porcelain are suitable materials, at least for gentle breezes!

WINE BOTTLE

Many fine bottles and **ewers** from East and West have been used for wine. Charming tin-glazed bottles labelled specifically "Whit" (white wine?), "Renish," "Claret," etc. were made in the mid-17th century at Lambeth, London. Stoneware bottles are still used for some special wines, though most have gone over to glass.

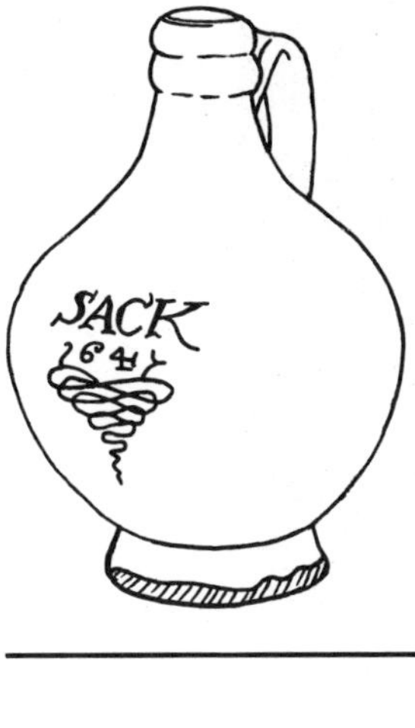

A typically attractive, slightly off center Lambeth wine bottle, probably for use at the table; i.e., as a carafe.

WINE CASK

A barrel-shaped vessel, closed but for two holes with corks, is referred to by Guilland (see G.EAFP in Booklist) from New England in 1821. See also **cask, barrel.**

WINE COOLER

The usual form was a tublike container which was filled with ice for cooling wine. This is still the kindest method for white wines and champagne, though largely ousted by the refrigerator. The **psykter** was a Greek wine cooler. Elaborately painted wine coolers were made in Italian majolica in the 15th century.

WINE LABEL

Sometimes curved wine labels, pleasantly shaped, with holes to take a fine chain so that they could be hung on the necks of bottles and carafes, were made in the 18th century (and probably also at an earlier date) in tin-glaze, creamware, and, more rarely, in porcelain. Such titles as "Orange Shrub," "Marcella," "Elderflower," etc. appear as well as the French wine types.

WINE POT/JAR

Early Far Eastern shapes, closely resembling teapots may have been used for wine; there are boldly shaped wine amphoras (see illustration E under **amphora**) from Roman Nubia; wine kettles were made in 17th century Japan (Shino) with **bail** handles and wide lids; the typical T'zu Chou shapes (**mei p'ing**), either rounded or with high shoulders, called "wine jars" by Charleston (see L.WC in Booklist); and in our own times, Picasso calls some of his fanciful and barely practical constructions "wine pitchers." Some wine pots are made by craftsmen potters (though rather more if one includes **cider** as an apple wine), but they are now less often made in pottery than at probably any other time in history. (Photograph: page 254.)

WINGED FORM

Flat, more or less solid, handles set on each side of a pot and resembling wings are found on Spanish/Moorish pottery of the 13/14th centuries; e.g., that from the Alhambra in Granada. A rather more wild and ornate "winged" pot from 400 A.D. Japan

The very delicately spouted and handled wine pot of Chinese Sung times (photo: facing page), with some resemblance to a modern coffeepot, but obviously intended for a thinner and more expensive drink. (Barlow Collection.)

is shown in E.EJP (see Booklist). Among modern potters, Colin Pearson has explored the idea more fully than any other. David Burnham has made winged spheres.

A

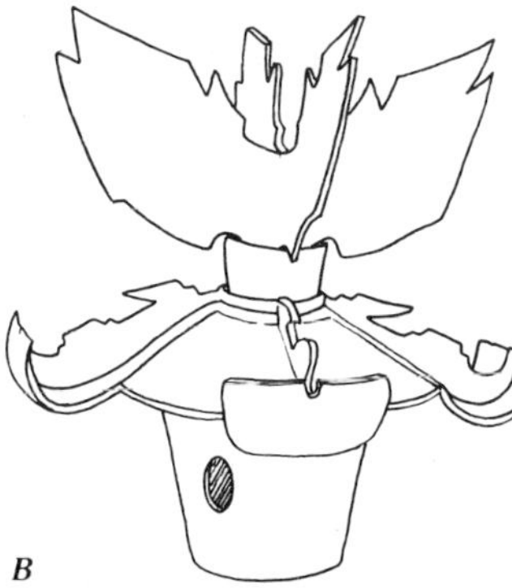

B

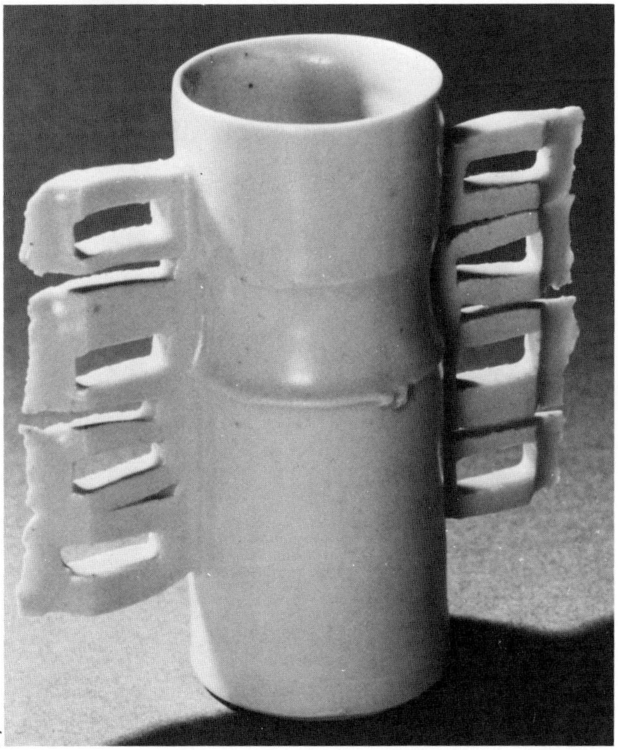

C

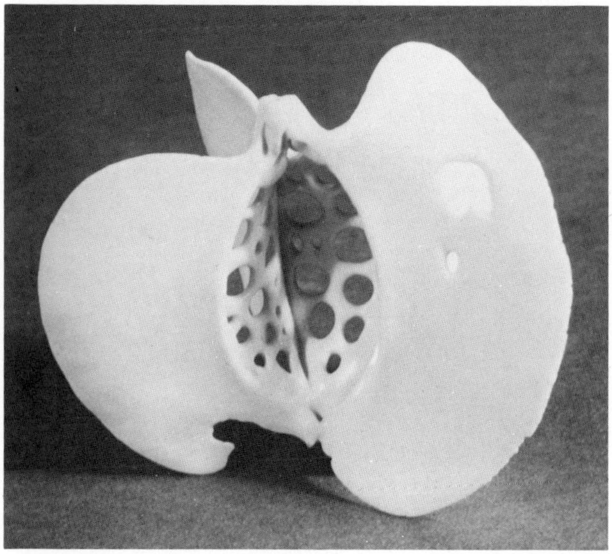

D

A. An Algerian 19th century pot with "wing" handles from Great Kabylia. The handle outline gives a second dimension to the body shape.
B. An astonishing construction for Iron Age Japan. The top part appears to be inset, almost a stopper. *The purpose of the piece is unknown.*
C. Colin Pearson has made the winged form his hallmark, both in stoneware and porcelain. Often the exaggerated "handles" are well-integrated into the form; sometimes they seem to be attached merely for their own sake.
D. In this fine piece of sculptured porcelain by Mary Rogers the "wings" are all and their "body" merely the space between them.

WISHBONE HANDLE

A flat handle or **lug handle** found especially on the so-called **milk ladles** or scoops of the 1st and 2nd millennia B.C. The base of the handle is divided; hence, the name. (Photograph: page 256.)

WITCH BOTTLE

Bellarmines and similar bottle/jugs are found full of rusting nails, pierced heart shapes, and other articles associated with the cult of witchcraft. Several are shown in Ipswich Museum, all giving, according to the captions "positive urine tests." An unlikely discovery site was Church Cottages. Instead of the usual mask or medallion, some were irregularly stamped with small horseshoe impressions, suggesting that the potter was a party to whatever was going on.

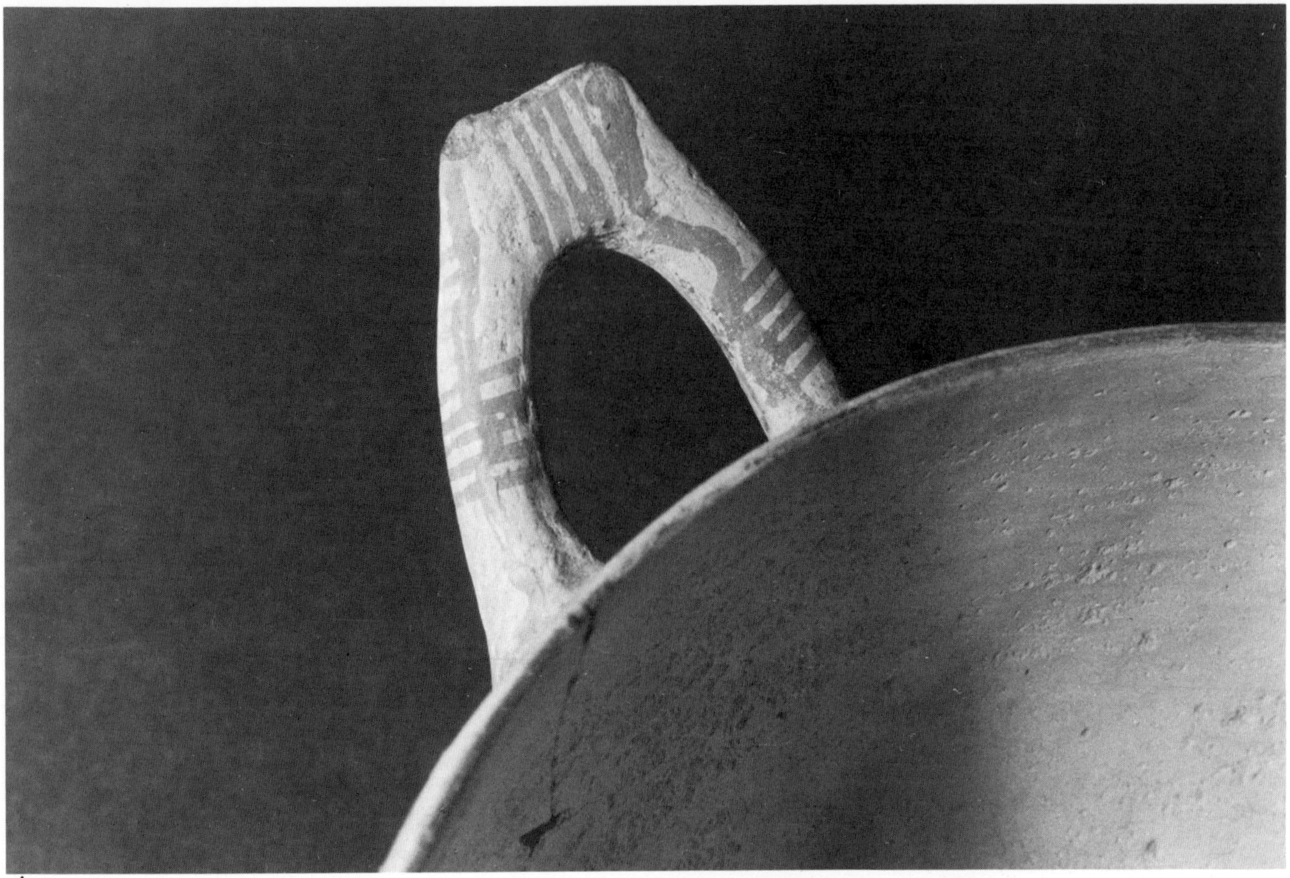

A

A. A typical wishbone handle on a milk ladle, circa 1500 B.C. Cyprus. B. In the author's opinion this is one of the world's finest pots, again from that treasure house of ceramics, Cyprus, and a fitting vessel with which to close this book.

B

Y

YA-SHOU PEI

A Chinese name for bowls with a flaring rim.

YEN-YEN

A dealer's name for a large Chinese vase with a wide neck and a trumpet mouth.

YUONOMI

A **tea bowl.**

Z

ZOOMORPHIC

In the form of animals; representations of animals. See **animal form.**

ABOUT THE AUTHOR

While studying at the Central School of Arts and Crafts in London, Robert Fournier built his first pottery in Hertfordshire, England, in 1947. He has been potting continuously since then, first in slipware and tin-glazed earthenware, followed by a period in ceramic mosaics. For the last twenty years, he has worked in oxidized stoneware with some porcelain and raku. Sheila Fournier, his wife, is known world wide for her inlaid porcelain. She is responsible for most of the line drawings in this book.

The Fournier Pottery is located in the medieval village of Lacock in Wiltshire, England. The Fourniers have shown their work in Europe and the United States. Both have taught in several schools and colleges and, together with John Anderson, they have made several films on potters. They have issued 500 slides of historical and modern pots, have published six books and numerous articles, and are responsible for the initiation of an archive of pottery for the Craftsmen Potters Association of Great Britain.

Mr. Fournier is the author of the *Illustrated Dictionary of Practical Pottery* and *Electric Kiln Construction for Potters,* both published by Van Nostrand Reinhold Company.